America's TEST KITCHEN

Light & Healthy

2011

THE YEAR'S BEST RECIPES LIGHTENED UP

BY THE EDITORS AT
AMERICA'S TEST KITCHEN

PHOTOGRAPHY BY
CARL TREMBLAY, KELLER + KELLER, AND DANIEL J. VAN ACKERE

AMERICA'S TEST KITCHEN
17 Station Street, Brookline, MA 02445

Library of Congress Cataloging-in-Publication Data
The Editors at America's Test Kitchen

AMERICA'S TEST KITCHEN LIGHT & HEALTHY 2011
The Year's Best Recipes Lightened Up

1st Edition

Hardcover: $35 US
ISBN-13: 978-1-933615-70-7 ISBN-10: 1-933615-70-2
1. Cooking. 1. Title
2011

Manufactured in the United States of America

10 9 8 7 6 5 4 3 2 1

Distributed by America's Test Kitchen
17 Station Street, Brookline, MA 02445

EDITORIAL DIRECTOR: Jack Bishop
EXECUTIVE EDITOR: Elizabeth Carduff
EXECUTIVE FOOD EDITOR: Julia Collin Davison
SENIOR EDITOR: Rachel Toomey Kelsey
ASSOCIATE EDITORS: Louise Emerick and Suzannah McFerran
TEST COOKS: Christie Morrison, Chris O'Connor, Adelaide Parker, and Kelly Price
DESIGN DIRECTOR: Amy Klee
ART DIRECTOR: Greg Galvan
DESIGNER: Beverly Hsu
FRONT COVER PHOTOGRAPH: Carl Tremblay
STAFF PHOTOGRAPHER: Daniel J. van Ackere
ADDITIONAL PHOTOGRAPHY: Keller + Keller
FOOD STYLING: Marie Piraino and Mary Jane Sawyer
PRODUCTION DIRECTOR: Guy Rochford
SENIOR PRODUCTION MANAGER: Jessica Quirk
SENIOR PROJECT MANAGER: Alice Carpenter
PRODUCTION AND TRAFFIC COORDINATOR: Kate Hux
ASSET AND WORKFLOW MANAGER: Andrew Mannone
PRODUCTION AND IMAGING SPECIALISTS: Judy Blomquist, Heather Dube, and Lauren Pettapiece
COPYEDITOR: Barbara Wood
PROOFREADER: Jeffrey Schier
INDEXER: Elizabeth Parson

PICTURED ON THE FRONT COVER: Broiled Salmon with Pineapple Salsa (page 106)
PICTURED OPPOSITE TITLE PAGE: Vietnamese Rice Noodle Salad with Pork (page 140)
PICTURED ON BACK OF JACKET: Easy Chicken Cordon Bleu (page 70), Cranberry Pork Loin (page 99), Spicy Beef Enchiladas (page 84), Plum-Peach Upside-Down Almond Cake (page 271)

Contents

SEVEN-LAYER DIP

APPETIZERS & SNACKS

M = TEST KITCHEN MAKEOVER

PARTY SNACK MIXES

CRUNCHY, SALTY, AND POSITIVELY ADDICTIVE, A homemade snack mix is guaranteed to be gone minutes after it's set out. The test kitchen had recently created three versions of this get-together favorite in an effort to beat the box: Asian Firecracker, Barbecue, and Fisherman's Friend. These recipes took one base and punctuated it with ingredients like oyster crackers, smoked almonds, and wasabi peas. They were packed with flavor and texture, but melted butter, nuts, and fried ingredients like sesame sticks and corn chips spoiled the fun. Could we develop low-fat versions that were just as irresistible?

Our first challenge was nailing down the right core components. All three versions contained low-fat ingredients like Chex cereal and pretzels that we agreed could remain. The other elements of Fisherman's Friend—goldfish, Melba toasts, and oyster crackers—were in good shape nutritionally. However, the other two recipes had some high-calorie heavy hitters that needed to be addressed. In the Asian Party Mix, additions like honey-roasted peanuts, sesame sticks, and fried chow mein noodles sent the calories sky-high. The Barbecue version wasn't much better, with smoked almonds and fried corn chips. We knew a couple of ingredient changes would pay dividends. Starting with some easy tweaks, we lowered the quantities of nuts and chow mein noodles in the Asian Party Mix and increased the amounts of flavor-boosting elements, like the wasabi peas. In the Barbecue mix, we swapped the fried corn chips for baked corn tortillas, which imparted great corn flavor and maintained the crucial crunch factor.

Limiting high-fat ingredients was one avenue to success, but could we go a step further and improve the nutritional value by adding whole grain ingredients? Our original recipes used Corn or Rice Chex, so we tested swapping in Whole Wheat Chex. It made our mixture unappealingly dry and dense, so we stuck with the original choices for cereal; however, tasters loved the nutty flavor of whole grain Melba toast in lieu of the plain Melbas used in the Fisherman's Friend and Barbecue mixes. We substituted sesame whole grain Melba toasts for the sesame sticks in the Asian Firecracker Mix, allowing us to further cut calories. The substitution not only added good hearty flavor to the mixes, but it also added a healthy dose of fiber.

With our mixtures in place, it was time to evaluate flavorings. Our original recipes, like the box version, used 6 tablespoons of butter to help distribute the seasonings and keep the mixes from being too dry. Tasters agreed the butter beat out olive oil and margarine because it added considerable flavor. Some butter seemed essential for flavor, but it was also an obvious place for calorie cutting. We tested different increments of butter and stopped at 4 tablespoons; any less resulted in a dry, unappetizing mix. The saturated fat was still too high for our liking, so we tested using a combination of butter and oil. We tested different ratios of oil and butter and found that equal parts gave us the taste and texture we were after and lowered the saturated fat significantly.

As for other liquid components, barbecue sauce was an obvious inclusion for our Barbecue mix, and after testing various increments we found that ¼ cup was just right. Soy sauce was a natural in the Asian Firecracker version, and tasters agreed that lemon juice and hot sauce were great starting points for the Fisherman's Friend. Now we just needed to figure out the right mix of dry spices.

Seasonings were the one area where we knew we could create big impact without having to worry too much about added fat and calories. Stale-tasting seasoned salts were nonstarters. After more than a few batches we unlocked the secret to spicing each mix. Bold seasonings were essential, but spices like paprika and onion powder lost their flavor during the baking process. Asian Firecracker Party Mix benefited from garlic powder, cayenne pepper, and ground ginger, which held their flavor through baking, while the Barbecue mix needed a strong spice like chili powder to stand up to the potent flavors in the barbecue sauce. We found that the favorite maritime spice, Old Bay, was the perfect seasoning for our Fisherman's Friend Party Mix.

Though nailing down the spices was relatively easy, getting them evenly distributed when tossed with the mix was a different story. In both our original full-fat recipes and the box recipe, the mix is drizzled with the butter, then tossed with the seasonings. But our lowered amount of fat left us with some bites that were bursting with flavor and others that were bare. We eventually found that adding the dry spices to the pan with the melting butter was the answer. It not only allowed the dry spices to distribute more evenly, but, as an added bonus, it allowed us to bloom the spices, a technique the kitchen relies on to maximize spices' potential and remove any raw or dusty flavors. With that final tweak, tasters agreed: We had tasty, low-fat snack mixes that were sure to get the party started and keep it going.

Asian Firecracker Party Snack Mix

MAKES ABOUT 10 CUPS

Wasabi peas can be found in the international aisle of most grocery stores.

- 5 cups Rice Chex cereal
- 5 ounces sesame Melba toasts, broken into ½-inch pieces (about 2½ cups)
- 1¼ cups wasabi peas
- ¾ cup honey-roasted peanuts
- ½ cup chow mein noodles
- 2 tablespoons unsalted butter
- 2 tablespoons canola oil
- 2 tablespoons low-sodium soy sauce
- 1 teaspoon ground ginger
- ¾ teaspoon garlic powder
- ¼ teaspoon cayenne pepper

1. Adjust an oven rack to the middle position and heat the oven to 250 degrees. Combine the cereal, Melba toasts, wasabi peas, peanuts, and chow mein noodles in a large bowl.

2. Cook the butter, oil, soy sauce, ginger, garlic powder, and cayenne together in a small saucepan over medium-low heat until fragrant and the butter is melted, about 1 minute. Drizzle the butter mixture over the cereal mixture and toss until well combined.

3. Spread the mixture on a rimmed baking sheet and bake, stirring every 15 minutes, until golden and crisp, about 45 minutes. Cool to room temperature, about 1 hour. Serve. (The snack mix can be stored in an airtight container at room temperature for up to 1 week.)

PER ¾-CUP SERVING: Cal 200; Fat 10g; Sat fat 2.5g; Chol 5mg; Carb 23g; Protein 5g; Fiber 2g; Sodium 320mg

VARIATIONS

Barbecue Party Snack Mix

MAKES ABOUT 10 CUPS

The test kitchen's favorite barbecue sauce is Bull's-Eye Original Barbecue Sauce for its great dark color, thick consistency, and smoky flavor.

- 5 cups Corn Chex cereal
- 2 cups baked tortilla chips, broken into ½-inch pieces
- 2 ounces whole grain Melba toasts, broken into ½-inch pieces (about 1 cup)
- 1¼ cups pretzel sticks
- ¾ cup smoked almonds
- ¼ cup barbecue sauce
- 2 tablespoons unsalted butter
- 2 tablespoons canola oil
- 1 teaspoon chili powder
- ½ teaspoon dried oregano
- ¼ teaspoon cayenne pepper

1. Adjust an oven rack to the middle position and heat the oven to 250 degrees. Combine the cereal, tortilla chips, Melba toasts, pretzels, and almonds in a large bowl.

2. Cook the barbecue sauce, butter, oil, chili powder, oregano, and cayenne in a small saucepan over medium-low heat until fragrant and the butter is melted, about 1 minute. Drizzle the barbecue sauce mixture over the cereal mixture and toss until well combined.

3. Spread the mixture on a rimmed baking sheet and bake, stirring every 15 minutes, until golden and crisp, about 45 minutes. Cool to room temperature, about 1 hour. Serve. (The snack mix can be stored in an airtight container at room temperature for up to 1 week.)

PER ¾-CUP SERVING: Cal 180; Fat 9g; Sat fat 2g; Chol 5mg; Carb 23g; Protein 4g; Fiber 2g; Sodium 310mg

Fisherman's Friend Party Snack Mix

MAKES ABOUT 10 CUPS

The test kitchen's preferred hot sauce is Frank's RedHot. If using a spicier brand, such as Tabasco, you may not need as much.

- 5 cups Corn Chex or Rice Chex cereal
- 2 cups oyster crackers
- 1 cup Pepperidge Farm Cheddar Goldfish
- 1 cup Pepperidge Farm Pretzel Goldfish
- 2 ounces whole grain Melba toasts, broken into ½-inch pieces (about 1 cup)
- 2 tablespoons unsalted butter
- 2 tablespoons canola oil
- 2 tablespoons hot sauce (see note)
- 1 tablespoon fresh lemon juice
- 1 tablespoon Old Bay Seasoning

1. Adjust an oven rack to the middle position and heat the oven to 250 degrees. Combine the cereal, oyster crackers, Cheddar Goldfish, Pretzel Goldfish, and Melba toasts in a large bowl.

2. Cook the butter, oil, hot sauce, lemon juice, and Old Bay in a small saucepan over medium-low heat until fragrant and the butter is melted, about 1 minute. Drizzle the butter mixture over the cereal mixture and toss until well combined.

3. Spread the mixture on a rimmed baking sheet and bake, stirring every 15 minutes, until golden and crisp, about 45 minutes. Cool to room temperature, about 1 hour. Serve. (The snack mix can be stored in an airtight container at room temperature for up to 1 week.)

PER ¾-CUP SERVING: Cal 160; Fat 6g; Sat fat 1.5g; Chol 5mg; Carb 24g; Protein 3g; Fiber 1g; Sodium 520mg

HUMMUS

HUMMUS IS A TRADITIONAL COMBINATION OF chickpeas and tahini (sesame seeds ground into a rich paste) seasoned with olive oil. The addition of tahini along with fruity olive oil gives hummus its characteristically rich nuttiness and creamy consistency, but those ingredients can also make this dip high in fat and calories. We wanted to create a lower-fat hummus—a dip mixed to a smooth, stiff, yet scoopable texture that would be perfect as a snack with pita chips or crudités, or as a sandwich spread.

Testing canned chickpeas against dried ones, we were impressed by the results obtained with canned chickpeas, so we saw no reason to fuss with the dried. Typically, canned chickpeas are packed in a slippery, water-based liquid, and we found that the hummus tasted cleaner when we rinsed the chickpeas before pureeing them. A 15-ounce can of chickpeas made a good-size batch of hummus, about 2 cups.

Tahini adds a signature toasted nutty flavor to hummus. The test kitchen had recently developed a hummus recipe, but it called for 6 tablespoons of tahini. With 9 grams of fat per tablespoon, it took our dip beyond the fat total we wanted in a light dip. We tried a few batches of hummus without any tahini at all, but this only resulted in weak-flavored dips that didn't taste anything like hummus. Trying various amounts of tahini, we found that ¼ cup yielded a rich and creamy dip with just enough of a distinct nutty flavor. Half a small clove of garlic along with a pinch of cayenne added just the right bite, and 3 tablespoons of lemon juice contributed citrusy brightness.

Last but not least, we needed to address the texture, as our dip was a bit stiff. Traditionally, hummus is thinned with a generous amount of olive oil (sometimes as much as ½ cup), which also serves to give the dip a rich flavor. We needed to thin our dip without so much oil but at the same time without compromising the flavor. We tried replacing the olive oil with chicken broth (a technique used in some recipes we found) and even water. Tasters found that the broth flavor was off and muddied, while the water washed out the dip's flavors. However, tasters did comment that the water had a nice clean taste, one that went well with the chickpeas. We found our answer in a combination of olive oil and water—just 1½ tablespoons of oil to bring all the flavors together and 5 tablespoons of water to make a smooth puree. Refrigerating the hummus for at least an hour allowed the flavors to meld.

Just before serving, we sprinkled our hummus with fresh parsley (though cilantro worked, too), which made for a nice presentation and added just the right herbal flavor. At last, we had reached our goal of creating a great-tasting hummus that was lighter too.

Hummus

MAKES ABOUT 2 CUPS

Be sure to stir the tahini thoroughly before measuring it.

- 1 **(15-ounce) can chickpeas, drained and rinsed**
- 5 **tablespoons water**
- ¼ **cup tahini**
- 3 **tablespoons fresh lemon juice**
- 1½ **tablespoons extra-virgin olive oil**
- ½ **small garlic clove, minced**
- **Salt**
- ⅛ **teaspoon ground cumin**
- **Pinch cayenne pepper**
- 1 **tablespoon minced fresh parsley or cilantro**

1. Process the chickpeas, water, tahini, lemon juice, oil, garlic, ½ teaspoon salt, cumin, and cayenne together in a food processor until smooth, 1 to 1½ minutes.

2. Transfer to a bowl, cover, and refrigerate until the flavors have blended, about 1 hour. Season with salt to taste and sprinkle with the parsley before serving. (The hummus can be refrigerated in an airtight container for up to 3 days. Season with additional lemon juice, salt, and cayenne to taste and sprinkle with the parsley before serving.)

PER ¼-CUP SERVING: Cal 100; Fat 7g; Sat fat 1g; Chol 0mg; Carb 7g; Protein 3g; Fiber 2g; Sodium 260mg

Lemon Hummus

Follow the recipe for Hummus, increasing the amount of lemon juice to ¼ cup and adding ½ teaspoon grated lemon zest to the food processor with the chickpeas.

PER ¼-CUP SERVING: Cal 100; Fat 7g; Sat fat 1g; Chol 0mg; Carb 7g; Protein 3g; Fiber 2g; Sodium 260mg

Roasted Red Pepper Hummus

Follow the recipe for Hummus, adding ¼ cup jarred roasted red peppers, chopped coarse, to the food processor with the chickpeas.

PER ¼-CUP SERVING: Cal 100; Fat 7g; Sat fat 1g; Chol 0mg; Carb 8g; Protein 3g; Fiber 2g; Sodium 270mg

Olive Hummus

Follow the recipe for Hummus, adding 2 tablespoons coarsely chopped pitted kalamata olives to the food processor with the chickpeas and stirring in 2 tablespoons more coarsely chopped pitted kalamata olives after transferring the mixture to the bowl.

PER ¼-CUP SERVING: Cal 120; Fat 9g; Sat fat 1g; Chol 0mg; Carb 8g; Protein 3g; Fiber 2g; Sodium 370mg

CREAMY DIPS

WHO CAN RESIST BOWLS OF CREAMY DIPS WITH PILES of chips and vegetables on the side? With a base of tangy sour cream and rich, velvety mayonnaise, and various flavorings like onion or cheese, there's a lot to love. But they can also carry with them 220 calories and more than 20 grams of fat for a mere 3-tablespoon serving. We went to the kitchen with a clear mission: creamy, flavorful dips, without the fat.

TEST KITCHEN **MAKEOVER**

Our first step was to create the base. The full-fat mayo and sour cream had to go. We tried their low-fat counterparts, but tasters gave mixed reviews. The low-fat sour cream passed the test; however, the mayo didn't fare as well. Although we like low-fat mayonnaise in certain situations, because it was such a predominant flavor in this application tasters found it added an unpleasantly sweet, artificial taste. We decided we could do better, so we began an onslaught of low-fat dairy product testing.

We went on to try mixing the low-fat sour cream with everything we could think of: low-fat cottage cheese, cream cheese, and yogurt, and part-skim ricotta. The chunky texture of the cottage cheese was all wrong for a creamy dip. The cream cheese was gluey. The yogurt was too thin, and the ricotta was unpleasantly grainy and watery. None of these could match the silky texture of mayonnaise. We needed to think outside the box.

We pureed almost anything that would stand still. The attempts with the most promise included hearts of palm, summer squash, white beans, cauliflower, and tofu. We even tried rehydrated potato flakes and rice cereal. But our efforts were futile. None of the options made tasters want to come back for a second dip.

Out of ideas, we returned to cottage cheese, which at least had the right neutral dairy flavor. It was the texture tasters couldn't get behind. We tried processing the cottage cheese in both the blender and the food processor but saw little change. Then a colleague suggested processing it with boiling water, which would help break down the curds and make it easier to puree. It worked perfectly. Combined with the low-fat sour cream, our dip base had the creamy texture and mildly tangy yet slightly rich taste we were after. Eager to see if the trick would work with nonfat cottage cheese, we whirled up a batch. Tasters agreed these dips lacked flavor and had a grainy texture, so nonfat cottage cheese was quickly ruled out.

We could now move on to flavoring our dips. We knew we wanted a French onion dip made with sweet caramelized onions, so we started by testing various types of onions. Tasters immediately eliminated red onions because they turned our dip an unappealing brown color. Sweet and yellow onions were both universally praised for the earthy sweetness they brought to the spread. We then turned our attention to the amount of caramelized onion. After some debate, tasters settled on 2 cups raw onions, which cooked down to about ½ cup. This amount imparted impressive onion flavor without overpowering the dip. Worcestershire sauce and a touch of garlic powder rounded out the flavors nicely.

We also wanted a dip that would capitalize on fresh herbs. After we went a few rounds with various options, it became obvious that basil, complemented by a touch of Parmesan, was the clear winner. While this pairing was good, we realized we could take it one step further by adding garlic and a little olive oil to create a creamy pesto dip.

We wanted one more spread to round out our trio. We chose assertive blue cheese and chives. This dip not only tasted great on crudités and chips (we opted for baked, of course), but we found it could even be a great topping for a baked potato.

After cutting around a whopping 150 calories and 20 grams of fat per serving, we could finally consider creamy dips a worthy addition to our healthy appetizer table.

MAKEOVER SPOTLIGHT: CREAMY FRENCH ONION DIP

	CALORIES	FAT	SAT FAT	CHOLESTEROL
BEFORE	220	22g	5g	25mg
AFTER	70	3g	0g	5mg

Creamy French Onion Dip

MAKES ABOUT 2 CUPS

Avoid red onion, which will turn the dip murky brown. For an accurate measurement of boiling water, bring a kettle of water to a boil, then measure out the desired amount. Serve with baked potato chips or crudités.

    2 onions, minced (about 2 cups)
    1 tablespoon olive oil
       Salt
    8 ounces 1 percent cottage cheese (about 1 cup)
    ¼ cup boiling water
    1 cup low-fat sour cream
    ½ teaspoon Worcestershire sauce
    ¼ teaspoon garlic powder
       Pepper

1. Combine the onions, oil, and ¼ teaspoon salt in a large nonstick skillet. Cover and cook, stirring occasionally, over medium-low heat until softened, 8 to 10 minutes. Uncover, increase the heat to medium-high, and continue to cook until the onions are well browned, 8 to 12 minutes longer.

2. Process the cottage cheese and boiling water together in a blender until no lumps remain, about 30 seconds. Add half of the caramelized onions and blend until completely smooth, about 30 seconds. Transfer the mixture to a medium bowl, and whisk in the remaining caramelized onions, sour cream, Worcestershire, garlic powder, and ¼ teaspoon pepper. Season with salt and

pepper to taste. Cover and refrigerate until the flavors blend, at least 1 hour or up to 3 days. Serve.

PER 3-TABLESPOON SERVING: Cal 70; Fat 3g; Sat fat 0g; Chol 5mg; Carb 3g; Protein 4g; Fiber 1g; Sodium 170mg

VARIATIONS
Creamy Blue Cheese Dip

MAKES ABOUT 2 CUPS

For an accurate measurement of boiling water, bring a kettle of water to a boil, then measure out the desired amount. Serve with baked potato chips or crudités.

    8 ounces 1 percent cottage cheese (about 1 cup)
  1⅓ ounces blue cheese, crumbled (about ⅓ cup)
    ¼ cup boiling water
    1 cup low-fat sour cream
    2 tablespoons minced fresh chives
    1 tablespoon olive oil
       Salt and pepper

Process the cottage cheese, 3 tablespoons of the blue cheese, and boiling water together in a blender until completely smooth, about 1 minute. Transfer the mixture to a medium bowl, then whisk in the remaining 2 tablespoons blue cheese, sour cream, chives, and oil. Season with salt and pepper to taste. Cover and refrigerate until the flavors blend, at least 1 hour or up to 3 days. Serve.

PER 3-TABLESPOON SERVING: Cal 70; Fat 4g; Sat fat 1g; Chol 10mg; Carb 1g; Protein 4g; Fiber 0g; Sodium 160mg

NOTES FROM THE TEST KITCHEN

SECRETS TO CREAMY LOW-FAT DIP
For creamy richness—without the calories—we turned to two substitute ingredients and one clever trick.

LOW-FAT SOUR CREAM
An easy substitution of low-fat sour cream for its full-fat counterpart provides the same appealing tang.

LOW-FAT COTTAGE CHEESE
Cottage cheese out of the container is lumpy and can taste grainy, but pureed with hot water, it mimics the creamy quality of full-fat mayonnaise.

CREAMY BLUE CHEESE DIP

Creamy Pesto Dip

MAKES ABOUT 2 CUPS

For an accurate measurement of boiling water, bring a kettle of water to a boil, then measure out the desired amount. Cherry tomatoes pair beautifully with the bright basil flavor in this dip.

- 8 ounces 1 percent cottage cheese (about 1 cup)
- ¼ cup boiling water
- 1 cup low-fat sour cream
- ⅓ cup grated Parmesan cheese
- ¼ cup finely chopped fresh basil
- 1 tablespoon olive oil
- 1 garlic clove, minced
- Salt and pepper

Process the cottage cheese and boiling water together in a blender until completely smooth, about 1 minute. Transfer the mixture to a medium bowl, then whisk in the sour cream, Parmesan, basil, oil, and garlic. Season with salt and pepper to taste. Cover and refrigerate until the flavors blend, at least 1 hour or up to 3 days. Serve.

PER 3-TABLESPOON SERVING: Cal 60; Fat 3.5g; Sat fat 0.5g; Chol 5mg; Carb 1g; Protein 4g; Fiber 0g; Sodium 135mg

CHIPS AND SALSA

PERUSE THE SUPERMARKET SNACK AISLE AND YOU'LL find countless variations of jarred and bottled salsa. With its simple combination of tomatoes, onions, spices, and seasoning, salsa is a great choice for a healthy snack. We've always liked the chunky texture and the cohesive sauce of this "thick and chunky" variety, but it's hard to get past the cooked-to-death flavor of the supermarket versions. Could we use fresh ingredients to perk up this all-time favorite? We also wanted an alternative to fried tortilla chips to go with it.

Most recipes call for chopping tomatoes, onions, and jalapeños into large pieces and tossing them with lime juice and cilantro. When we gave this a go, tasters loved the freshness but found the texture disconcerting. The tomatoes shed their juice and diluted the salsa, and the big pieces of crunchy onion and jalapeño were overwhelming. Plus, with no binder, the salsa seemed more like chopped salad or a weak attempt at *pico de gallo*.

The watered-down texture was easy to solve: We used the proven technique of seeding and salting the chopped tomatoes before we tossed them with the other ingredients. After roughly chopping 2 pounds of ripe tomatoes, we placed them in a strainer, sprinkled them with salt, and let them drain for 30 minutes. Almost ¼ cup of liquid drained out in that time.

Next, we finely chopped the onion and jalapeño to ensure that little pieces would work their way into each bite but not dominate. Then, along with the vibrant cilantro and lime juice flavors, we added chili powder to give the salsa depth. Tasters agreed our recipe was improving, but it didn't have the proper saucy liquid binding it.

To remedy this, we tested an idea we'd found that called for stirring in canned tomato sauce. The texture was right, but the spent tomato flavor was disappointing. We moved on to other tomato products: juice, then pureed canned tomatoes. Neither produced the results we were after. Canned products weren't getting us anywhere. We would need to make our own binder. We blended some of the fresh, already diced tomatoes in the food processor, then stirred this puree into the rest of the ingredients. After this move, the salsa was thick, chunky, and fresh. All it needed was a good chip to go with it.

We needed an alternative to fried tortilla chips. Store-bought baked chips, while healthier, typically have an unappealing, dry texture. We could do better. We cut 6-inch corn tortillas into wedges and sprinkled them with salt. After spreading them on a rimmed baking sheet and moving them to the oven, a few minutes later we got a mixed bag: some somewhat crisp chips and a lot that were leathery. Spraying them with a little vegetable oil spray helped, and it also helped the salt stick to the chips, but after a few tests we realized it was imperative that the chips be spread in a single layer to ensure even crispness. By spreading the chips across two baking sheets, placing them on the upper-middle and lower-middle oven racks and flipping the tortilla chips halfway through their cooking time, we were able to achieve the consistent results we were after. We also tried various oven temperatures and found that cooking the chips at 350 degrees for about eight minutes on each side yielded a consistently crisp chip. With that, we had healthier, crispy chips that easily beat out the grocery store products, and they were the perfect match for our fresh, chunky salsa.

Thick and Chunky Salsa

MAKES ABOUT 3 CUPS

To make this salsa spicier, add the chile seeds. Serve with Homemade Baked Corn Tortilla Chips (recipe follows).

 2 pounds ripe tomatoes (5 to 6 medium), cored, seeded, and chopped medium

 ½ teaspoon salt

 ¼ cup minced red onion

 ¼ cup minced fresh cilantro

 1 jalapeño chile, stemmed, seeded, and minced

 1 tablespoon fresh lime juice

 ¾ teaspoon chili powder

1. Place the tomatoes in a fine-mesh strainer set over a bowl, sprinkle with the salt, and let drain until the tomatoes begin to soften, about 30 minutes. Discard the liquid.

2. Meanwhile, combine the onion, cilantro, jalapeño, lime juice, and chili powder in a medium bowl.

3. Process one-third of the drained tomatoes in a food processor until smooth, about 30 seconds. Transfer the pureed tomatoes to the bowl with the onion mixture. Add the remaining drained tomatoes to the bowl and toss to combine. Cover and let sit at room temperature until the flavors blend, about 1 hour. Serve. (The salsa can be refrigerated in an airtight container for up to 2 days; let sit at room temperature for 1 hour before serving.)

PER ¼-CUP SERVING: Cal 15; Fat 0g; Sat fat 0g; Chol 0mg; Carb 4g; Protein 1g; Fiber 1g; Sodium 110mg

NOTES FROM THE TEST KITCHEN

KEEPING TOMATOES FRESH LONGER

We've heard that storing a tomato with its stem end facing down can prolong shelf life. To test this theory, we placed one batch of tomatoes stem-end up and another stem-end down and stored them at room temperature. A week later, nearly all the stem-down tomatoes remained in perfect condition, while the stem-up tomatoes had shriveled and started to mold. Why? We surmised that the scar left on the tomato skin where the stem once grew provides both an escape route for moisture and an entry point for mold and bacteria. Placing a tomato stem-end down blocks air from entering and moisture from exiting the scar. To confirm this theory, we ran another test, this time comparing tomatoes stored stem-end down with another batch stored stem-end up, but with a piece of tape sealing off their scars. The taped stem-up tomatoes survived just as well as the stem-down batch.

SEEDING JALAPEÑOS

Most of the heat in a chile pepper is in the ribs and seeds. To easily remove both, cut the pepper in half lengthwise, then, starting at the end opposite the stem, use a melon baller to scoop down the inside of each half.

Homemade Baked Corn Tortilla Chips

MAKES 48 CHIPS

Be sure to bake the chips until they are good and crisp before removing them from the oven. Serve with Thick and Chunky Salsa or Seven-Layer Dip (page 11).

 8 (6-inch) corn tortillas, each cut into 6 wedges

 Vegetable oil spray

 1 teaspoon salt

1. Adjust the oven racks to the upper-middle and lower-middle positions and heat the oven to 350 degrees. Spread the tortilla wedges in an even layer on 2 rimmed baking sheets. Spray the tops of the tortilla wedges with vegetable oil spray, then sprinkle with the salt.

2. Bake the tortilla wedges until they are lightly browned and begin to crisp, 8 to 12 minutes. Flip the tortilla wedges and continue to bake until the chips are fully toasted, 8 to 12 minutes longer. Remove the baking sheets from the oven and let the chips cool before serving.

PER SERVING (6 CHIPS): Cal 70; Fat 1g; Sat fat 0g; Chol 0mg; Carb 14g; Protein 1g; Fiber 1g; Sodium 330mg

SEVEN-LAYER DIP

WITH ITS TEX-MEX FLAVORS AND CONTRASTING textures, this classic dip made with layers of refried beans, sour cream, shredded cheese, guacamole, diced tomatoes, scallions, and black olives is easily recognizable to most people as seven-layer dip. It's a snap to make and has an everyday, football-game-watching "everyman's" appeal that makes it seem like a sure winner. But sadly, it never tastes as good as it sounds or looks. The flavors are always muddled, tired, and bland, and there's nary a hint of freshness. Then there's the fact that seven-layer dip is well known as a real heavyweight, tallying more than 300 calories and 25 grams of fat per serving. We wanted to reevaluate this classic, one layer at a time, to find out if we could breathe new (lighter) life into this staple and at the same time maintain its crowd-pleasing appeal.

We began our overhaul at the bottom, with the beans. Though canned refried beans (made with pinto beans) are the typical choice for this party snack, tasters agreed they tasted stale and tinny, and their dense consistency made them far from dip-friendly. Making our own refried beans from scratch with dried beans would take more time than we wanted to devote to this humble appetizer, so we started with canned beans. At this point, we decided that swapping the pinto beans for black beans would give our dip more appealing color contrast. So we grabbed a can of black beans off the shelf, drained them, and set to work making a flavorful, nicely textured refried black bean layer. To make the beans silky without adding fat, we broke test kitchen protocol by not rinsing them. A simple seasoning of fresh garlic, chili powder, and lime juice gave these quick refried beans the depth and touch of freshness they needed. We all agreed that the five minutes of extra work these beans required was worth it. One layer down, six to go.

Next, we focused on the guacamole. Store-bought guacamole, with its stale (and sometimes rancid) flavor, was a nonstarter. Most guacamole recipes we came across used four avocados, but this was clearly too much fat for our lightened dip. Could we substitute a filler ingredient with a similar texture to avocado but with less fat? We tested cutting the avocados with lima beans, edamame, and peas. Tasters complained that the "mock-a-mole" tasted too lean and that it had an off-putting vegetal flavor. So we settled for less of the real deal, just two avocados mashed with lime juice and salt.

On to the sour cream and cheese layers. For the sour cream, the low-fat variety was the obvious choice, and while it provided plenty of creamy appeal, it was a little bland. Stirring in 1 tablespoon of minced chipotle chiles in adobo sauce did the trick. For the cheese, some recipes call for as much as 2 pounds of shredded Monterey Jack or cheddar. We tried making one batch substituting reduced-fat cheddar and another with a lesser amount of the full-fat stuff. To our surprise, tasters were fairly indifferent about the cheese. Amid the beans, avocados, and sour cream, tasters didn't even know it was there, so we decided to save ourselves the calories and forgo the cheese altogether.

Next up was the tomato layer. While a lot of recipes turn to jarred salsa, it just didn't taste fresh, and tasters said straight fresh tomatoes lacked punch. We found our solution in the form of a homemade pico de gallo, a relish made with chopped fresh tomatoes, jalapeños, cilantro, scallions, lime juice, and salt. As we did with our Thick and Chunky Salsa (page 9), we salted the tomatoes and let them drain before adding them to the dip—this kept excess water from the salsa from diluting the dip and ruining its layers.

After sprinkling on a layer of sliced scallions for fresh bite and good color, we were almost in the end zone. But the final layer of canned sliced black olives needed work. Rinsing the olives helped mitigate their metallic flavor, but they were still bland. After several frustrating rounds of testing, we decided to eliminate the olives.

True, our recipe has just five layers, but with all its textures, flavors, and colors, and just 120 calories and 7 grams of fat per serving, we didn't hear anyone complaining.

MAKEOVER SPOTLIGHT: SEVEN-LAYER DIP

	CALORIES	FAT	SAT FAT	CHOLESTEROL
BEFORE	310	25g	11g	60mg
AFTER	120	7g	0.5g	5mg

Seven-Layer Dip

SERVES 12

To make this dip spicier, add the chile seeds. This recipe is usually served in a clear dish so you can see the layers. Serve with Homemade Baked Corn Tortilla Chips (see page 9).

- 2 pounds ripe tomatoes (5 to 6 medium), cored, seeded, and chopped
  Salt
- 6 scallions, 2 minced and 4 with green parts sliced thin (white parts discarded)
- 5 tablespoons plus 2 teaspoons fresh lime juice (about 3 limes)
- 3 tablespoons minced fresh cilantro
- 2 jalapeño chiles, stemmed, seeded, and minced
- 1 (15-ounce) can black beans, drained but not rinsed
- 2 garlic cloves, minced
- ¾ teaspoon chili powder
- 1½ cups low-fat sour cream
- 1 tablespoon minced canned chipotle chiles in adobo sauce
- 2 ripe avocados, pitted, peeled, and cubed (see photos)

1. Place the tomatoes in a fine-mesh strainer set over a bowl, sprinkle with ½ teaspoon salt, and let drain until the tomatoes begin to soften, about 30 minutes. Discard the liquid. Stir in the minced scallions, 2 tablespoons of the lime juice, cilantro, and jalapeños. Season with salt to taste and set aside.

2. Pulse 2 teaspoons more lime juice, beans, garlic, and chili powder together in a food processor until the mixture resembles a chunky paste. Season with salt to taste and set aside. Whisk the sour cream and chipotles together in a bowl and set aside.

3. Combine the remaining 3 tablespoons lime juice, avocados, and ¼ teaspoon salt in a large bowl, and mash with a potato masher until smooth. Season with salt to taste.

4. Spread the bean mixture evenly over the bottom of an 8-inch square glass baking dish or 1-quart glass bowl. Spread the avocado mixture evenly over the bean layer. Spread the sour cream mixture over the avocado, then top with the tomato mixture. Sprinkle with the sliced scallions and serve. (The dip can be covered tightly with plastic wrap and refrigerated for up to 1 day; let sit at room temperature for 1 hour before serving.)

PER ⅓-CUP SERVING: Cal 120; Fat 7g; Sat fat 0.5g; Chol 5mg; Carb 12g; Protein 5g; Fiber 5g; Sodium 250mg

PREPARING AVOCADOS

1. After slicing the avocado in half around the pit, lodge the edge of the knife blade into the pit and twist to remove. Use a large wooden spoon to pry the pit safely off the knife.

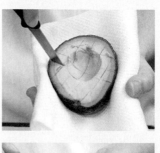

2. Use a dish towel to hold the avocado steady. Make ½-inch crosshatch incisions in the flesh of each avocado half with a knife, cutting down to but not through the skin.

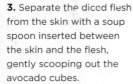

3. Separate the diced flesh from the skin with a soup spoon inserted between the skin and the flesh, gently scooping out the avocado cubes.

CANNED BLACK BEANS

Most canned black beans have three main ingredients: beans, water, and salt. So how different could they taste? Plenty different, we found out when we sampled six national brands in a blind test. The three brands that scored the highest all have more than 400 milligrams of sodium per ½-cup serving; simply adding salt to the low-scoring brands that had far less salt didn't help. Tasters also disliked mushy beans. The difference between firm and mushy beans hinges on a balance between chemistry (in the form of salt and other additives) and how hot and how long the beans are cooked during canning. The beans need salt for good flavor, but too much can make them mushy. This is why two of our salty, highly ranked brands include calcium chloride, which counteracts the softening power of sodium. But **Bush's Best**, our winning brand, does not. How they achieve firm beans with lots of salt and no calcium chloride is proprietary manufacturing information, we're told, but odds are that to preserve more of their firm texture, Bush's quickly processes their beans with less heat than the other brands.

CROSTINI

PERFECT TWO-BITE COCKTAIL PARTY APPETIZERS with Italian roots, crostini are crusty, rustic pieces of toast lightly flavored with garlic and olive oil that serve as a vehicle for a variety of spreads and toppings. There wasn't much we wanted to change about the already light toasts themselves; the toppings, however, were another story.

Most Italian cookbooks offer similar directions for crostini, wherein the bread is toasted and then rubbed lightly with a clove of raw garlic. The slightly rough texture of the toast acts like sandpaper against the garlic, releasing its flavorful, perfumed oil. The dry, garlic-infused toasts are then allowed to soak up a bit of olive oil to give them just the right texture and hint of richness.

We discovered that the toasting technique is the most important part of the crostini process. It is best to toast the bread for about 10 minutes in a 400-degree oven. Although this may seem like a slow way to make toast, it dries the interior of the bread so that the crostini are crunchy throughout.

The amount of olive oil to use on the toasts was the next issue to tackle. We wanted to limit the fat in our recipe, but we certainly didn't want to eliminate the olive oil altogether, as it lent richness and subtle flavor and improved the texture of the toasts. Although traditionally the toasts are brushed with olive oil, we found it was difficult to control the amount of oil used, so we turned to olive oil spray. The spray evenly dispersed a light coating of olive oil, just enough to season the toasts without making them greasy or adding too much fat.

When it came to deciding on the toppings for the crostini, we focused on classic Italian-inspired flavor combinations: white bean and arugula, tomato and basil, and spinach and Parmesan. Starting with the white bean topping, we pureed a few cans of cannellini beans with extra-virgin olive oil, lemon juice, garlic, shallot, and a pinch of cayenne for heat. We spread the smooth and creamy beans on the crostini and sprinkled chopped arugula over the top, which added just the right bitter-herbal counterpoint. For the tomato and basil topping, we began by salting the tomatoes, just as we had done in several other recipes we'd recently developed so they didn't release their liquid onto the toasts and make them soggy. A touch of extra-virgin olive oil and some basil was all it took to take the tomatoes to the next level.

Spinach and Parmesan are natural partners, but the spinach needed something creamy to bind it together (not unlike spinach dip). Ricotta is traditional on crostini, but we found that part-skim ricotta was just too bland, and full-fat ricotta upped the calorie count too much. We needed to come up with an alternative. Looking back to our recently developed Creamy Dips (page 5), we turned to 1 percent cottage cheese, which has an appealingly salty, tangy flavor that isn't overwhelming. We pureed the cottage cheese with the spinach, Parmesan, lemon juice, basil, oil, garlic, and cayenne to make a smooth, creamy spread. We spread the mixture on the crostini, then topped them off with a sprinkling of freshly grated Parmesan.

We found that the crostini were best when toasted at the last possible moment, and it's a huge bonus if they are served slightly warm. With such a great variety of toppings that were all appealingly fresh, there was no doubt these crostini would be a big hit on our next party spread.

Toasts for Crostini

MAKES ABOUT 30 CROSTINI

You want small rounds for crostini, so try to find a baguette with a diameter of 2½ to 3 inches.

1 **large baguette, cut on the bias into**
   ½-inch-thick slices (about 30 slices) (see note)
1 **large garlic clove, peeled**
   Olive oil spray
   Salt and pepper

1. Adjust an oven rack to the middle position and heat the oven to 400 degrees. Arrange the bread slices in a single layer on a baking sheet. Bake until the bread is dry and crisp, 8 to 10 minutes, turning the slices over halfway through.

2. Remove the toasts from the oven and, while still hot, rub one side of each toast with the raw garlic clove. Spray with the olive oil spray and sprinkle liberally with salt and pepper. (The toasts are best topped and served shortly after they come out of the oven, but you can set the toasts themselves aside for several hours and then top them just before serving.)

PER SERVING (3 CROSTINI): Cal 80; Fat 0.5g; Sat fat 0g; Chol 0mg; Carb 14g; Protein 2g; Fiber 1g; Sodium 180mg

Crostini with White Beans and Arugula

MAKES ABOUT 30 CROSTINI

We found that thoroughly pureeing the beans until smooth and using a high-quality extra-virgin olive oil make all the difference here.

- 2 (15-ounce) cans cannellini beans, drained and rinsed
- 2 tablespoons extra-virgin olive oil
- 2 tablespoons fresh lemon juice
- 2 garlic cloves, minced
- 1 shallot, minced (about 3 tablespoons)
  Pinch cayenne pepper
  Salt and black pepper
- 1 recipe Toasts for Crostini (page 12)
- 1 ounce arugula, chopped (about ½ cup)

1. Process the beans, oil, lemon juice, and garlic together in a food processor until smooth, 1 to 1½ minutes, scraping down the sides of the bowl as needed. Transfer the mixture to a bowl and stir in the shallot and cayenne. Season with salt and black pepper to taste.

2. Cover and let sit at room temperature until the flavors blend, about 1 hour.

3. Spread about 1 tablespoon of the bean puree over each crostini and sprinkle with the arugula. Serve. (The spread can be prepared through step 2 and refrigerated in an airtight container for up to 2 days; let sit at room temperature for 1 hour before proceeding with step 3.)

PER SERVING (3 CROSTINI): Cal 150; Fat 4g; Sat fat 0g; Chol 0mg; Carb 23g; Protein 5g; Fiber 3g; Sodium 300mg

VARIATIONS

Crostini with Tomato and Basil

MAKES ABOUT 30 CROSTINI

If desired, ¼ cup minced fresh chives can be substituted for the basil.

- 1½ pounds ripe tomatoes (about 4 medium), cored, seeded, and chopped medium
  Salt
- ⅓ cup shredded fresh basil
- 1 tablespoon extra-virgin olive oil
  Pepper
- 1 recipe Toasts for Crostini (page 12)

1. Place the tomatoes in a fine-mesh strainer set over a bowl, sprinkle with ½ teaspoon salt, and let drain until the tomatoes begin to soften, about 30 minutes. Discard the liquid.

2. Stir in the basil and oil and season with salt and pepper to taste. Spoon about 1 tablespoon of the tomatoes over each crostini and serve.

PER SERVING (3 CROSTINI): Cal 100; Fat 2.5g; Sat fat 0g; Chol 0mg; Carb 17g; Protein 3g; Fiber 2g; Sodium 300mg

Crostini with Spinach and Parmesan

MAKES ABOUT 30 CROSTINI

Be sure to squeeze the spinach dry so it doesn't make the crostini soggy.

- 12 ounces 1 percent cottage cheese (about 1½ cups)
- 1 (10-ounce) box frozen chopped spinach, thawed and squeezed dry
- 1 ounce Parmesan cheese, grated (about ½ cup)
- ¼ cup packed fresh basil leaves
- 1 tablespoon fresh lemon juice
- 1 tablespoon olive oil
- 1 garlic clove, minced
  Pinch cayenne pepper
  Salt and black pepper
- 1 recipe Toasts for Crostini (page 12)

1. Process the cottage cheese, spinach, ¼ cup of the Parmesan, basil, lemon juice, oil, garlic, and cayenne together

---

NOTES FROM THE TEST KITCHEN

MAKING CROSTINI

When the bread is toasted but still warm, briefly rub a peeled garlic clove over just one side. The coarse texture of the toast acts like sandpaper against the garlic, scenting the bread with just the right amount of garlic flavor.

STORING FRESH HERBS

Most of our appetizer recipes use some fresh herbs, but rarely do we go through a whole bunch in a single recipe, so we know firsthand that their shelf life is short. To get the most life out of your herbs, loosely roll them in a few paper towels, put the roll of herbs in a zipper-lock bag, and place it in the crisper drawer of your refrigerator. Stored in this manner, your herbs will stay fresh for a week or longer.

in a food processor until smooth, 1 to 1½ minutes, scraping down the sides of the bowl as needed. Transfer the mixture to a bowl and season with salt and black pepper to taste.

2. Cover and let sit at room temperature until the flavors blend, about 1 hour.

3. Spread about 1 tablespoon of the spinach mixture over each crostini and sprinkle with the remaining ¼ cup Parmesan. Serve. (The spread can be prepared through step 2 and refrigerated in an airtight container for up to 2 days; let sit at room temperature for 1 hour before proceeding with step 3.)

PER SERVING (3 CROSTINI): **Cal** 130; **Fat** 3g; **Sat fat** 1g; **Chol** 5mg; **Carb** 17g; **Protein** 8g; **Fiber** 1g; **Sodium** 400mg

ARTICHOKE TART

AMONG ALL THE APPETIZERS TO CHOOSE FROM, ONE of our favorites is the vegetable tart. It is guaranteed to stand out on your cocktail party spread, making a nice break from the cheeses and dips. Thinly cut, warm slices of a vegetable tart are sure to impress. Artichokes are a staple on the party table, featured in numerous dips and spreads, so we had to wonder, Could we find a way to incorporate them into an elegant, low-fat tart that had big artichoke flavor? We imagined a creamy artichoke-based filling topped off with even more artichokes.

The crust was our first hurdle, but luckily we had a head start. The test kitchen recently developed a whole wheat olive oil crust, which saved us from all the fat and calories found in traditional butter-laden tart crust. We were also able to streamline the method used for conventional rolled-out dough, switching to a much easier press-in method. And as an added bonus, the olive oil in the crust provided a subtlety that complemented the Mediterranean flavors of the artichokes.

In our previous testing, we had found that the correct amount of oil was the crucial determinant for the crisp, tender tart crust we were after. Not enough oil resulted in a crumbly texture similar to that of shortbread; too much oil and the dough was tough and chewy. Six tablespoons proved to be the happy medium. No only did whole wheat flour add a healthy element, but tasters also loved its rustic, nutty flavor. Parbaking the crust before adding the filling ensured a crisp, evenly baked crust that would hold our filling perfectly.

With our crust ready to go, we moved on to the tart construction, starting with the filling. We often employ a creamy cheese layer to hold the vegetables in place, but we wanted to cut back on the fat and take the opportunity to create even more artichoke flavor. We decided that pureeing artichokes with a creamy component was a good starting point. We tested various combinations of a creamy ingredient (goat cheese, part-skim ricotta, cottage cheese, low-fat cream cheese, and low-fat sour cream) with artichokes in some form (we tried fresh, canned, and frozen). Fresh artichokes were a lot of work to prepare, but luckily it didn't matter; tasters found the texture of the canned artichokes preferable because they pureed into a velvety smooth spread most easily. As for the binder, the ricotta and cream cheese both tasted watery and bland. Tasters thought the low-fat cream cheese and sour cream didn't perform any better, creating a strange off-flavor in the filling. The standout was the goat cheese. Tasters overwhelmingly praised it for making a filling with a pleasant tang that didn't overwhelm the artichoke flavor. A little lemon juice and garlic rounded out the flavor of the puree. Some tasters noted that our filling tasted similar to hot artichoke dip, which no one had a problem with.

With the filling ironed out, we turned our attention to the topping. We needed to determine the best form of artichoke to use. After our filling tests, we decided the limited growing season and labor-intensive nature of fresh artichokes eliminated them from the running. This left canned and frozen artichokes, but even then, neither was without its limitations. While we liked canned artichokes in the filling, when used whole or in chunks on the top of the tart they tasted tinny and a little slimy. They also leached water when baked, which created a soggy crust.

Frozen artichoke quarters were better, but they tasted a little bland. Because they were baked for only 10 minutes on top of the tart, they didn't have a chance to develop a fuller flavor. We found that roasting them before putting them on the tart helped immensely. They didn't even need to be thawed; they could go straight from freezer to oven and emerge nicely roasted and flavorful after about 20 minutes. For our first test, we arranged the quarters artfully on the top of the tart. While it looked impressive, tasters found that the large pieces made cutting even slices nearly impossible. After a few pulses in the food processor we had a roasted artichoke confetti that could be easily spread over the tart filling. With our topping in place, all we had to do was heat up the assembled tart in the oven for 10 to 15 minutes to warm it through. To round out the flavors, we topped it off just before serving with a tablespoon of shredded basil. This added the touch of freshness our artichoke tart needed.

Satisfied that we had packed as much artichoke flavor into this tart as possible, we developed two variations that would build on the recipe by adding complementary flavors. Sun-dried tomatoes added a rich, briny punch of flavor against the mild artichokes, and sautéed prosciutto added a crisp salty element when sprinkled on top.

Artichoke Tart

SERVES 12

The filling in this tart is relatively thin, so you need to press the dough only ¾ inch up the sides of the tart pan.

CRUST

- ¾ cup plus 3 tablespoons (about 4⅔ ounces) unbleached all-purpose flour
- ¼ cup plus 1 tablespoon (about 1¾ ounces) whole wheat flour
- 1 tablespoon sugar
- ½ teaspoon salt
- 6 tablespoons extra-virgin olive oil
- 4–6 tablespoons ice water

FILLING

- 1 (14-ounce) can artichoke hearts, drained
- 2 ounces goat cheese, crumbled (about ½ cup)
- 1 teaspoon fresh lemon juice
- 1 garlic clove, minced
- Salt and pepper

TOPPING

- 2 (9-ounce) boxes frozen artichoke hearts (do not thaw)
- Olive oil spray
- 2 teaspoons extra-virgin olive oil
- Salt and pepper
- 1 tablespoon shredded fresh basil

1. FOR THE CRUST: Process the all-purpose flour, whole wheat flour, sugar, and salt together in a food processor until combined. Drizzle the oil over the flour mixture and pulse until the mixture resembles coarse sand, about 12 pulses. Add 4 tablespoons of the ice water and process until large clumps of dough form and no powdery bits remain, about 5 seconds. If the dough doesn't clump, add the remaining 2 tablespoons water, 1 tablespoon at

NOTES FROM THE TEST KITCHEN

FORMING A PRESS-IN TART CRUST

1. Transfer the processed dough to a 9-inch tart pan with a removable bottom.

2. Working outward from the center, press the dough into an even layer, sealing any cracks.

3. Working around the edge, press the dough firmly into the corners of the pan with your fingers.

4. Go around the edge once more, pressing the dough up the sides and into the fluted ridges.

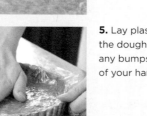

5. Lay plastic wrap over the dough and smooth out any bumps using the palm of your hand.

a time, and pulse to incorporate, about 4 pulses. (The dough should feel quite sticky.)

2. Following the photos on page 15, transfer the dough to a 9-inch tart pan with a removable bottom and pat into an even layer. Press the dough up the sides of the pan. Lay plastic wrap over the dough and smooth out any bumps using the palm of your hand. Leaving the plastic on top of the dough, place the tart pan on a large plate and freeze the tart shell until firm, about 30 minutes.

3. Adjust an oven rack to the middle position and heat the oven to 375 degrees. Set the tart pan on a large baking sheet. Remove the plastic, press a double layer of foil into the frozen tart shell and over the edges of the pan, and fill with pie weights. Bake until the tart shell is golden brown and set, 40 to 50 minutes, rotating the baking sheet halfway through. Transfer the baking sheet to a wire rack and carefully remove the weights and foil.

4. Let the tart shell cool on the baking sheet while making the filling. Increase the oven temperature to 450 degrees.

5. FOR THE FILLING: Process the canned artichokes, goat cheese, lemon juice, and garlic together in the food processor until smooth, about 1 minute. Transfer to a bowl and season with salt and pepper to taste.

6. FOR THE TOPPING: Lightly coat the frozen artichokes with olive oil spray. Roast the artichokes until browned at the edges, 20 to 25 minutes, stirring halfway through.

7. Transfer the roasted artichokes to the food processor and pulse until coarsely chopped, about 4 pulses. Transfer to a bowl, stir in the oil, and season with salt and pepper to taste.

8. Spread the artichoke-cheese filling evenly over the tart crust, then spread the roasted artichoke topping over the top. Bake the tart on the baking sheet until heated through, 10 to 15 minutes.

9. Let the tart cool on the baking sheet for 5 minutes, then sprinkle with the basil. To serve, remove the outer metal ring of the tart pan, slide a thin metal spatula between the tart and the tart pan bottom, and carefully slide the tart onto a platter or cutting board. Serve warm. (The tart can be assembled through step 8 but do not bake. Cover with plastic wrap and refrigerate for up to 1 day. Remove plastic wrap and proceed as directed.)

PER SERVING: Cal 160; Fat 9g; Sat fat 2g; Chol 0mg; Carb 15g; Protein 4g; Fiber 3g; Sodium 210mg

VARIATIONS

Artichoke Tart with Sun-Dried Tomatoes

Follow the recipe for Artichoke Tart, stirring ½ cup chopped sun-dried tomatoes into the chopped roasted artichokes in step 7.

PER SERVING: Cal 170; Fat 10g; Sat fat 2g; Chol 0mg; Carb 16g; Protein 4g; Fiber 3g; Sodium 230mg

Artichoke Tart with Crispy Prosciutto

Heat 1 teaspoon canola oil in a 10-inch nonstick skillet over medium heat. Cook 2 ounces finely chopped prosciutto until crisp, 3 to 5 minutes. Transfer to a paper towel–lined plate and set aside. Follow the recipe for Artichoke Tart, sprinkling the cooked prosciutto over the top when the tart comes out of the oven in step 8.

PER SERVING: Cal 170; Fat 10g; Sat fat 2g; Chol 5mg; Carb 16g; Protein 5g; Fiber 3g; Sodium 340mg

SMOKED SALMON ROLLS

LET'S FACE IT, SMOKED SALMON IS A TRIED-AND-TRUE choice for many a cocktail party spread, and the fact that it is naturally healthy makes it even more appealing. But when you tire of smoked salmon dip or pumpernickel toasts topped with smoked salmon, crème fraîche, and capers, what are the options? After seeing a few recipes for smoked salmon rolls as well as premade versions at the deli counter in our local supermarket, we decided it was time to try our own hand at coming up with a smoked salmon roll recipe. We wanted to create a light and healthy appetizer that was both visually appealing and easy to make.

Many salmon rolls rely on a creamy spread to hold them together, but this component is problematic if you are trying to eat light. Typically dairy-based (cream cheese, sour cream, and not much else), it packs on the calories and lacks flavor, not to mention there's usually so much spread it overwhelms the salmon.

We decided to begin by putting the fat and calories of the spread in check. The obvious jumping-off point was to take out the cream cheese and sour cream and swap in the low-fat counterparts. This worked OK, but we missed the luscious texture of the full-fat versions; this spread was denser, almost pasty. We tried using both

SMOKED SALMON ROLLS

low-fat yogurt and part-skim ricotta, but the yogurt was too watery and its tang was too overwhelming, and the ricotta had a grainy texture that didn't work at all. Because we liked the flavor of the light cream cheese and low-fat sour cream combination (tasters approved a 1-to-1 ratio), we decided to move ahead with those ingredients and focus on correcting the texture.

The cream cheese was not incorporating into our mixture well, but when we tried lessening the amount, tasters felt that the flavor balance was off. So first we tried to beat the cream cheese before mixing it with the sour cream, hoping that incorporating some air would lighten the texture. This helped a little, but not enough to justify dirtying our mixer for marginal results. We then tested incorporating various amounts of water to soften the texture, but this only gave the spread an unappealingly loose texture. Ultimately, the answer was simpler than we thought. The whole time we had been working with chilled ingredients. We wanted this appetizer to come together quickly, but we realized it was critical to let the cream cheese come to room temperature first. With that small change, we could move on to boosting the flavor.

Our goal was to give our spread a nice, subtle balance of flavors. Too many flavors and we would overwhelm the salmon; too few and our appetizer would fall flat. To balance the richness of the cheese and sour cream, this spread needed an acidic component. We tried lemon juice, and white wine, red wine, and cider vinegars, to name a few. Tasters unanimously agreed that 1 tablespoon of lemon juice lent the right clean flavor; it was a logical match for the salmon as well. Minced shallots added depth; capers (also a classic choice for smoked salmon) lent a nice briny bite, and chives added a touch of freshness (though tasters also liked dill, so we left that as an option).

It was time to assemble the rolls. We laid the salmon slices out and topped each one with 1 teaspoon of our cream cheese–sour cream mixture. Originally, we thought this would seem skimpy, but in a side-by-side taste test of a slice of salmon (each was just short of 1 ounce) paired with 1 teaspoon, 2 teaspoons, and 1 tablespoon of filling, tasters preferred the balance of salmon to spread offered by 1 teaspoon. We then gently rolled the salmon into tight cylinders, cut them in half, and stood them on their cut ends.

These rolls looked pretty and tasted great, but something was still missing. In search of both a garnish and a touch of freshness, we landed on one leaf of baby arugula to garnish each roll. Its peppery crunch also lent a new textural element to the dish that tasters unanimously agreed was a welcome addition.

These salmon rolls tasted as fresh and good as they looked, and they didn't have any fat or calories to hide.

Smoked Salmon Rolls

MAKES ABOUT 18 ROLLS

Be sure to use good-quality, fresh smoked salmon for this recipe; it should glisten and have a bright, rosy color.

- 1 tablespoon light cream cheese, softened
- 1 tablespoon low-fat sour cream
- ½ teaspoon fresh lemon juice
- Pinch salt
- Pinch pepper
- 1 teaspoon minced shallot
- 1 teaspoon drained capers, rinsed and minced

NOTES FROM THE TEST KITCHEN

MAKING SALMON ROLLS

1. After spreading the cheese mixture over the slices of salmon, roll up the salmon around the filling.

2. Using a sharp knife, slice each salmon roll in half.

3. Stand up each roll on its cut end and garnish with a small leaf of arugula.

1 teaspoon minced fresh chives or dill

8 ounces sliced smoked salmon (about 9 slices)

18 small leaves baby arugula

1. Mix the cream cheese, sour cream, lemon juice, salt, and pepper together in a bowl until uniform, then stir in the shallot, capers, and chives.

2. Spread about 1 teaspoon of the cheese mixture evenly over each slice of salmon. Following the photos on page 18, roll up the salmon around the cheese mixture. (The salmon rolls can be made up to this point, covered tightly with plastic wrap, and refrigerated for up to 4 hours.)

3. Slice each salmon roll in half with a sharp knife. Stand each roll on its cut end, garnish with an arugula leaf, and serve.

PER SERVING (3 ROLLS): Cal 50; Fat 2g; Sat fat 0.5g; Chol 10mg; Carb 0g; Protein 7g; Fiber 0g; Sodium 350mg

SHRIMP COCKTAIL

NOTHING IS MORE BASIC THAN SHRIMP COCKTAIL: cooked shrimp served cold with "cocktail" sauce, typically a blend of bottled ketchup or chili sauce spiked with horseradish. Could something so simple and good be improved upon? It seems like such a basic dish that it would be foolproof to make, but after testing more than a few recipes, it became obvious to us, between the rubbery, tasteless shrimp and sauces that were either bland or searingly hot, that there was plenty of room for improvement.

Boosting the shrimp's sweet flavor was first on the list. Conventional shrimp cocktail recipes call for boiling or simmering the shrimp in salted water to bring out their natural flavor. The salted water produced acceptable results, but we really wanted to amplify the shrimp flavor. First we tried cooking the shrimp with the shells on. This created more shrimp-y flavor, but it had a few problems. Peeling cooked shrimp was hardly something we would want to deal with while mingling at a get-together, especially when it is much harder to peel cooked shrimp than raw.

Next we tried adding flavors to the water itself. Everyone we talked to had a secret concoction to recommend, and the combinations we tried seemed endless: Lemon juice, lemon zest, a range of spices and herbs, vinegars, and even wine and beer were just some of our tests. Seasonings like garlic, parsley, oregano, paprika, and lemon zest were quickly eliminated because they covered up the shrimp flavor. We found that wine and beer also overpowered the delicate shrimp. In the end, we settled on a simple blend of lemon juice, Old Bay, a few bay leaves, and salt and pepper.

These complementary seasonings definitely helped to bring out the natural flavor of the shrimp, but we still weren't satisfied. Adding more seasonings to the cooking liquid would simply cover up the flavor of the shrimp, so we needed to increase the amount of time the shrimp were in contact with the liquid, while at the same time avoiding overcooking them.

The traditional method of boiling the shrimp allowed us only a small window before they overcooked, not to mention that it happened so quickly that it gave the seasonings little time to permeate. We found that the best method was to bring the liquid and aromatics to a boil, then turn off the heat, add the shrimp, and cover with a lid. The residual heat allowed the shrimp to cook much more gently. After tests of various time increments, we found that we could leave the shrimp in the broth for up to seven minutes before they ran the risk of turning tough. A full seven minutes meant our shrimp could be in contact with the flavorful cooking liquid for much longer than they would in the traditional method.

Two-thirds of the way there, we finally turned to the sauce. Cocktail sauce is one of those recipes that everyone knows and appreciates for what it is, so we didn't want to stray too far from the classic. We started with the tomato product and tested both canned and fresh tomatoes as well as more familiar choices like ketchup and bottled chili sauce. We even went so far as to make our own homemade ketchup. Tasters spoke unanimously in favor of bottled ketchup. Fresh tomatoes were too watery, canned tomatoes tasted tinny, and the chili sauce was too vinegary.

With the base of the sauce sorted out, we moved to flavorings. Prepared horseradish is a classic inclusion and we saw no reason to change it. We fiddled with the correct ratio and found that 2 tablespoons of horseradish to 1 cup of ketchup worked best. It offered good heat without overwhelming the tomato flavor or the shrimp. We then tried various seasonings to add some depth.

An acidic component would add some brightness, so we tested nearly every vinegar we could think of (white wine, balsamic, cider, rice, and sherry vinegars), only to decide that lemon juice was the best choice for its bright, clean flavor that highlighted the other ingredients without adding any distracting flavors. A few shots of hot sauce for a little peppery heat, and we were satisfied.

Content that we had accomplished all of our goals, we whipped together another sauce variation. Though we like rémoulade, another classic choice for pairing with seafood, we decided to spice things up by making a creamy sauce with a Southwestern flair. Adding cilantro, chipotle chiles, and lime to light mayonnaise gave our Creamy Chipotle Sauce just the right combination of flavors, making another great match for our perfectly cooked shrimp.

Classic Shrimp Cocktail

SERVES 8

You can use larger or smaller shrimp if desired; however, the cooking time will vary by a few minutes. The recipe can easily be doubled; use a large Dutch oven and increase the cooking time to about 10 minutes. For a bolder sauce, add more horseradish and hot sauce to taste.

SHRIMP

- 2 teaspoons fresh lemon juice
- 2 bay leaves
- 1 teaspoon salt
- 1 teaspoon black peppercorns
- 1 teaspoon Old Bay Seasoning
- 1 pound extra-large shrimp (21 to 25 per pound), peeled and deveined (see page 120)

COCKTAIL SAUCE

- 1 cup ketchup
- 2 tablespoons prepared horseradish
- 2 tablespoons fresh lemon juice
- 2 teaspoons hot sauce
- ½ teaspoon salt
- ¼ teaspoon pepper

1. FOR THE SHRIMP: Bring the lemon juice, bay leaves, salt, peppercorns, Old Bay, and 4 cups water to a boil in a large saucepan, and boil for 2 minutes. Remove the pan from the heat and add the shrimp. Cover and steep until the shrimp are firm and pink, about 7 minutes.

2. Drain the shrimp and plunge immediately into ice water. Drain and refrigerate the shrimp in an airtight container until thoroughly chilled, at least 1 hour or up to 1 day.

3. FOR THE COCKTAIL SAUCE: Meanwhile, stir the ketchup, horseradish, lemon juice, hot sauce, salt, and pepper together in a bowl. Cover and refrigerate until the flavors blend, at least 1 hour or up to 2 days. Serve the shrimp with the sauce.

PER SERVING (3 SHRIMP WITH 2 TABLESPOONS SAUCE): Cal 90; Fat 1g; Sat fat 0g; Chol 85mg; Carb 9g; Protein 12g; Fiber 0g; Sodium 680mg

VARIATION

Shrimp Cocktail with Creamy Chipotle Sauce
Follow the recipe for Classic Shrimp Cocktail, substituting the following for the Cocktail Sauce: Stir 1 cup light mayonnaise, 4 teaspoons water, 4 teaspoons fresh lime juice, 1 tablespoon minced fresh cilantro, 1 minced garlic clove, ½ teaspoon minced canned chipotle chiles in adobo sauce, ¼ teaspoon salt, and ⅛ teaspoon pepper together in a bowl. Cover and refrigerate until the flavors blend, at least 1 hour or up to 1 day.

PER SERVING (3 SHRIMP WITH 2 TABLESPOONS SAUCE): Cal 120; Fat 7g; Sat fat 1g; Chol 90mg; Carb 2g; Protein 12g; Fiber 0g; Sodium 420mg

---

NOTES FROM THE TEST KITCHEN

OUR FAVORITE KETCHUP
You think you know ketchup. It's red, thick, sweet, salty, and tangy—and you can't imagine a burger and fries without it. And you think you know which brand tastes best. Heinz is ketchup and ketchup is Heinz, right? No one in the test kitchen likes to accept things at face value, so we rounded up eight brands (all available nationwide and fairly traditional) and asked 29 tasters to taste them plain and with french fries. Our panel had some shocking news for ketchup lovers. According to tasters, there's a better option than Heinz—and it's sitting right there on the shelf of your local supermarket. **Hunt's**, America's number-two ketchup, was the clear winner of our tasting. Tasters praised its "tangy" flavor and found it "well balanced," whereas Heinz was criticized for being "too bland."

SPRING ROLLS

WHILE THE NAME "SPRING ROLLS" SOUNDS LIGHT, order them at a Chinese restaurant and you'll end up with a plate of the smaller version of egg rolls. They may be appetizer-size and have a more delicate exterior than egg rolls, but they're still deep-fried, heavy, and greasy. However, look to Vietnamese cuisine and you will discover another kind of spring roll, those that are fresh. Made by filling translucent softened rice paper wrappers with shrimp, pork, or tofu, as well as chilled rice vermicelli, raw vegetables, and fragrant herbs, this variety of spring roll is light and refreshing. When made well, these spring rolls offer great textural appeal as well as simple, fresh contrasting flavors, but they can easily miss the mark with gummy noodles, soggy rice paper, shriveled herbs, and saccharine "peanut" sauces that taste nothing like peanuts. Given that spring rolls require only a short list of fresh ingredients and minimal cooking, we felt up to the challenge of producing a four-star spring roll recipe of our own with perfect wrappers surrounding a fresh filling and an appealing peanut dipping sauce.

We began with the wrapper. Straight from the package, rice paper wrappers are hard and inedible and so must be soaked in water before use. It quickly became apparent that timing was crucial here. When soaked too long, the wrappers simply disintegrated; when soaked for just two or three seconds, the wrappers remained stiff. We found that a two-minute soak was just right. But even with the correct soaking time, the wrappers were so delicate that they tore easily as soon as we started working with them. The trick, we discovered, was to place the softened wrappers on top of a damp kitchen towel spread out on the counter.

With the wrappers ready to go, we turned to the filling, starting with the noodles. The instructions on the package of thin vermicelli-style rice noodles call for bringing water to a boil, then pouring the hot water over the noodles in another dish and letting them soak. We found that this technique was a little too gentle, and the noodles never quite softened properly. We next tried dropping the noodles right into a pot of boiling water that had just been removed from the heat and letting them sit for 10 minutes. This small increase in residual heat was the answer. Next we moved on to the protein. While the combination of shrimp and pork is a classic spring roll choice, we decided to keep things simple and use only shrimp. We found that extra-large shrimp worked best, as they portioned well and meant we needed only a few for each spring roll. We had to slice the shrimp in half lengthwise in order to make them lie properly; whole shrimp had a tendency to break through the wrapper.

For the vegetables, carrot, daikon radish, and cucumber are the traditional choices. Daikon can be difficult to find, so we eliminated it from the options. Carrots contributed a pleasantly sweet flavor and nice texture when shredded. We tried grating cucumber as well but ended up with watery, soggy rolls. When sliced into matchstick-size pieces, however, the cucumber added significant crunch without dampening the wrappers. Shredded lettuce added more crunch to round out our vegetable selection.

For the herbs, fragrant cilantro and mint, both classic choices, are usually added as whole leaves in a single pile before rolling. Tasters agreed they added a burst of freshness and lent visual appeal, but we didn't like the single bunch of leaves in a mouthful. The solution was twofold: We sprinkled both herbs over the rice paper before any other ingredients were added, and we tore any large mint leaves into smaller pieces.

These rolls had great textures, but despite our liberal dose of herbs, the rolls remained a little bland and dry. We went back to our library of cookbooks and discovered spring roll recipes that included an acidic marinade for the vegetables and noodles that would lend both flavor and moisture. We eventually settled on a simple mixture of fish sauce and lime juice. Whisking in a teaspoon of sugar and some chopped fresh jalapeño balanced the

---

NOTES FROM THE TEST KITCHEN

SPRING ROLL WRAPPERS

Made from a paste of rice flour and water that is stamped into bamboo mats and dried, rice paper wrappers are translucent, brittle, and delicate—meaning they can be difficult to work with. They are almost impossible to make at home but can be purchased at Asian grocery stores, natural foods stores, and gourmet grocers. Make sure you look for all-rice wrappers, not the thin wrappers made with tapioca starch or the thick wheat flour wrappers.

ASSEMBLING SPRING ROLLS

1. Lay the cucumber over the herbs on the wrapper, leaving a 2-inch border at the bottom, followed by the carrots, lettuce, noodles, and shrimp.

2. Fold the bottom of the wrapper up over the filling.

3. Fold the sides of the wrapper over the filling.

4. Finish by rolling the wrapper up into a tight roll.

SEEDING CUCUMBERS

Halve the peeled cucumber lengthwise. Run a small spoon inside each cucumber half to scoop out the seeds and surrounding liquid.

acidity and gave the rolls a sweet-hot punch.

For the dipping sauce, we began with a standard recipe for peanut sauce made with hoisin sauce, sugar, peanut butter, and a little water to reach the proper consistency. Tasters agreed we could live without the sugar; it made the sauce too sweet on top of the peanut butter, and it added unnecessary calories. To minimize the fat, we cut back on the peanut butter as much as we could while still maintaining good peanut flavor and creamy texture. Next we added lime juice, garlic, and Asian chili-garlic sauce for heat. The resulting sauce was gently sweet and spicy with a subtle richness, the perfect counterpoint to the spring rolls.

These spring rolls were so good and easy to make, we were sure we wouldn't be ordering them off a menu anytime soon.

Vietnamese Spring Rolls with Hoisin-Peanut Dipping Sauce

MAKES 8

Both rice paper wrappers and rice vermicelli can be purchased in Asian markets as well as in the international food aisle of many supermarkets. The thickness of rice vermicelli varies from brand to brand, so it's best to taste the noodles periodically to make sure they are tender before draining. You can buy already cooked shrimp, or follow our method for cooking shrimp in Classic Shrimp Cocktail (page 20). To make this dish spicier, add the chile seeds.

SAUCE
- ¼ cup creamy peanut butter
- ¼ cup hot water
- ⅓ cup hoisin sauce
- 1 tablespoon fresh lime juice
- 1 garlic clove, minced
- ½ teaspoon Asian chili-garlic sauce

SPRING ROLLS
- 3 ounces dried rice vermicelli (see page 31)
- 2½ tablespoons fresh lime juice (about 2 limes)
- 1½ tablespoons fish sauce
- 1 teaspoon sugar
- 1 carrot, peeled and shredded
- 1 jalapeño chile, stemmed, seeded, and minced

1 cucumber (about 8 ounces), peeled, halved, seeded (see photo), and cut into matchsticks

8 (8-inch) round rice paper wrappers (see page 21)

½ cup fresh mint, leaves torn into pieces

½ cup fresh cilantro

4 large leaves red leaf or Boston lettuce, shredded

8 ounces cooked and fully peeled extra-large shrimp (21 to 25 per pound), halved lengthwise (see note)

1. FOR THE SAUCE: Whisk the peanut butter and hot water together in a bowl until smooth, then whisk in the hoisin, lime juice, garlic, and chili-garlic sauce until combined. Cover and refrigerate until needed. (The sauce can be refrigerated in an airtight container for up to 2 days; season with additional lime juice to taste before serving.)

2. FOR THE ROLLS: Bring 4 quarts water to a boil in a large pot. Remove from the heat, add the rice vermicelli, and let sit, stirring occasionally, until the noodles are tender, about 10 minutes. Meanwhile, whisk the lime juice, fish sauce, and sugar together until the sugar dissolves.

3. Drain the noodles, transfer to a bowl, and toss with 2 tablespoons of the lime juice mixture. In another bowl, toss the carrot and jalapeño with 1 tablespoon more lime juice mixture. In a third bowl, toss the cucumber with the remaining 1 tablespoon lime juice mixture.

4. Spread a clean, damp kitchen towel on the counter. Fill a pie plate with 1 inch room-temperature water. Working with 1 rice paper wrapper at a time, immerse it in the water until it is just pliable, about 2 minutes, then transfer it to the towel.

5. Sprinkle with about 6 pieces mint leaves and 6 cilantro leaves. Following the photos on page 22, arrange 5 cucumber sticks horizontally on the wrapper and top with 1 tablespoon of the carrot mixture, 2 tablespoons of the lettuce, 2½ tablespoons of the noodles, and 3 shrimp halves.

6. Roll the rice paper wrapper around the filling into a spring roll, transfer it to a large platter, and cover with another clean, damp kitchen towel. Repeat with the remaining rice paper wrappers and filling ingredients. Serve with the sauce. (The spring rolls can be prepared and refrigerated, covered with a damp kitchen towel, for up to 4 hours.)

PER SERVING (1 ROLL WITH ABOUT 1½ TABLESPOONS SAUCE): Cal 190; Fat 5g; Sat fat 1g; Chol 45mg; Carb 26g; Protein 11g; Fiber 2g; Sodium 420mg

CHICKEN SKEWERS

MOST EVERYONE LIKES CHICKEN WHEN IT'S SEASONED well and cooked just right, and skewers are ideally portioned so that you can eat one and feel satisfied but not weighed down. But chicken dishes quickly become unappealing when the meat is bland and overcooked. We wanted to come up with a recipe for flavorful, well-seasoned chicken skewers with tender meat and a dipping sauce that complemented the skewers.

Chicken breasts are a relatively blank canvas and require a flavorful spice rub or marinade to make them stand out. We settled on an Indian-spiced recipe since we could use a lot of seasoning without adding a lot of calories or fat. First we tried a wet marinade with coconut milk, curry, paprika, red pepper flakes, garlic powder, and salt, but tasters agreed its flavor seemed diluted. Using the same spices, we dropped the coconut milk to make a dry rub. To help the spices adhere to the meat, we also added honey, which would have the additional benefit of promoting browning.

Next up was the cooking method. We wanted to make enough skewers to feed a crowd, so we needed a cooking method that could churn out a lot of skewers in little time. Grilling was an option, but the idea of all the back-and-forth between the grill outside and greeting guests at the front door nixed that idea. Broiling was a better option—it allowed us to prepare about 30 skewers at a time, keeping our guests satisfied and our sanity intact.

Although we typically prefer metal skewers in the test kitchen because they are more durable and heat-resistant and their flattened shape ensures food won't flip around, this situation was a little different. Because these hors d'oeuvres would be eaten out of hand, tasters preferred bamboo to metal skewers since the bamboo ones are disposable and easier to handle immediately after cooking. The only downside to bamboo skewers, as we were well aware, is that they run the risk of smoldering, or even catching fire, under the broiler. To combat this issue, we lined up the meat ends of the skewers on the same side of the broiler pan and protected the exposed bamboo with a strip of aluminum foil. Positioned about 6 inches below the broiler element, the chicken cooked through in about eight minutes and the skewers remained in good shape for serving.

Skewered chicken is often served with a dipping sauce, and we naturally wanted one that would complement and enhance its partner in terms of flavor and consistency.

CURRIED CHICKEN SKEWERS WITH YOGURT-MINT DIPPING SAUCE

A thin sauce wouldn't work well for this style of appetizer—we needed a thick sauce that wouldn't run down our arms or drip on our shirts. Yogurt is often used to finish Indian dishes, and tasters really liked the cool and creamy richness of a dipping sauce made from low-fat plain yogurt and low-fat sour cream. Finishing it with mint and scallions gave it a fresh, bright flavor that made it the perfect accompaniment to the spicy chicken. At last we had easy-to-prepare chicken skewers with tender, well-seasoned meat and a perfect dipping sauce to serve alongside.

Curried Chicken Skewers with Yogurt-Mint Dipping Sauce

MAKES ABOUT 30 SKEWERS

You will need thirty 6- to 8-inch-long wooden skewers for this recipe. The spice-honey mixture is thick; you will need to toss the chicken in it for several minutes, until it loosens up, to achieve even coating. The cooking time will depend on the strength and type of your broiler.

SAUCE

- ¾ cup plain low-fat yogurt
- ¼ cup low-fat sour cream
- 2 tablespoons minced fresh mint
- 2 scallions, sliced thin
- 1 small garlic clove, minced
- ¼ teaspoon salt
- ⅛ teaspoon pepper

CHICKEN

- ¼ cup honey
- 1 tablespoon curry powder
- 1 teaspoon salt
- ½ teaspoon paprika
- ¼ teaspoon red pepper flakes
- ¼ teaspoon garlic powder
- 2 pounds boneless, skinless chicken breasts, trimmed and frozen for 30 minutes

1. FOR THE SAUCE: Whisk the yogurt, sour cream, mint, scallions, garlic, salt, and pepper together in a bowl until smooth. Cover and refrigerate until the flavors blend, at least 1 hour or up to 1 day.

2. FOR THE CHICKEN: Combine the honey, curry powder, salt, paprika, pepper flakes, and garlic powder in a large bowl. Following the photos, slice the partially frozen chicken diagonally into ¼-inch-thick strips. Add the chicken strips to the honey-spice mixture and toss to coat. Cover the bowl and refrigerate for at least 1 hour or up to 1 day.

3. Weave each piece of marinated chicken onto a bamboo skewer. Position an oven rack 6 inches from the heating element and heat the broiler. Line the bottom of a broiler pan with foil, cover with the slotted broiler pan top, and lightly coat with vegetable oil spray.

4. Lay half of the skewers on the broiler pan and cover the skewer ends with foil. Broil until the chicken is fully cooked, about 8 minutes, flipping the skewers halfway through. Transfer the skewers to a large platter and serve with the sauce. Repeat with the remaining chicken skewers.

PER SERVING (3 SKEWERS WITH 1½ TABLESPOONS SAUCE): Cal 150; Fat 2g; Sat fat 0.5g; Chol 55mg; Carb 9g; Protein 22g; Fiber 0g; Sodium 370mg

---

NOTES FROM THE TEST KITCHEN

MAKING CHICKEN SKEWERS

1. Using a chef's knife, slice the partially frozen chicken on the diagonal into ¼-inch-thick strips.

2. After marinating the chicken in the spice rub, weave each strip back and forth onto a skewer until the entire strip is firmly on the skewer.

3. To keep the exposed portions of the skewers from burning, cover the ends of the skewers with a narrow strip of aluminum foil.

CHICKEN AND DUMPLINGS

SOUPS & STEWS

M = TEST KITCHEN MAKEOVER

HEARTY CHICKEN NOODLE SOUP

AT THE SAME TIME BOTH HEALTHY AND SATISFYING, a bowl of chicken noodle soup comforts better than most foods out there. And while it may seem like the simplest of recipes—broth, chicken, noodles, a few vegetables—a lot of work actually goes into a good bowl of chicken noodle soup. The time-honored tradition for making it, however, takes hours. It starts with a homemade stock made with chicken bones and scraps, a few aromatic vegetables, and herbs. After this stock is simmered for hours, it is strained, and vegetables (often only onion, carrot, and celery), chicken, and noodles are added. Then the soup is cooked until the flavors meld. We had to wonder, Was there a simpler way to deliver similar results? We wanted a deeply flavorful, healthy chicken soup, with more vegetables than is typical, as well as perfectly cooked meat, soft noodles, not to mention a satisfying broth. But (and this was a big *but*) this recipe also had to be fast and convenient to prepare. We weren't sure if it was possible, but we decided to give it a shot.

True, shortcut recipes already exist, but a few recipes we tested from this category revealed we would do just as well to heat up a bowl of canned soup from the supermarket. Most of these easy recipes have you add chunks of cooked chicken and chopped vegetables to canned broth, then simmer until the vegetables are soft. Fast, yes. But not worth even the small effort given the results: watery and bland broth; dry, overcooked meat; and "soft" vegetables that are really mushy and blown out. Even if we were using store-bought broth, we knew we could do better.

The biggest question was how to boost the flavor of store-bought broth quickly and easily. In the test kitchen, we've had great success boosting the flavor of store-bought broth by first sweating aromatic vegetables in the pot in oil or butter to coax out their natural sweetness. Once the broth is added, the vegetables' flavors enrich and add depth to the otherwise flat-tasting broth. This seemed like an obvious starting point for our recipe. The veggies traditionally used (onion, carrot, and celery) were givens here as well. However, the substantial amount of fat was not. We opted for the healthier test kitchen technique for sweating vegetables, which requires only

a minimum of fat. We added our veggies, some salt, and a scant amount of oil to the pot, put on the lid, and cooked until the veggies were soft. The salt helped pull the moisture from the vegetables, concentrating their flavor, and the lid trapped the moisture, preventing the vegetables from burning without the need for much oil.

Another way we typically improve the flavor of store-bought broth is by poaching the chicken right in the broth, which gives it more genuine chicken flavor. We ruled out fattier dark meat (thighs and legs) in favor of white meat to keep up our healthy theme. And while bone-in, skin-on chicken breasts lent a lot of flavor, we wondered if they were necessary since they took some time to cook and required a little work. In the end, boneless, skinless chicken breasts, the easiest and quickest to cook of all the options, won out, and poaching them in our broth not only bolstered the flavor of the liquid but also ensured that the meat stayed moist and tender.

At this point our soup was developing pretty good flavor, but tasters agreed something earthy added to the pot would contribute a necessary depth. We found that we liked a slightly nontraditional chicken noodle soup addition: a hearty green. We eventually settled on Swiss chard, whose leaves held up well without being tough, and we liked the fact that we could also incorporate the stems to add more texture to our soup. We added the chopped stems to the pot with the other vegetables, and the leaves went into the pot toward the end.

Of course, what is chicken noodle soup without the noodles? It was a given that the traditional choice, wide egg noodles, were a logical fit. With that, our soup was nearly there: We had a great-tasting broth, a nice mix of vegetables, and perfectly tender chicken. But still, tasters complained that the broth was too thin. This wasn't a surprising flaw, since our quick-version broth was prepared without the chicken bones that are used in a long-simmered broth to contribute not only flavor but also gelatin, which gives the soup a richer texture. To thicken our quick broth, we tried varying amounts of both cornstarch and flour. Cornstarch gave the broth a slimy feel so we crossed it off the list. However, flour worked well, thickening the soup without adding a strange texture or flavor. Two tablespoons proved just right. After adding the noodles, we had a soup that was great-tasting, healthy, and quick and easy to make. No one missed the extra work involved in many other chicken noodle soups.

Hearty Chicken Noodle Soup

SERVES 8

Kale or curly-leaf spinach can be substituted for the chard; if using kale, discard the stems and simmer for an additional 5 minutes in step 3.

- 8 ounces Swiss chard, stems and leaves separated, stems chopped fine and leaves cut into 1-inch pieces (see photos)
- 2 carrots, peeled and cut into ½-inch pieces
- 1 onion, halved and sliced thin
- 1 celery rib, cut into ½-inch pieces
- 1 tablespoon canola oil
- 1 teaspoon minced fresh thyme or ¼ teaspoon dried
- 1 bay leaf
  Salt
- 2 tablespoons unbleached all-purpose flour
- 8 cups low-sodium chicken broth
- 12 ounces boneless, skinless chicken breasts, trimmed
- 1 cup wide egg noodles
  Pepper

1. Combine the Swiss chard stems, carrots, onion, celery, oil, thyme, bay leaf, and ⅛ teaspoon salt in a large Dutch oven. Cover and cook over medium-low heat, stirring occasionally, until the vegetables are softened, 8 to 10 minutes. Uncover, stir in the flour, and cook for 1 minute.

2. Slowly whisk in the broth and bring to a simmer. Reduce the heat to medium-low, add the chicken, and cook until the chicken registers 160 to 165 degrees on an instant-read thermometer, 10 to 15 minutes. Transfer the chicken to a plate. When cool enough to handle, shred the meat into bite-size pieces.

3. Remove and discard the bay leaf. Add the noodles and continue to simmer until the vegetables and noodles are tender, about 7 minutes longer. Stir in the shredded chicken and chard leaves and cook until the chard is tender, about 5 minutes. Season with salt and pepper to taste and serve.

PER 1½-CUP SERVING: Cal 120; Fat 3g; Sat fat 0g; Chol 30mg; Carb 11g; Protein 13g; Fiber 2g; Sodium 710mg

VARIATIONS

Hearty Chicken Soup with Leeks, Fennel, and Orzo

Follow the recipe for Hearty Chicken Noodle Soup, substituting 3 leeks, white and light green parts only, halved and sliced ¼ inch thick, for the onion, ½ bulb fennel, chopped, for the celery, and ½ cup orzo for the egg noodles.

PER 1½-CUP SERVING: Cal 170; Fat 3g; Sat fat 0g; Chol 25mg; Carb 20g; Protein 14g; Fiber 2g; Sodium 720mg

Hearty Chicken Soup with Corn, Bell Peppers, and Ditalini

This variation makes a little extra soup and serves 9.

Follow the recipe for Hearty Chicken Noodle Soup, omitting the carrots and adding 2 finely chopped red bell peppers to the pot with the onion. Add 2 cups fresh corn kernels (from 3 ears corn) to the pot with the broth. Substitute ¾ cup ditalini for the egg noodles.

PER 1½-CUP SERVING: Cal 160; Fat 3g; Sat fat 0g; Chol 20mg; Carb 22g; Protein 13g; Fiber 3g; Sodium 630mg

NOTES FROM THE TEST KITCHEN

PREPARING LEAFY GREENS

These steps will work for Swiss chard, kale, collard greens, and bok choy.

1. Cut away the leafy green portion from either side of the stalk or stem using a chef's knife.

2. Stack several leaves on top of one another and either slice the leaves crosswise or chop them into pieces (as directed in the recipe). Use a salad spinner to wash and dry the leaves after they are cut.

3. For both bok choy and chard, we like to include the stems in our recipes. Wash the stems, then trim and cut them into small pieces (or as directed in each recipe).

VIETNAMESE RICE NOODLE SOUP WITH BEEF

THE NATURALLY LIGHT RICE NOODLE SOUP FROM Southeast Asia known as *pho* (pronounced "fuh") has won a lot of fans in the States for its unique combination of ingredients—those that are both hot and cold, raw and cooked—that makes it at once satisfying and refreshing. To make pho, a rich, but not heavy, beef stock infused with warm spices is poured over rice noodles and meat (anything from thinly sliced brisket to tripe to meatballs), then the soup is garnished with fresh scallions, crisp bean sprouts, and fresh herbs like Thai basil and cilantro. These days a bowl of pho can be bought from any neighborhood Vietnamese restaurant, but because of its year-round appeal we thought it was time to develop a recipe of our own so we could make it whenever the craving hit.

Pho relies heavily upon the quality of the broth, but traditional recipes call for five hours or more of simmering, an impractical expectation for a weekday meal. When faced with this issue for our Hearty Chicken Noodle Soup (page 29), we worked around it by punching up otherwise mildly flavored store-bought broth with extra aromatics. We didn't see why that technique wouldn't work for our pho as well.

A slow-simmered, deeply flavored beef stock is usually central to this dish, but for the results we wanted, the effort seemed impractical. Store-bought beef stock made for a poor substitute; we had better luck using a combination of water and chicken broth and boosting its flavor with seasoning and aromatics. We began by sweating onions, garlic, and lemon grass, all typical aromatics in Asian recipes, in a scant amount of oil. We added the broth and water to the pot and simmered the mixture briefly to allow the flavors to meld. This was a good start, but the broth needed an infusion of Asian flavors to take it to the next level. Soy sauce lent a meatiness that homemade beef stock would normally contribute, and fish sauce added just the right combination of saltiness and musky sweetness. Clove, star anise, coriander, and cinnamon are all commonly used to season pho, and tasters agreed clove and star anise provided just the right warmth and depth to our version (we just made sure to strain both out before serving). Last, we added a pinch of sugar, which balanced the other seasonings. This was the well-rounded, flavorful, yet light broth we were after.

Next up were the rice noodles. We found that cooking the noodles in the simmering broth tended to turn them to mush and—if left in the hot soup for any length of time—caused them to break apart. It would be best to parcook them, then add them to the serving bowls and let the warm broth finish cooking them through. Just as we had found when making our Vietnamese Spring Rolls (page 22), soaking the noodles in water that had been brought to a boil and then removed from the heat was the way to go. We drained the noodles when they had softened to the point that they were tender but still had a little chew, then put them in the bowls to wait for the broth.

Next we looked at what meat to add and how to cook it. Traditional choices run the gamut—beef tenderloin, sirloin steak, tendons, tripe, meatballs, chicken, and chicken organs are all common additions—so we started by narrowing the field to the healthiest and most readily available choices that wouldn't be a headache to prepare. We settled on making two versions of the soup, one with boneless, skinless chicken breasts and another with some type of lean beef steak. We tested a variety of steaks and concluded that beef tenderloin, a traditional choice, was the best because it is naturally lean yet extremely tender.

Traditionally the beef is sliced paper-thin and added to the individual soup bowls raw with the idea that it can cook directly in the hot broth. We liked the authenticity of this method but had trouble getting the beef to cook through consistently in the individual bowls. It seemed like a safer bet to cook the beef in the simmering broth before serving it. As for the soup with chicken, we poached the whole breasts in the broth to infuse them with flavor and keep them moist, then shredded the meat into bite-size pieces and returned it to the pot before serving.

After we added a generous helping of garnishes—bean sprouts, fresh herbs, lime juice, and some minced chile for heat—one spoonful of our pho confirmed we had two recipes as healthy and flavorful as anything we'd find at a restaurant.

Vietnamese Rice Noodle Soup with Beef
SERVES 6

To make slicing the steak easier, freeze it for 15 minutes. Serve the soup immediately after cooking the beef in step 5; if the beef sits in the hot broth for too long it will become tough. If you cannot find Thai basil, substitute regular basil. To make this dish spicier, add the chile seeds.

BROTH

2 onions, minced (about 2 cups)

¼ cup fish sauce

4 garlic cloves, minced

1 lemon grass stalk, bottom 5 inches only, trimmed and sliced thin (see photos)

1 teaspoon canola oil

8 cups low-sodium chicken broth

1 cup water

2 tablespoons low-sodium soy sauce

2 tablespoons sugar

4 star anise pods

4 whole cloves

Salt and pepper

NOODLES, MEAT, AND GARNISH

12 ounces (¼-inch-wide) dried flat rice noodles

3 cups bean sprouts

1 cup fresh Thai basil

1 cup fresh cilantro

2 scallions, sliced thin on the bias

1 fresh Thai, serrano, or jalapeño chile, stemmed, seeded, and minced

1 lime, cut into wedges

12 ounces beef tenderloin, sliced in half lengthwise, then sliced crosswise into ¼-inch-thick pieces

1. FOR THE BROTH: Combine the onions, 1 tablespoon of the fish sauce, garlic, lemongrass, and oil in a large Dutch oven. Cover and cook over medium-low heat, stirring occasionally, until the onions are softened, 8 to 10 minutes.

2. Stir in the remaining 3 tablespoons fish sauce, broth, water, soy sauce, sugar, star anise, and cloves and bring to a simmer. Cover, reduce the heat to low, and cook until the flavors have blended, about 10 minutes. Strain the broth, discarding the solids, season with salt and pepper to taste, and return to a clean pot.

3. FOR THE NOODLES, MEAT, AND GARNISH: Bring 4 quarts water to a boil in a large pot. Remove from the heat, add the noodles, and let sit, stirring occasionally, until the noodles are tender but still chewy, about 10 minutes.

4. Drain the noodles, divide them evenly among 6 individual serving bowls, top each with ½ cup of the bean sprouts, and set aside. Arrange the basil, cilantro, scallions, chile, and lime wedges on a platter and set aside.

SLICING LEMON GRASS

1. Trim and discard all but the bottom 5 inches of the lemon grass stalk.

2. Remove the tough outer sheath from the trimmed lemon grass. If the lemon grass is particularly thick or tough, you may need to remove several layers to reveal the tender inner portion of the stalk.

3. Cut the trimmed and peeled lemon grass in half lengthwise, then slice it thin crosswise.

RICE NOODLES

In Southeast Asia and southern regions of China, delicate pasta made from rice flour and water is used in an array of dishes including soups, stir-fries, and salads. Unlike other pasta, you don't want to boil these delicate noodles. They have a tendency to overcook quickly, resulting in a mushy, sticky mess. We have found it is best to bring water to a boil, then steep the noodles in the water gently off the heat.

FLAT RICE NOODLES
This variety comes in several different widths, from extra-small to extra-large. We use a medium-width noodle, similar to linguine in size (about ¼ inch wide), for our Vietnamese Rice Noodle Soup recipes.

ROUND RICE NOODLES
Called *bun* or rice vermicelli, the round noodles also come in a variety of sizes. We use the smallest size we can get our hands on in our Vietnamese Rice Noodle Salad and Vietnamese Spring Rolls.

5. Return the strained broth to a simmer over medium-high heat, then reduce the heat to low. Add the beef and cook until no longer pink, about 1 minute (do not overcook). Ladle the soup over the noodles and serve, passing the garnishes separately.

PER 1½-CUP SERVING: Cal 360; Fat 5g; Sat fat 1.5g; Chol 40mg; Carb 60g; Protein 18g; Fiber 2g; Sodium 1440mg

VARIATION

Vietnamese Rice Noodle Soup with Chicken

Follow the recipe for Vietnamese Rice Noodle Soup with Beef, omitting the beef and adding 12 ounces boneless, skinless chicken breasts with the broth in step 2 and simmering until the chicken registers 160 to 165 degrees on an instant-read thermometer, 10 to 15 minutes. Remove the breasts from the broth before straining; when cool enough to handle, shred the meat into bite-size pieces. Substitute the shredded chicken for the beef in step 5.

PER 1½-CUP SERVING: Cal 340; Fat 2.5g; Sat fat 0g; Chol 35mg; Carb 60g; Protein 18g; Fiber 2g; Sodium 1450mg

TOMATO SOUP WITH MEATBALLS AND PASTA

TWO OF OUR FAVORITE COMFORT FOODS HAVE TO BE pastas and soups, and it doesn't get much better than meatballs and spaghetti for the former and tomato soup for the latter. So a recipe for tomato soup that incorporated meatballs and pasta sounded like a winner (think grown-up SpaghettiOs!), but we knew we'd have some challenges since we wanted to keep our recipe healthy.

We set out to build a base with big tomato flavor and a full, thick texture, and we wanted to avoid using fatty dairy components. In most simple tomato soup recipes we found, onions, carrots, celery, and garlic were sautéed in olive oil and then simmered in chicken broth and canned tomatoes before being pureed until smooth. We found that many of these recipes contained such a small amount of vegetables that the results were watery and thin once pureed. Others had so much canned tomato in them that we felt as if that's all we were eating.

The key was to find a balance between aromatic vegetables, canned tomatoes, and chicken broth. A few tests revealed that a small but not skimpy amount of onion, carrot, and celery added the right amount of depth to the soup without turning it into vegetable (instead of tomato) soup. Looking for the right ratio of tomatoes to broth that would balance the quantity of liquid and flavor, we eventually found that one 28-ounce can of diced tomatoes and 2½ cups of chicken broth were just the right proportions. The tomato flavor was front and center, and the tomatoes maintained a little texture, ensuring that our soup didn't turn into tomato sauce.

As for the meatballs, they obviously start with ground meat. Our first step was switching from ground beef to ground chicken, which would keep this recipe in the healthy realm. But when we made a test batch with ground white breast meat, they were far too lean and bland, not to mention dry. We needed a little fat and a little moisture in the mix. A combination of white and dark meat gave us superior meatballs with a lot more flavor and far better texture.

We all know there's more to meatballs than just meat. Traditional inclusions are herbs, Parmesan, and garlic for flavor and egg and bread (typically as a panade, or paste made with milk and bread) as binder and tenderizer. Looking over the flavors, we realized the three chief ingredients were in what make up pesto. Requiring no mincing or grating—just measure and add—jarred pesto greatly simplified our recipe. And instead of the panade as a tenderizer, we found we could cut a few calories and omit the milk. Bread crumbs alone mixed into the meat did the job just fine. These meatballs held together well without the egg, so we skipped that addition, too.

Typically meatballs are fried in about 1¼ cups of oil for a crisp crust. The crust not only adds flavor but also helps keep the meatballs from drying out during cooking. But this much oil clearly went against our healthy goal. While we could have decided to just pan-fry them in less oil, we realized that poaching them right in the soup would be a great way to infuse flavor into both the soup and the meatballs, and if we watched our poaching time they were guaranteed to be perfectly tender and moist. We found that about 12 to 15 minutes was all they needed.

The final item was the pasta. We liked the idea of spaghetti to reinforce the spaghetti and meatballs concept, but even when broken into small pieces it was too difficult to scoop up with a spoon. We found that any small, tubular pasta (we liked ditalini) worked best, and

TOMATO SOUP WITH MEATBALLS AND PASTA

adding it to the soup at the same time as the meatballs gave us perfect al dente pasta by the time the meatballs were ready. We found we didn't need much, just 1 ounce of pasta per serving. A sprinkle of Parmesan on top of each serving sealed the deal. This was satisfying, hearty comfort food at its best.

Tomato Soup with Meatballs and Pasta

SERVES 4

You can use any small, bite-size pasta in this recipe; pasta alphabets are fun if you can find them. Do not use ground chicken breast here (also labeled 99 percent fat-free) or the meatballs will be dry and grainy. You can make your own pesto, or use your favorite store-bought variety. Serve with a light sprinkling of grated Parmesan cheese, if desired. If you are concerned about sodium intake, substitute low-sodium diced tomatoes.

> 6 **ounces ground chicken (see note)**
>
> 3 **tablespoons pesto**
>
> 3 **tablespoons plain bread crumbs**
>
>   **Salt and pepper**
>
> 1 **onion, minced (about 1 cup)**
>
> 1 **carrot, peeled and chopped medium**
>
> 1 **small celery rib, chopped medium**
>
> 1 **tablespoon olive oil**
>
> 3 **garlic cloves, minced**
>
> 2½ **cups low-sodium chicken broth**
>
> 1 **(28-ounce) can diced tomatoes**
>
> 4 **ounces ditalini (about ¾ cup)**

1. Mix the chicken, pesto, bread crumbs, ⅛ teaspoon salt, and a pinch pepper together in a bowl and combine the mixture with your hands until it is uniform. Scoop heaping teaspoonfuls and gently form into ¾-inch round meatballs (you should have about 30 meatballs). Refrigerate until ready to use.

2. Combine the onion, carrot, celery, oil, and ¼ teaspoon salt in a large Dutch oven. Cover and cook over medium-low heat, stirring occasionally, until the vegetables are softened, 8 to 10 minutes. Stir in the garlic and cook until fragrant, about 30 seconds. Stir in the broth and tomatoes with their juice. Bring to a simmer, reduce the heat to medium-low, cover, and cook until the carrot is softened, 15 to 20 minutes.

3. Working in 2 batches, process the soup in a blender until completely smooth, 2 to 3 minutes. Return the soup to the pot and bring to a simmer.

4. Stir the meatballs and pasta into the pot and cook until the pasta is al dente and the meatballs are cooked through, 12 to 15 minutes. Season with salt and pepper to taste and serve.

PER 1½-CUP SERVING: Cal 350; Fat 13g; Sat fat 3g; Chol 40mg; Carb 42g; Protein 17g; Fiber 6g; Sodium 1260mg

NOTES FROM THE TEST KITCHEN

PUREEING SOUPS SAFELY

To prevent getting sprayed or burned by an exploding blender top, fill the blender jar only two-thirds full, hold the lid in place with a folded kitchen towel, and pulse rapidly a couple of times before blending continuously.

A BETTER BLENDER

A blender has one basic job—to blend food into a uniform consistency, whether it's crushing ice or producing lump-free purees for smoothies, soups, or hummus. And just two things matter for success at this basic job: the configuration of the blender blades and a V-shaped jar that keeps food close to the blade edges. We gathered nine models of blenders, including basic machines as well as those that boasted fancy new features (such as "dual-wave action" and "reversible motion" blade design), to find out which brand is best. After crushing hundreds of ice cubes and pureeing our way through countless soups and smoothies, we found two winners. The **KitchenAid 5-Speed Blender** (left), $149.99, impressed us with its brute strength and efficiency, and the **Kalorik BL Blender** (right), $49.99, though noticeably slower than our winner, performed nearly as well and was also the quietest of the bunch, making it our best buy.

ITALIAN PASTA AND BEAN SOUP

PASTA E FAGIOLI ("PASTA AND BEANS") IS A HEARTY, nutritious peasant soup made throughout Italy. The type of beans and pasta shapes used vary from region to region, but the broad outline of this classic soup is always the same. Aromatics (vegetables and often some pork product) are sautéed in olive oil. The tomatoes and broth then go into the pot, followed by the beans, and last the pasta. Ultimately this is a simple soup made with minimal ingredients that meld so well that none stands out. Our goal was to create a healthy, full-flavored version of this soup that was streamlined and could be on the table in less than an hour.

Many authentic pasta e fagioli recipes call for pancetta, unsmoked Italian bacon, though Americanized recipes call for regular bacon. In a side-by-side comparison, our tasters actually preferred bacon's smoky flavor to the mild pancetta, and just two slices, finely chopped, distributed its flavor throughout the soup without packing on a lot of fat.

Most Italian recipes use the same quartet of aromatic vegetables: onions, celery, carrots, and garlic. Tasters liked the onions, celery, and garlic but were divided about the sweetness imparted by the carrots, so we decided to cut them. Using the fat rendered from the bacon to cook the vegetables, rather than simply oil, helped boost their flavor even further.

In most recipes, once the aromatics have been sautéed, tomatoes or broth is used to deglaze the pan. We tested both, as well as white wine. The wine proved to be a bad idea; the tomatoes provided plenty of acidity on their own, so adding the wine just made the soup sour. Both the tomatoes and the broth worked fine, but we liked the way the tomatoes and aromatics blended, so we decided to add them to the pot first to deglaze the pan before stirring in the broth.

Pasta e fagioli usually starts with dried beans, but we wanted to keep things simple for our streamlined recipe so we turned to canned. The challenge, of course, would be getting some flavor into them. We wondered if adding the beans to the tomato mixture and letting them simmer together before adding the broth would help infuse the beans with the flavors of the bacon and aromatics.

We prepared two batches of soup to find out—one with beans and broth added simultaneously after the tomatoes had gone into the pan, and one with beans added to the tomatoes and cooked for 10 minutes before the broth went into the pot. We found that simmering the beans in the thick tomato mixture was a far better method of infusing them with flavor.

We next focused on the type of beans. Cannellini beans, also known as white kidney beans, are a common choice in this soup, so they were a given for our recipe as well. Another popular choice in Italy is the cranberry bean, a pink-and-white mottled variety with a sweet, delicate flavor. But this variety can be hard to find in the United States, so we tested two common substitutes, pinto and red kidney beans. Neither bean has the sweet, delicate flavor of a cranberry bean, but tasters felt that the red kidneys were the closest approximation and worked well in our soup.

Our recipe was coming together, but we had a few more ingredients to go. Many versions of this soup rely on chicken broth for the base, but a number of our tasters complained that the chicken flavor was too strong. First, we tried using water instead of chicken broth, but the resulting soup lacked depth. Then we gave various combinations of chicken broth and vegetable broth a shot, but like the carrots earlier, the vegetable broth imparted too much sweetness. We eventually settled on half water and half chicken broth. This soup was rich but not overly chicken-y, and chicken broth helped lend more body than water alone could accomplish.

Our last ingredient to investigate was the pasta. A few tests proved that smaller shapes worked best in our version of pasta e fagioli; larger ones crowded out the other ingredients and soaked up too much liquid. Ditalini (small tubes), tubettini (very small tubes), and orzo (rice-shaped pasta) were the top favorites among our tasters. We also liked conchigliette (very small shells with ridges), but this shape is hard to find.

We were nearly there, but our soup was tasting a little lean. Small amounts of two classic Italian ingredients, we realized, were a must, and worth the fat and calories they would add. A drizzle of olive oil and a sprinkling of grated Parmesan cheese were all that was needed to take our healthy, streamlined pasta and bean soup from good to great.

Italian Pasta and Bean Soup

SERVES 8

We prefer ditalini here, but orzo and tubettini are great substitutions.

    2 slices bacon, chopped fine
    1 onion, minced (about 1 cup)
    1 celery rib, chopped fine
       Salt
    4 garlic cloves, minced
    1 tablespoon minced fresh oregano or 1 teaspoon dried
    ¼ teaspoon red pepper flakes
    2 (14.5-ounce) cans diced tomatoes
    2 (15-ounce) cans cannellini beans, drained and rinsed
    4 cups low-sodium chicken broth
    4 cups water
    8 ounces ditalini (1½ cups)
    ¼ cup minced fresh parsley
       Pepper
    1 ounce Parmesan cheese, grated (about ½ cup)
    2 teaspoons extra-virgin olive oil

1. Cook the bacon in a large Dutch oven over medium-low heat, stirring often, until the fat is rendered and the bacon is crisp, 8 to 10 minutes. Add the onion, celery, and ⅛ teaspoon salt, cover, and cook, stirring occasionally, until the vegetables begin to soften, 2 to 4 minutes. Uncover, stir in the garlic, oregano, and pepper flakes, and cook until fragrant, about 30 seconds.

2. Stir in the tomatoes with their juice and beans, bring to a simmer, and cook until the flavors meld, about 10 minutes. Stir in the broth and water and bring to a simmer. Add the pasta and cook until tender, 10 to 12 minutes.

3. Off the heat, stir in the parsley and season with salt and pepper to taste. Sprinkle individual portions with the Parmesan and drizzle with the oil before serving.

PER 1⅔-CUP SERVING: Cal 250; Fat 6g; Sat fat 1.5g; Chol 5mg; Carb 39g; Protein 10g; Fiber 6g; Sodium 860mg

BLACK BEAN SOUP

HIGH IN FIBER AND PROTEIN, RICH IN IRON, AND WITH virtually no fat, black beans have been a healthy staple in Mexican, Cuban, and Caribbean diets for years. One of the most popular preparations, now well known in the States as well, is in a robust, hearty, peasant-style soup. The beans create a soup with an earthy, rich taste and a dark color that makes a striking backdrop for a colorful array of garnishes like cilantro, chopped tomato, and sour cream. We wanted to create an easy black bean soup recipe that went beyond a basic bowl of beans, with an appealing combination of depth and richness.

Although dried beans would have been the most authentic choice, for the sake of ease we opted to stick with canned beans and would find complementary ingredients to boost their flavor. We settled on chicken broth to add subtle depth and richness. Most recipes include some sort of meat; ham hock, bacon, ham, and pork loin are all common choices. We gave each one a test run. The ham hock and ham were both too strong. Pork loin, though appealingly lean, had a flavor that was too subtle. Ultimately, we settled on bacon since its smoky flavor was a nice complement to the earthiness of the beans.

We moved on to the aromatics next. In many Caribbean recipes, a *sofrito* (a mixture of aromatic vegetables—usually onion, garlic, and bell pepper—sautéed in olive oil until soft) is added to flavor cooked beans. We gave the traditional sofrito ingredient trio a try, but tasters felt the bell pepper tasted out of place, and it did not hold up well during cooking. Substituting carrots and celery for the bell pepper gave the soup the aromatic flavor and depth we were looking for. We also found that if we sautéed the bacon first, it gave off enough fat to cook our aromatics, adding another layer of smoky flavor to the soup.

Spices are an integral part of black bean soup. Recipes vary, but most include cumin. Other spices such as coriander, chipotle, red pepper flakes, chili powder, and cayenne are also common additions. Ground chipotle was a bit too strong and smoky, but more subtle cumin, not surprisingly, earned a spot in our recipe. A judicious amount of red pepper flakes imparted the perfect amount of heat without being too hot.

With the spices and aromatics set, we moved on to the texture of our soup. Black bean soup should be thick, not soupy. In some recipes some of the beans and cooking liquid are pureed or mashed to create a thicker texture, while in other recipes all of the beans are blended to create a soup that is essentially a thick puree. At the outset, we decided we wanted our soup to have some whole beans in it, so we dismissed the pureed-only version. We tried a variety of thickening methods and proportions with a portion of the beans (always reserving some to stay whole): We mashed them into the sofrito, whizzed them in the blender, and pulsed them in the food processor. In the end, pureeing about one-third of the soup in the blender, then mixing it back into the pot with the remaining whole beans, resulted in the best texture.

Our last addition was finding the right acid to incorporate into our soup, which was key for adding a necessary brightness. We tested red wine, balsamic and cider vinegars, as well as lime juice and lemon juice. We generally liked all of our options, except for the cider vinegar (it was too harsh), but the winner was lime juice. It brought just the right hint of acidity to complement the richness of the bacon and earthy flavor of the beans without adding any sort of distraction. Garnished with a dollop of low-fat sour cream, cilantro, and lime wedges, our healthy black bean soup is as easy as it is good.

Black Bean Soup

SERVES 6

To make this soup vegetarian, omit the bacon and substitute vegetable broth for the chicken broth. The canned beans are the primary source of sodium in this recipe; if you are concerned about sodium intake, substitute low-sodium or salt-free canned beans. Serve with low-fat sour cream, cilantro, and lime wedges, if desired.

- 2 slices bacon, chopped fine
- 3 celery ribs, chopped fine
- 2 onions, minced (about 2 cups)
- 1 carrot, peeled and cut into ¼-inch pieces
  Salt
- 6 garlic cloves, minced
- 4½ teaspoons ground cumin
- ¼ teaspoon red pepper flakes
- 4 (15-ounce) cans black beans, drained and rinsed
- 4 cups low-sodium chicken broth
- 2 tablespoons fresh lime juice
  Pepper

1. Cook the bacon in a large Dutch oven over medium-low heat, stirring often, until the fat is rendered and the bacon is crisp, 8 to 10 minutes. Add the celery, onions, carrot, and ⅛ teaspoon salt, cover, and cook, stirring occasionally, until the vegetables are softened, 8 to 10 minutes. Uncover, stir in the garlic, cumin, and pepper flakes, and cook until fragrant, about 30 seconds.

2. Stir in the beans and broth, bring to a simmer, and cook until the beans are very tender and the broth is flavorful, about 30 minutes.

3. Process 1½ cups of the beans and 2 cups of the broth in a blender until completely smooth, 2 to 3 minutes. Return the pureed mixture to the pot. Stir in the lime juice, season with salt and pepper to taste, and serve.

PER 1½-CUP SERVING: **Cal** 240; **Fat** 6g; **Sat fat** 1.5g; **Chol** 5mg; **Carb** 38g; **Protein** 13g; **Fiber** 13g; **Sodium** 1220mg

MULLIGATAWNY

LITERALLY TRANSLATED TO MEAN "PEPPER WATER," *mulligatawny* is a pureed vegetable soup from southern India that is mildly spicy, but not hot, with a faint sweetness, usually from coconut, and is often garnished with chicken or lamb. At its best, mulligatawny is silky and elegant with potent yet balanced spices and aromatics. But very often this soup falls short, with poorly incorporated, raw-tasting spices and an overly thin base. With its vegetable base and flavor that relies primarily on spices, it made a good choice for adding a little pep to our selection of healthy soups. We wanted to reclaim this soup's velvety texture and deep, complex flavor, all the while keeping an eye toward developing a healthy and straightforward recipe.

We decided to start with the soup's base. Research told us that chicken broth, lamb broth, beef broth, vegetable broth, and water were all possibilities. We tried each in a test recipe to settle on the best choice. Tasters found vegetable broth too sweet and beef broth too strong, even a bit sour. None of us were surprised that the lamb broth was overpowering (not to mention that it's not a broth that can be purchased ready-made, and we weren't going to commit to making homemade). In the end, we decided that mild, well-balanced chicken broth was the ideal base for the wide range of spices and vegetables that would go into our soup. (Water made a tasty vegetarian version that was not quite as flavorful as the soup made with chicken broth, but it was still acceptable.)

Curry powder, which is actually a blend of up to 20 different spices, is a central ingredient in most mulligatawny recipes, so we tackled it next. We wanted to keep our recipe as simple as possible, but after experimenting with several store-bought curry powders, we agreed they all made soups that were muted and muddy-tasting. We decided to make our own simple curry powder blend. After a little tinkering, we came up with a winning combination of garam masala, cumin, coriander, and turmeric.

Following the curry powder, it made sense next to address the aromatics—garlic and ginger—and the coconut, which is key for providing a balancing cool sweetness to the spices. We tested various ratios of garlic and ginger, and we found we preferred an even balance of 4 teaspoons each. As for the coconut, some recipes we found called for coconut milk, others for fresh coconut meat, and still others dried coconut. Light coconut milk was too thin and not flavorful enough against the spices. Regular coconut milk gave the soup a great silky consistency, but it took a fair amount to get the coconut flavor to come through, at which point it was adding too much fat and too many calories. Fresh coconut was not flavorful enough to merit the work it required to prepare, so it was ruled out. Sweetened dried coconut was the best option, and ⅓ cup added just enough flavor to balance the soup without taking over or adding too much fat. We cooked the coconut with the onions to allow its flavor to develop before the rest of the ingredients were added.

With our aromatics and spices under control it was time to work on the vegetables, which would add not only flavor, but also bulk and color. We tested onions, carrots, celery, cauliflower, spinach, and peas, all of which we'd seen in at least a few recipes. Not surprisingly, we found that onions were a must. Carrots added color and sweetness, and the celery provided a cool flavor that contrasted nicely with the hot spices, so they also made the cut. Cauliflower was rejected for the cabbage-like flavor it gave to the soup. Spinach and peas did little to enhance the soup's flavor, and since they gave our soup an undesirable muddy appearance once pureed, we cut them from the list.

Several recipes suggested using pureed rice or lentils to thicken the soup, and while tasters didn't oppose these flavors (in fact they liked the additional flavor of the lentils), they didn't like the thick, porridge-like texture they produced once pureed. After a bit more testing, we found that sprinkling a little flour over the sautéed aromatics (to make a sort of roux) gave the soup a thickened yet velvety consistency—silky and substantial but not heavy.

Returning to the idea of including lentils, we decided that incorporating them whole (adding them after the soup was pureed) would add a nice earthiness and contrasting texture to the soup, so we tested several varieties. Chana dal, a smaller cousin to chickpeas, also known as yellow split peas, imparted an overly earthy, vegetal flavor that didn't meld with the flavor of the soup (not to mention that they took over an hour to cook). Red lentils all but disintegrated, leaving a grainy texture. We finally settled on standard brown lentils or green French lentils, both of which held their shape and readily absorbed the surrounding flavors.

A dollop of low-fat yogurt and a sprinkle of cilantro were all our spicy soup needed for a fresh, cool finish.

Mulligatawny

SERVES 6

French green lentils (*lentilles du Puy*) will also work well here; the cooking time will remain the same. Do not use red lentils because they turn very soft when cooked and will disintegrate into the soup.

- 2 **tablespoons unsalted butter**
- 2½ **teaspoons garam masala**
- 1½ **teaspoons ground cumin**
- 1½ **teaspoons ground coriander**
- 1 **teaspoon ground turmeric**
- 2 **onions, minced (about 2 cups)**
- ⅓ **cup sweetened shredded or flaked coconut**
  Salt
- 4 **garlic cloves, minced**
- 4 **teaspoons grated or minced fresh ginger**
- 1 **teaspoon tomato paste**
- ¼ **cup unbleached all-purpose flour**
- 7 **cups low-sodium chicken broth**
- 2 **carrots, peeled and cut into ½-inch pieces**
- 1 **celery rib, cut into ½-inch pieces**
- ½ **cup brown lentils, rinsed and picked over**
  Pepper
- 6 **tablespoons plain low-fat yogurt**
- 2 **tablespoons minced fresh cilantro**

1. Melt the butter in a large Dutch oven over medium heat. Add the garam masala, cumin, coriander, and turmeric and cook until fragrant, about 10 seconds. Turn the heat to medium-low, add the onions, coconut, and ⅛ teaspoon salt, cover, and cook until the onions are softened, 8 to 10 minutes. Stir in the garlic, ginger, and tomato paste and cook until fragrant, about 30 seconds. Stir in the flour and cook for 1 minute.

2. Gradually whisk in the broth. Stir in the carrots and celery, bring to a simmer, and cook until the vegetables are tender, 20 to 25 minutes.

3. Working in 2 batches, process the soup in a blender until completely smooth, 2 to 3 minutes. Return the soup to the pot, add the lentils, and bring to a simmer. Cover and cook until the lentils are tender, about 40 minutes.

4. Season with salt and pepper to taste. Ladle the soup into bowls, dollop with the yogurt, and sprinkle with the cilantro before serving.

PER 1⅓-CUP SERVING: Cal 200; Fat 7g; Sat fat 4.5g; Chol 10mg; Carb 28g; Protein 8g; Fiber 5g; Sodium 770mg

FRENCH ONION SOUP

TODAY'S IDEAL FRENCH ONION SOUP IS A SATISFYING broth bursting with sweet caramelized onion flavor topped with toasted baguette and melted cheese. You should be able to taste the time and effort that went into making it. But in reality, most onion soup isn't very good. Once you manage to dig through the layer of congealed cheese to unearth a spoonful of broth, it doesn't even taste like onions. And most recipes for French onion soup require a watchful eye and constant stirring. We hoped to find a way to make a deeply flavored, oniony soup using an easier, foolproof method.

We began by reviewing existing recipes and looked for a way to streamline. Most start with heating butter and/or oil, adding sliced onions (and sometimes sugar), and cooking over low to medium-low heat, stirring frequently, for up to two hours, until they are cooked down and caramelized. We knew from experience that trying to shorten stirring time by cranking up the heat would only result in burned onions. We tried keeping the heat as low as possible and simply stirring the onions less frequently but over a longer period of time. Unfortunately, without continual attention, these onions burned as well.

What the onions needed was steady, low, even heat. The stovetop was concentrating too much heat at the bottom of the pot, so why not use the oven? We spread lightly oiled sliced onions on a sheet pan and roasted them at 450 degrees. Instead of caramelizing, they dried out. We tried lower temperatures but this only gave us steamed onions. When we cooked as many sliced onions as we could squeeze into a Dutch oven (4 pounds), covered, the results were far more promising. These onions cooked slowly and evenly, building flavor all the while. Lightly coating the pot with vegetable oil spray ensured the onions wouldn't stick and helped keep the onions around the pot's edge from burning. The vegetable oil spray helped us lighten the recipe by eliminating the butter.

After some trial and error, we settled on cooking the onions, covered, in a 400-degree oven for an hour, then continued cooking with the lid ajar for another hour and a half. Covering for the first phase kept the heat even and the onions moist, and it didn't require any babysitting on our part. After the onions had released their moisture, it was time for the browning to begin, so we cracked the lid to let excess moisture evaporate. At this point, we had to stir the onions every half hour to prevent burning.

These onions emerged from the oven golden, soft, and sweet, and a nice fond had begun to collect on the bottom of the pot. The few stirs required were a far cry from the demands of the old-fashioned recipes. We continued the caramelization process on the stovetop so we could take advantage of the fond. Deglazing the pan once boosted the flavor noticeably, but what if we deglazed multiple times, allowing the onions to recaramelize each time? The result was fantastic, deeply flavorful onions. Once the onions were as dark as possible, we poured in some dry sherry, which tasters preferred to sweet sherry, white wine, Champagne, red wine, and vermouth.

Settling on a type of standard supermarket onion was a snap. We dismissed red onions—they bled out, producing a dingy soup. White onions were too mild, and Vidalia made the broth candy-sweet. Yellow onions offered just the sweet-savory notes we were after. After making batches with water, chicken broth, and beef broth alone and in combination, we decided the soup was best with a combination of all three for a balanced complexity.

It was time to focus on the soup's finishing touches: the croutons and cheese. We didn't want to obscure the depth of our broth, so we dialed back the typically hefty amount of cheese most recipes call for, allowing the broth to take center stage and also cutting out unnecessary fat and calories. Tasters agreed just 1 tablespoon of grated Gruyère per crouton was the perfect amount. We toasted slices of baguette, then floated them on the soup, sprinkled on the cheese, and ran the crocks quickly under the broiler. This French onion soup is so rich and flavorful, no one will ever guess how easy it is to make.

French Onion Soup

SERVES 6

Be patient when caramelizing the onions in step 3; the entire process takes 45 to 60 minutes. Use broiler-safe crocks and keep the rims of the bowls 4 to 5 inches from the heating element to obtain a proper gratinée of melted, bubbly cheese. If using ordinary soup bowls, sprinkle the toasted bread slices with Gruyère and return them to the broiler until the cheese melts, then float them on top of the soup.

SOUP

- 4 pounds yellow onions (about 8 medium), halved and sliced ¼ inch thick
  Salt
- 2 cups water, plus more for deglazing
- ½ cup dry sherry
- 4 cups low-sodium chicken broth
- 2 cups beef broth
- 6 sprigs fresh thyme, tied with kitchen twine
- 1 bay leaf
  Pepper

CROUTONS

- 4 ounces baguette, cut ½ inch thick on the bias into 6 slices
- 1½ ounces Gruyère cheese, shredded (about 6 tablespoons)

1. FOR THE SOUP: Adjust an oven rack to the lower-middle position and heat the oven to 400 degrees. Lightly coat the inside of a heavy-bottomed large Dutch oven with vegetable oil spray. Add the onions and ½ teaspoon salt. Cover, place the pot in the oven, and cook for 1 hour (the onions will be moist and slightly reduced in volume).

2. Working carefully, remove the pot from the oven and stir the onions, scraping the bottom and sides of the pot. Partially cover, return the pot to the oven, and continue to cook until the onions are deep golden brown, 1½ to 1¾ hours longer, stirring the onions and scraping the bottom and sides of the pot every 30 minutes.

3. Remove the pot from the oven and place over medium-high heat. Cook, stirring often and scraping the bottom and sides of the pot, until the liquid evaporates, 15 to 20 minutes, reducing the heat if the onions are browning too quickly. Continue to cook, stirring often, until the pot bottom is coated with a dark crust, 6 to 8 minutes. Stir in ¼ cup of the water, scrape the pot bottom to loosen the crust, and cook until the water evaporates and another dark crust has formed on the pot bottom, 6 to 8 minutes. Repeat 2 or 3 more times, until the onions are very dark brown. Stir in the sherry and cook, stirring frequently, until evaporated, about 5 minutes.

4. Stir in the remaining 2 cups water, the chicken broth, beef broth, thyme sprigs, and bay leaf, scraping up any browned bits. Bring to a simmer, cover, and cook for 30 minutes. Remove and discard the thyme sprigs and bay leaf. Season with salt and pepper to taste.

5. FOR THE CROUTONS: While the soup simmers, arrange the baguette slices in a single layer on a baking sheet and bake until the edges are golden, about 10 minutes; set aside.

6. TO SERVE: Adjust an oven rack to the upper-middle position and heat the broiler. Set individual broiler-safe crocks on a baking sheet and fill each with 1½ cups of the soup. Top each bowl with 1 baguette slice and sprinkle evenly with 1 tablespoon of the cheese. Broil until the cheese is melted and bubbly around the edges, 3 to 5 minutes. Let the soup cool for 5 minutes before serving.

PER 1½-CUP SERVING WITH 1 CROUTON: Cal 240; Fat 3.5g; Sat fat 1.5g; Chol 10mg; Carb 44g; Protein 10g; Fiber 7g; Sodium 1010mg

---

NOTES FROM THE TEST KITCHEN

THE SECRET TO SERIOUS ONION FLAVOR

Most classic recipes for French onion soup call for deglazing—loosening the dark brown crust, or fond, that forms on the bottom of the pot—only once, if at all. The key to our recipe is to deglaze the pot at least three times.

CREAMY ASPARAGUS SOUP

TEST KITCHEN
MAKEOVER

CREAM OF ASPARAGUS SOUP SHOULD BE BRIGHT green, bursting with asparagus flavor, and flawlessly smooth, yet often these requirements are not met. Most recipes for creamy asparagus soup use the same basic technique: Sauté chopped asparagus and onion in butter, add liquid (a touch of wine, broth, or milk), simmer until tender, then puree, finally stirring in cream at the end. But the cream and the butter used to sauté the asparagus make an otherwise light springtime soup heavier and fattier than it should be. So it's no surprise that a number of low-fat versions of this recipe exist.

Most of these recipes rely on reduced-fat dairy products like milk, sour cream, and condensed milk, but a few tests proved they were all poor choices for the delicate asparagus, turning out soups that were thin and bland or had tangy or overly sweet off-flavors. In another low-fat recipe we came across, steamed asparagus was pureed with water; you can imagine the lack of flavor. It was time to develop our own asparagus soup that was low-fat but could hold its own against the full-fat version. It needed to be not too thick, not too thin, with the sweet, nutty asparagus, not cream, serving as the star.

Starting with 2 pounds of asparagus, the standard in most recipes, we removed the tough ends of the spears and chopped the remainder into rough pieces. We set aside the asparagus tips, saving them for a garnish down the road. We cranked up the heat and browned the rest of the asparagus in butter in the hope of bringing out a deeper flavor than sautéing alone could accomplish. No luck; the browned asparagus made the soup bitter and brown. Broiling the asparagus yielded similar results.

We clearly needed to avoid browning the asparagus. One way to keep green vegetables green is to blanch them (quickly cook them in boiling water, then plunge them into ice water). We gave it a shot, and while the asparagus was bright green, most of the asparagus flavor went down the drain with the blanching water. We had the best results when we turned down the heat to medium-low, sautéing the asparagus to slowly coax out its flavor. And with the lid on we needed only 1 tablespoon of butter to get the job done (we tried oil but tasters agreed the richness of butter was a must). We learned the hard way not to let the asparagus spears overcook, for their fresh flavor to make it into the soup, they should be just tender enough to puree but no more. We also had

to be careful to avoid spears that were too thick. These did not cook through before the color started to fade. We found that ½-inch-thick spears were perfect, cooking through fairly quickly and not turning army green.

We already knew from early tests that water-based asparagus soup would be bland and thin, so we started by making asparagus stock from asparagus trimmings. This was not nearly flavorful enough to justify the effort. Ultimately, our tasters favored store-bought chicken broth, which added a bit of richness without overwhelming.

Now for the "creamy" dairy component. Cream was too fatty for the amount of soup needed. Just as we had found with our Creamy Mushroom Soup (page 46), half-and-half provided good richness and creaminess without so much fat. If we went beyond ¼ cup of half-and-half, however, tasters started to comment that the asparagus flavor was getting masked, but we still wanted more creaminess. Then leeks occurred to us, which are great for adding a silkiness to soups once pureed without muddling the flavor. We sautéed two leeks with our asparagus in the butter and indeed, they did the trick, adding not only creaminess but also a sweet complexity.

The soup tasted good, but it wasn't the bright green we wanted. You eat with your eyes, too, after all. We had come across some recipes in which spinach was added to asparagus soup to intensify its color. We gave it a shot, adding half a bunch of spinach to our next batch. The spinach gave the soup a stunning color, but its mineral-like taste was too aggressive for the asparagus. We needed a green vegetable that would work with, not against, the asparagus. What about peas? We stirred a handful into the pot with the asparagus just before it was time to puree the mixture. The peas added sweetness, an emerald hue, and a little body because of their starch. Would our tasters pick up on the switch? Not a chance. One after another commented on the intense asparagus flavor and the lovely color of this batch. None was the wiser.

A couple of tablespoons of Parmesan lent a nuttiness that echoed the asparagus, while lemon juice brightened it up. This soup tasted elegant, was bright green, and saved 90 calories and 11 grams of fat in the process.

MAKEOVER SPOTLIGHT: CREAMY ASPARAGUS SOUP

	CALORIES	FAT	SAT FAT	CHOLESTEROL
BEFORE	260	17g	11g	50mg
AFTER	170	6g	3.5g	15mg

CREAMY ASPARAGUS SOUP

Creamy Asparagus Soup

SERVES 4

Look for asparagus spears that are no more than ½ inch thick. If using thicker spears (thicker than ½-inch diameter), use a vegetable peeler to peel the length of the spears before cooking to ensure a silky soup.

> 2 bunches thin asparagus (about 2 pounds), tough ends trimmed (see photos)
>
> 2 leeks, white and light green parts only, halved lengthwise, sliced thin, and rinsed thoroughly
>
> 1 tablespoon unsalted butter
>
>   Salt and pepper
>
> 3½ cups low-sodium chicken broth
>
> ½ cup frozen peas (2 ounces)
>
> 2 tablespoons grated Parmesan cheese
>
> ¼ cup half-and-half
>
> ½ teaspoon fresh lemon juice

NOTES FROM THE TEST KITCHEN

TRIMMING ASPARAGUS SPEARS

1. Remove one stalk of asparagus from the bunch and bend it at the thicker end until it snaps.

2. With the broken asparagus as a guide, trim the tough ends from the remaining asparagus bunch with a chef's knife.

THE SECRET TO BRIGHT ASPARAGUS SOUP

Some recipes boost the color of asparagus soup with spinach, but we found its mineral flavor didn't work quite right. Instead, we rely on just ½ cup of frozen peas to give our soup a boost of green color without obscuring the flavor.

1. Cut the tips off the asparagus spears and chop the remaining spears into ½-inch pieces. Bring ½ cup water to a boil in an 8-inch skillet over medium-high heat. Add the asparagus tips, cover, and cook until the tips are tender, about 2 minutes. Remove the asparagus tips, pat dry, and set aside.

2. Combine the remaining asparagus pieces, leeks, butter, ⅛ teaspoon salt, and ⅛ teaspoon pepper in a large saucepan. Cover and cook over medium-low heat, stirring occasionally, until softened, 8 to 10 minutes.

3. Add the broth to the pot, bring to a simmer, and cook until the vegetables are completely tender, about 5 minutes. Stir in the peas and Parmesan.

4. Working in 2 batches, process the soup in a blender until completely smooth, 2 to 3 minutes. Return the soup to the pot. Stir in the reserved asparagus tips, half-and-half, and lemon juice and cook until heated through, about 2 minutes. Season with salt and pepper to taste and serve.

PER 1½-CUP SERVING: Cal 170; Fat 6g; Sat fat 3.5g; Chol 15mg; Carb 21g; Protein 8g; Fiber 7g; Sodium 630mg

CREAMY LEEK AND POTATO SOUP

COOKS HAVE BEEN MAKING LEEK AND POTATO SOUP for centuries, but these days it runs the gamut from elegant and refined to something tasting like a pureed baked potato. At its best, it is a marriage of leeks and potatoes, supported by a cast of background ingredients. The result should be a velvety and subtle soup without complex flavorings. The versions we encountered inevitably fell short, turning out stodgy and gluey, or with so much cream or butter blended in it was hard to detect the leek—or the potato. Others had so much bacon or cheese we were unsure if we were actually tasting leek and potato soup. Heading into the test kitchen, we were certain we could find the right spark to reignite the marriage between leek and potato, and at the same time get the fatty ingredients in check so that the starring ingredients were front and center.

When a colleague reminded us Julia Child thought so highly of the soup that she made it her first recipe in *Mastering the Art of French Cooking*, we were stunned. We decided to give her recipe a closer look. Like a lot of other cooks, she simmered equal parts potatoes and chopped leeks in water until tender. The only notable difference: Instead of pureeing the vegetables in a blender, as virtually all contemporary recipes specify, Child passed them through a food mill. Wondering if this little-used tool made a difference, we hunted down the test kitchen's model and gave it a try. The result? The best soup of this kind we'd ever had: mellow but clear vegetable flavor, and a consistency that was remarkably creamy—even with just 2 tablespoons of cream.

That meant the blender was the culprit in most recipes, which made sense. When overwhipped (as in a blender), potatoes leach too much starch and turn gluey. Some recipes try to fix this problem by creating another: They go overboard on the cream—as much as a cup per pound of potato—which not only makes the soup a caloric heavyweight but also dulls the potato and leek flavors. In the test kitchen, we all agreed that for such a simple soup it was too involved to require today's cooks to unearth a food mill; instead, we would fix the blender problem.

Putting the glueyness problem on hold, we drew up a basic recipe based on existing versions to evaluate potato types. It went like this: Sweat the thinly sliced white and light green parts of four leeks in butter, then add a quart of water and a pound of potatoes. Working through the potatoes, we agreed Yukon Golds tasted too distinct, and waxy Red Bliss potatoes failed to break down completely. Russets broke down well and had the right mild flavor, so we stopped there.

But even with the right potato, we found that the leek flavor was barely discernible. Simply adding more leeks didn't help; their flavor became sulfur-like. Caramelizing them to ramp up the sweetness lent an off-putting browned-vegetable aroma to the soup, and the addition of sugar was too cloying. But incorporating a single onion amplified and complemented the leeks' flavor and sweetness just enough. However, we still wanted more leek flavor, and we found the answer in the potent dark green leek tops that we had been throwing away. We simply simmered them in the cooking liquid, only discarding them after they had spent 20 minutes in the pot.

Now that our vegetables were in check, we fine-tuned the remaining flavors. We replaced half the water with store-bought chicken broth and dropped a bay leaf and a sprig of thyme into the pot. The soup's flavor was spot-on.

Now back to that gummy texture. Outside of changing our cookware options, the only thing left to tinker with was the potato. The correlation was obvious: Less potato would mean less starch, and less starch would mean less glueyness. To make any impact, we actually had to drop down from a pound of potatoes to just 6 ounces. The resulting soup was good, yet flawed. Surprisingly it wasn't the flavor of the potatoes we missed most but their thickening power. This low-starch version had a thin, broth-like consistency.

Brainstorming for a potato-free way to thicken the soup, we tested a few techniques. Combining flour and butter to make a traditional roux was a nonstarter for our healthy recipe. Cornstarch lent an off-putting texture to the soup. Then we remembered a test kitchen trick used to thicken another recently developed recipe: sandwich bread. We lightly toasted a slice of sandwich bread to remove its moisture, tossed it into the pot with the soup, and waited until it started to break down before pureeing the soup in the blender. Voilà! Just like Julia's recipe, this soup "smelled good, tasted good, and was simplicity itself to make." And it didn't have a lick of cream.

NOTES FROM THE TEST KITCHEN

PREPARING LEEKS

1. Trim the root and dark green leaves.

2. If using the dark green leaves, slice them in half lengthwise, then cut into 2-inch pieces (otherwise, discard). Cut the trimmed leek base in half lengthwise, then slice it into ½-inch pieces.

3. Rinse the cut leeks thoroughly to remove the dirt and sand using either a salad spinner or bowl of water.

Creamy Leek and Potato Soup

SERVES 4

Tarragon can be substituted for the thyme, if desired. Use the lowest setting on your toaster to dry out the bread without browning it too much.

- 4 leeks, white and light green parts halved lengthwise, sliced thin, and rinsed thoroughly (about 4 cups), dark green leaves halved lengthwise, cut into 2-inch pieces, and rinsed thoroughly (about 2 cups) (see page 44)
- 2 cups low-sodium chicken broth
- 2 cups water
- 1 onion, minced (about 1 cup)
- 1 tablespoon unsalted butter
  Salt
- 1 small russet potato (about 6 ounces), peeled and cut into ¼-inch slices
- 1 sprig fresh thyme
- 1 bay leaf
- 1 slice high-quality white sandwich bread, lightly toasted and torn into ½-inch pieces
  Pepper

1. Bring the leek greens, broth, and water to a boil in a large saucepan over high heat. Reduce the heat to low, cover, and simmer for 20 minutes. Pour the broth through a fine-mesh strainer into a medium bowl, pressing on the solids to extract as much liquid as possible, and set aside. Discard the solids in the strainer and rinse out the saucepan.

2. Combine the leek white and light green parts, onion, butter, and ⅛ teaspoon salt in the saucepan. Cover and cook over medium-low heat, stirring occasionally, until the onion is softened, 8 to 10 minutes.

3. Uncover, increase the heat to high, stir in the reserved broth, potato, thyme sprig, and bay leaf, and bring to a boil. Reduce the heat to low and simmer until the potato is tender, about 10 minutes. Add the toasted bread and simmer until the bread starts to break down, about 5 minutes.

4. Remove and discard the thyme sprig and bay leaf. Working in 2 batches, process the soup in a blender until completely smooth, 2 to 3 minutes. Return the soup to the saucepan and bring to a simmer. Season with salt and pepper to taste and serve.

PER 1¼-CUP SERVING: Cal 150; Fat 3.5g; Sat fat 2g; Chol 10mg; Carb 27g; Protein 3g; Fiber 3g; Sodium 410mg

CREAMY MUSHROOM SOUP

WHEN MOST PEOPLE THINK OF CREAM OF MUSHROOM soup, they picture the pasty, flavorless glop in the iconic red and white can (we don't remember it fondly). While the best of the homemade versions have a deep, woodsy flavor and luxurious texture, they rely on expensive wild mushrooms that are an impractical choice for an everyday meal. And the recipes that use less expensive, less flavorful white button supermarket mushrooms try, without success, to remedy the blandness by using an excess of butter and cream. The results aren't much better than the canned stuff, not to mention the fact that they typically tally somewhere in the ballpark of 360 calories and 30 grams of fat. We wanted to come up with a practical, affordable cream of mushroom soup that put the deep mushroom flavor center stage and at the same time limited the dairy components to only what was necessary.

Most recipes start with sautéing 2 pounds of mushrooms in as much as 6 tablespoons of butter. This was the first place we could quickly cut away the fat; for other recipes we had developed a sweating technique that allowed us to get away with far less. We cooked the mushrooms with ½ teaspoon of salt and a mere 1 tablespoon of oil, covered at first; then we removed the lid, allowing the moisture to evaporate and the mushrooms to brown. The mushrooms looked perfect, but tasters missed some of the rich butter flavor; the saturated fat added by swapping in 1 tablespoon of butter for the oil helped bring a bit of richness back to the soup.

With just mushrooms and broth (we were working with chicken broth for now), our soup had good mushroom flavor, but not surprisingly, it tasted flat and lean. Many recipes include onions, shallots, or leeks for complexity. We tried all three, sautéing them with the mushrooms. Each provided a bit of sweetness, but the delicate leeks won out over the onions (which were too strong) and the shallots (which were too sweet). We also knew from experience that once pureed, leeks add an element of creaminess to soups. To further round out the flavor, a few cloves of garlic and a couple of teaspoons of fresh thyme were added before any of the liquid.

Now that our soup base was coming together, we decided to hone the liquid components next. Most recipes use either chicken or beef broth and a heavy dose of cream for the base, with a touch of wine (or other

TEST KITCHEN
MAKEOVER

alcohol) to complement the musky mushroom flavor. We decided to work out the nondairy components first. We tested countless combinations of a broth—chicken, beef, and vegetable as well as water—with an alcohol component—we narrowed this group to white wine, Madeira, sherry, and brandy. While all but the water resulted in some success, a combination of beef broth and Madeira gave our soup just the right complexity for pairing with the meatiness of the mushrooms.

For the dairy component, typical full-fat recipes started with a whole cup of heavy cream. We tried to simply omit the cream, but this soup didn't have any of the luxurious qualities this type of soup requires. We decided to test various lower-fat dairy products. Milk—whether 1 percent, 2 percent, or whole—only thinned out our soup. Evaporated milk, with which we've had luck when lightening some creamy soups in the past, was too sweet here. Half-and-half was the happy medium, lower in fat than the heavy cream but thicker than the milk, and just ½ cup gave our soup the right richness and appealing texture without overwhelming the mushroom flavor. We sautéed our mushrooms and leeks, added the aromatics, broth, and Madeira, and simmered until the vegetables were tender. We then pureed the mixture in the blender, and once we had returned this base to the pot, we added the half-and-half.

To add a touch of texture to our velvety soup, we considered our garnishes. Many mushroom soups are garnished with additional sautéed mushrooms. To avoid the extra work, and the extra butter, we simply removed some of the mushrooms and leeks once they were sautéed, then finely chopped the vegetables and added them back to the soup before serving. To complete the dish, we found a few teaspoons of lemon juice and a little Madeira drizzled over the soup before serving brightened our soup and cut through the richness. No one could have guessed we had cut the calories of the original by more than half and brought the fat all the way down from 30 grams to a mere 5. This was a decadent soup we could feel good about eating.

MAKEOVER SPOTLIGHT: CREAMY MUSHROOM SOUP

	CALORIES	FAT	SAT FAT	CHOLESTEROL
BEFORE	360	30g	20g	95mg
AFTER	130	5g	3g	15mg

Creamy Mushroom Soup
SERVES 6

Since this soup is pureed, don't waste time slicing the mushrooms. Just break them into rough pieces with your hands. Use the blender, not the food processor, for the smoothest possible soup. You can use brandy or dry sherry in place of the Madeira.

- 2 **pounds white mushrooms, broken into rough pieces**
- 2 **leeks, white and light green parts only, halved lengthwise, sliced thin, and rinsed thoroughly (see page 44)**
- 1 **tablespoon unsalted butter**
  Salt and pepper
- 4 **garlic cloves, minced**
- 2 **teaspoons minced fresh thyme or ½ teaspoon dried**
- 5 **cups beef broth**
- ½ **cup Madeira, plus extra for serving**
- ½ **cup half-and-half**
- 2 **teaspoons fresh lemon juice**

1. Combine the mushrooms, leeks, butter, ½ teaspoon salt, and ¼ teaspoon pepper in a large Dutch oven. Cover and cook over medium-low heat, stirring occasionally, until the mushrooms are softened, 8 to 10 minutes. Uncover, increase the heat to medium-high, and continue to cook, stirring occasionally, until the mushrooms are well browned, 8 to 12 minutes longer. Transfer ⅔ cup of the mushroom mixture to a cutting board, chop fine, and set aside.

2. Stir the garlic and thyme into the pot and cook until fragrant, about 30 seconds. Stir in the broth and Madeira, bring to a simmer, and cook until the mushrooms and leeks are completely tender, about 20 minutes.

3. Working in 2 batches, process the soup in a blender until completely smooth, 2 to 3 minutes. Return the soup to the pot. Stir in the chopped mushroom mixture, half-and-half, and lemon juice and cook until heated through. Season with salt and pepper to taste and serve, drizzling individual portions with additional Madeira.

PER 1⅓-CUP SERVING: Cal 130; Fat 5g; Sat fat 3g; Chol 15mg; Carb 12g; Protein 6g; Fiber 1g; Sodium 690mg

CHICKEN TAGINE

TAGINES ARE A NORTH AFRICAN SPECIALTY— exotically spiced, assertively flavored stews slow-cooked in earthenware vessels of the same name. They can include all manner of meats, vegetables, and fruit, though our hands-down favorite is a combination of chicken, briny olives, and tart lemon. Unfortunately, the traditional recipes we found required time-consuming, labor-intensive cooking methods, a special pot (the tagine), and hard-to-find ingredients. We're usually game for a day in the kitchen or a hunt for exotica, but isn't tagine, at its most elemental level, just stew? Could we find a way to make this exotic dish into a healthy everyday meal with supermarket ingredients?

A little research proved that we weren't the first to take a stab at making tagine more accessible. While most of the recipes we tried lacked the depth of an authentic tagine, they did hold promise, proving that a Western cooking method (braising in a Dutch oven) is a serviceable substitution for stewing for hours in a tagine. We also discovered that the flavors we associated with Moroccan cooking weren't necessarily "exotic"—they were a strategic blend of ingredients we already had in our cupboard.

Almost all of the recipes we collected called for a whole chicken broken down into pieces. Looking to save calories, fat, and time, we decided to try substituting boneless, skinless chicken breasts into a basic recipe. Batches made with diced white meat, while quick to cook, turned out rubbery and tasteless chicken pieces. For our next test, we seared the chicken breasts, then poached them whole in the stew. Once they were cooked through, we removed them, shredded the meat, and returned it to the stew. This chicken was juicy and perfectly cooked, and poaching it right in the soup infused it with flavor. Dusting the breasts with a small amount of flour helped create a better fond and protected the chicken since the breasts were without skin. This small amount of flour also helped to thicken the stew, which tasters agreed was a plus.

Some carrots, a sliced onion, and a healthy dose of garlic rounded out the basic flavors, so we moved on to the spices. Many recipes called for a spice blend called

ras el hanout, which translates loosely as "top of the shop" and may contain more than 30 spices. Since it's hard to find, we experimented with coming up with our own combination, but the final list was always too unwieldy. We decided to take a look at spice blends and see if one could approximate the flavor we were after. With its combination of coriander, black pepper, cumin, cardamom, and cinnamon, garam masala fit right in. We also included paprika, which added sweetness and a deep, attractive red color to the stew's broth.

As for the olives, finding the right variety proved harder than we anticipated. Big, meaty, green Moroccan olives were the obvious choice for the stew, but they were a rarity at our local markets. Other meaty green olives, like Manzanilla, Cerignola, and Lucques, were either too mild or too assertive to match the other flavors in the stew. Greek green "cracked" olives, which have been partially split open to allow a marinade (typically olive oil and vinegar seasoned with oregano and lemon zest) to penetrate the meat, offered complex flavor to our tagine, and they were easy to find next to regular jarred olives in the supermarket.

The lemon flavor in authentic tagines comes from preserved lemon, a long-cured Moroccan condiment that's hard to find outside of specialty stores. "Quick" preserved lemons can be produced at home in a few days, but we wanted to keep our recipe as simple as possible. Part tart citrus, part pickled brine, traditional preserved lemon has a unique flavor that's tough to imitate. So we chose not to try; instead, we aimed for a rich citrus back note in the dish. We added a few broad ribbons of lemon zest along with the onions. The heat coaxed out the zest's oils and mellowed them, giving our stew a good lemony infusion. Adding 2 tablespoons of juice just before serving reinforced the bright flavor.

To balance the spices, we added a spoonful of honey, and chopped cilantro added a hint of freshness and color. But the stew still lacked a certain spark. Chickpeas, a common tagine ingredient, added good texture and an appealing nuttiness. Apricots, another typical inclusion, provided bright, fruity notes and a slight tartness. Our healthy tagine boasted an exotic flavor and tender, juicy meat, and unlike most recipes it was a snap to make.

CHICKEN TAGINE

Chicken Tagine

SERVES 6

If you cannot find pitted olives and don't want to pit them yourself, substitute pimiento-stuffed green olives. The olives are one of the main sources of sodium in this recipe; omit them if you are concerned about sodium intake.

- ½ cup unbleached all-purpose flour
- 1½ pounds boneless, skinless chicken breasts, trimmed
  Salt and pepper
- 4 teaspoons canola oil
- 2 onions, halved and sliced ¼ inch thick
- 4 (2-inch) strips lemon zest plus 2 tablespoons fresh lemon juice
- 8 garlic cloves, peeled
- 2½ teaspoons paprika
- 2 teaspoons garam masala
- 4 cups low-sodium chicken broth
- 1 tablespoon honey
- 1 pound carrots (about 6), peeled, halved lengthwise, and sliced 1 inch thick
- 1 (15-ounce) can chickpeas, drained and rinsed
- 1 cup Greek green olives, rinsed, pitted, and halved
- 1 cup dried apricots, chopped medium
- ¼ cup minced fresh cilantro

1. Spread the flour in a shallow dish. Pat the chicken breasts dry with paper towels and season with ⅛ teaspoon salt and ⅛ teaspoon pepper. Lightly dredge the chicken in the flour, shaking off the excess. Heat 2 teaspoons of the oil in a large Dutch oven over medium-high heat until just smoking. Carefully lay the chicken breasts in the pot and cook until well browned on the first side, 6 to 8 minutes. Transfer the chicken breasts to a plate.

2. Add the remaining 2 teaspoons oil, onions, lemon zest, and ⅛ teaspoon salt to the pot, cover, and cook over medium-low heat, stirring occasionally, until the onions are softened, 8 to 10 minutes. Uncover, stir in the garlic, paprika, and garam masala, and cook until fragrant, about 30 seconds. Slowly stir in the broth and honey, scraping up any browned bits.

3. Stir in the carrots, chickpeas, olives, and apricots. Arrange the chicken breasts in a single layer over the top and bring to a simmer. Cover, reduce the heat to medium-low, and cook until the chicken registers 160 to 165 degrees on an instant-read thermometer, 10 to 15 minutes.

4. Transfer the chicken to a plate; when cool enough to handle, shred the meat into bite-size pieces. Meanwhile, continue to simmer the stew until the liquid has thickened slightly and the carrots are tender, 5 to 10 minutes longer.

5. Remove and discard the lemon zest strips. Stir in the shredded chicken, lemon juice, and cilantro, season with salt and pepper to taste, and serve.

PER 1½-CUP SERVING: Cal 400; Fat 9g; Sat fat 0.5g; Chol 65mg; Carb 47g; Protein 32g; Fiber 7g; Sodium 980mg

CHICKEN AND DUMPLINGS

THERE'S PROBABLY NO STEW MORE CLASSIC IN American home cooking than chicken and dumplings. And given the fat in the dark meat chicken, the cream and butter in the filling, and the butter and shortening

TEST KITCHEN
MAKEOVER

in the dumplings, there are few stews as fatty (25 grams of fat and 650 calories in a serving, in fact). We didn't want to have to think of this everyday comfort food as a meal we could eat only on a special occasion, so we set out to create a lighter and healthier version that had all the comfort-food appeal of the original.

To keep this recipe healthy, we wanted to use only white meat. But dark meat also adds flavor, so we needed to bolster the flavor of our cooking liquid another way. Replacing the water, which old-fashioned recipes relied on for the cooking liquid, with store-bought broth was a good start, as was browning bone-in, skin-on chicken breasts before adding the broth to the pot (after browning we discarded the skin). This latter step would leave behind a flavorful fond in the pot. Sweating aromatic vegetables—carrots, onions, and celery—in this fond and adding ¼ cup of sherry (preferred by tasters over white wine and vermouth) contributed acidity, depth, and sweetness.

Now we had the flavor of the broth where we wanted it, but we still had to address the body. Most recipes turn to flour as a thickener, but some recipes leave well enough alone. We compared straight broth to broth we thickened with ½ cup of flour (an amount typical in many recipes we found), added just before deglazing with the sherry. We were actually surprised when the straight broth style won out; tasters agreed that the bready dumplings would add plenty of heartiness, and forgoing the thickener saved us some calories and at the same time allowed the chicken flavor to take center stage.

There are two styles of dumplings. There are those made of dough rolled out to about ¼ inch and cut into squares that are then added to the pot. It was a tedious and messy process that yielded dense, doughy dumplings. The other style of dumplings, on the other hand, we found to be far simpler. These dumplings are closely related to oven-baked drop biscuits. You simply mix flour and leavener in one bowl and fat and a liquid in another, combine the two mixtures rapidly, and drop biscuit-size balls into the broth. Tasters vastly preferred these lighter biscuits—although they weren't really all that light.

We tried using our standard drop biscuit recipe (flour, salt, sugar, baking powder and soda, butter, and buttermilk) to see if it would produce more pillowy results. These dumplings had great tangy buttermilk flavor, and because they had more leavener and butter than the earlier recipes we had tried, they were far from leaden. In fact, they had the opposite problem: They were so fragile, they disintegrated into the broth as they cooked.

The ideal dumpling should have all the lightness of our drop biscuits, but enough structure to hold together in the broth. Knowing that fat coats flour and weakens its structure, we tried gradually cutting down on the 8 tablespoons of butter in the recipe (which we would have had to address from a healthy aspect at some point anyway). At 2 tablespoons, their structure improved somewhat; removing any more compromised flavor. Since we were cooking our dumplings in a moist environment instead of a dry oven, our next thought was to cut back on the liquid in the dumplings. Reducing the amount of buttermilk from a full cup to ¾ cup was another improvement—but the dumplings were still too delicate.

Perhaps the problem was too much leavener, which can lead to over-rising and poor structure. Completely eliminating the baking powder (only baking soda remained) gave the dumplings just the right density in the center, but they were still mushy around the edges. While eggs are not traditional biscuit ingredients, we tried adding one, hoping that the extra protein would help the dumplings hold together. A whole egg was too much; tasters didn't like the eggy flavor. A single egg white whisked into the buttermilk added just the right amount of structure without affecting flavor, and it was a bonus that we could successfully omit the fatty yolk. Waiting until the broth was simmering before adding the dumplings reduced their time in the broth and helped keep them whole.

Now, just one last problem remained: Steam was condensing on the inside of the pot's lid and dripping onto the dumplings, turning their tops soggy. Wrapping a kitchen towel around the lid of the Dutch oven worked like a charm, trapping the moisture before it had a chance to drip down and saturate our light-as-air dumplings and flavor-packed broth. With 340 calories and 6 grams of fat in a bowl, we felt pretty good about making chicken and dumplings into a regular comfort-food favorite in our own kitchen.

MAKEOVER SPOTLIGHT: CHICKEN AND DUMPLINGS

	CALORIES	FAT	SAT FAT	CHOLESTEROL
BEFORE	650	25g	9g	260mg
AFTER	340	6g	2.5g	75mg

Chicken and Dumplings

SERVES 8

After dropping the dumplings into the simmering broth, be sure to wrap the lid of the Dutch oven with a clean kitchen towel (keep the towel away from the heat source) and cover the pot. The towel absorbs moisture that would otherwise drip onto the dumplings and turn their tops soggy.

STEW

- 3 **pounds bone-in, skin-on split chicken breasts, trimmed (see page 61)**
- **Salt and pepper**
- 1½ **teaspoons canola oil**
- 4 **carrots, peeled and cut into ¾-inch pieces**
- 2 **onions, minced (about 2 cups)**
- 1 **celery rib, chopped fine**
- ¼ **cup dry sherry**
- 6 **cups low-sodium chicken broth**
- 1 **teaspoon minced fresh thyme or ¼ teaspoon dried**
- ½ **cup frozen peas (2 ounces)**
- ¼ **cup minced fresh parsley**

DUMPLINGS

- 2 **cups (10 ounces) unbleached all-purpose flour**
- 1 **teaspoon sugar**
- 1 **teaspoon salt**
- ½ **teaspoon baking soda**
- ¾ **cup cold buttermilk**
- 2 **tablespoons unsalted butter, melted and cooled slightly**
- 1 **large egg white**

1. FOR THE STEW: Pat the chicken breasts dry with paper towels and season with ⅛ teaspoon salt and ⅛ teaspoon pepper. Heat the oil in a large Dutch oven over medium-high heat until just smoking. Carefully lay the chicken, skin side down, in the pot and cook until golden brown on both sides, 10 to 12 minutes, flipping the breasts halfway through. Transfer the chicken to a plate and remove and discard the skin.

2. Add the carrots, onions, celery, and ⅛ teaspoon salt to the oil left in the pot, reduce the heat to medium-low, cover, and cook, stirring occasionally, until the vegetables are softened, 8 to 10 minutes. Stir in the sherry, scraping up any browned bits. Add the chicken to the pot, along with any accumulated juice, broth, and thyme. Bring to a simmer, cover, and cook until the chicken registers 160 to 165 degrees on an instant-read thermometer, about 20 minutes.

3. Remove the pot from the heat and transfer the chicken to a plate. When cool enough to handle, shred the meat into large pieces, discarding the bones.

4. FOR THE DUMPLINGS: Whisk the flour, sugar, salt, and baking soda together in a large bowl. Stir the buttermilk and melted butter together in a bowl until the butter forms small clumps, then whisk in the egg white. Add the buttermilk mixture to the flour mixture and stir with a rubber spatula until just incorporated and the batter pulls away from the sides of the bowl.

5. Return the stew to a simmer, then stir in the shredded chicken, peas, and parsley. Season with salt and pepper to taste. Using a greased tablespoon measure, scoop a level amount of batter and drop 24 dumplings on top of the stew about 1 inch apart. Wrap the lid of the Dutch oven with a clean kitchen towel (keeping the towel away from the heat source) and cover the pot. Cook over low heat until the dumplings have doubled in size, 13 to 16 minutes. Serve.

PER 1½-CUP SERVING WITH 3 DUMPLINGS: Cal 340; **Fat** 6g; **Sat fat** 2.5g; **Chol** 75mg; **Carb** 36g; **Protein** 32g; **Fiber** 3g; **Sodium** 1010mg

---

BEEF AND VEGETABLE STEW

TEST KITCHEN MAKEOVER

AT ITS HEART, BEEF STEW IS SIMPLE COMFORT FOOD, rich and satisfying. Plenty of tender chunks of meat are surrounded by a rich, deeply flavorful, and slightly thickened broth. Typically a few vegetables, probably some carrots, potatoes, and onions (and perhaps a handful of peas for color), are dotted throughout to add contrasting texture. But tallying a whopping 720 calories and 26 grams of fat per serving, beef stew makes for anything but light dining. Sure, light beef stew recipes exist, but they usually cut back on the beef so much that you are left wondering "Where's the beef?" We set before ourselves one of our biggest challenges yet. Could we make a beef stew with big, beefy flavor but also make it healthy? We wanted to give the vegetables more of a presence, but not so much that they took away the dish's identity.

We started by reviewing what we already knew about making beef stew, since we've had plenty of experience in the test kitchen nailing down the basics. Chuck roasts are our preferred cut—they're flavorful, tender, juicy, and available at a reasonable price; we like to buy a whole roast and cut it ourselves rather than buy precut stew meat. Browning the meat, once cubed, is the first step to adding deep flavor to beef stew. Choosing the right stewing liquids is another. For our classic beef stew we found that chicken broth with a little red wine worked best. For thickening our stew, a few tablespoons of flour added to the pot with the onions and garlic, before the liquids, was the easiest way and didn't interfere with our stew's rich color as some thickeners will. So with those basics already under our belt, we set out to see what we could do.

Starting with the meat in our classic stew, we trimmed the amount down from 3 pounds of meat to 2 pounds. This put the stew's fat and calories in the right ballpark for a healthy stew, and tasters agreed it still gave each serving plenty of meat. We were counting on heft to come from the vegetables anyway, so we weren't too worried about bulk.

Next we focused on the stewing liquids. Now that we had taken some of the meat out of our original, we were missing some of that beefy flavor that infused the liquid. Instead of using just wine and chicken broth, we found that substituting some beef broth for part of the chicken broth put back the flavor we were missing. We also gave a stew with all beef broth and wine a shot, but it was too tinny-tasting.

Now we needed to find vegetables that would work in harmony with the beef. We knew from experience that mushrooms provide a meaty, earthy flavor that works well with beef. We tried several varieties, including white button, cremini, and portobello. Taster preferred the portobello because it added more intense mushroom flavor than the others and had more meatiness to it, and because they are large we needed only a single mushroom. After browning the meat, we cooked the mushroom in the fond left behind, boosting its flavor and ensuring that the mushroom didn't have a spongy texture in the final stew.

To balance the rich and earthy flavors of the mushroom and meat, root vegetables seemed like a good fit, and they are always a welcome addition to hearty stews. Starchy potatoes went a long way toward cutting some of the richness. Of the three varieties we tested (Yukon Golds, red potatoes, and russets), red potatoes won out for their ability to maintain their shape. Carrots and parsnips also earned a spot, providing a bit of sweetness that helped round out our stew.

Hoping to boost the healthy qualities of our stew even further, we decided it was time to go beyond the expected in a beef stew and add some hearty greens. Neither Swiss chard nor escarole provided the right flavor profile, but kale, a hearty braising green, was a perfect

fit. It added just the right amount of bitterness without being too strong and ruining the balance. A last-minute addition of frozen peas provided the freshness needed to complement the other vegetables and finish off our stew.

With plenty of beef and vegetables, at 440 calories and 10 grams of fat per serving, our beef stew was both comfort food and healthy. We couldn't ask for much more than that.

MAKEOVER SPOTLIGHT: BEEF AND VEGETABLE STEW

	CALORIES	FAT	SAT FAT	CHOLESTEROL
BEFORE	720	26g	10g	150mg
AFTER	440	10g	2g	50mg

Beef and Vegetable Stew

SERVES 6

Make this stew in a large Dutch oven, preferably one with an 8-quart capacity.

- 2 **pounds beef chuck-eye roast, trimmed of all visible fat and cut into 1½-inch chunks (see page 53)**
  Salt and pepper
- 5 **teaspoons canola oil**
- 1 **medium portobello mushroom cap (about 6 ounces), cut into ½-inch pieces**
- 2 **onions, minced (about 2 cups)**
- 3 **garlic cloves, minced**
- 1 **tablespoon minced fresh thyme or ¾ teaspoon dried**
- 3 **tablespoons unbleached all-purpose flour**
- 1 **tablespoon tomato paste**
- 1½ **cups dry red wine**
- 2 **cups low-sodium chicken broth**
- 2 **cups beef broth**
- 2 **bay leaves**
- 12 **ounces red potatoes (about 2 medium), cut into 1-inch pieces**
- 4 **carrots, peeled, halved lengthwise, and sliced 1 inch thick**
- 3 **parsnips, peeled, halved lengthwise, and sliced 1 inch thick**
- 1 **pound kale, stemmed, leaves cut into ½-inch pieces (see page 29)**
- ½ **cup frozen peas (2 ounces)**
- ¼ **cup minced fresh parsley**

1. Adjust an oven rack to the lower-middle position and heat the oven to 300 degrees. Pat the beef dry with paper towels and season with ⅛ teaspoon salt and ⅛ teaspoon pepper. Heat 1 teaspoon of the oil in a large Dutch oven over medium-high heat until just smoking. Add half of the meat and cook until well browned on all sides, 5 to 10 minutes, turning as needed. Transfer the beef to a bowl and repeat with 1 teaspoon more oil and the remaining beef.

2. Add the mushroom to the fat left in the pot, cover, and cook over medium-low heat, stirring occasionally, until softened, 8 to 10 minutes. Uncover, increase the heat to medium-high, and continue to cook until well browned, 8 to 12 minutes longer.

3. Stir in the remaining 1 tablespoon oil and onions and cook until the onions are softened, about 5 minutes. Stir in the garlic and thyme and cook until fragrant, about 30 seconds. Stir in the flour and tomato paste and cook until lightly browned, about 1 minute.

4. Slowly whisk in the wine, scraping up any browned bits. Slowly whisk in the chicken broth and beef broth until smooth. Stir in the browned meat, along with any accumulated juice, and bay leaves and bring to a simmer. Cover, transfer the pot to the oven, and cook for 1½ hours.

5. Stir in the potatoes, carrots, and parsnips and continue to cook in the oven until the meat and vegetables are tender, about 1 hour longer.

6. Stir in the kale and continue to cook in the oven until tender, about 10 minutes longer. Remove the stew from the oven. Remove and discard the bay leaves. Stir in the peas and parsley and let the stew sit for 5 to 10 minutes. Season with salt and pepper to taste and serve.

PER 1½-CUP SERVING: **Cal** 440; **Fat** 10g; **Sat fat** 2g; **Chol** 50mg; **Carb** 45g; **Protein** 34g; **Fiber** 9g; **Sodium** 630mg

NOTES FROM THE TEST KITCHEN

CUTTING STEW MEAT

1. Pull apart the roast at its major seams (delineated by lines of fat and silver skin). Use a knife as necessary.

2. With a knife, trim off excess fat and silver skin.

3. Cut the meat into 1½-inch chunks.

NEW ENGLAND FISH STEW

IN NEW ENGLAND, FISH STEW IS SIMILAR TO CLAM chowder. Chunks of white fish take the place of the clams, but otherwise the two are fairly similar—onions, potatoes, and bacon or salt pork are added with the fish to a briny, creamy broth. Still, there are some other minor but important differences. Clams shed so much juice that there's no need for fish stock in a clam chowder. Meanwhile, the firm, meaty white fish used in a hearty fish stew sheds no liquid, so another source for the liquid is a must. The other important difference has to do with heft. The potatoes in a clam chowder are cut fairly small so they don't overwhelm the clams—you want everything to fit on the spoon at the same time. It makes for a chowder that is fairly delicate. A New England fish stew is traditionally a little heartier. The fish and potatoes are cut into large chunks, and the broth is thicker and less plentiful so that the other components can take center stage. This stew is definitely a main course. With this profile in mind, we set out to lighten this recipe without sacrificing its flavor.

After preparing several versions of this stew, we noticed two big problems. The first issue was the fish—in many recipes the fish fell apart into small flakes. Some flaking was fine, but we wanted the fish to remain for the most part in large chunks to maintain the character of a stew. The second issue we flagged was the number of ingredients that had no place in this simple stew. This, unlike the fish, was an easy fix to make off the cuff. We jettisoned tomatoes, cayenne, and any other ingredients that just didn't fit the simple, hearty New England character of the recipe.

As for the fish issue, we had found several tips in other recipes for keeping the fish from falling apart. One suggested laying whole fillets on top of the liquid and letting the fish naturally fall apart into large chunks as it cooked. We found that this method worked when there was a lot of liquid in the pot, but we wanted a thicker stew. When we tried cooking the fish this way in a pot with less liquid, it was a failure. The potatoes pushed the fish up above the stew liquid, and without the cooking liquid surrounding the fish, it emerged from the pot a bit bland-tasting—it had steamed above the liquid rather than poaching in it.

We found that cutting each fillet into 4-ounce pieces (roughly the size of your palm) yielded the best results. The pieces were small enough to sink into the stew liquid but large enough to hold their shape, making for only a minimum amount of flaking.

To add some meaty depth, most recipes include salt pork or bacon. We prepared stews with each pork product, and while the salt pork is a more traditional choice, tasters favored the smoky flavor of the bacon. One slice, chopped fine, was enough to infuse our soup, and cooking the bacon first allowed us to use the rendered fat to cook the onion, giving the stew a smoky flavor that oil alone could not match.

Once the onion had softened, the liquid and potatoes went into the pot and simmered until the potatoes were tender before the fish was added. Homemade fish stock was excellent at reinforcing the fish flavor, but as for most of our soup recipes, we wanted to keep things simple. Bottled clam juice mixed with a little water added just the bit of brininess we missed and didn't require anything more of the cook than using a bottle opener.

Most fish stew recipes rely on cream, but to keep things light we looked for alternatives. We tested whole milk but were disappointed with the results; the liquid was too thin and broke under the heat. Just as in our other creamy soup recipes, half-and-half was the right choice, providing creaminess, richness, and body without so much fat. But even with the half-and-half, we wanted this soup to be thicker. A few teaspoons of flour did the trick, and because the flavors in this recipe were so simple, we found that cooking the flour before adding the liquid deepened its flavor.

Our stew was almost finished. For the final touches and seasoning, we added a bay leaf and a small amount of thyme with the potatoes, then stirred in a touch of parsley just before serving. Our finished stew was healthy and quick, while maintaining its restrained and dignified New England pedigree.

New England Fish Stew

SERVES 4

Haddock or cod is the best choice for this recipe, although striped bass, hake, or halibut can also be used. We prefer thicker fillets, but you can use thinner fillets as long as you reduce the cooking time by 2 to 3 minutes.

- 1 **slice bacon, chopped fine**
- 1 **onion, chopped coarse (about 1 cup)**
- 1 **teaspoon canola oil**
  Salt
- 4½ **teaspoons unbleached all-purpose flour**
- 1 **(8-ounce) bottle clam juice**
- ½ **cup water**
- ¼ **cup dry white wine**
- 8 **ounces red potatoes (about 2 medium), cut into 1-inch cubes**
- ½ **teaspoon minced fresh thyme or ⅛ teaspoon dried**
- 1 **bay leaf**
- 1½ **pounds haddock or cod fillets (¾ to 1 inch thick), rinsed, patted dry, and cut into 4-ounce pieces**
- ⅓ **cup half-and-half**
- 2 **tablespoons minced fresh parsley**
  Pepper

1. Cook the bacon in a large Dutch oven over medium-low heat, stirring often, until the fat is rendered and the bacon is crisp, 8 to 10 minutes. Add the onion, oil, and ⅛ teaspoon salt, cover, and cook, stirring occasionally, until softened, 8 to 10 minutes. Stir in the flour and cook until lightly browned, about 1 minute. Slowly whisk in the clam juice, water, and wine and bring to a simmer.

2. Stir in the potatoes, thyme, and bay leaf, return to a simmer, cover, and cook until the potatoes are almost tender, about 15 minutes.

3. Nestle the fish pieces into the liquid, return to a simmer over medium heat, and cook for 7 minutes, gently stirring occasionally. Remove the pot from the heat, cover, and let sit until the fish is just cooked through, 2 to 3 minutes.

4. Remove and discard the bay leaf. Stir in the half-and-half and parsley, season with salt and pepper to taste, and serve.

PER 1½-CUP SERVING: Cal 280; Fat 7g; Sat fat 2.5g; Chol 85mg; Carb 15g; Protein 33g; Fiber 2g; Sodium 360mg

TEN-VEGETABLE STEW

MOST GREAT STEW RECIPES ARE CHOCK-FULL OF meat because, honestly, in the dead of winter nothing sounds as satisfying. But with so many heavy, meaty wintertime recipes out there, we felt the need for a reprieve from the beef, the chicken, and the pork. We wanted a vegetarian vegetable stew packed with a variety of vegetables that could satisfy just as well. Unfortunately, the vegetable stews we've come across are just vegetables thrown into a pot and simmered away. They are either watery and bland or muddy and overloaded. There had to be a way to bring the vegetables to the forefront yet maintain balance, and at the same time win over even the most adamant carnivores.

Based on previous test kitchen experience, we knew that onion, carrot, celery, and red bell pepper were in for their essential aromatic flavor, so we started by sautéing them until brown to coax out their natural sweetness. Garlic, thyme, and tomato paste added further depth, and a little flour helped thicken the stew. At this point we deglazed the pot with wine, which would pick up the browned bits and at the same time add depth. Red wine overpowered the vegetables; white proved to be a much better choice, adding brightness, slight acidity, and depth all at once. After the wine reduced, we were ready to add the other liquid components. We began testing various amounts of vegetable broth and canned tomatoes, but the tomatoes brought too much acidity. This stew was better off with the vegetable broth alone.

Now for the real hurdle: What vegetables should be featured in our stew? With their earthy flavor and hearty makeup, root vegetables made a logical starting point. Turnips proved to be slightly bitter, not what we were looking for, and russet potatoes and sweet potatoes fell apart. In the end, parsnips, celery root, and red potatoes won out for their unique flavors and appealing textures.

We added them to the pot right after the broth, then we simmered the stew until the vegetables were tender. The size to which these vegetables were cut proved key. Too small and they disappeared into the stew, too large and they didn't cook through. We found that 1-inch pieces cooked through properly and gave the stew just the right hearty appearance. However, at this point we noticed a new problem. The stew was developing an overly sweet quality.

Mushrooms, with their earthy flavor, could work as an obvious counter to the sweet flavors. First we tried portobellos, always a top choice for a meaty mushroom, but they weren't right here. Working through the other supermarket mushroom options, we were surprised that everyday white button mushrooms won out. But how we incorporated them was crucial. Adding them straight to the broth resulted in chewy, spongy mushrooms. Sautéing the mushrooms until they were well browned helped to deepen the mushrooms' flavor, kept them from being spongy, and created even more flavorful fond to further the earthiness.

Still needing a bit more earthiness, we looked toward hearty greens. Mustard greens and escarole were both too bitter. Tasters liked both kale and curly-leaf spinach, but the real winner was Swiss chard. It was hearty but not too tough. We added the stems with the aromatics and the leaves toward the end of the cooking to ensure that they didn't disintegrate. This helped to tip the scales further from the sweet side, but still, not enough.

Vegetable broth has a natural sweetness that we realized was a major contributor to the problem. Using a mixture of vegetable broth and water went a long way toward bringing the stew into balance. We settled on a ratio of nearly equal parts water and vegetable broth. The water helped cut the sweetness and allowed the earthy flavors to come through.

This stew was almost there, but it needed a touch of freshness and acidity. Summery zucchini struck us as a good addition, but it turned to mush when added with the root vegetables. Waiting to add it until the end of cooking with the chard leaves was an easy fix. A splash of lemon juice and a sprinkle of fresh parsley were the perfect finishing touches of freshness and acidity. This vegetable stew was hearty (we had managed to squeeze in a whopping 10 vegetables) and satisfying, yet balanced and healthy. It could definitely hold its own against even the best of the beef stews.

HEARTY TEN-VEGETABLE STEW

Hearty Ten-Vegetable Stew

SERVES 8

Kale or curly-leaf spinach can be substituted for the chard; if using kale, discard the stems and simmer for an additional 5 minutes in step 4.

- 1 pound white mushrooms, sliced thin
- 2 tablespoons canola oil
   Salt
- 8 ounces Swiss chard, stems and leaves separated, stems chopped fine and leaves cut into ½-inch pieces (see page 29)
- 2 onions, minced (about 2 cups)
- 1 celery rib, cut into ½-inch pieces
- 1 carrot, peeled, halved lengthwise, and sliced 1 inch thick
- 1 red bell pepper, stemmed, seeded, and cut into ½-inch pieces
- 6 garlic cloves, minced
- 2 teaspoons minced fresh thyme or ½ teaspoon dried
- 2 tablespoons unbleached all-purpose flour
- 1 tablespoon tomato paste
- ½ cup dry white wine
- 3 cups vegetable broth
- 2½ cups water
- 8 ounces red potatoes (about 2 medium), cut into 1-inch pieces
- 2 parsnips, peeled and cut into 1-inch pieces
- 8 ounces celery root, peeled and cut into 1-inch pieces
- 2 bay leaves
- 1 zucchini, seeded and cut into ½-inch pieces
- ¼ cup minced fresh parsley
- 1 tablespoon fresh lemon juice
   Pepper

1. Combine the mushrooms, 1 tablespoon of the oil, and ¼ teaspoon salt in a large Dutch oven. Cover and cook over medium-low heat, stirring occasionally, until softened, 8 to 10 minutes. Uncover, increase the heat to medium-high, and continue to cook until well browned, 8 to 12 minutes longer.

2. Stir in the remaining 1 tablespoon oil, chard stems, onions, celery, carrot, bell pepper, and ⅛ teaspoon salt and cook until the vegetables are well browned, 7 to 10 minutes.

3. Stir in the garlic and thyme and cook until fragrant, about 30 seconds. Stir in the flour and tomato paste and cook until lightly browned, about 1 minute. Stir in the wine, scraping up any browned bits, and simmer until nearly evaporated, about 2 minutes. Stir in the broth, water, potatoes, parsnips, celery root, and bay leaves and bring to a simmer.

4. Reduce the heat to medium-low, partially cover, and cook until the stew is thickened and the vegetables are tender, about 1 hour. Stir in the chard leaves and zucchini and continue to simmer until tender, 5 to 10 minutes longer.

5. Remove and discard the bay leaves. Stir in the parsley and lemon juice, season with salt and pepper to taste, and serve.

PER 1½-CUP SERVING: Cal 160; Fat 4g; Sat fat 0g; Chol 0mg; Carb 26g; Protein 4g; Fiber 5g; Sodium 450mg

NOTES FROM THE TEST KITCHEN

VEGETABLE BROTH
There are a slew of vegetable broth options available today, but how do they all taste? We sampled 10 broths, heated and served plain and also cooked into soups and risotto. Flavors ranged from bland to overpowering; some broths were astonishingly salty or sweet, others oddly sour, and many tasted nothing like vegetables. What we learned is that broths listing vegetable content (whether from fresh whole vegetables or extracts) first on the ingredient list fared best. Also important were generous amounts of flavor-enhancing additives (such as MSG) and salt. Of the 10 brands, Swanson Vegetarian Vegetable Broth was the overall winner; tasters praised its "good balance of vegetable flavors." But with 940 milligrams of sodium per cup, it was too sodium-laden for healthier recipes. We used our runner-up, **College Inn Garden Vegetable Broth**, which was deemed "one of the best," with only 590 milligrams of sodium per cup.

EASY CHICKEN CORDON BLEU

ROAST CHICKEN AND VEGETABLES

THE BEAUTY OF ROASTED CHICKEN AND VEGETABLES lies in its simplicity. The two should bring out each other's best qualities, making it the perfect light supper. And if you swap out the whole bird for chicken breasts, you've got all the comfort and appeal of the classic in less time. In our dream recipe, the lightly caramelized vegetables offer a sweetness and an earthiness that complement the moist, delicate chicken. A test of as many recipes as we could find quickly brought our heads out of the clouds with results that ran the gamut: Vegetables were variously barely cooked through or overdone to mush, while the chicken ranged from still raw in the middle to impossibly dry. We set out to create a foolproof recipe that would give us both perfect chicken and vegetables, every time.

We settled early on bone-in, skin-on chicken breasts. Boneless, skinless breasts were too thin and delicate for oven roasting. They overcooked before they could develop the deep roasted flavor of the bone-in chicken. We also made the crucial decision to roast the chicken with the skin on. While the skin contains the majority of the fat, it would protect the meat during its time in the oven, guarding it from drying out, and would provide the vegetables with essential moisture so that they, too, could cook through properly. After the chicken was cooked, we found we could easily remove the skin before eating.

Next we focused on the vegetables. Our testing of existing recipes showed there is no one combination of vegetables that works best. We did find, however, some simple guidelines were helpful. It was best to stay away from vegetables with high water content like tomatoes, because they washed out the other flavors. We liked various combinations of root vegetables such as potatoes, carrots, and parsnips because they held their shape and developed a sweet, slightly caramelized flavor. Often the vegetables are tossed with as much as ¼ cup of oil for flavor and to promote browning. We found a mere tablespoon for 3 pounds of vegetables along with a bit of fresh rosemary, salt, and pepper could get the job done nicely.

We could finally hammer out our cooking method. With our quicker-cooking bone-in breasts, we figured the meat and vegetables would cook through in about the same amount of time. So, starting as simply as possible, we spread the chicken breasts and the vegetables in a single layer in a baking dish and popped it into a 450-degree oven. Thirty minutes later we pulled out moist, tender chicken breasts and half-cooked vegetables. For the next test, we gave the vegetables a 15-minute head start, then layered the chicken on top and cooked for an additional 30 minutes. An improvement, no doubt, but with the vegetables pinned under the chicken, they didn't roast but instead steamed in the meat's juice. We wanted to keep this recipe as efficient as possible and use only one pan, but we weren't sure what to do next. That's when a colleague suggested elevating the breasts above the vegetables in the pan somehow. We use a roasting rack to elevate a whole chicken when roasting to ensure even circulation of the heat, so why not do the same here? For the next test, we set a wire rack over the roasting pan, placed the chicken breasts on the rack, and scattered the vegetables underneath. This allowed the chicken's juice to drip onto the vegetables and infuse them with flavor without causing them to steam. Jackpot. The vegetables were tender and perfectly roasted and the chicken was tender and juicy.

We ran one final test, just to confirm that we were all set, and lo and behold, the vegetables were not cooked through properly. It turned out that the chicken we used was simply not as juicy as the previous batch. This called for an easy fix; for those instances when the chicken didn't release as much juice as the vegetables needed, we removed the chicken from the oven when it was done, stirred a little chicken broth into the pan with the vegetables, and let them finish cooking through while the chicken rested. With that, we had a recipe that was as foolproof as it was flavorful, easy to make, and healthy.

Roast Chicken Breasts with Red Potatoes, Carrots, and Parsnips

SERVES 4

Choose parsnips no wider than 1 inch; larger parsnips are likely to have tough cores. If using kosher chicken, do not brine. If brining, do not season with salt in step 3.

1 **pound red potatoes (about 3 medium), scrubbed and cut into 1-inch chunks**
1 **pound carrots, peeled, halved lengthwise, and cut into 1-inch lengths**

1 pound parsnips, peeled, halved, and cut
   into 1-inch lengths
2 shallots, peeled and quartered
8 garlic cloves, peeled
1 tablespoon olive oil
2 teaspoons minced fresh rosemary
   Salt and pepper
4 (12-ounce) bone-in, skin-on split chicken breasts,
   trimmed, brined if desired (see at right)
¼ cup low-sodium chicken broth, if needed
   Lemon wedges, for serving

1. Adjust an oven rack to the middle position and heat the oven to 450 degrees.

2. Toss the potatoes, carrots, parsnips, shallots, garlic, oil, rosemary, ½ teaspoon salt, and ½ teaspoon pepper together in a bowl. Spread the vegetables in a 13 by 9-inch baking dish and roast for 15 minutes.

3. Pat the chicken breasts dry with paper towels and season with ⅛ teaspoon salt and ⅛ teaspoon pepper. Lay the chicken, skin side up, on a wire rack. Following the photo, carefully place the wire rack over the dish of partially cooked vegetables (the rack may overhang the dish slightly). Roast until the chicken registers 160 to 165 degrees on an instant-read thermometer, 30 to 35 minutes.

4. Transfer the chicken to a platter, then remove and discard the skin. Tent the chicken loosely with foil and let rest for 5 minutes. (If the vegetables are not yet tender, stir in the broth and continue to cook until they are tender, up to 15 minutes longer.) Season the vegetables with salt and pepper to taste and transfer to the platter with the chicken. Serve with the lemon wedges.

PER SERVING: **Cal** 510; **Fat** 7g; **Sat fat** 1.5g; **Chol** 130mg; **Carb** 54g; **Protein** 56g; **Fiber** 11g; **Sodium** 640mg

VARIATIONS

Roast Chicken Breasts with Red Potatoes, Fennel, and Cauliflower

Follow the recipe for Roast Chicken Breasts with Red Potatoes, Carrots, and Parsnips, substituting 1 thinly sliced fennel bulb and ½ head cauliflower, cut into 1-inch florets, for the carrots and parsnips. Omit the rosemary and sprinkle the vegetables with 1 tablespoon minced fresh tarragon before serving.

PER SERVING: **Cal** 420; **Fat** 7g; **Sat fat** 1.5g; **Chol** 130mg; **Carb** 33g; **Protein** 57g; **Fiber** 7g; **Sodium** 610mg

NOTES FROM THE TEST KITCHEN

TRIMMING SPLIT CHICKEN BREASTS

Using kitchen shears, trim off the rib section from each breast

MAKING ROAST CHICKEN BREASTS AND VEGETABLES

Roast the vegetables alone for 15 minutes, then lay the chicken, skin side up, on a wire rack and place the rack over the dish of partially cooked vegetables. Continue roasting until the chicken is done.

BRINING

Both poultry and pork are lean, and in some preparations they can cook up dry. The salt in a brine changes the structure of the muscle proteins and allows them to hold on to more moisture when exposed to heat. Though we leave brining optional, if you have the time it will give you juicier meat in recipes.

To brine, dissolve table salt in water following the chart below in a container large enough to hold the brine and meat. Submerge the meat in the brine. Cover and refrigerate, following the chart's times (do not overbrine or the meat will taste too salty). Remove the meat from the brine, rinse, and pat dry with paper towels. The meat is ready to be cooked.

There is one exception to brining: If you've purchased kosher poultry, frozen injected turkey, or enhanced pork (pork injected with a salt solution), don't brine them. These treatments will keep the chicken, turkey, and pork moist, and brining will make the meat way too salty.

Our nutrition data does not account for brining or using any of the types of meat or poultry that should not be brined. As such, be aware that the final sodium content for those recipes will be higher than what we have listed.

POULTRY OR MEAT	COLD WATER	SALT	TIME
Chicken 4 (12-ounce) bone-in, skin-on split chicken breasts	2 quarts	½ cup	½ to 1 hour
Pork 1 (3-pound) pork loin	2 quarts	¼ cup	1 hour

Roast Chicken Breasts with Squash, Carrots, and Brussels Sprouts

Follow the recipe for Roast Chicken Breasts with Red Potatoes, Carrots, and Parsnips, substituting 8 ounces butternut squash, peeled and cut into 1-inch chunks (about 2 cups), and 10 ounces Brussels sprouts, halved, for the potatoes and parsnips. Substitute 1 tablespoon minced fresh thyme for the rosemary.

PER SERVING: Cal 400; Fat 7g; Sat fat 1.5g; Chol 130mg; Carb 29g; Protein 56g; Fiber 7g; Sodium 640mg

MEDITERRANEAN CHICKEN

CHICKEN WITH ARTICHOKES AND OLIVES, SIMMERED in a sauce of tomatoes, white wine, garlic, and herbs, is a naturally healthy, Mediterranean-inspired dish. Traditional recipes for this combination are fairly easy to find, but they don't lend themselves well to a quick weeknight dinner. Weeknight casserole versions exist, but those we have come across are halfhearted efforts that produce subpar results. Most of these recipes focus on convenience, using canned artichokes and olives tossed with cubed chicken and a jarred pasta sauce. We wanted tender chicken with fresh Mediterranean flavors. Not willing to make sacrifices, we set out to create a version with all the flavor of the traditional recipes that was simple enough to be made in one pan on a weeknight.

Our first issue to tackle was the chicken. Traditionally this dish involves cutting up a whole chicken and slowly braising the bone-in pieces—not an option on a Tuesday night. The weeknight chicken scene is often dominated by boneless, skinless chicken breasts, but they weren't well suited to this recipe. We needed a cut of chicken that would cook slowly enough to allow the other ingredients to cook through and the flavors to meld. Bone-in, skin-on chicken breasts fit the bill nicely and had a rustic appeal that worked well in the recipe. Breasts alone rather than a combination of breasts and thighs were not only a lighter choice but also a faster-cooking one; we would simply remove the fatty skin before serving. After browning the chicken in a skillet to deepen its flavor (and create fond in the pan to help build our sauce), we set it aside so we could build our sauce in the pan.

We knew we wanted a Mediterranean-inspired combination of tomatoes, olives, and artichokes. We quickly settled on briny kalamata olives and canned diced tomatoes, the latter of which we knew from experience would hold their structure best among the canned tomato options during the cooking time and give the sauce the right chunky, rustic texture. However, the artichokes presented a problem. Trimming and prepping fresh artichokes was well beyond the scope of a quick supper, and canned artichokes didn't maintain the structure we wanted in this recipe. Frozen artichokes had a firm, appealing texture, but tasters found them in need of a flavor boost. To solve this, we sautéed them briefly after browning the chicken.

After browning and setting aside both the chicken and the artichokes, we deglazed the pan with white wine and added our olives and diced tomatoes. We nestled the chicken and artichokes back into the sauce, then put the skillet in a 450-degree oven until the chicken cooked through, allowing the juice exuded by the chicken to add further flavor to the sauce. The results weren't bad, but we had seriously underestimated the amount of liquid that four chicken breasts would give off while roasting. The chicken went in with a fairly dry sauce and emerged swimming in a liquid that tasted as watery as it looked.

We needed to both thicken the sauce and boost the flavors. The first task was simple: We drained off the juice from the canned tomatoes, reduced the wine, and added 2 teaspoons of tomato paste to give the sauce some body. This sauce was so dry going into the oven that it resembled a chunky relish, giving us serious reason for doubt, but when it came out of the oven it was the perfect consistency for spooning over the chicken.

Tasters liked the flavor of the dish, but the combination of wine, olives, and garlic came on a little strong on just one side of the spectrum. We considered adding a pinch of sugar to the sauce to balance things out, then reconsidered and tried orange juice, hoping to boost the acidity along with the sweetness. We simply substituted ¼ cup of orange juice for half of the wine, then reduced them together in the pan. The resulting sauce was flavorful and bright, and a little parsley sprinkled into the sauce before serving sealed the deal on this easy weeknight dinner.

Mediterranean Chicken with Tomatoes, Olives, and Artichokes

SERVES 4

To thaw the frozen artichokes quickly, microwave them on high, covered, for 3 to 5 minutes, then drain them thoroughly in a colander.

- 4 (12-ounce) bone-in, skin-on, split chicken breasts, trimmed
- Salt and pepper
- 1 tablespoon olive oil
- 1 (9-ounce) box frozen artichokes, thawed and drained
- 1 onion, minced (about 1 cup)
- 3 garlic cloves, minced
- 2 teaspoons tomato paste
- 1 teaspoon minced fresh thyme or ¼ teaspoon dried
- ¼ cup dry white wine
- ¼ cup orange juice
- 1 (14.5-ounce) can diced tomatoes, drained
- ½ cup kalamata olives, pitted and chopped coarse
- 1 tablespoon minced fresh parsley

1. Adjust an oven rack to the middle position and heat the oven to 450 degrees.

2. Pat the chicken breasts dry with paper towels and season with ⅛ teaspoon salt and ⅛ teaspoon pepper. Heat 1 teaspoon of the oil in a 12-inch skillet over medium-high heat until just smoking. Carefully lay the chicken, skin side down, in the skillet and cook until well browned on the first side, about 5 minutes. Transfer the chicken to a plate.

3. Heat 1 teaspoon more oil in the skillet over medium heat until shimmering. Add the artichokes and cook until well browned on all sides, 5 to 7 minutes, turning them as needed. Transfer the artichokes to a bowl.

4. Add the remaining 1 teaspoon oil to the skillet and return to medium heat. Add the onion and cook, stirring often, until golden, about 6 minutes. Stir in the garlic, tomato paste, and thyme and cook until fragrant, about 30 seconds. Add the wine and orange juice, scraping up any browned bits. Bring to a simmer and cook until reduced by half, about 2 minutes. Add the tomatoes, bring to a simmer, and cook until the sauce is thickened slightly, about 2 minutes. Stir in the browned artichokes and olives.

5. Nestle the chicken breasts into the sauce, skin side up. Transfer to the oven and bake until the breasts register 160 to 165 degrees on an instant-read thermometer, 15 to 20 minutes.

6. Transfer the chicken to a platter, tent loosely with foil, and let rest for 5 minutes. Remove and discard the skin. Stir the parsley into the sauce and season with salt and pepper to taste. Spoon the artichokes and sauce over the chicken and serve.

PER SERVING: Cal 400; Fat 11g; Sat fat 1.5g; Chol 130mg; Carb 17g; Protein 54g; Fiber 6g; Sodium 680mg

VARIATION

Mediterranean Chicken with Tomatoes, Olives, Artichokes, and Feta

Follow the recipe for Mediterranean Chicken with Tomatoes, Olives, and Artichokes, substituting 1 tablespoon shredded fresh basil for the parsley and sprinkling ½ cup crumbled feta cheese over the chicken before serving.

PER SERVING: Cal 430; Fat 14g; Sat fat 4g; Chol 140mg; Carb 17g; Protein 56g; Fiber 6g; Sodium 830mg

POLLO CANZANESE

BOTH SIMPLE AND SATISFYING, THIS BRAISED CHICKEN dish from the Abruzzo region of Italy consists of chicken slow-cooked in a sauce of white wine, prosciutto, sage, garlic, and cloves until fork-tender. While

TEST KITCHEN
MAKEOVER

we love our original recipe, we quickly realized all that flavor doesn't come for free. Chicken cooked with the skin on in a sauce with fatty prosciutto and finished with butter came with a price tag of almost 800 calories and more than 50 grams of fat. Could we take out the fat but still keep the flavor?

Our original recipe called for bone-in, skin-on chicken thighs. Though they are fattier than chicken breasts, the tenderness and flavor of the thighs were central to our original recipe, so we decided not to stray from the original choice. The bulk of the fat is found in the chicken's skin, so we decided to remove it for our lightened version, which would save us 11 grams of fat per serving. However, it wasn't quite so easy. When we made the dish without the skin, tasters noted that the sauce lacked depth; it was lacking the fond, or bits that had been left behind in the skillet from browning the skin-on meat. When we had added our liquid ingredients, those bits were incorporated into the sauce, adding substantial flavor. To remedy the problem, we seared the thighs with the skin on, then removed the skin. A fair amount of fat had rendered into the pan, so we poured off most of it, leaving a couple of teaspoons for making our sauce.

With the chicken settled, we turned our focus to the sauce. Our original recipe started with 2 cups of white wine and 1 cup of chicken broth and was finished with 1 tablespoon of lemon juice. With the help of the rendered fat (about ⅓ cup) from browning the chicken and a generous helping of butter, all that acidity from the wine and lemon juice was brought into balance, resulting in a bright yet rich sauce. So removing the fatty ingredients left us with, no surprise, a mouth-puckering, acidic sauce. To compound the issue, the prosciutto added a saltiness that only heightened the astringent flavors.

We started by cutting the amount of prosciutto in half, which not only helped cut back the salinity but also eliminated some fat. But tasters still felt the sauce was overwhelming. Testing different ratios of wine to broth, we found that 1½ cups of wine to 1 cup of broth was the ideal balance. Any more wine and the sauce was too acidic; any less and we had generic chicken gravy. Noting that the sauce seemed to have lost a little of its original punch, we decided to bump up the aromatics. Increasing the amounts of garlic and sage helped round out our lightened sauce nicely.

With the sauce completed, we had one final problem to sort out. The original recipe started on the stove and finished in the oven, but our skinless chicken was turning leathery on top because the skin was no longer there to protect the meat during the stint in the oven. The solution was simple: We covered the skillet. We found that with the help of the lid we didn't even need to use the oven; the meat could cook through entirely on the stovetop.

We used to consider Canzanese a once-in-a-while indulgence, but with our new lighter version containing only 370 calories and 12 grams of fat, we were ready to welcome it into our light cooking routine.

MAKEOVER SPOTLIGHT: POLLO CANZANESE

	CALORIES	FAT	SAT FAT	CHOLESTEROL
BEFORE	790	52g	17g	250mg
AFTER	370	12g	2.5g	165mg

Pollo Canzanese

SERVES 4

If thick prosciutto is unavailable, substitute thinly sliced prosciutto (which will be slightly tougher when cooked), thickly sliced pancetta, or bacon. Because the prosciutto adds a fair amount of sodium, be careful when seasoning with salt. Serve with boiled potatoes, noodles, or polenta.

- 1 teaspoon canola oil
- 1 (1-ounce) piece prosciutto, ¼ inch thick, chopped medium
- 6 garlic cloves, sliced thin
- 8 (6-ounce) bone-in, skin-on chicken thighs, trimmed
  Pepper
- 1 tablespoon unbleached all-purpose flour
- 1½ cups dry white wine
- 1 cup low-sodium chicken broth
- 14 whole fresh sage leaves
- 2 bay leaves
- 2 whole cloves
- ½ teaspoon minced fresh rosemary
- ⅛ teaspoon red pepper flakes
- 1 teaspoon fresh lemon juice
- 1 tablespoon minced fresh parsley
  Salt

1. Heat the oil in a 12-inch skillet over medium heat until shimmering. Add the prosciutto and cook, stirring frequently, until just starting to brown, about 3 minutes. Stir in the garlic and cook until golden brown, 1 to 2 minutes. Using a slotted spoon, transfer the prosciutto and garlic to a bowl and set aside.

2. Pat the chicken thighs dry with paper towels and season with ⅛ teaspoon pepper. Heat the fat in the skillet over medium-high heat until just smoking. Carefully lay half of the chicken thighs, skin side down, in the skillet and cook until well browned on both sides, 7 to 10 minutes, flipping them halfway through. Transfer the chicken to a plate and remove and discard the skin. Repeat with the remaining thighs.

3. Pour off all but 2 teaspoons of the fat and return the skillet to medium heat. Stir in the flour and cook for 1 minute. Add the wine, scraping up any browned bits. Bring to a simmer and cook until the liquid is reduced slightly, about 2 minutes. Stir in the reserved prosciutto and garlic, broth, sage leaves, bay leaves, cloves, rosemary, and pepper flakes.

4. Return the chicken, along with any accumulated juice, to the skillet. Cover and cook over low heat until the chicken is very tender and almost falling off the bone, about 1 hour.

5. Transfer the chicken thighs to a platter and tent loosely with foil. Remove and discard the sage leaves, bay leaves, and cloves. Return the skillet to high heat, bring the sauce to a simmer, and cook until reduced to 1¼ cups, 5 to 7 minutes. Off the heat, stir in the lemon juice and parsley and season with salt and pepper to taste. Spoon the sauce over the chicken and serve.

PER SERVING: **Cal** 370; **Fat** 12g; **Sat fat** 2.5g; **Chol** 165mg; **Carb** 6g; **Protein** 41g; **Fiber** 0g; **Sodium** 500mg

SPA CHICKEN

BONELESS, SKINLESS CHICKEN BREASTS HAVE ALL THE qualities needed to make it a healthy diet all-star. They are a great low-fat protein source, quick-cooking, affordable, and adaptable to a variety of flavors and cooking methods. If you make a trip to a spa resort, you'll likely see a lot of boneless, skinless chicken on the café menu for these very reasons. But they aren't trouble-free, as we all know. A healthy recipe (one that minimizes added fat and calories) for boneless, skinless chicken can easily result in nothing more than dry, rubbery, and bland chicken, with a sauce that is one-dimensional. We didn't see why we couldn't develop light recipes for boneless, skinless chicken that would consistently deliver moist, flavorful chicken—without any added fat—as well as some balanced sauces that offered intriguing flavor combinations.

We've often turned to methods like sautéing, baking, broiling, and grilling as a lean way to prepare chicken breasts, but even these require at least some fat to get the ball rolling, and we wanted to see what we could do without any added fat whatsoever. Moist-heat methods—like boiling, steaming, and poaching—cook the meat in some amount of liquid, no added fat necessary. For our version of spa chicken, we knew one of these moist-heat techniques would be the way to go.

We started by testing our way through the moist-heat cooking methods one by one, and we were quickly reminded of an important lesson: It is just as easy to dry out a piece of chicken when cooking in liquid as it is in a dry environment. That's because, like most other meats,

a chicken breast is made up of long muscle fibers that resemble tightly packed straws filled with liquid. As the meat approaches doneness (160 to 165 degrees), these muscle fibers squeeze out their juice, resulting in tough, dry meat no matter how much liquid the meat is cooked in. So while the method certainly could achieve the goal of cooking with no added fat, we would still have to be diligent when it came to timing.

As we worked down the list, we were quick to make our eliminations. To no one's surprise, boiling gave the chicken a tough texture and turned it an unappealing gray color, and microwaving with a little liquid produced inconsistent results. Steaming seemed promising but it wasn't without issues. Even with flavored steaming liquid, we could impart only a negligible amount of flavor to the meat.

We found that we got the best results by poaching the chicken breasts in just enough water to cover the meat. By using a cooking liquid that never reached a boil, we ensured gentle, even heat which was our best bet for moist, evenly cooked chicken. And because the meat was cooking right in the liquid, it could absorb some of the flavors in whatever cooking liquid we used.

But even with poaching we had to be careful. For our first tests we poached by the book: We brought the cooking liquid up to temperature, added the meat, then removed the chicken breasts from the liquid when they landed in the 160- to 165-degree range (which took about 20 minutes). This resulted in rubbery meat. It wasn't that it was overcooked—it was cooked to the right temperature—but the simmering liquid was too aggressive and led to tough meat. For the next test, we didn't preheat the poaching liquid. Instead, we placed the chicken in the pan with the cold water and aromatics, slowly brought the liquid to a low simmer over medium-low heat, and covered the pan until the chicken cooked through. This slow, gentle technique took a few extra minutes, but it was worth it—the chicken was juicy and tender every time.

With our technique settled, we focused our attention on flavoring the liquid. We wanted to get as much flavor into our poaching liquid with as few ingredients and as little prep as possible. For the liquid component, we wanted to use only the minimum quantity of water needed to cook four chicken breasts in order to get the most concentrated flavor, and we settled on 1½ cups. A few cloves of garlic, smashed, and some sprigs of thyme gave us a good start. But still, it seemed to fall flat; the chicken missed a necessary richness or depth. Scouring the pantry, we fell upon soy sauce, which we've often used in the test kitchen in small quantities to add meaty flavor to non-Asian dishes. Just 2 teaspoons was enough to give the chicken a complex, savory flavor that tasters noticed but couldn't identify. Just before serving, we sprinkled the chicken with chives and gave it a spritz of lemon for a fresh finish.

We were pretty happy with our chicken—simple, clean, infused with flavor—so now we needed to develop a few sauces to spruce it up. A traditional pan sauce was out: We had no fond in the pan as you would from sautéing chicken, which serves as the base for a pan sauce, and this type of sauce often calls for the addition of butter toward the end. We wanted fresh, intriguing, easy-to-make sauces with flavorful ingredients that would give our sauces intensity without adding fat. Dried apricots, fresh orange, and smoky chipotle chiles produced a sauce with a bright, sweet-spicy flavor. For a deeper, more savory flavor profile, we created another sauce that paired the earthy sweetness of carrots with the

pungency of fresh ginger and warm spices like coriander and turmeric. This was a healthy chicken dish we'd be happy to eat again and again.

Spa Chicken
SERVES 4

Do not let the poaching liquid boil or the chicken will be tough. You can substitute parsley, cilantro, or tarragon for the chives if desired. Serve with one of our flavorful sauces (recipes follow).

- 4 (6-ounce) boneless, skinless chicken breasts, trimmed
- ⅛ teaspoon salt
- ⅛ teaspoon pepper
- 1½ cups water
- 4 garlic cloves, peeled and smashed
- 4 sprigs fresh thyme
- 2 teaspoons low-sodium soy sauce
- 1 tablespoon minced fresh chives
   Lemon wedges, for serving

1. Pat the chicken breasts dry with paper towels and season with the salt and pepper. Combine the water, garlic, thyme sprigs, and soy sauce in a 12-inch skillet. Add the chicken and bring to a simmer over medium-low heat, 10 to 15 minutes.

2. When the water simmers, flip the chicken, cover, and continue to cook until the chicken registers 160 to 165 degrees on an instant-read thermometer, 10 to 15 minutes longer.

3. Transfer the chicken to a carving board, tent loosely with foil, and let rest for 5 minutes. Cut the chicken breasts on the bias into ½-inch-thick slices. Sprinkle with the chives and serve with lemon wedges (and sauce, if using).

PER SERVING: Cal 190; Fat 2g; Sat Fat 0.5g; Chol 100mg; Carb 0g; Protein 39g; Fiber 0g; Sodium 180mg

NOTES FROM THE TEST KITCHEN

BONELESS CHICKEN BREASTS

Given that they're affordable, easy to prepare, and an excellent low-fat source of protein, it's not surprising that boneless, skinless chicken breasts are standard in many home kitchens. To find out which brand is best, we gathered six popular brands of boneless, skinless chicken breasts, broiled them without seasoning, and had 20 tasters sample them side by side. Among the contenders were one kosher bird, two "natural," and one "free-range." The remaining two were just "chicken."

The koshering process involves coating the chicken with salt to draw out any impurities; this process, similar to brining, results in moist, salty meat. Natural—in the case of chicken—simply means there are no antibiotics or hormones, and the birds are fed a vegetarian diet. "Free-range" means exactly what it says: The birds are not confined to small cages but are allowed to roam freely. The tie for first place went to **Empire Kosher** (left) and the all-natural **Bell & Evans** (right). The kosher bird in our tasting, Empire won points with tasters for its superior flavor.

Apricot-Orange Chipotle Sauce
MAKES ABOUT 1 CUP

- 1 teaspoon olive oil
- 1 small shallot, minced (about 1 tablespoon)
- 2 garlic cloves, minced

½ teaspoon minced canned chipotle chiles in
adobo sauce

1 cup orange juice

⅓ cup dried apricots, chopped fine

1 orange, peeled and cut into ½-inch pieces

1 tablespoon minced fresh cilantro

Salt and pepper

Heat the oil in a small saucepan over medium heat until shimmering. Add the shallot and cook until softened, about 2 minutes. Stir in the garlic and chipotles and cook until fragrant, about 30 seconds. Stir in the orange juice and apricots, bring to a simmer, and cook until the apricots are plump and the sauce measures ¾ cup, 3 to 5 minutes. Off the heat, stir in the orange pieces and cilantro, and season with salt and pepper to taste.

PER ¼-CUP SERVING: Cal 90; Fat 1.5g; Sat Fat 0g; Chol 0mg; Carb 20g; Protein 1g; Fiber 2g; Sodium 0mg

Carrot-Ginger Sauce
MAKES ABOUT 1 CUP

1 teaspoon olive oil

2 shallots, minced (about 6 tablespoons)

¼ teaspoon ground coriander

¼ teaspoon ground turmeric

2 carrots, peeled and sliced thin

1 cup low-sodium chicken broth

¾ cup hot water

1 teaspoon grated fresh ginger

Salt and pepper

Heat the oil in a small saucepan over medium heat until shimmering. Add the shallots and cook until softened, 2 to 3 minutes. Stir in the coriander and turmeric and cook until fragrant, about 30 seconds. Stir in the carrots and cook until softened, 6 to 8 minutes. Add the broth, cover, and cook until the carrots mash easily, 25 to 30 minutes. Uncover and continue to cook until any remaining liquid has evaporated. Process the sauce in a blender with the water and ginger until completely smooth, about 30 seconds. Season with salt and pepper to taste.

PER ¼-CUP SERVING: Cal 40; Fat 1.5g; Sat Fat 0g; Chol 0mg; Carb 6g; Protein 1g; Fiber 1g; Sodium 170mg

SKILLET CHICKEN VESUVIO

THOSE WHO HAVE TRIED THE CHICAGO CLASSIC known as chicken vesuvio—browned chicken and potatoes with a garlicky wine sauce finished with a healthy garnish of peas—will agree it's at once comforting and elegant. But the old-fashioned cooking method, which goes back to the recipe's 1930s origin, calls for several pots and pans and multiple trips to the oven. To bring chicken vesuvio into the 21st century, the test kitchen had recently streamlined the process by limiting cookware to a skillet and keeping it on the stovetop. This was a great start, but now we needed to take it one step further; it was too high in fat for our lighter standards. We headed into the kitchen to see what we could do.

Classic chicken vesuvio starts with browning chicken parts in a skillet; then the browned parts are set aside and potato wedges are browned in the rendered fat. Then the potatoes come out of the pan so the sauce can be built, then it's all transferred to a roasting pan and moved to the oven. Finally, the sauce goes back on the stovetop to reduce. The test kitchen had already taken care of some of the lightening work when we streamlined the recipe for the stovetop. We had found that boneless, skinless chicken breasts were the easiest to cook evenly given our revised method, not to mention quicker-cooking and lower in fat. We started by browning the breasts on both sides to develop their flavor and give them appealing color, then set them aside while we tackled the potatoes.

Testing various amounts of oil for the potatoes, we were able to cut back to a modest 2 teaspoons. Any less and they didn't brown properly. Choosing the right potato variety was key. Fluffy russets broke apart; Yukon Golds were better, but in the end waxy baby red potatoes were our best choice since they held their shape and texture throughout cooking. Traditionally the potatoes in chicken vesuvio are wedges, but we had better success with halved baby red potatoes. They cooked more evenly and achieved better browning with just one cut side.

The procedure for the rest of our skillet version was simple. To finish cooking the chicken and potatoes through, we would add the sauce components to the skillet (with the potatoes), return the chicken to the pan, cover, and simmer until done. So now we needed to tackle what would go into our sauce. Wine was a given, and chicken broth provided the right complementary

SKILLET CHICKEN VESUVIO

liquid component. We found that ½ cup of white wine combined with 1½ cups of chicken broth cooked the potatoes through properly and gave us the right amount of sauce by the end of cooking. To stay true to the recipe's Italian-American roots, we added garlic, oregano, and rosemary to the mix. The sauce is traditionally finished with a big hunk of butter, but in the interest of keeping the fat to a minimum, we left it out. We added the sauce ingredients to the pan, nestled the chicken on top of the potatoes, covered the skillet, and about 12 minutes later we had perfectly cooked chicken and potatoes. The sauce, however, needed some help.

Since we had left out the butter, we weren't surprised the sauce was lacking the silky, rich texture integral to chicken vesuvio, and tasters weren't going to overlook this. In the hope of achieving a similar texture, we added a tablespoon of flour to the pan after we browned the potatoes. The flour helped by thickening the sauce slightly, but tasters still felt that something was missing. Everyone agreed that adding back some of the butter was a must, but we found that with the help of the flour we could keep it down to half of the original amount.

Stirring in green peas and lemon juice at the end with the butter lent the right fresh finish. Now this Chicago favorite was not only easy, but it was also healthy.

Skillet Chicken Vesuvio
SERVES 4

Be sure to use potatoes about 1 inch in diameter. If your potatoes are larger, cut them into 1-inch pieces before cooking.

- 4 **(6-ounce) boneless, skinless chicken breasts, trimmed**
  Salt and pepper
- 4 **teaspoons canola oil**
- 10 **small red potatoes (about 1¼ pounds), halved (see note)**
- 2 **garlic cloves, minced**
- 1 **teaspoon minced fresh rosemary**
- ½ **teaspoon dried oregano**
- 1 **tablespoon unbleached all-purpose flour**
- 1½ **cups low-sodium chicken broth**
- ½ **cup dry white wine**
- 1 **cup frozen peas (4 ounces), thawed**
- 1 **tablespoon unsalted butter**
- 2 **teaspoons fresh lemon juice**

1. Pat the chicken breasts dry with paper towels and season with ⅛ teaspoon salt and ⅛ teaspoon pepper. Heat 2 teaspoons of the oil in a 12-inch nonstick skillet over medium-high heat until shimmering. Carefully lay the chicken breasts in the skillet and cook until golden brown on the first side, about 5 minutes. Flip the breasts and continue to cook until lightly browned on the second side, about 3 minutes longer. Transfer the chicken to a plate.

2. Heat the remaining 2 teaspoons oil in the pan over medium heat until shimmering. Arrange the potatoes in the pan, cut side down, and cook until golden brown, about 7 minutes. Stir in the garlic, rosemary, oregano, and ¼ teaspoon salt and cook until fragrant, about 30 seconds. Stir in the flour and cook for 1 minute. Add the broth and wine, scraping up any browned bits, and bring to a simmer.

3. Nestle the chicken breasts into the potatoes. Cover and cook over medium-low heat until the chicken registers 160 to 165 degrees on an instant-read thermometer and the potatoes are tender, about 12 minutes. Transfer the chicken and potatoes to a platter and tent loosely with foil.

4. Increase the heat to medium-high and cook until the sauce is reduced to 1 cup, about 5 minutes. Stir in the peas and cook until heated through, about 1 minute. Off the heat, whisk in the butter and lemon juice and season with salt and pepper to taste. Spoon the sauce over the chicken and potatoes and serve.

PER SERVING: Cal 420; Fat 10g; Sat fat 3g; Chol 105mg; Carb 30g; Protein 45g; Fiber 4g; Sodium 410mg

---

NOTES FROM THE TEST KITCHEN

GIVE (FROZEN) PEAS A CHANCE
In the test kitchen, we've come to depend on frozen peas. Not only are they more convenient than their fresh comrades in the pod, but they also taste better. In test after test, we've found that frozen peas are tender and sweet, whereas fresh peas are starchy and bland. Finding good frozen peas is not hard. After tasting peas from the major national brands, including Birds Eye and Green Giant, along with organically grown peas from Cascadian Farm, our panel found little difference in flavor or texture. All of the peas were sweet and fresh, with a bright green color.

CHICKEN CORDON BLEU

TEST KITCHEN
MAKEOVER

AT THE HEIGHT OF ITS POPULARITY IN THE 1960S, chicken cordon bleu was considered an elegant dish. Its combination of breaded and fried chicken breast stuffed with ham and Swiss cheese was an adaptation of centuries-old dishes (including Austria's schnitzel cordon bleu and Switzerland's veal cordon bleu) variously made with veal, prosciutto, and seasoned butter. But today you're more likely to encounter it as a tired selection at wedding halls. Nearly as fussy as it is fatty (chicken breasts have to be pounded thin, painstakingly rolled with ham and cheese, and then breaded and fried in butter), we wondered if it wasn't time to give chicken cordon bleu the overdue lift it deserved.

Boneless, skinless chicken breasts are the traditional choice for chicken cordon bleu, and since they are a naturally healthy option we saw no need to deviate. The ham-and-cheese filling, however, needed some refiguring. The recipes we collected contained varying amounts of ham and Swiss cheese, most calling for a quarter-pound of ham and ½ cup of cheese per breast. After testing different levels of ham and cheese, we found that tasters were perfectly happy when we halved those amounts, resulting in substantial calorie savings. We tried using low-fat Swiss cheese instead of the full-fat, but tasters were lukewarm about the results and the low-fat variety was tough to find anyway.

When it came to the assembly process, our patience quickly ran out. We pounded, stuffed, and rolled countless breasts to test our filling amounts, only to be constantly disappointed by breasts that unrolled and cheese that oozed out the sides, wrecking our crispy coating (we were using a traditional full-fat breading at this point). We knew we would have to address this before moving forward. In the past, we have cut a pocket in chicken breasts and pork chops to make stuffing easier, so we decided it was worth a shot here. Indeed, this method proved far easier, but the amount of cheese in our cordon bleu was greater than in our similar recipes, and once melted, it still wouldn't stay put. Next we tried blocking the opening of the pocket with a slice of ham, but this failed to make a tight seal, plus the elegant cordon bleu turned homely—there was no pretty ham-and-cheese swirl when we cut into it. After a little tinkering with the method, we found our answer in simply rolling a ham slice into a cylinder around some shredded cheese and tucking a cylinder into each chicken breast.

With our filling now securely inside the chicken, we could return our focus to eliminating calories. Our next hurdle was replacing the traditional fried coating. Rather than deal with the calories and the mess of frying, we decided to move our recipe to the oven. We hoped to save ourselves work by using store-bought bread crumbs, but tasters wanted a fresher take for our revitalized cordon bleu. Homemade bread crumbs, tossed with a modest amount of melted butter and toasted, fared better, adding color and some crispness to the chicken, but tasters complained that they missed the richness that came with the deep-fried coating. Could something other than buttery bread crumbs fill the need? We tested low-fat corn chips, low-fat potato chips, and preshredded cheese mixed with the bread, but in each instance tasters' reactions were lukewarm. Finally, we hit the jackpot by combining our bread crumbs with low-fat Ritz crackers. This coating was savory, buttery, and a tad sweet.

The flavor of the coating was finally right on, but it was coming out of the oven somewhat soggy. We'd been baking the cordon bleus on a rimmed baking sheet, but the crumbs on the bottom were sodden. We tried an old test kitchen trick and elevated the chicken on a wire rack set inside a baking sheet to let any juice drip away—a moderate improvement. Next, we fiddled with oven temperatures and rack positioning as we tried to achieve the trinity of moist chicken, melted cheese, and crispy golden crumbs simultaneously. Eventually we discovered that starting the chicken on the lowest rack of a 450-degree oven (this made escaping moisture evaporate quickly) and finishing it on the middle rack at a lower heat (400 degrees) yielded the best results.

Having cut the fat more than in half (from 33 grams down to 16 grams) and streamlined the preparation method, we were happy to welcome chicken cordon bleu back to the dinner table.

MAKEOVER SPOTLIGHT: CHICKEN CORDON BLEU

	CALORIES	FAT	SAT FAT	CHOLESTEROL
BEFORE	780	33g	19g	195mg
AFTER	590	16g	7g	150mg

Easy Chicken Cordon Bleu

SERVES 4

Chilling the stuffed chicken breasts helps them stay closed during breading. After resting, the cooked chicken may be cut on the bias into ½-inch-thick slices for an attractive presentation.

- 4 (6-ounce) boneless, skinless chicken breasts, trimmed
- 2 ounces Swiss cheese, shredded (about ½ cup)
- 8 ounces Black Forest ham (about 8 slices)
- 3 slices high-quality white sandwich bread, torn into pieces
- 20 reduced-fat Ritz crackers
- 2 tablespoons unsalted butter, melted
- 1 cup unbleached all-purpose flour
- 3 large egg whites
- 2 tablespoons Dijon mustard
- ⅛ teaspoon salt
- ⅛ teaspoon pepper
-    Vegetable oil spray

1. Following the photos, cut a pocket in the thickest part of each chicken breast. Tightly roll 2 tablespoons of the cheese in 2 pieces of the ham. Repeat with the remaining cheese and ham. Stuff each chicken breast with 1 roll. Transfer the chicken to a plate, cover with plastic wrap, and refrigerate until firm, at least 20 minutes or up to 3 hours.

2. Meanwhile, adjust the oven racks to the lowest and middle positions and heat the oven to 400 degrees. Pulse the bread and crackers together in a food processor to coarse crumbs, about 10 pulses. Transfer the crumbs to a bowl and toss with the melted butter. Spread the crumbs on a rimmed baking sheet and bake, stirring occasionally, until golden brown and dry, 7 to 9 minutes. Let the crumbs cool to room temperature.

3. Turn the oven to 450 degrees and set a wire rack inside a second rimmed baking sheet. Place the flour in a shallow dish. In a second shallow dish, whisk the egg whites and mustard together until combined. Spread the cooled crumb mixture in a third shallow dish.

4. Pat the chicken breasts dry with paper towels and season with the salt and pepper. Dredge the chicken in the flour and shake off the excess. Coat the chicken with the egg mixture, allowing the excess to drip off. Coat all sides of the chicken with the crumb mixture, pressing

STUFFING CHICKEN FOR CORDON BLEU

After weeks of trying to make it work, we decided pounding and butterflying chicken breasts was for the birds. Our method is easier and makes a neater cordon bleu.

1. Using a paring knife, make a small opening in the thickest part of the chicken breast and work the knife back and forth until the pocket extends deep into the breast.

2. Place two slices of ham on top of each other, sprinkle with 2 table-spoons of cheese, and with the short side facing you, roll tightly into a cylinder.

3. Stuff each pocket with a ham-and-cheese roll and refrigerate at least 20 minutes before breading.

RATING BLACK FOREST DELI HAM

In Germany, this boneless ham is a traditional regional specialty produced according to strict "Protected Geographic Indication" regulations. The dark exterior comes from smoke and a mixture of salt and spices, including garlic, sugar, and juniper berries. The curing and smoking can take up to three months. In North America, the hams are usually cured quickly by brining, the smoke flavor is often artificial, and the exterior is painted with caramel coloring. We compared a German-produced Black Forest ham with four domestic brands. When tasted raw, the German-made Black Forest ham was outstanding, whereas some domestic imitators tasted like "processed," "rubbery" canned ham. But when we used the hams to make our Easy Chicken Cordon Bleu, the smoked, paper-thin slices of the import became "dry" and "leathery," and the rich flavor was "overpowering." Our top-rated domestic brand, **Dietz & Watson Black Forest Smoked Ham with Natural Juices**, provides "good ham flavor" and "balance." Save the imported ham to savor on its own.

to help the crumbs adhere. Lay the breaded chicken on the prepared wire rack. Lightly coat each breast with vegetable oil spray.

5. Bake the chicken on the lowest rack for 10 minutes. Lower the oven temperature to 400 degrees and transfer the baking sheet to the middle rack. Continue to bake until the chicken breasts register 160 to 165 degrees on an instant-read thermometer, about 20 minutes longer. Let the chicken rest for 5 minutes before serving.

PER SERVING: **Cal** 590; **Fat** 16g; **Sat fat** 7g; **Chol** 150mg; **Carb** 44g; **Protein** 62g; **Fiber** 1g; **Sodium** 1480mg

DEVILED CHICKEN

WE'RE ALWAYS ON THE LOOKOUT FOR FAST AND healthy meals, so when we came across deviled chicken—marinated chicken breasts touting big, fiery heat and a crunchy coating, all accomplished with a minimum of added fat—we were all ears. But we tried a few recipes and found them meek; the hallmark ("deviled") flavors of mustard, black pepper, and chili spice barely registered. The bread-crumb toppings didn't impress us, either. They were variously soggy, sandy, or prone to sloughing off. We headed to the kitchen to return the spark to deviled chicken.

We began by focusing on flavoring the chicken. For speedy marinating and cooking—and a neutral backdrop for a spicy marinade—we used boneless, skinless breasts. Sorting through the marinades used in existing recipes we found, we noticed that a wide variety of ingredients were used. We tested dried mustard, prepared mustard, black pepper, fresh chiles, hot sauce, cayenne pepper, and red pepper flakes, combined with ingredients ranging from vinegar, lemon juice, Worcestershire sauce, and soy sauce to ketchup, sour cream, butter, garlic, horseradish, and fresh and dried herbs.

After seemingly endless rounds of tests, tasters finally settled on an assembly of winners. They liked straight yellow mustard for its bright flavor (when we tried adding dry mustard powder as well, they pronounced it "overkill"). A full tablespoon of freshly ground black pepper was deemed essential, and tangy hot sauce (Frank's RedHot or another mild brand) got the nod

over cayenne, crushed chili flakes, and minced chiles. Lemon juice, garlic, and a little fresh thyme provided ample background flavor. Just 30 minutes in this potent marinade was enough to thoroughly season the chicken.

With the marinade settled, we moved on to the crunchy crumb coating. Over the years we've tested numerous crumb coatings for a variety of recipes. Store-bought bread crumbs, fresh bread crumbs, panko, saltines, Ritz—we've tried them all and found there is no one choice that can do every job. In this instance, we found our winner in the fresh bread crumbs; their slightly sweet flavor was a perfect match to the spicy marinated meat, and tasters liked the fact that they were crunchy without being overly so (like crackers or panko).

However, tasters felt that for this particular dish, a coating all the way around the chicken wasn't necessary. While the crunch from a surrounding coating adds an essential textural contrast to the gooey, cheesy filling in our Easy Chicken Cordon Bleu (page 71), here it wasn't a must. In fact, tasters actually preferred less of a coating on the deviled chicken to allow the spicy flavors to come to the forefront, leaving the crunchy crumbs to play a supporting role. We would simply sprinkle the crumbs over the top of the chicken breasts.

We seasoned the crumbs with salt and pepper, then added a modest amount of melted butter for richness, adhesion, and browning. When we tried making them without the butter, we got a firm thumbs down; 1 tablespoon was as low as we could go. Tasters liked the flavor of the crumbs, but they didn't stick to the chicken as well as we wanted. To help them stick, one test cook suggested adding a little light mayonnaise to the marinade to act like glue between the bread crumbs and the chicken. That did the trick, but we still had a few coating problems to tackle before we were finished. The bread crumbs came out of the oven unevenly browned and slightly dusty and dry. For the next test we toasted the crumbs in a skillet until golden and sprayed the chicken breasts with vegetable oil spray to help keep the crumbs moist throughout cooking. This ensured that every bite had browned (not dusty) crumbs when the chicken emerged from the oven. And they all stayed put on top of our spicy chicken breasts.

With that, we had finally put the firepower back into deviled chicken.

Deviled Chicken

SERVES 4

Be sure to use a mild hot sauce in this recipe, such as Frank's RedHot. Spicier brands like Tabasco will make the dish too hot.

- 3 tablespoons yellow mustard
- 2 tablespoons light mayonnaise
- 1½ tablespoons hot sauce (see note)
- 1 tablespoon fresh lemon juice
- 3 garlic cloves, minced
- ½ teaspoon minced fresh thyme
- 1 teaspoon salt
- 3¼ teaspoons pepper
- 4 (6-ounce) boneless, skinless chicken breasts, trimmed
- 2 slices high-quality white sandwich bread, torn into pieces
- 1 tablespoon unsalted butter
  Vegetable oil spray

1. Adjust an oven rack to the upper-middle position and heat the oven to 450 degrees. Line a rimmed baking sheet with aluminum foil and set a wire rack inside the baking sheet.

2. Combine the mustard, mayonnaise, hot sauce, lemon juice, garlic, thyme, ¾ teaspoon of the salt, and 1 tablespoon of the pepper in a large bowl. Add the chicken breasts and toss until coated. Cover with plastic wrap and refrigerate for at least 30 minutes or up to 3 hours.

3. Meanwhile, pulse the bread, the remaining ¼ teaspoon salt, and remaining ¼ teaspoon pepper together in a food processor to coarse crumbs, about 10 pulses. Melt the butter in a 12-inch nonstick skillet over medium heat. Add the bread crumbs and cook, stirring frequently, until golden, 5 to 7 minutes.

4. Remove the chicken from the bowl and transfer to the prepared wire rack. Sprinkle the toasted bread crumbs evenly over the chicken, pressing gently to adhere. Lightly coat the tops of the chicken with vegetable oil spray.

5. Bake until the crumbs are deep golden brown and the chicken registers 160 to 165 degrees on an instant-read thermometer, 20 to 25 minutes, rotating the pan halfway through. Let the chicken rest for 5 minutes before serving.

PER SERVING: Cal 290; Fat 8g; Sat fat 3g; Chol 105mg; Carb 11g; Protein 41g; Fiber 2g; Sodium 1040mg

CHICKEN CHILAQUILES

THE MEXICAN DISH KNOWN AS *CHILAQUILES* WAS originally created to use up leftovers, hence its alias, "poor man's dish." Traditionally, chicken (or chorizo or shredded beef) and fried corn tortillas are simmered in a thin, silky red or green chile sauce until the tortillas start to soften, then the casserole is topped with cheese and whatever else might be handy, perhaps avocado or sour cream, before serving. Sometimes chilaquiles is layered in a casserole dish like lasagna, giving it even more comfort-food appeal. We loved the sound of a layered chilaquiles, but between the fried tortillas, a copious amount of oil in the sauce, and the toppings of cheese, sour cream, and avocado, it packed too many calories and too much fat for our light and healthy lifestyle. And even though these days people make chilaquiles from scratch, the results often get no more attention than what you'd give to a dish made from leftovers. We thought chilaquiles deserved more than its just-for-leftovers stigma. We wanted a recipe for freshly made chilaquiles with tender chicken, a flavorful sauce, and tortillas that added texture and didn't bog down our casserole, all topped off with judiciously chosen toppings that lent the right finishing touches. And we wanted to get there without all the fat.

We started by gathering a number of traditional recipes, then focused on the chicken. The recipes we'd turned up were a mixed bag: Some used breasts, some used thighs, others used a combination of the two. We baked up test batches of each and compared them side by side. Tasters felt they were all comparable, but we decided to go with the leaner, milder breast meat since it allowed the flavor of the sauce to shine through.

Next we tackled the tortillas. Traditionally, stale tortillas are fried in oil until crisp and then layered into a casserole with the other ingredients. To eliminate the added fat, we followed the method we'd developed for our Homemade Baked Corn Tortilla Chips (page 9). We cut the tortillas into wedges, spread them out in an even layer on two baking sheets, sprayed them with vegetable oil, and baked them in a moderate 350-degree oven.

The next obstacle was the sauce. Whether red or green, this sauce is a simple combination of onions, chiles, aromatics, and either tomatoes or tomatillos. Testing basic recipes for both a red and a green sauce, tasters overwhelmingly preferred the red for its deep, peppery flavor. Unfortunately, the richness and velvety body of

CHICKEN CHILAQUILES CASSEROLE

the best sauces we came across were a result of copious amounts of oil used to sauté the onions, peppers, and aromatics. To achieve a similar savory flavor and silky texture, we started by sautéing poblano chiles and onions in 2 teaspoons of oil using our lighter sweating technique of low heat and a lid to trap moisture, then cooking off the liquid so the flavors would concentrate. Next we stirred in chipotle chiles for smoky depth, a little cilantro, and six garlic cloves. The smell of our sautéing aromatics told us we were on the right track, and a can of whole peeled tomatoes (canned offered a better guarantee of year-round quality) sealed the deal. Then all we had to do was puree the mixture until smooth and velvety.

Our sauce flavor was as good as we could have hoped, but we wondered if we could use it to pull double duty. Up to this point we had been poaching our chicken separately in water, then shredding it and layering it with the tortillas and sauce in our casserole dish. What if we poached the chicken in the sauce? This would infuse our chicken with even more flavor, we thought, and one test proved we were right.

Our process was streamlined and simple: Toast the tortilla chips while making the sauce and poaching the chicken. Then puree the sauce, return it to the skillet, and add the chips, cooking until they just soften. Then we transferred it all to a baking dish and it was ready for the oven. We opted for a piping-hot 500-degree oven; we found that at lower temperatures the casserole needed more time to heat through, and those extra minutes led to soggy, unappealing tortilla wedges. At high heat the tortillas kept some crunch, and those that were exposed at the top of the casserole became extra-crunchy. Tasters gave our casserole two thumbs up.

All we needed before we were finished was the toppings. Traditional toppings like sour cream, cheese, and avocado threatened to derail all of our calorie-cutting efforts. We enlisted low-fat sour cream as a substitute for its full-fat counterpart and added a little lime juice to create a zesty *crema* to drizzle over our chilaquiles. The cheese was slightly harder to settle. Tasters were not wild about the taste of low-fat cheese in this recipe. Instead they preferred a restrained amount of full-fat *queso fresco* (which is also lower in fat than many other cheeses), which punctuated our chilaquiles with just the right tangy, salty bite. (We found that feta cheese could be substituted in a pinch.) A diced fresh tomato, onion, and cilantro sprinkled on top added the final touch of freshness our revamped chilaquiles needed.

Chicken Chilaquiles Casserole

SERVES 4

If you cannot find poblano chiles, substitute 2 green bell peppers. To make this dish spicier, add the chile seeds.

10	(6-inch) corn tortillas, each cut into 8 wedges
	Vegetable oil spray
2	poblano chiles, stemmed, seeded, and chopped coarse
2	onions, minced (about 2 cups)
2	teaspoons canola oil
	Salt
¼	cup minced fresh cilantro
6	garlic cloves, minced
2	teaspoons minced canned chipotle chiles in adobo sauce
1	(14.5-ounce) can whole peeled tomatoes
¾	cup low-sodium chicken broth
1½	pounds boneless, skinless chicken breasts, trimmed
	Pepper
3	ounces crumbled queso fresco or feta cheese (about ¾ cup)
¼	cup low-fat sour cream
1	tablespoon fresh lime juice
1	tomato, cored, seeded, and chopped medium

1. Adjust the oven racks to the upper-middle and lower-middle positions and heat the oven to 350 degrees. Spread the tortilla wedges on 2 rimmed baking sheets. Lightly coat both sides of the tortilla wedges with vegetable oil spray.

2. Bake the tortilla wedges until they are lightly browned and begin to crisp, 8 to 12 minutes. Flip the tortilla wedges and continue to bake until the chips are fully toasted, 8 to 12 minutes longer. Set the tortilla wedges aside and turn the oven to 500 degrees.

3. Combine the poblano chiles, 1 cup of the onions, oil, and ⅛ teaspoon salt in a 12-inch skillet. Cover and cook over medium-low heat until the vegetables are softened, 8 to 10 minutes. Uncover, increase the heat to medium-high, and continue to cook, stirring occasionally, until the vegetables are lightly browned, 4 to 6 minutes longer.

4. Stir in 2 tablespoons of the cilantro, garlic, and chipotles and cook until fragrant, about 30 seconds. Stir in the tomatoes with their juice and the broth. Pat the chicken breasts dry with paper towels and season with ⅛ teaspoon salt and ⅛ teaspoon pepper. Nestle the chicken breasts into the sauce and bring to a simmer over medium-low heat, about 5 minutes. When the sauce simmers, flip the chicken, cover, and continue to cook until the chicken registers 160 to 165 degrees on an instant-read thermometer, 10 to 12 minutes longer.

5. Transfer the chicken to a plate. When cool enough to handle, shred the meat into bite-size pieces. Process the sauce in a blender until completely smooth, about 1 minute. Return the sauce to the skillet, season with salt and pepper to taste, and bring to a simmer over medium heat.

6. Stir in the tortillas and cook until they begin to soften, about 2 minutes. Stir in the shredded chicken, then transfer the mixture to an 8-inch square baking dish. Sprinkle with the cheese and bake on the lower-middle rack until hot throughout, 5 to 10 minutes.

NOTES FROM THE TEST KITCHEN

QUESO FRESCO

We love the tangy, creamy counterpoint that queso fresco provided to our chilaquiles. Popular in Mexico, queso fresco (also called *queso blanco*) is a fresh, mild cheese made from either cow's or goat's milk. Although it's not a great melting cheese, its crumbly-soft texture makes it an excellent option for topping enchiladas or tacos, sprinkling over bean soups, or tossing into a salad. If you can't find queso fresco, a mild feta is a suitable substitute.

THE BEST CANNED WHOLE TOMATOES

A ripe, fresh tomato should balance elements of sweetness and tangy acidity; ideally, canned tomatoes, which are a better option than fresh for much of the year because they are packed at the height of ripeness, should reflect the same combination of characteristics. Whole tomatoes are steamed to remove their skins and then packed in tomato juice or puree. We prefer tomatoes packed in juice; they generally have a fresher, livelier flavor than tomatoes packed in puree, which has a cooked-tomato flavor that imparts a slightly stale, tired taste to the whole can. We tasted whole tomatoes both straight from the can and in a simple tomato sauce. **Progresso Whole Peeled Tomatoes with Basil** finished at the head of the pack, with a bright flavor and firm texture. Be sure to buy the tomatoes packed in juice; Progresso has another, similar-looking can of whole peeled tomatoes packed in puree.

7. Stir the sour cream and lime juice together in a bowl and drizzle over the casserole. Sprinkle with the remaining 1 cup onion, remaining 2 tablespoons cilantro, and tomato and serve.

PER SERVING: **Cal** 510; **Fat** 10g; **Sat fat** 2g; **Chol** 110mg; **Carb** 51g; **Protein** 47g; **Fiber** 6g; **Sodium** 700mg

CHICKEN AND BROWN RICE

CHICKEN AND RICE MIGHT BE A CLASSIC CHOICE FOR an easy one-dish dinner, but the typical outcome— bland, overcooked chicken, mushy white rice, a smattering of peas and carrots, and a sauce made from a can—leaves a lot to be desired. We wanted to bring new life to chicken and rice while at the same time maintaining its simple cooking method. We wanted a flavorful, healthy, one-pot dish with both the chicken and the rice cooked perfectly.

Because we wanted to boost the nutritional worth of the typical chicken and rice, we decided off the bat we'd lose the white rice in favor of brown rice. However, we knew this was no insignificant swap. One of the best things about traditional chicken and rice is that when done right, the chicken (usually boneless, skinless chicken breasts) and the white rice go into the skillet together and emerge perfectly cooked at once because they have comparable cooking times. Brown rice upsets this harmony because it requires more than twice the cooking time of white rice. Boneless, skinless chicken breasts would be woefully overdone if cooked for the 50 minutes needed to get brown rice tender.

For our first test, we started by adding brown rice and some cooking liquid (we began with the usual 3-to-1 ratio of liquid to brown rice) to the skillet, got it simmering, and simply added the chicken when 20 minutes of cooking time remained for the rice. We put the lid on and waited. What we saw when we lifted the lid after 20 minutes was not at all what we had hoped for. The chicken looked OK, but there was liquid in the bottom of the pan and the rice was mushy. We tried cutting back on the added liquid, but that got us only so far. We realized the chicken was causing issues we hadn't been accounting for. Added midway through the cooking time, it was contributing moisture that the brown rice couldn't absorb in those last 20 minutes. Next we tried using bone-in chicken breasts (and a roughly 2-to-1 ratio

LATIN-STYLE CHICKEN AND BROWN RICE

of liquid to rice); since they cook more slowly, we could add them earlier in the cooking process, which we hoped would give the rice more time to absorb the released liquid. But the results were more of the same. The chicken was well cooked; the rice was not.

It was pretty clear at this point that chicken breasts and brown rice weren't meant to be cooked together. Obviously the brown rice was not coming out of our recipe; the chicken breasts had to go. While we always try to use the leanest choice, all-white-meat chicken breasts, sometimes (including here) it just isn't a workable option. A colleague's suggestion to use boneless, skinless chicken thighs, which would take about as long to cook as brown rice, seemed like our best bet. So for our next test, we added the rice, some chicken broth (a better choice than water for a boost in flavor), and chicken thighs all at once to our skillet. While in the past we've cooked chicken and rice on the stovetop, the extended cooking time required for brown rice and chicken thighs inspired us to move our skillet to the oven, where our dish could cook in the even heat without worry of scorching. After about an hour in the oven, we pulled out our skillet and happily found we were definitely on the right track. The rice was cooked somewhat unevenly, but we weren't too surprised. The oven provided gentler heat than the stovetop, and together with the liquid leached from both the meat and the vegetables, we were sure that tweaking the amount of chicken broth would set things straight. After a few more tests, we found that a ratio of 1 cup of rice to 1¼ cups of liquid produced perfect rice every time.

With the chicken and rice cooked to our liking, we turned our attention to the flavoring. Looking for a big hit of flavor, we took a cue from the traditional Mexican preparation of *arroz con pollo* and created a blend of vegetables and aromatics (red bell pepper, corn, onion, jalapeños, and garlic) that added appealing color and flavor. We simply sautéed them in the skillet before stirring in the rice. We also tested a range of spices: Cumin and coriander were out (they lent flavors more suited to tacos), while chili powder and ½ teaspoon of hot sauce added just the right kick, bringing new life to simple rice. We were so close, but tasters felt the chicken itself could be more flavorful. A quick wet rub for the chicken with some of our key seasonings—chili powder, hot sauce, and garlic—did the trick, and the meat absorbed these flavors in the brief time needed to cook the aromatics and vegetables.

Tasters loved our Tex-Mex recipe, so we developed a few more flavor combinations. Thai-Style Chicken and Brown Rice with lemon grass, carrots, and snow peas and Latin-Style Chicken and Brown Rice with pimientos, green olives, and capers made everyone happy.

Tex-Mex Chicken and Brown Rice
SERVES 4

Fresh corn really makes this dish, but when it's not available, you can substitute 1½ cups thawed frozen corn. White rice cannot be substituted for the brown rice in this recipe. To make this dish spicier, add the chile seeds. Serve with sliced avocado if desired.

- 8 garlic cloves, minced
- 2 teaspoons chili powder
- ½ teaspoon hot sauce
  Salt and pepper
- 1 pound boneless, skinless chicken thighs, trimmed
- 1 onion, minced (about 1 cup)
- 1 red bell pepper, stemmed, seeded, and chopped medium
- 2 ears corn, kernels removed from cobs (see page 79)
- 2 jalapeño chiles, stemmed, seeded, and minced
- 1 teaspoon canola oil
- 1 cup long-grain brown rice, rinsed (see page 79)
- 1¼ cups low-sodium chicken broth
- 4 scallions, sliced thin
- 1 tablespoon fresh lime juice

1. Adjust an oven rack to the lower-middle position and heat the oven to 300 degrees. Combine half of the garlic, 1 teaspoon of the chili powder, hot sauce, ⅛ teaspoon salt, and ¼ teaspoon pepper in a large bowl. Stir in the chicken thighs to coat and set aside.

2. Combine the onion, bell pepper, corn, jalapeños, oil, and ⅛ teaspoon salt in a large Dutch oven. Cover and cook over medium-low heat, stirring occasionally, until the vegetables are softened, 8 to 10 minutes. Stir in the remaining garlic, remaining 1 teaspoon chili powder, and rice and cook until fragrant, about 30 seconds. Stir in the broth, scraping up any browned bits.

3. Lay the chicken on top of the rice. Bring to a simmer, cover, and transfer to the oven. Cook until the rice is tender and the liquid is almost fully absorbed, 50 to 65 minutes.

4. Transfer the chicken to a plate. Cover the pot and let the rice steam for 10 minutes. Meanwhile, when cool enough to handle, shred the meat into bite-size pieces.

5. Stir the shredded chicken, scallions, and lime juice into the rice. Season with salt and pepper to taste and serve.

PER 1½-CUP SERVING: **Cal** 410; **Fat** 9g; **Sat fat** 1.5g; **Chol** 95mg; **Carb** 54g; **Protein** 30g; **Fiber** 5g; **Sodium** 460mg

VARIATIONS

Thai-Style Chicken and Brown Rice

SERVES 4

White rice cannot be substituted for the brown rice in this recipe.

8	garlic cloves, minced
2	tablespoons grated or minced fresh ginger
4	teaspoons fish sauce
1	pound boneless, skinless chicken thighs, trimmed
1	onion, minced (about 1 cup)
2	teaspoons canola oil
	Salt
1	cup long-grain brown rice, rinsed (see photo)
1	stalk lemongrass, trimmed and smashed (see photo)
1¼	cups low-sodium chicken broth
3	carrots, peeled and sliced thin on the bias
4	ounces snow peas (about 2 cups), trimmed and halved
¼	cup minced fresh cilantro
2	teaspoons fresh lime juice
	Pepper

1. Adjust an oven rack to the lower-middle position and heat the oven to 300 degrees. Combine half of the garlic, 1 tablespoon of the ginger, and fish sauce in a large bowl. Stir in the chicken thighs to coat and set aside.

2. Combine the onion, oil, and ⅛ teaspoon salt in a large Dutch oven. Cover and cook over medium-low heat, stirring occasionally, until softened, 8 to 10 minutes. Stir in the remaining garlic, remaining 1 tablespoon ginger, rice, and lemon grass and cook until fragrant, about 30 seconds. Stir in the broth, scraping up any browned bits.

3. Lay the chicken on top of the rice. Bring to a simmer, cover, and transfer to the oven. Cook for 40 minutes, then add the carrots and snow peas, cover, and continue to cook in the oven until the rice is tender and the liquid is almost fully absorbed, 10 to 15 minutes longer.

NOTES FROM THE TEST KITCHEN

RINSING RICE

Before cooking rice, it's best to rinse it. This washes away any excess starch and prevents the final dish from turning out sticky or gummy.

Simply place the rice in a fine-mesh strainer and rinse under cool water until the water runs clear, occasionally stirring the rice around lightly with your hand. Set the strainer of rinsed rice over a bowl to drain until needed.

THE BEST BROWN RICE

Brown rice is essentially a less-processed version of white rice, and it tends to have a firmer texture and a nuttier, earthier flavor than white rice. For a product with so little processing, we wondered if the brand of brown rice really mattered. We tasted five brands of long-grain brown rice prepared two ways: steamed in a rice cooker and baked in the oven. While most were fairly neutral in flavor, one brand boasted distinct nutty and toasty flavors. In both taste tests, **Goya Brown Rice** came out on top—though by a slim margin. What separated it from the rest of the group was a bolder, more distinct flavor.

SMASHING LEMON GRASS

Smashing lemon grass helps release its flavorful oils. To smash lemon grass, set the stalk on a cutting board and smash it with a meat pounder. This keeps the stalk intact so it can be easily removed from the pan.

CUTTING CORN OFF THE COB

Standing the corn upright inside a large bowl, carefully cut the kernels from the ear of corn using a paring knife.

4. Transfer the chicken to a plate. Cover the pot and let the rice steam for 10 minutes. Meanwhile, when cool enough to handle, shred the meat into bite-size pieces.

5. Remove and discard the lemon grass. Stir the shredded chicken, cilantro, and lime juice into the rice. Season with salt and pepper to taste and serve.

PER 1½-CUP SERVING: Cal 390; Fat 9g; Sat fat 1.5g; Chol 95mg; Carb 50g; Protein 29g; Fiber 5g; Sodium 620mg

Latin-Style Chicken and Brown Rice
SERVES 4

White rice cannot be substituted for the brown rice in this recipe. Serve with sliced avocado if desired.

- 8 garlic cloves, minced
- 1 tablespoon cider vinegar
- 2 teaspoons minced fresh oregano or ½ teaspoon dried
-    Salt and pepper
- 1 pound boneless, skinless chicken thighs, trimmed
- 1 onion, minced (about 1 cup)
- 1 green bell pepper, stemmed, seeded, and chopped medium
- 1 teaspoon canola oil
- 1 cup long-grain brown rice, rinsed (see page 79)
- ⅛ teaspoon red pepper flakes
- 1 (14.5-ounce) can diced tomatoes
- ¾ cup low-sodium chicken broth
- ½ cup pimientos or jarred roasted red peppers, rinsed, patted dry, and sliced thin
- ½ cup pitted green olives, chopped coarse
- ¼ cup minced fresh cilantro
- 2 tablespoons drained capers, rinsed
-    Lemon wedges, for serving

1. Adjust an oven rack to the lower-middle position and heat the oven to 300 degrees. Combine half of the garlic, vinegar, oregano, ⅛ teaspoon salt, and ¼ teaspoon pepper in a large bowl. Stir in the chicken to coat and set aside.

2. Combine the onion, bell pepper, oil, and ⅛ teaspoon salt in a large Dutch oven. Cover and cook over medium-low heat, stirring occasionally, until the vegetables are softened, 8 to 10 minutes. Stir in the remaining garlic, rice, and pepper flakes and cook until fragrant,

about 30 seconds. Stir in the tomatoes with their juice and the broth, scraping up any browned bits.

3. Lay the chicken on top of the rice. Bring to a simmer, cover, and transfer to the oven. Cook until the rice is tender and the liquid is almost fully absorbed, 50 to 65 minutes.

4. Transfer the chicken to a plate. Cover the pot and let the rice steam for 10 minutes. Meanwhile, when cool enough to handle, shred the meat into bite-size pieces.

5. Stir the shredded chicken, pimientos, olives, cilantro, and capers into the rice. Season with salt and pepper to taste and serve with the lemon wedges.

PER 1½-CUP SERVING: Cal 420; Fat 11g; Sat fat 2g; Chol 95mg; Carb 51g; Protein 28g; Fiber 5g; Sodium 980mg

TURKEY CUTLETS

ONE QUICK LOOK AT THE SUPERMARKET MEAT CASE will confirm it: Turkey has spread its wings far beyond Thanksgiving. There's ground turkey, smoked turkey, turkey parts, turkey sausage, and turkey burgers—to name just a few. And for home cooks in need of a light, quick-cooking dinner, there are turkey cutlets. However, they do take some know-how to prepare. Because they are thin, usually no more than about ⅜ inch thick, and very lean, the margin of error between a perfectly cooked turkey cutlet and shoe leather is slim. Most recipes turn out flavorless meat with a tough, pale exterior. We knew we could do better, so we headed to the kitchen, determined to bring out the best in turkey cutlets by perfecting our cooking technique and coming up with a flavorful, easy pan sauce to pair with them.

Our first obstacle was settling on a cooking method. We knew for the best flavor and appearance, our cutlets needed to be nicely browned. Because the cutlets are so thin, we knew a high-heat cooking method (sautéing, grilling, broiling) was essential; low or moderate heat (baking, poaching) would overcook the delicate meat before it could form that flavorful browned exterior. We ruled out grilling from the start because we wanted to keep this an easy, year-round recipe. Broiling yielded mediocre results; some cutlets were cooked perfectly and others were overdone. Sautéing on the stovetop was our best bet as it required a minimal amount of fat (cutlets are so thin they don't require very much) and offered us the most control. And as an added bonus, once we sautéed the cutlets, we could build a sauce in the same pan.

We found recipes that called for butter, olive oil, canola oil, and a combination of butter and oil. To keep the saturated fat to a minimum, we opted for canola oil. In side-by-side testing, we wanted to see how much oil was really necessary to brown the cutlets without scorching them. Ultimately we realized that we needed 1 tablespoon for every three cutlets; any less and our cutlets browned unevenly. A 12-inch skillet was key to giving our cutlets enough room to brown, rather than steam in their own juice. We took a cue from past test kitchen experience and tried flouring our cutlets, which would not only encourage browning but would also protect the delicate meat and prevent the outside of the cutlets from overcooking before the inside cooked through. Two minutes on each side over medium-high heat did the trick.

The hard part was over; now we could focus on the sauce. We settled on a red wine sauce that was slightly rich but wouldn't overpower our delicate turkey. After gently sautéing shallots, garlic, and thyme in the skillet, we used wine and broth to loosen the flavorful browned bits left in the pan from browning the turkey. Dried cranberries added just the right tartness (and carried out our Thanksgiving-anytime theme), and a touch of honey lent just the right balancing sweetness. Because the thin cutlets cooled while we made our sauce, we kept them warm in a low oven once they came out of the pan while we finished up.

Now we had a fast, elegant, and healthy dinner ready in minutes.

Turkey Cutlets with Cranberries and Red Wine

SERVES 4

One cutlet per person makes a skimpy serving, so we call for a total of 6 cutlets to serve four people.

CUTLETS

- ½ cup unbleached all-purpose flour
- 6 (4-ounce) turkey cutlets, pounded ¼ inch thick
- ⅛ teaspoon salt
- ⅛ teaspoon pepper
- 2 tablespoons canola oil

SAUCE

- 2 shallots, sliced thin
- 1 garlic clove, minced
- 1 teaspoon minced fresh thyme
- 1 tablespoon unbleached all-purpose flour
- ¾ cup dry red wine
- ½ cup low-sodium chicken broth
- ½ cup dried cranberries
- 1 teaspoon honey
- Salt and pepper

1. FOR THE CUTLETS: Adjust an oven rack to the middle position and heat the oven to 200 degrees. Spread the flour in a shallow dish. Pat the turkey cutlets dry with paper towels and season with the salt and pepper. Dredge the cutlets in the flour to coat and shake off any excess.

2. Heat 1 tablespoon of the oil in a 12-inch skillet over medium-high heat until just smoking. Add half of the cutlets to the pan and cook until light golden brown on both sides, about 4 minutes, flipping them halfway through. Transfer the cutlets to a plate and keep warm in the oven. Repeat with the remaining 1 tablespoon oil and remaining cutlets. Do not wipe out the skillet.

3. FOR THE SAUCE: Add the shallots to the skillet and cook over medium heat until softened, about 2 minutes. Stir in the garlic and thyme and cook until fragrant, about 30 seconds. Stir in the flour and cook for 30 seconds. Whisk in the wine, broth, cranberries, and honey, scraping up any browned bits.

4. Bring to a simmer and cook until the sauce has reduced to 1 cup, about 3 minutes. Stir in any accumulated turkey juice, season with salt and pepper to taste, and serve with the cutlets.

PER SERVING: Cal 370; Fat 8g; Sat fat 0.5g; Chol 65mg; Carb 25g; Protein 44g; Fiber 1g; Sodium 300mg

VARIATION

Turkey Cutlets with Cranberries and Apple
Follow the recipe for Turkey Cutlets with Cranberries and Red Wine, adding ½ Granny Smith apple, peeled and chopped fine, to the skillet with the shallots. Substitute ¾ cup apple juice and 1 tablespoon cider vinegar for the wine and omit the honey.

PER SERVING: Cal 370; Fat 8g; Sat fat 0.5g; Chol 65mg; Carb 31g; Protein 44g; Fiber 2g; Sodium 300mg

STEAK TIPS WITH MUSHROOM–ONION GRAVY

BEEF ENCHILADAS

TRADITIONAL BEEF ENCHILADAS, WITH SILKY, slow-cooked meat and a blanket of hearty chile sauce and sprinkling of cheese, are the ultimate in Mexican comfort food. But as with many comfort-food favorites, from-scratch enchiladas aren't exactly easy to make, nor are they high on the list of healthy dinner options. We wanted to see if we could simplify the enchilada-making process but still maintain some of the authentic flavor—all without packing on unnecessary fat and calories.

A lot of simplified enchilada recipes exist. Many use ground beef instead of stew meat and canned enchilada sauce instead of making it from scratch with dried chiles and tomatoes. But the enchiladas we tested with these tricks, while certainly easy, had none of the richness of the original, and they typically tried to make up for marginal flavor by overloading the cheese. Could we shorten the traditional process, all the while cutting calories and fat without shortchanging the flavor?

We started with the sauce. Red chile sauce—made with dried red chiles, tomatoes, and a mix of spices and aromatics—is the most common choice for enchiladas, so we began by preparing a half-dozen traditional recipes. The flavor of all these sauces was spicy and complex, the texture smooth and somewhat thick, the color deep orange-red. The problem was that whole dried chiles, a key player in all these sauces, are not only hard to find but require substantial preparation time, including toasting, seeding, stemming, rehydrating, and processing in a blender. For approachability, we would have to find a way to achieve similar results without the dried chiles.

We started with the tomatoes. Since we were after simplicity and convenience, we explored canned tomato products first. We tried cooking diced tomatoes with a handful of aromatics (onion and garlic for now) and then pureed the mixture. Tasters agreed the texture of the sauce was too thin. Thicker canned tomato sauce, combined with some water, worked better, giving us a smooth enchilada sauce that wasn't overly acidic.

To infuse our tomato sauce with flavor, store-bought chili powder seemed like an obvious place to begin since dried chiles weren't an option. We knew that heating the chili powder in oil, a process known as blooming, would intensify the flavor of the dried spice, but before adding it to the pan we sautéed a little onion and garlic to give our sauce bite and texture. Cumin and coriander, ingredients often found in authentic red chile sauces, brought our sauce depth and complexity. After sautéing the aromatics and blooming the spices, we added the tomato sauce and water and simmered briefly. This sauce, simple yet deeply flavored, was right on track. Now we needed to figure out the filling for our enchiladas.

In traditional recipes an inexpensive cut of meat is slow-cooked in the sauce, which tenderizes the meat and infuses both with flavor. Cuts from the chuck (the shoulder) are particularly good here, but a whole chuck roast would take at least four hours. We got what we were looking for using another cut from the chuck: smaller, inexpensive top blade steaks. Browning the meat in the pan first deepened its flavor and left behind a nice fond, which we could use in turn to enrich the sauce. So with the meat browned, we built the sauce in the same pan, then returned the meat to the pot and cooked it through. Although this took an hour and a half, the resulting deep flavors and tender meat were well worth it.

To prepare the filling, we separated the cooked meat from the sauce with a strainer, then broke the tender meat into smaller chunks. Adding back ½ cup of the sauce would give the filling the right amount of moistness. To help bind it together, cheese seemed like the right choice, but we would need to be careful how much we added to maintain a healthy profile. *Queso fresco*, a tangy, crumbly-soft cheese popular in Mexico that is similar to a mild feta, is lower in fat than cheddar or Monterey Jack, so we tested adding varying amounts to see how little we could get away with. Ultimately, 1 cup of queso fresco gave our filling the right consistency and balanced the deeply flavored, rich sauce and meat.

Looking for more heat in our filling, we tested minced fresh jalapeños, chipotle chiles in adobo sauce, and pickled jalapeños. Chipotles added a distinctive warm heat and smoky flavor that some tasters enjoyed but that most found too assertive for our already deeply flavorful sauce. The fresh jalapeños were good, but surprisingly, the convenient pickled jalapeños were the hands-down favorite. The vinegar pickling solution added spicy, bright, and tart notes to the filling that took it to the next level.

Some recipes suggest frying the corn tortillas and then dipping them in sauce to simultaneously soften and season them. Deciding against this involved, messy procedure, we opted to simply microwave the tortillas to soften them before filling them. We filled and rolled the tortillas, then topped them with our flavorful sauce and a sprinkling of reduced-fat cheddar cheese, for just the right amount of gooey appeal. After just 20 minutes in

SPICY BEEF ENCHILADAS

the oven, they were warmed through and ready to eat. These spicy beef enchiladas tasted every bit as good as an authentic version, and with just the right balance of beef, cheese, and sauce, they were a perfect comfort food that didn't leave us feeling weighed down.

Spicy Beef Enchiladas

SERVES 6

Don't be tempted to use either preshredded or nonfat cheddar cheese in this dish; the texture and flavor will suffer substantially. For best results, choose a low-fat cheddar cheese that is sold in block form and has roughly 50 percent of the fat and calories of regular cheddar cheese (we like Cabot and Cracker Barrel brands). Garnish the enchiladas with shredded lettuce, if desired.

1½	pounds top blade steaks, trimmed of all visible fat (see photos)
	Salt and pepper
2	teaspoons canola oil
2	onions, minced (about 2 cups)
3	garlic cloves, minced
3	tablespoons chili powder
2	teaspoons ground coriander
2	teaspoons ground cumin
1	teaspoon sugar
1	(15-ounce) can tomato sauce
¾	cup water
4	ounces queso fresco (about 1 cup) (see page 76)
⅓	cup minced fresh cilantro
1	(4-ounce) can chopped pickled jalapeños, drained
12	(6-inch) corn tortillas
2	ounces 50 percent light cheddar cheese, shredded (about ½ cup)

1. Pat the beef dry with paper towels and season with ⅛ teaspoon salt and ⅛ teaspoon pepper. Heat the oil in a large Dutch oven over medium-high heat until just smoking. Add the beef and cook until well browned on all sides, 4 to 6 minutes, turning as needed. Transfer the beef to a plate.

2. Add the onions to the fat left in the pot, cover, and cook over medium-low heat, stirring occasionally, until softened, 8 to 10 minutes. Stir in the garlic, chili powder, coriander, cumin, and sugar and cook until fragrant, about 1 minute.

3. Stir in the tomato sauce and water, scraping up any browned bits, and bring to a simmer. Stir in the beef, along with any accumulated juice, cover, and simmer until the meat is tender, about 1½ hours.

4. Adjust an oven rack to the middle position and heat the oven to 350 degrees. Strain the beef mixture over a bowl, reserving the sauce. Transfer the meat to a second bowl and break into small pieces. Mix ½ cup of the reserved sauce, queso fresco, cilantro, and jalapeños into the beef and season with salt and pepper to taste.

5. Spread ¾ cup more reserved sauce in the bottom of a 13 by 9-inch baking dish. Microwave 6 of the tortillas on a plate on high until soft, about 1 minute. Spread a heaping ¼ cup of the beef mixture down the center of a tortilla, roll the tortilla tightly, and set it in the baking dish seam side down. Repeat with the remaining tortillas and beef mixture (you may have to fit 2 or more enchiladas down the sides of the baking dish).

6. Pour the remaining sauce over the enchiladas and spread to coat evenly. Sprinkle the cheddar cheese evenly over the enchiladas, cover tightly with aluminum foil, and bake until heated through, 20 to 25 minutes. Remove the foil and continue to bake until the cheese browns slightly, 5 to 10 minutes longer. Let sit for 5 minutes before serving.

PER SERVING: Cal 430; Fat 16g; Sat fat 5g; Chol 75mg; Carb 42g; Protein 32g; Fiber 6g; Sodium 710mg

NOTES FROM THE TEST KITCHEN

TRIMMING BLADE STEAKS

1. Halve each steak lengthwise, leaving the gristle on one half.

2. Cut away the gristle from the half to which it is attached.

SLOPPY JOES

SLOPPY JOES, WHILE POPULAR AND QUICK, ARE OFTEN little more than a can of sweet sauce dumped over greasy, third-rate burger meat that is brought to a simmer in a skillet. Though the base for Sloppy Joes is pretty constant among published recipes—ground beef, onion, garlic, spices, something sweet, something sour, and something tomato—many of the recipes we tried were either greasy, dry, crumbly, bland, too sweet, too sour, or too saucy—and they were all high in fat. On average, a typical Sloppy Joe can come in at 500 calories and 26 grams of fat. With a little research and a few tests, we felt that we could turn the ho-hum Sloppy Joe around—time well spent if we could make over this childhood favorite into a quick, flavorful skillet supper that didn't weigh us down.

A typical Sloppy Joe gets its heft from onions browned with ground beef; the mixture is then simmered in a caloric combination of ketchup, bottled chili sauce, and sugar. We decided to test out a few adventurous low-calorie recipes we had found, all of which relied on an assortment of nontraditional ingredients: wheat berries, ground vegetable protein, and tofu, to name a few (and not a grain of sugar). Tasters didn't even recognize these sandwiches as Sloppy Joes; most were too vegetal in flavor, and the texture of the imitation meat fooled no one. We unanimously agreed the only route to take was to start with the traditional recipe and cut calories where we could.

We began with the sauce. Ketchup is a must, but too much made the sauce excessively sweet (many recipes call for ½ cup to ¾ cup). We were able to reduce the amount to ¼ cup, but to give our Sloppy Joes the right tomatoey flavor, we would need to add another tomato product. Canned crushed and whole tomatoes both needed lengthy cooking to break down, so we ruled them out of our easy weeknight recipe. Tomato paste made the sauce dry and stiff. Tomato sauce, however, which we'd successfully used to make tomato sauces for both our Spicy Beef Enchiladas (page 86) and Spicy Mexican Shredded Pork Tostadas (page 97), was once again a winner with its deep tomato flavor and slightly sweet notes. Sautéed minced onion and just a teaspoon of brown sugar (which has more robust flavor than granulated) added the right sweetness, and a teaspoon

of cider vinegar gave the sauce its trademark tang.

Many recipes cut fat and calories by using ground chicken or turkey, but we wanted to keep the beefy flavor. After crunching the numbers, we were happy to find that 93 percent lean ground beef was comparable in calories and fat to a mixture of dark and white meat chicken or turkey (all-white was not an option since it would make an unpalatably dry sandwich). But when we browned the lean beef, as is done for full-fat versions to deepen the meat's flavor, it turned chewy and tough, and no matter how long we simmered it in the sauce, it never became tender. We ruled out browning and began testing when it was best to add the beef to the pan. Unexpectedly, we found that when we stirred it into the cooked sauce and simmered the mixture for just a few minutes, the meat cooked through yet stayed perfectly tender.

Although our Sloppy Joes were leaner, the amount of beef needed to create four properly portioned sandwiches still pushed the nutrition numbers too high. Cutting back on the portion size was a no-go for the hearty recipe we were after, so we tried "stretching" the beef by adding various grains, like oatmeal and barley, to fill out our recipe. They all gave our Sloppy Joes off-flavors and textures. Might mushrooms, which are often described as "meaty," work? Unlike the meat, these we browned; then we chopped them in the food processor to get the appearance and texture of ground meat. A few tests showed that we could switch out 6 ounces of the beef (which contains 260 calories and 12 grams of fat) for an equal amount of mushrooms (35 calories and zero fat) before anyone caught on. Adding a splash of Worcestershire sauce to the tomato sauce boosted the sandwich's meaty flavor even further.

Tasters gave the thumbs-up to our overhauled Joes, which had the mild spice, sweet tang, and tender texture of the original sandwich. And with 190 fewer calories and 17 grams of fat less than the original, these sandwiches were addictive for kids and adults alike.

MAKEOVER SPOTLIGHT: SLOPPY JOES

	CALORIES	FAT	SAT FAT	CHOLESTEROL
BEFORE	500	26g	8g	75mg
AFTER	310	9g	2.5g	45mg

Sloppy Joes

SERVES 4

If the onions remain firm after cooking in the tomato sauce mixture, simmer for an additional 5 minutes before adding the beef. If the mixture becomes too dry during cooking, add water, 1 tablespoon at a time, to reach the desired consistency.

6	ounces white mushrooms, sliced thin
2	teaspoons canola oil
	Salt
1	onion, minced (about 1 cup)
1¼	teaspoons chili powder
1	(8-ounce) can tomato sauce
¼	cup ketchup
¼	cup water
1	tablespoon Worcestershire sauce
1	teaspoon brown sugar
1	teaspoon cider vinegar
10	ounces 93 percent lean ground beef
	Pepper
4	hamburger buns

1. Combine the mushrooms, 1 teaspoon of the oil, and ¼ teaspoon salt in a 12-inch nonstick skillet. Cover and cook over medium-low heat until softened, 8 to 10 minutes. Uncover, increase the heat to medium-high, and continue to cook, stirring occasionally, until the mushrooms are well browned, 8 to 12 minutes longer. Transfer to a food processor and pulse until the mushrooms are finely ground, about 6 pulses.

2. Heat the remaining 1 teaspoon oil in the skillet over medium heat until shimmering. Add the processed mushrooms and onion, cover, and cook until the onion is softened, 8 to 12 minutes. Stir in the chili powder and cook until fragrant, about 30 seconds. Add the tomato sauce, ketchup, water, Worcestershire, sugar, and vinegar. Bring to a simmer and cook over medium-low heat until the sauce is thickened slightly, about 15 minutes.

3. Add the beef and simmer, breaking up the meat with a wooden spoon, until no longer pink, about 5 minutes. Season with salt and pepper to taste. Divide the mixture among the buns and serve.

PER SERVING: Cal 310; Fat 9g; Sat fat 2.5g; Chol 45mg; Carb 35g; Protein 21g; Fiber 3g; Sodium 940mg

---

NOTES FROM THE TEST KITCHEN

SECRETS TO A SLIMMER SANDWICH
Two key ingredients ensure big, beefy flavor in our Sloppy Joes, without all the fat.

WHITE MUSHROOMS	**LEAN BEEF**
Browned, finely ground mushrooms contribute beefy flavor and bulk but no fat and few calories.	Rather than resorting to ground poultry or oddball ingredients like tofu, we use 93 percent lean ground beef to cut fat, not beefiness.

STEAK TIPS WITH MUSHROOM-ONION GRAVY

STEAK TIPS WITH MUSHROOM AND ONION GRAVY IS A pub classic that always beckons with its promise of juicy meat and hearty flavors, but often it's just overcooked beef swimming in a thin, generic brown sauce or thick, bland gravy. Most recipes call for small, easily overcooked strips of beef and flavor-sacrificing shortcuts like canned cream of mushroom soup, dried onion soup mix, or ketchup. They all come across tasting tired and uninspired. We knew we could create a better, more balanced version with tender, meaty pieces of steak covered in a sauce that emphasized the mushrooms and onions.

After some initial tests, we developed a basic framework. We would sear the beef and set it aside, then build the gravy in the same pan, and finally add the meat back to the gravy to cook through. Aside from the convenience of using only one pan, this method offered two key advantages. The initial searing left the skillet full of fond, which provided a flavorful base for the sauce. Second, cooking the beef through in the gravy would allow the flavors to mingle and build depth.

First, we needed to find the right cut of beef for the job. Though you occasionally find this dish made with tender, flavorful, and expensive cuts like strip steak, rib-eye steak, and tenderloin, we didn't want to pay top dollar for a midweek meal. We turned to testing cheaper cuts: flank steak, round steak, and the most common choice, sirloin steak tips (aka flap meat). This latter beefy cut becomes incredibly tender when cooked between medium-rare and medium as its internal marbling melts into the coarse muscle fibers of the steak. Flank steak made a suitable substitute if steak tips were unavailable but wasn't nearly as meaty-tasting. Round steak was too lean and easily turned dry and chalky. Even though the steak tips had more fat than several of the options, we agreed they were the ideal choice. We would just keep an eye on portioning and create a hearty dish with the help of the gravy.

We wanted to develop a flavorful, well-seared crust yet leave the interior slightly underdone so it wouldn't turn tough when we returned it to the pan with the gravy. We experimented with cutting the meat into various sizes to see what would cook through most efficiently and offer appealing texture and portioning. Eventually we settled on 1½-inch chunks.

One of the test kitchen's proven methods to make steak taste beefier and juicier is a quick soak in soy sauce, so we opted to apply the technique here. The salty soy draws juice out of the steak, and then the reverse happens as the soy, along with the moisture, flows back in, bringing deep flavor into the meat. We have also used sugar to promote caramelization and the development of a good crust, so we figured adding sugar to the soy sauce might get the job done with minimal work. After a 30-minute soak and a quick sear, we produced our most flavorful steak yet, with a substantial crust and plenty of fond left behind. With a rich flavor base now encrusting the pan, we were ready to move on to the gravy.

Even with a full pound of white mushrooms (the most we could reasonably fit in a skillet), the mushroom flavor in our gravy came up short. We tried using costlier creminis and portobellos. The creminis were incrementally more earthy, the portobellos much more so. Unfortunately, tasters also found them leathery, and they left the gravy unappealingly gray. Looking beyond fresh mushrooms, we then gave dried porcinis a try. Adding ¼ ounce of porcinis to our white mushrooms gave us the intense mushroom flavor we were after.

To further boost the gravy's flavor, we needed to make sure the mushrooms released moisture quickly enough to dissolve the beef's fond before it burned. We added the sliced mushrooms, along with some onions and salt, and covered the pan. The salt helped to break down the

KEYS TO FULL-FLAVORED STEAK TIPS AND GRAVY

1. Soak the steak tips in soy sauce and sugar to boost the meaty flavor and browning.

2. Sear the steak tips to create flavorful browned bits (fond) that serve as the base for a rich gravy.

3. Cook mushrooms and onions in the unwashed pan until deeply caramelized to form an extra layer of flavorful fond on top of the beef's fond.

vegetables' cell walls and set their juices flowing more quickly. Once the vegetables had "deglazed" the pan, we removed the lid and allowed them to brown, creating a second fond before adding the liquid components of the gravy. We now had a doubleheader for flavor: a classic meat fond compounded by a layer of vegetable fond.

For the liquid component, we settled on convenient beef broth. Adding cornstarch seemed like an easy way to thicken the broth into gravy, but it created a gelatinous sauce. Sprinkling flour over the mushrooms as they sautéed was equally simple but much more effective in creating a rich, lump-free gravy. A minced garlic clove lent depth and ½ teaspoon of minced thyme accented the woodsy flavor of the mushrooms nicely.

After building the gravy, we returned the seared beef to the pan and gently simmered the meat and gravy together for five minutes, just long enough to meld their flavors. We garnished our steak tips with a little parsley and agreed that our recipe was better than any version we'd ever been served in a pub.

Steak Tips with Mushroom-Onion Gravy

SERVES 6

Steak tips, also known as flap meat, are sold as whole steaks, cubes, and strips. To ensure evenly sized chunks, we prefer to purchase whole steak tips and cut them ourselves. If you can find only cubes or strips, reduce the cooking time slightly to avoid overcooking any smaller or thinner pieces. Serve over rice or egg noodles.

1	tablespoon low-sodium soy sauce
1	teaspoon sugar
1½	pounds sirloin steak tips, trimmed of all visible fat and cut into 1½-inch chunks (see note)
	Pepper
4	teaspoons canola oil
1	pound white mushrooms, sliced thin
1	onion, halved and sliced thin
¼	ounce dried porcini mushrooms, rinsed and minced
	Salt
1	garlic clove, minced
½	teaspoon minced fresh thyme or ⅛ teaspoon dried
4	teaspoons unbleached all-purpose flour
1¾	cups beef broth
1	tablespoon minced fresh parsley

1. Combine the soy sauce and sugar in a medium bowl. Add the beef, toss to coat, and marinate for at least 30 minutes or up to 1 hour, tossing once.

2. Season the meat with ⅛ teaspoon pepper. Heat 2 teaspoons of the oil in a 12-inch skillet over medium-high heat until just smoking. Carefully add the beef and cook until well browned on all sides, 4 to 6 minutes, turning as needed. Transfer the beef to a plate and set aside.

3. Return the skillet to medium-low heat and add the remaining 2 teaspoons oil, white mushrooms, onion, porcini mushrooms, and ⅛ teaspoon salt. Cover and cook until the vegetables are softened, 8 to 10 minutes. Uncover, increase the heat to medium-high, and continue to cook, stirring occasionally, until the vegetables are well browned, 8 to 12 minutes longer. Stir in the garlic and thyme and cook until fragrant. Stir in the flour and cook for 1 minute. Stir in the broth, scraping up any browned bits, and bring to a simmer.

4. Return the beef, along with any accumulated juice, to the skillet. Reduce the heat to medium-low and simmer until the meat registers 130 degrees on an instant-read thermometer, 3 to 5 minutes, stirring occasionally. Season with salt and pepper to taste, sprinkle with the parsley, and serve.

PER SERVING: Cal 210; Fat 6g; Sat fat 1.5g; Chol 60mg; Carb 8g; Protein 28g; Fiber 1g; Sodium 380mg

HORSERADISH-CRUSTED BEEF TENDERLOIN

BEEF TENDERLOIN IS A FAVORITE SPECIAL-OCCASION dinner choice. While this cut is ultra-tender, it is also very lean, a great attribute if you are keeping an eye on fat; but this leanness also means a tenderloin doesn't offer much in terms of flavor. A bold, spicy horseradish sauce is a classic choice for giving tenderloin the flavor boost it needs. We wondered if we could take this favorite duo to the next level by creating a horseradish-crusted tenderloin roast.

The handful of existing recipes we found were disastrous. Most consisted of nothing more than adding horseradish to a basic bread-crumb mixture, spreading it over the beef, and roasting the meat in the oven. More often than not, the crust absorbed the meat's juice, causing most of it to turn mushy and fall off, and what "shell" still remained had only a trace of horseradish flavor. We wanted to make a recipe that would give us a beef tenderloin with a crisp, golden crust surrounding rosy, perfectly juicy meat.

A center-cut tenderloin roast—also known as Châteaubriand—was the ideal choice, since its uniform shape would cook evenly (other tenderloin roasts, from either end, would be uneven). For the crust, we figured we'd work with a test kitchen favorite for creating ultra-crispy bread coatings, Japanese panko crumbs, and apply them using a basic breading technique: lightly flouring the meat, applying a thin wash of egg white, and then rolling the roast in a horseradish-crumb mixture.

As for horseradish, we tried both fresh, thinking a few grated tablespoons straight from the gnarly-looking root might have the best punch, as well as jarred. Unfortunately, the fresh horseradish turned unpleasantly bitter when cooked, and the crumb coating failed to crisp. Bottled prepared horseradish, made with grated horseradish and vinegar, proved a better and easier choice. To avoid an overly wet coating, we pressed the horseradish through a strainer, but even after pressing it, the resulting crust was still too moist.

Perhaps we needed to reevaluate our choice of breading. Crackers and Melba toast were OK but added too much of their own flavor. On a whim, we tried crushed baked potato chips. They contributed a salty potato flavor that tasters loved; the problem was their processed, slightly stale taste. Could we whip up our own fresher potato coating? We shredded a potato on a box grater, rinsed the shreds to remove surface starch (which would help avoid clumping), and then, borrowing a technique for baked tortilla chips, lightly sprayed them with vegetable oil spray and baked them until golden brown. A test run proved that combining them with the panko (which was pretoasted) was the best option: The panko coated the nooks in the meat that the potatoes couldn't reach, while the potato shreds jutted out, making for a craggy, golden crust full of savory flavor. Adding shallot, parsley, garlic, and thyme gave the coating just the right boost.

Still, the results weren't ideal. In order to keep the crust truly crisp, the most horseradish we could add to the crumb mixture was 2 tablespoons. We'd have to find another way to up the horseradish flavor. We tried adding some horseradish to the egg white wash before applying the coating, but the egg wash was too thin and the horseradish dripped off the meat. In the past we have used mayonnaise to act as a "glue" to help coatings adhere; we tried to create a flavorful paste of egg white, light mayonnaise, Dijon mustard, and horseradish. This made a horseradish-flavored paste that clung firmly to the tenderloin before we rolled it in the panko-potato coating. Everything seemed to be going well until we tried to slice our cooked roast and everything came apart—literally. The crust cracked into pieces that fell straight onto the carving board.

Stumped, we consulted our science editor, who came up with a novel idea: Replace the egg white with gelatin. Gelatin's properties allow it to create a stronger bond with meat than egg whites are able to form, and its slight elasticity would help our coating stick to the meat during slicing. We added just half a teaspoon to the horseradish paste mixture, applied it to the tenderloin, rolled it in the coating, and roasted the meat. Unlike the crackly egg-based paste, the gelatin bound the bread crumbs firmly to the meat, yet yielded slightly as we sliced it. At long last, each slice delivered rosy beef topped by a cohesive horseradish crust that stayed put.

Only one problem remained: Given the half hour of cooking time plus the necessary 20 minutes of resting to allow the juice to redistribute, the crust still became slightly soggy from the released meat juice. Three tweaks fixed this problem. First, we raised the oven temperature from 300 degrees to 400 degrees, which helped keep the crust a little crispier. Second, we seared the meat in a hot skillet, then let it rest on a wire rack set inside a baking sheet so that its juice could drain off before we applied the paste and the crumbs. Finally, we coated only the top and sides of the tenderloin, leaving an "opening" on the bottom for meat juice to escape as the meat roasted.

Served with a low-fat horseradish sauce, this beef tenderloin was a standout, combining succulent meat with a crisp, salty, pungent crust.

NOTES FROM THE TEST KITCHEN

TESTING MEAT FOR DONENESS

An instant-read thermometer is the most reliable method for checking the doneness of chicken, beef, and pork. To use an instant-read thermometer, simply insert it through the side of a chicken breast, steak, or pork chop. The chart below lists temperatures at which the meat should be removed from the heat, as the temperature of the meat will continue to climb between 5 and 10 degrees as it rests. (Cutlets cook too quickly for an actual doneness test and you will have to rely more on visual cues and cooking times.)

MEAT	COOK UNTIL IT REGISTERS	SERVING TEMPERATURE
Chicken and Turkey Breasts	160 to 165 degrees	160 to 165 degrees
Chicken Thighs	175 degrees	175 degrees
Pork	140 to 145 degrees	150 degrees
Beef		
Rare	115 to 120 degrees	125 degrees
Medium-rare	120 to 125 degrees	130 degrees
Medium	130 to 135 degrees	140 degrees
Medium-well	140 to 145 degrees	150 degrees
Well-done	150 to 155 degrees	160 degrees

Horseradish-Crusted Beef Tenderloin

SERVES 6

Add the gelatin to the horseradish paste at the last moment, or the mixture will become unspreadable. If you prefer your meat more or less done, see "Testing Meat for Doneness" on page 91. Serve this roast with Creamy Horseradish Sauce (recipe follows) if desired.

  2   teaspoons kosher salt or 1 teaspoon table salt
  1   (2-pound) center-cut beef tenderloin, silver skin
       removed, trimmed of all visible fat
  1   small russet potato (about 6 ounces), peeled and
       shredded on the large holes of a box grater
  3   tablespoons panko
       Vegetable oil spray
  ¼   cup drained prepared horseradish
  2   tablespoons minced fresh parsley
  1   small shallot, minced (about 1 tablespoon)
  2   garlic cloves, minced
  ½   teaspoon minced fresh thyme or ⅛ teaspoon dried
  ¼   teaspoon pepper
  2   teaspoons canola oil
  1½ teaspoons light mayonnaise
  1½ teaspoons Dijon mustard
  ½   teaspoon powdered gelatin

1. Sprinkle the salt evenly over the roast. Place the roast on a plate, cover with plastic wrap, and let sit at room temperature for 1 hour or refrigerate for up to 24 hours. (If refrigerated, let the roast sit at room temperature for 1 hour before cooking.)

2. Adjust the oven racks to the upper-middle and lower-middle positions and heat the oven to 400 degrees. Set a wire rack inside a foil-lined rimmed baking sheet and set aside.

3. Rinse the shredded potato under cold water, then squeeze dry in a kitchen towel. Spread the shredded potato on a rimmed baking sheet. Spread the panko on a second rimmed baking sheet. Lightly coat the shredded potato and panko with vegetable oil spray. Bake the shredded potato on the upper-middle rack until golden brown, 20 to 30 minutes, stirring occasionally to break up the clumps; set aside to cool to room temperature. Bake the panko on the lower-middle rack until golden brown, 5 to 10 minutes, stirring occasionally; set aside to cool to room temperature.

4. Toss the panko with 2 tablespoons of the horseradish, parsley, shallot, garlic, and thyme and return to the baking sheet. Place the potatoes in a large zipper-lock bag and crush until coarsely ground. Transfer the potatoes to the baking sheet with the panko mixture and toss to combine.

5. Pat the tenderloin dry with paper towels and season with ¼ teaspoon pepper. Heat the oil in a 12-inch non-stick skillet over medium-high heat until just smoking. Carefully lay the roast in the skillet and cook until well browned on all sides, 6 to 10 minutes, turning as needed. Transfer the roast to the prepared wire rack and let sit for 10 minutes.

6. Combine the remaining 2 tablespoons horseradish, mayonnaise, and mustard in a bowl. When ready to coat the tenderloin, stir the gelatin into the horseradish mixture. Spread the horseradish mixture on the top and sides of the roast, leaving the bottom and ends bare. Roll the coated sides of the roast in the crumb mixture, pressing gently so the crumbs adhere. Pat off any excess crumbs.

7. Return the roast to the wire rack and roast until the meat registers 120 to 125 degrees (for medium-rare) on an instant-read thermometer, 25 to 30 minutes. Transfer the roast to a carving board and let rest for 20 minutes. Cut the roast crosswise into ½-inch-thick slices and serve.

PER SERVING: Cal 220; Fat 8g; Sat fat 2g; Chol 80mg; Carb 9g; Protein 31g; Fiber 1g; Sodium 540mg

Creamy Horseradish Sauce

MAKES ABOUT 1 CUP

This sauce will keep in an airtight container in the refrigerator for up to 1 day.

  ½   cup light mayonnaise
  ¼   cup low-fat sour cream
  3   tablespoons drained prepared horseradish
  2   tablespoons fresh lemon juice
  ½   teaspoon garlic powder
       Water
       Salt and pepper

Mix the mayonnaise, sour cream, horseradish, lemon juice, and garlic powder together in a bowl, adding water as needed to thin the sauce. Season with salt and pepper to taste. Cover and refrigerate until the flavors blend, about 30 minutes.

PER 2-TABLESPOON SERVING: Cal 50; Fat 4g; Sat fat 0.5g; Chol 5mg; Carb 2g; Protein 0g; Fiber 0g; Sodium 150mg

HORSERADISH–CRUSTED BEEF TENDERLOIN

FRENCH PORK AND WHITE BEAN CASSEROLE

MAKING FRENCH CASSOULET, A 700-YEAR-OLD peasant dish, is usually a three-day affair, combining an assortment of meats, including braised pork, homemade sausage, and duck confit, with white beans and topping it off with buttery bread crumbs. It's the ultimate choice when it comes to a satisfying winter meal, but this time-consuming recipe has a lengthy grocery list that makes it intimidating to make, and it isn't exactly light cooking given the fatty pork products, duck cooked in its own fat, and buttery bread crumbs. But come January in Boston and the prospect of a few more months of winter ahead of us, the idea of a casserole brimming with creamy beans and rich meat sounded irresistible. We had to wonder, Could we develop a healthier, more streamlined version that would bring this homey classic back into our regular rotation? The test kitchen had recently developed a cassoulet recipe that simplified the process, so we decided this was a great starting point for us to develop a light and healthy version.

Following our recently developed recipe, we started by blanching the sausage and salt pork, which would remove excess salt from the salt pork and firm up the sausages so they could better maintain their shape throughout the long cooking time. Then we browned the meat along with some pork shoulder in a Dutch oven. After the meat was browned, we built our flavor base, sautéing onion, carrot, garlic, and tomato paste. We deglazed the fond with white wine, then added diced tomatoes, chicken broth, the beans, and some thyme, celery, and bay leaves for aromatic notes (we would remove these latter three ingredients before serving). Once it was up to a simmer, we placed the whole thing in the oven for 1½ hours, just until the beans were tender. Then we added the bread crumbs in stages, a process that allowed us to slowly develop a "bread-crumb raft," ensuring a crunchy, nicely browned topping. This process was certainly more streamlined than the traditional method, and it eliminated some of the more obscure ingredients like duck confit, but it certainly needed some tweaking in terms of fat and calories.

We started with the meat. The original combination of salt pork, fresh garlic pork sausage, and pork shoulder was certainly flavorful, but we knew we'd need to reevaluate them, one by one. First, we cooked two batches of cassoulet, one with the salt pork and one without it, and while the salt pork added a mellow richness that tasters liked, it didn't make enough of a difference to merit keeping it in a lightened recipe.

Next, we tried substituting chicken and turkey sausage for the pork sausage. Tasters were pleased with the flavor of both but not the texture. Because these poultry sausages lack the fat found in pork sausage, they dried out after the long two-hour stint in the oven. Adding the sausage to the pot toward the end of the cooking time easily solved the problem. We also wondered how much sausage was really necessary; in the end we were able to reduce the amount from 1½ pounds down to 1 pound and still have a cassoulet with plenty of meatiness to it. Inadvertently, by eliminating the salt pork and changing the cooking time for the sausage, we simplified the recipe further, eliminating the blanching step completely.

Keeping pork shoulder in our recipe was a must for both authenticity and flavor, but we wondered if we could cut back on how much of it we added. We eventually found we could reduce the amount of pork shoulder from 1½ pounds to 1 pound without taking away from the heartiness of our recipe. (As a bonus, since we had less meat to brown, we could also reduce the amount of oil from 2 tablespoons to 2 teaspoons.)

It was time to evaluate the bread-crumb topping. Our original recipe called for combining crumbs from four slices of bread with 2 tablespoons of oil, which facilitated browning and helped build a shield between the crumbs and the liquid in the pot. Nevertheless, we felt this was a significant amount of oil, and since we were counting calories and fat we would have to go without it. But without the oil, the crumbs, not surprisingly, turned soggy. Next we tried pre-toasting them. The results were not much better. We tried adding only a portion of the oil back to the crumbs, but anything less than 2 tablespoons resulted in a soggy, unappealing topping. We eventually realized our best path was to separate the crumbs from the dish completely. By tossing them with only 1 tablespoon of oil, then toasting them and serving them tableside, we achieved the same textural contrast as in our original. Doing this also eliminated 40 minutes from the cooking time since we weren't incrementally layering on the crumb topping anymore.

This cassoulet was a recipe we wouldn't think twice about making the next time we craved a hearty winter stew, and we wouldn't feel a shred of guilt about eating it.

French Pork and White Bean Casserole

SERVES 8

This recipe calls for raw turkey sausage; do not use pre-cooked sausages. Chicken sausage can be substituted for the turkey sausage.

  4 slices high-quality white sandwich bread,
     torn into pieces
  5 teaspoons canola oil
  ½ cup minced fresh parsley
     Salt and pepper
  2 celery ribs
  4 sprigs fresh thyme
  1 bay leaf
  1 pound pork shoulder, trimmed of all visible fat and
     silver skin and cut into 1-inch chunks
  2 carrots, peeled and chopped medium
  1 onion, minced (about 1 cup)
  4 garlic cloves, minced
  1 tablespoon tomato paste
  ½ cup dry white wine
  1 (14.5-ounce) can diced tomatoes
  1 pound (about 2½ cups) dried cannellini beans,
     rinsed, picked over, and soaked (see page 214)
  4 cups low-sodium chicken broth
  1 pound garlic turkey sausage, sliced 1 inch thick

1. Adjust an oven rack to the lower-middle position and heat the oven to 400 degrees. Pulse the bread in a food processor to ¼-inch pieces, about 5 pulses. Transfer the crumbs to a bowl and toss with 1 tablespoon of the oil. Spread the crumbs on a rimmed baking sheet and bake, stirring occasionally, until golden brown, 7 to 12 minutes. Let the crumbs cool to room temperature, then transfer to a bowl, stir in the parsley, and season with salt and pepper to taste.

2. Adjust the oven to 300 degrees. Using kitchen twine, tie the celery, thyme sprigs, and bay leaf together.

3. Heat the remaining 2 teaspoons oil in a large Dutch oven over medium-high heat until just smoking. Carefully add the pork shoulder and cook until well browned on all sides, 4 to 6 minutes, turning as needed. Stir in the carrots and onion and cook, stirring constantly, until the onion is beginning to soften, about 2 minutes. Stir in the garlic and tomato paste and cook until fragrant, about 30 seconds. Stir in the wine, scraping up any browned bits, and cook until reduced

slightly, about 30 seconds. Stir in the celery bundle and diced tomatoes with their juice.

4. Stir in the soaked beans and broth, pressing the beans into an even layer, and bring to a simmer over high heat. Cover, transfer to the oven, and cook until the beans are tender, about 1½ hours.

5. Adjust the oven to 350 degrees. Remove and discard the celery bundle. Season the beans with salt and pepper to taste, then stir in the sausage pieces. Bake, uncovered, until the sausage is cooked and the liquid has reduced slightly, 30 to 40 minutes. Let the cassoulet rest for 15 minutes. Sprinkle the bread crumbs over each portion before serving.

PER SERVING: Cal 380; Fat 17g; Sat fat 4.5g; Chol 75mg; Carb 27g; Protein 26g; Fiber 5g; Sodium 990mg

MEXICAN SHREDDED PORK

TRUE MEXICAN SHREDDED PORK—OR *TINGA*—IS A far cry from the bland version we typically find in the States at quick-serve burrito joints. As in good barbecued pulled pork, tinga's moist, tender shreds boast an intense, sweet meatiness. After a slow braise, the shredded pork is sautéed until it acquires deeply browned edges, which stay crisp even after the quick simmer in a rich chipotle-infused tomato sauce. Then the meat is served on crunchy tostadas and garnished with avocado, sour cream, queso fresco, cilantro, and lime. Our goal was to come up with a lightened version of this traditional Mexican favorite that could easily be made at home with supermarket ingredients.

First we'd focus on the pork. Boston butt and picnic shoulder were the two most likely candidates, since these well-marbled cuts would benefit from long, gentle cooking, but we wanted to test pork tenderloin since it offered a leaner profile. Not surprisingly, the tenderloin failed, ending up tough and dry (shortening the cooking time was not an option since it would shortchange flavor). Going back to the picnic shoulder and Boston butt, we cubed one of each cut into 1-inch pieces and simmered the cubes in a saucepan of salted water, as most recipes directed. The two samples were equally tender after about an hour and a half of simmering, but since pork butt contains less sinew, we opted for it (the sinew, since it is inedible, would mean additional butchering).

We liked the clean, sweet taste of the pork butt, but could we give it a bit more complexity? Replacing the 4 cups of water used to braise the meat with chicken broth might do the trick, but this seemed wasteful since the bulk of the liquid would be discarded. Instead, we tried simply adding an onion and a few smashed garlic cloves to the simmering water, along with several sprigs of thyme. This imparted a subtle vegetal flavor to the meat that tasters approved.

Now for the step that really separates tinga from pulled pork: its crisp texture. Since pulled pork is smoked as a roast, only its ends have the crunchy browned bits known as bark. Because the pork for tinga is shredded before sautéing, it has far more surface area available for browning. We began by draining the meat, reserving a cup of cooking liquid for the sauce, then returned the meat to the pot to shred (we found the meat was so tender, it came apart with nothing more than the pressure of a potato masher). We placed the meat in a hot pan with a couple of teaspoons of olive oil and sautéed it with the requisite additions of finely chopped onion

and oregano. It took about 10 minutes for the pork to develop crackling edges crisp enough to survive the final step of simmering in a tomato sauce.

Instead of the sweet and tangy sauce typical of American barbecue, tinga relies on a complex, smoky tomato sauce. We began with the tomatoes. Some all-out versions specify fresh tomatoes charred on a hot *comal* (a cast-iron griddle) and then pureed until smooth, but most simply call for some form of canned tomatoes. We found that whole canned tomatoes had a nice bright flavor, but we wondered if we could avoid getting out the blender and use tomato puree instead. While the puree's concentrated flavor proved too sweet, canned tomato sauce worked well, contributing a smooth texture and bright taste. A cup of reserved cooking liquid diluted it to an ideal consistency, and two bay leaves added herbal complexity.

Next we considered the all-important smoky flavor, which in tinga comes from chipotle chiles (smoked jalapeños). This flavor-packed ingredient is generally available in two forms: canned in adobo sauce and ground into powder. As we made tinga after tinga, tasters noticed that the flavor of canned chipotles varied greatly from brand to brand. Some were more salty, sweet, and vinegary than spicy, while others offered searing heat more than anything else. Ground chipotle powder, though a little harder to track down, turned out to be far more consistent, with the deeper, complex smokiness that was needed in this recipe.

Now our tinga tasted great, but to keep this recipe on the light side, we would need to cut back on some of the meat. Beans seemed like a logical substitution. Pinto beans, with their mild flavor and creamy texture, were the perfect replacement for some of the meat. Adding them with the tomato sauce ensured that they absorbed plenty of flavor and blended seamlessly with the dish.

With our tinga finished, it was time to address the tostadas. While traditional, deep-frying tortillas is time-consuming and would add far too much fat. Instead, we looked to the technique we had used to make Homemade Baked Corn Tortilla Chips (page 9). We lightly coated tortillas with vegetable oil spray and toasted them in a 350-degree oven for about 10 minutes. While this had worked for the tortilla chips, we found whole tortillas were coming out tough, not crispy. Upping the oven temperature to 450 degrees did the trick.

After topping our lightened crispy tostadas with the smoky, rich tinga, we felt confident our new recipe could win fans from either side of the border.

NOTES FROM THE TEST KITCHEN

KEYS TO PERFECT MEXICAN SHREDDED PORK

1. Simmer the pork with aromatics to infuse it with vegetal flavors. Drain the pork, reserving 1 cup of the cooking liquid to flavor the sauce.

2. Mash the pork with a potato masher to maximize the surface area available for browning.

3. Sauté the pork with onion, garlic, and oregano until its exterior is deeply brown and crisp, then finish by simmering it in the sauce.

Spicy Mexican Shredded Pork Tostadas

SERVES 6

We prefer the complex flavor and aroma of ground chipotle powder, but 2 teaspoons minced canned chipotle chiles in adobo sauce can be used in its place. The tostadas are best garnished with queso fresco, low-fat sour cream, diced avocado, cilantro, and lime wedges.

TOSTADAS

- 12 (6-inch) corn tortillas
-     Vegetable oil spray

TINGA

- 4 cups water
- 1 pound boneless pork butt, trimmed of all visible fat and cut into 1-inch chunks
- 2 onions, 1 minced (about 1 cup) and 1 quartered
- 5 garlic cloves, 2 minced and 3 peeled and smashed
- 4 sprigs fresh thyme
- 2 teaspoons olive oil
- ½ teaspoon dried oregano
- 1 (15-ounce) can tomato sauce
- 1 (15-ounce) can pinto beans, drained and rinsed
- 1 tablespoon ground chipotle powder
- 2 bay leaves
-   Salt and pepper

1. FOR THE TOSTADAS: Adjust the oven racks to the upper-middle and lower-middle positions and heat the oven to 450 degrees. Spread the tortillas on 2 rimmed baking sheets. Lightly coat both sides of the tortillas with vegetable oil spray.

2. Bake until lightly browned and crisp, 8 to 10 minutes, switching and rotating the baking sheets halfway through. Set the tostadas aside.

3. FOR THE TINGA: Bring the water, pork, quartered onion, smashed garlic cloves, and thyme sprigs to a simmer in a large saucepan over medium-high heat, skimming off any foam that rises to the surface. Reduce the heat to medium-low, partially cover, and cook until the meat is tender, 1¼ to 1½ hours.

4. Drain the pork, reserving 1 cup of the cooking liquid. Discard the onion, garlic, and thyme sprigs. Return the pork to the saucepan and, using a potato masher, mash until the pork is shredded into rough ½-inch pieces.

5. Heat the oil in a 12-inch nonstick skillet over medium-high heat until just smoking. Add the shredded pork and minced onion and cook, stirring often,

until the pork is well browned and crisp, 5 to 7 minutes. Stir in the minced garlic and oregano and cook until fragrant, about 30 seconds.

6. Stir in the reserved pork cooking liquid, tomato sauce, beans, chipotle powder, and bay leaves. Bring to a simmer and cook until almost all the liquid has evaporated, 5 to 7 minutes. Remove and discard the bay leaves and season with salt and pepper to taste.

7. Spoon ⅓ cup of the shredded pork mixture into the center of each tostada and serve.

PER SERVING: Cal 370; Fat 16g; Sat fat 4g; Chol 40mg; Carb 41g; Protein 15g; Fiber 7g; Sodium 590mg

MUSTARD AND FRUIT BRAISED PORK CHOPS

PORK CHOPS ARE A FAVORITE FOR LIGHT COOKING since they are traditionally a lean cut, but they need some dressing up to be flavorful. In many recipes they are paired with a rich pan sauce or smothered in a cream sauce, but we were after a healthier option. One of our test cooks recalled a recipe from his days as a restaurant chef for meaty pork chops paired with a classic and highly flavorful Italian condiment called *mostarda*.

Intrigued, we did a little research, which revealed that sweet, spicy mostarda is traditionally made by combining preserved (essentially candied) fruit with a healthy dose of mustard seed, or more obscure options like mustard oil or mustard essence, and it is often served with various kinds of meat or cheese. We also learned that making a traditional mostarda at home is no simple feat; it can take anywhere from hours to days to weeks, depending on how long the fruit should slow-cook or "steep" in the mustard and syrup. We liked the idea of the mostarda, but not the time or obscure ingredients required, so we decided to come up with our own version of a fruit and mustard sauce for pairing with pork chops for an easy weeknight meal. To make our recipe as streamlined as possible, we also settled on braising our pork chops right in the sauce. Our goal was not only to come up with a recipe for a sweet, spicy mustard-and-fruit sauce that was easy to make, but also to perfect a method for cooking our chops right in the sauce.

We entered the test kitchen with a straightforward braising framework in mind. We would brown the chops, remove them from the pan, then add the liquid components, return the chops to the pan, nestle them into the mostarda, and braise them until tender. Then we'd set them aside and cook the mostarda to just the right thickness. First up, the components of our mostarda. Traditionally mostarda is composed of fresh fruits such as pears, apricots, grapes, cherries, quinces, or figs (alone or in combination). These fruits are cooked down in a syrup—usually a mix of wine, sugar, and vinegar—until they are essentially candied. The addition of mustard in some form brings a heat that balances the sweetness of the fruit. We were able to rule out several fruits quickly: Grapes needed to be peeled, and figs and quinces were expensive and hard to find. Pears, apricots, and cherries were our favorites, holding up well and providing a mix of tartness and sweetness. To shorten the cooking time, we replaced some of the fresh fruit with dried, which had the benefit of not breaking down during cooking. A few test runs with a working recipe led us to a mix of underripe pears (ripe ones broke down too much), dried apricots, and dried cherries.

For our cooking liquid, which would double as braising liquid for the pork chops and syrup for the mostarda, we settled on a combination of water, sugar, and white wine vinegar. We knew we would need to use more water than would be necessary for making a mostarda alone so that the chops could properly braise. We settled on 1 cup of water, with 3 tablespoons of vinegar and 2 tablespoons sugar for the right balance of sweet and sour.

For the mustard component, hard-to-find mustard essence was a nonstarter. We tested Dijon and whole grain mustard, dry mustard powder, and mustard seeds. Tasters agreed that dry mustard brought too much raw heat. We liked the texture mustard seeds provided but felt whole grain mustard could perform the same job and was likely an ingredient that most people already have on hand. In combination with the whole grain mustard, Dijon brought the right heat and spice. All we had to do was stir together the mustards with our fruit and add them to the pan.

Next, we tackled the choice of chop. Considering blade, center-cut loin, and rib chops, we eventually settled on rib chops. The blade chops were a little fattier than we wanted, and the center-cut were hard to cook evenly since they have two types of muscle that cook at different rates. As for thickness, we tried rib chops ranging from ½ inch to 1½ inches thick (any thinner than ½ inch and the chops were likely to overcook). Tasters unanimously chose the ½-inch-thick chops; in a short amount of time, they were tender and infused with flavor.

Next we determined the optimum amount of cooking time once the browned chops and mostarda ingredients were together in the skillet. Although we typically cook pork only just through to ensure tenderness, this was one time when we wanted to go a little longer to really infuse the meat with the flavor of the fruit and mustard and achieve fall-apart-tender pork. After their initial stint in the pan, the chops registered 140 degrees on an instant-read thermometer. After 15 minutes of braising in the mostarda, the chops had good flavor but they were tough—the meat fibers had contracted and expelled moisture, but the fat and connective tissue between the fibers had not had a chance to melt fully and turn into gelatin, which is what makes braised meats especially rich and tender. Another 15 minutes of braising time solved the problem; the meat turned tender and succulent, and it was pleasantly sweet from the braising liquid.

After the chops were done, we set them aside and reduced the liquid to create a sauce with just the right syrupy consistency. Another tablespoon of Dijon mustard stirred in just before serving took our mostarda from good to great, giving it a fresh hit of mustard flavor. A final sprinkle of parsley gave our tender braised pork chops and mostarda the perfect fresh, finishing touch—and all in under an hour.

Mustard and Fruit Braised Pork Chops
SERVES 4

Be sure to use an unripe pear here; if the pear is too ripe it will become too mushy once cooked.

- 1 cup water
- 1 unripe pear, peeled and cut into ¾-inch pieces
- ⅓ cup dried apricots, quartered
- ¼ cup dried cherries
- 3 tablespoons white wine vinegar
- 2 tablespoons sugar
- 2 tablespoons whole grain mustard
- 2 tablespoons Dijon mustard
- 2 bay leaves
- 4 (6-ounce) bone-in pork rib chops, ½ inch thick, trimmed of all visible fat
  Salt and pepper
- 2 teaspoons canola oil
- 1 tablespoon minced fresh parsley

1. Combine the water, pear, apricots, cherries, vinegar, sugar, whole grain mustard, 1 tablespoon of the Dijon mustard, and bay leaves in a bowl and set aside.

2. Pat the pork chops dry with paper towels and season with ⅛ teaspoon salt and ⅛ teaspoon pepper. Heat the oil in a 12-inch skillet over medium-high heat until just smoking. Carefully arrange the pork chops in the skillet in a pinwheel formation with the tips of the ribs pointing toward the pan's edge. Cook the chops until browned on both sides, about 6 minutes, flipping them halfway through. Transfer the pork chops to a plate.

3. Add the fruit mixture to the pan, scraping up any browned bits. Bring to a simmer, reduce the heat to low, and nestle the pork chops into the sauce. Cook until the pork chops are tender, about 30 minutes.

4. Transfer the pork chops to a platter and tent loosely with foil. Increase the heat to medium and continue to simmer the sauce, uncovered, until thickened, 5 to 7 minutes. Remove and discard the bay leaves, stir in the remaining 1 tablespoon Dijon mustard and parsley, and season with salt and pepper to taste. Spoon the sauce over the pork chops and serve.

PER SERVING: Cal 410; Fat 11g; Sat fat 3g; Chol 95mg; Carb 34g; Protein 38g; Fiber 4g; Sodium 510mg

CRANBERRY PORK LOIN

WHEN A COWORKER BEGAN TELLING US ABOUT a cranberry-glazed pork roast he had recently been served at a friend's house, we were immediately all ears. Mild pork, much like turkey, is perfect paired with sweet-tart cranberries, and using the cranberries as a way to not only dress up a simple roast but also infuse the meat with flavor sounded like a great idea. While the particular version he had tasted wasn't much of a success (with canned cranberry sauce pooling around a ghostly beige roast), we were inspired to come up with our own recipe.

A little research into existing recipes didn't turn up much promise. Most, similar to what our colleague had come across, began with a can of jellied cranberry sauce mixed with frozen cranberries and broth or water. This mixture was simply poured over a roast and baked. The results were almost predictably wan, dry meat and under-developed sauces. We felt confident we could develop our own version, boasting pork that was juicy and tender

paired with a jammy cranberry sauce offering bright cranberry flavor.

We started with a center-cut pork loin roast, which we purchased with its fat cap intact. We knew from experience that once rendered, the fat would melt into the roast, keeping it moist and infusing it with flavor. But for our lighter recipe, the typical ¼-inch-thick fat cap was just too much. We trimmed it back to ⅛ inch, which would still help keep our roast moist throughout cooking. To encourage the fat to render, we cut a crosshatch pattern into the layer of fat.

Our first step was getting color on the roast. We tried browning the roast in a skillet, as we often do with pork roasts, before moving it to the oven to cook through. This worked fine, but we missed the ease of our trial recipes (failed though they were), for which we simply combined the ingredients and popped it all in the oven. Maybe we could use the cranberry glaze to our advantage. In an effort to maintain similar simplicity, we tried basting the roast with the canned cranberry mixture, thinking it would caramelize and brown the roast. That was a bust: The thin sauce ran off the roast as fast as we could spoon it on. For our next go-round, we tried putting the sauced pork in a hotter oven. We typically roast a pork loin at a gentle 325 degrees, but we wondered if we couldn't crank it up in this case to 425 degrees since we had the moisture from the sauce to protect our meat. We gave it a shot, and voilà! The fat cap browned and blistered beautifully, allowing us to skip the usual skillet sear.

For the glaze, tasters demanded more berry texture and flavor, so we tested various combinations of jellied cranberry sauce, whole berry cranberry sauce, and cranberry juice. A few tests revealed the jellied cranberry sauce added minimal flavor, just loads of sugar, so we cut it. Tasters gave the thumbs-up to whole berry cranberry sauce, which lent texture and a truer cranberry flavor. Sweetened cranberry juice was a better choice than the commonly used chicken broth, and reducing the double-cranberry mixture intensified the flavor. A little cornstarch gave it the right consistency, turning the sauce into a glaze that would adhere to the pork.

Now we had good cranberry flavor, but the glaze was ending up too sweet. To create better balance, we tried adding ingredients we'd seen in other cranberry pork recipes. Baking spices were overwhelming, and orange peel distracted from our goal of a pure cranberry flavor. Bottled barbecue sauce was too smoky, but it did set us on the right path. A mix of ketchup, Dijon mustard,

CRANBERRY PORK LOIN

and vinegar cut through the sweetness nicely and gave the sauce a bit of tang. The addition of garlic and thyme rounded it out.

Still, something was missing. We tried stirring in fresh berries, but tasters agreed they were too acidic. Seeking a less assertive tartness, we tried dried cranberries instead. These berries plumped in the simmering sauce and added bright pockets of tart chew. The sauce snapped into focus with a final addition of 2 tablespoons of brown sugar. We placed the pork in a baking pan, poured the sauce around it, and roasted it until the top rendered and browned. We opened the oven just once, to spoon some of the thickened sauce over the top of the roast, and then continued to cook the pork through. After a 15-minute rest, our perfectly juicy pork loin with jammy sweet-tart cranberry sauce was ready for the table.

Cranberry Pork Loin

SERVES 8

If the pork is enhanced (see at right), do not brine. If brining the pork, do not season with salt in step 1. We found that leaving a ⅛-inch-thick layer of fat on top of the roast is ideal; if your roast has a thicker fat cap, trim it to be about ⅛ inch thick. For the best texture, use whole berry cranberry sauce, not jellied cranberry sauce. Avoid unsweetened cranberry juice in this recipe—cranberry juice cocktail will work just fine.

    1 (3-pound) boneless center-cut pork loin roast,
       trimmed, brined if desired (see page 61)
       Salt and pepper
    2 garlic cloves, minced
    2 teaspoons minced fresh thyme
    1 teaspoon canola oil
    1 (16-ounce) can whole berry cranberry sauce
 1½ cups plus 2 tablespoons cranberry juice
    1 cup dried cranberries
    3 tablespoons ketchup
    2 tablespoons light brown sugar
    1 tablespoon Dijon mustard
    1 teaspoon white vinegar
    1 tablespoon cornstarch

1. Adjust an oven rack to the upper-middle position and heat the oven to 425 degrees. Pat the pork loin dry with paper towels and season with ¼ teaspoon salt and

TRIPLE CRANBERRY WHAMMY

CRANBERRY SAUCE
Whole berry cranberry sauce provides the backbone for our sauce/glaze.

CRANBERRY JUICE
Cranberry juice reinforces the berry flavor.

DRIED CRANBERRIES
Dried cranberries hold their shape and add concentrated bursts of tartness.

⅛ teaspoon pepper. Following the photo on page 178, score the fat on top of the roast in a crosshatch pattern at ½-inch intervals.

2. Combine the garlic, thyme, and oil in a large sauce-pan over medium-high heat and cook until fragrant, about 30 seconds. Stir in the cranberry sauce, 1½ cups of the cranberry juice, dried cranberries, ketchup, sugar, mustard, and vinegar and bring to a simmer. Reduce the heat to medium-low and cook until thickened slightly, about 5 minutes. Whisk the remaining 2 tablespoons cranberry juice and cornstarch together in a bowl, then whisk into the sauce and simmer until thickened, 1 to 2 minutes.

3. Place the pork, fat side up, in a 13 by 9-inch baking dish. Pour the sauce around the pork and roast until the top of the pork is golden brown, about 45 minutes. Spoon the sauce over the pork and continue to cook until the meat registers 140 to 145 degrees on an instant-read thermometer, 15 to 25 minutes longer.

4. Transfer the roast to a carving board, tent loosely with foil, and let rest for 15 minutes. Transfer the sauce to a serving bowl and cover to keep warm. Cut the roast crosswise into thin slices and serve, passing the sauce separately.

PER SERVING: Cal 480; Fat 16g; Sat fat 5g; Chol 115mg; Carb 47g; Protein 35g; Fiber 2g; Sodium 290mg

GARLIC PORK ROAST

BONELESS PORK LOIN IS A GREAT OPTION WHEN IT comes to choosing a low-fat dinner, but its mild, lean meat garners a lot more appeal when prepared with bright or bold flavorings. We had just developed a sweet-tart cranberry-glazed pork roast (see page 101), so next we wanted a pork roast that had a more savory profile. Garlic is one of our favorite choices for adding a big hit of flavor without many added calories or fat, so we decided to put our focus there. With a little research, we uncovered three basic techniques for uniting pork and garlic: rubbing a garlic paste on a raw roast, brushing garlic butter on a cooked roast, and putting pungent slivers of raw garlic into the meat before cooking it. A few quick tests proved none of these methods provided enough garlic flavor. We were after a recipe that infused every bite of our pork loin with the sweet, mellow essence of garlic, yet without tasting raw or overly bracing.

First, we settled on how to prepare and cook the pork. The test kitchen has plenty of experience roasting boneless pork loin: Score the fat (so it renders during cooking), sear the meat on the stovetop for flavorful browning, then roast gently (in a 325-degree oven) on a rack to ensure moist, tender meat. We also have a technique we like for adding flavor throughout a roast: Butterfly the loin (cutting it open like a folded business letter), layer on a seasoning component, then roll and tie the meat into a cylinder to create a spiral of flavor throughout.

We began making our garlic pork roast by mashing several cloves of minced garlic with oil, salt, and pepper, then we spread the mixture on the butterflied pork, rolled, and roasted it. The garlic was so strong it burned. To soften its bite, we tried cooking the garlic with oil on the stovetop until it was soft and golden, then spreading it on our roast, but this muted the garlic almost entirely. Was there no middle ground?

We knew that toasting whole, unpeeled cloves in a dry skillet tames the intensity and enhances their nutty flavor. So for our next test we toasted a full dozen cloves until the exteriors were browned, then peeled, minced, and again mixed the garlic with a scant amount of oil, salt, and pepper to make the paste for the swirl. Inside the roast, the garlic spiral had found its sweet spot—neither too strong nor meek. But tasters demanded that the meat itself taste garlicky.

We often brine meat to season it and keep it juicy. Our gentle cooking method already ensured juicy meat, but we wondered if we could use a "garlic brine" to give the pork more flavor. We added crushed raw garlic cloves to our standard saltwater brine, but the garlic was barely detectable. How could that be? Our science editor reminded us that garlic loses its flavor rapidly when exposed to oxygen, even the oxygen present in water. But there was hope. Oil protects the garlic from oxygen, so if we used oil instead of water, he told us (effectively turning the brine into a marinade), the meat should end up plenty garlicky. Yep, the garlic flavor was far more pronounced when the pork was marinated in garlic and oil. Butterflying the pork before marinating let more of the meat's surface come into contact with the marinade, further intensifying the garlic flavor.

Finishing our roast with garlic butter, one of the methods we came across in our initial testing, still held promise. While slathering our roast with loads of butter was out of the question, we felt just 1 tablespoon could make a big difference in the final result. We tried simply mincing a few of the toasted garlic cloves and tossing them with the melted tablespoon of butter, but the result was a tad too pungent. A few pinches of sugar and a minute in the microwave mellowed out the flavor. We brushed this butter over the cooked roast after it came out of the oven. The extra hit of garlic was exactly what our roast had been missing.

With a triple dose of garlic, our recipe had succeeded where others had failed. This was one Garlic Pork Roast that really lived up to its name.

Garlic Pork Roast

SERVES 8

We found that leaving a ⅛-inch-thick layer of fat on top of the roast is ideal; if your roast has a thicker fat cap, trim it back to be ⅛ inch thick. For easier butterflying, look for a pork roast that is short and wide (7 to 8 inches long and 4 to 5 inches wide). You will need 2 heads of garlic for this recipe.

1	(3-pound) boneless center-cut pork loin roast, trimmed
22	garlic cloves (10 peeled and crushed, 12 unpeeled)
4	teaspoons olive oil
½	teaspoon salt
¾	teaspoon pepper
1½	teaspoons minced fresh thyme
½	teaspoon red pepper flakes
1	tablespoon unsalted butter
¼	teaspoon sugar

1. Following the photos, butterfly the pork roast. Whisk the crushed garlic, 1 teaspoon of the oil, salt, and ¼ teaspoon of the pepper together in a bowl. Transfer the garlic mixture to a large zipper-lock bag, add the pork, seal, and turn to coat thoroughly. Refrigerate the pork for at least 1 hour or up to 24 hours.

2. Toast the unpeeled garlic cloves in a large skillet over medium heat until fragrant and the color deepens slightly, about 8 minutes; set aside. When cool enough to handle, peel the garlic. Mince 10 of the cloves, transfer to a bowl, and add 1 teaspoon more oil, thyme, red pepper flakes, and ¼ teaspoon more pepper. Mash the mixture to a paste and set aside.

3. Adjust an oven rack to the lower-middle position and heat the oven to 325 degrees. Set a wire rack inside a foil-lined rimmed baking sheet and set aside.

4. Remove the roast from the marinade and pat dry with paper towels. Spread the inside surface of the meat with the garlic paste, leaving a ½-inch border on all sides.

BUTTERFLYING A BONELESS PORK LOIN
To expose more surface area to the potent garlic oil, we butterfly the pork loin before marinating it.

1. Place the roast, fat side up, on a cutting board. Starting about 1 inch up from the cutting-board surface, cut through the roast horizontally, stopping about 1½ inches before the edge of the roast.

2. Cut into the thicker half of the roast again, starting about 1 inch from the cutting-board surface and stopping about ½ inch before the edge. Open the pork roast the way you would a letter.

Roll tightly into a cylinder, then tie the roast at 1-inch intervals with kitchen twine. Season the outside of the roast with the remaining ¼ teaspoon pepper.

5. Heat the remaining 2 teaspoons oil in the skillet over medium-high heat until just smoking. Carefully lay the roast in the skillet and cook until well browned on all sides, 6 to 10 minutes, turning as needed. Transfer the roast to the prepared wire rack and roast in the oven until the meat registers 140 to 145 degrees on an instant-read thermometer, 50 to 60 minutes.

6. Meanwhile, mince the remaining 2 toasted garlic cloves and place in a microwave-safe bowl. Add the butter and sugar and microwave on high until the garlic is golden and the butter is melted, about 1 minute, stirring halfway through.

7. Transfer the roast to a carving board and brush with the garlic butter. Tent loosely with foil and let rest for 15 minutes. Cut the roast crosswise into ½-inch-thick slices and serve.

PER SERVING: Cal 330; Fat 19g; Sat fat 6g; Chol 120mg; Carb 2g; Protein 36g; Fiber 0g; Sodium 240mg

BROILED SALMON WITH PINEAPPLE SALSA

FISH & SHELLFISH

M = TEST KITCHEN MAKEOVER

BROILED SALMON

SEAFOOD IS A GREAT CHOICE WHEN YOU'RE TRYING to eat more healthfully, and salmon in particular gets a lot of attention since it is an excellent source of heart-healthy Omega-3 fatty acids. We love salmon's naturally rich flavor, and when it's pan-seared, the textural contrast between the crisp, golden crust and the moist flesh inside is unbeatable. However, proper pan-searing, though easy and fast, typically requires a good amount of oil. Under the high heat of the broiler, could salmon fillets achieve a similarly crisp crust without the need for so much added oil and fat? We wanted to come up with a fast broiled salmon recipe with succulent flesh topped with a crisp crust that boasted plenty of flavor, appealing texture, and visual appeal.

Adding a good slather of oil (alone, as a vinaigrette, or as a marinade) would of course help create a crisp crust, but additional oil was a nonstarter. Topping the salmon with a spice rub seemed like our best route for adding bold flavor and simultaneously helping to form the crust. After some initial testing, we settled on a combination of coriander, ginger, garlic powder, salt, and pepper, with a touch of allspice to round it out. Tasters were happy with the flavor of the rub, but in the short amount of time the fish needed to cook through using our broiling method (about eight minutes), there was little crust to speak of, and the spice rub was a bit dry and powdery.

We needed something to help speed up the caramelization. Brown sugar was our first thought. After a few tests, tasters agreed they liked the balancing, slightly maple-y sweetness the brown sugar added to the bold spice rub, but we weren't satisfied with the level of caramelization—we weren't getting the crisp crust we hoped for, and the spices still tasted powdery.

What about honey? We brushed the salmon lightly with honey, sprinkled on the spices (we kept a touch of brown sugar), and placed the salmon under the broiler—finally, we saw some progress. The honey caramelized quickly under the broiler, and better yet, it helped solve the problem of the powdery spices. As the honey bubbled under the heat, it quickly cooked the spices, creating a unified caramelized crust. We tested various amounts of honey and settled on 1 teaspoon per salmon fillet. Any more than that and the honey pooled and ran off the salmon, taking our spice rub with it.

We weren't finished yet. We kept running into one nagging problem with our new honey technique: The honey was really difficult to spread on the salmon. We didn't want to heat the honey; this would require another pot, and we didn't want to spread a warm mixture on the fish and affect the cooking. The answer was simply stirring some water into the honey to thin it. We found that just ¼ teaspoon of water stirred into the honey made the application process surprisingly easier; any more prevented the honey from sticking to the salmon.

We had made real progress, but we were still troubled by a few powdery pockets where the spice rub had not cooked in the honey. We reconsidered the idea of adding oil to the fish. We tried lightly spraying the salmon with vegetable oil spray—a far cry from brushing it on—and this did the trick. Just a light coating ensured that no dry bits remained, and it added negligible fat. Our salmon was now a deep golden color, with a flavorful crisp crust and moist fish beneath.

Finally, we turned our attention to accompaniments. We wanted something light to top the fish, and we came up with a few quick salsas that offered a lot of appeal in terms of ease and fresh flavor. We started with pineapple and added a bit of jalapeño for a kick; lime juice added punch and acidity, and cilantro added a fresh finish. We developed a second salsa with mango in lieu of the pineapple, and a third with honeydew and radishes. This summer, simple broiled salmon is sure to become a weeknight favorite.

Broiled Salmon with Pineapple Salsa
SERVES 4

We find it easiest to buy fresh pineapple that has already been peeled and cored, but you can also buy a whole pineapple and prepare it yourself (see page 107); you will need a little less than half of a medium pineapple for this salsa. To make this dish spicier, add the chile seeds. If you can't find skinless salmon at the store, you can easily remove the skin yourself, following the photos on page 107.

SALSA
- 7 **ounces peeled and cored fresh pineapple, chopped medium (about 1¼ cups) (see page 107)**
- 1 **scallion, sliced thin**
- ½ **jalapeño chile, stemmed, seeded, and minced**
- 4 **teaspoons fresh lime juice**
- 1 **teaspoon minced fresh cilantro**
  Salt and pepper

FISH

4 teaspoons honey

¼ teaspoon water

1 teaspoon light brown sugar

¾ teaspoon ground coriander

½ teaspoon ground ginger

½ teaspoon garlic powder

½ teaspoon pepper

¼ teaspoon salt

¼ teaspoon ground allspice

4 (6-ounce) skinless center-cut salmon fillets,
about 1½ inches thick

Vegetable oil spray

1. FOR THE SALSA: Combine the pineapple, scallion, jalapeño, lime juice, and cilantro in a bowl and season with salt and pepper to taste. Set aside.

2. FOR THE FISH: Position an oven rack 6 inches from the heating element and heat the broiler. Stir the honey and water together in a bowl. In a second bowl, combine the sugar, coriander, ginger, garlic powder, pepper, salt, and allspice.

3. Pat the salmon fillets dry with paper towels and place them, skinned side down, on a foil-lined rimmed baking sheet. Brush each fillet with the honey. Sprinkle the spice mixture evenly over the salmon and gently press to adhere. Lightly coat the tops of the salmon fillets with vegetable oil spray.

4. Broil until golden, the sides are opaque, and the salmon registers 125 degrees on an instant-read thermometer, 6 to 9 minutes. Transfer the salmon to individual plates and serve with the salsa.

PER SERVING (WILD SALMON): Cal 310; Fat 12g; Sat fat 1.5g; Chol 95mg; Carb 15g; Protein 34g; Fiber 1g; Sodium 220mg

PER SERVING (FARMED SALMON): Cal 370; Fat 19g; Sat fat 3.5g; Chol 100mg; Carb 15g; Protein 34g; Fiber 1g; Sodium 250mg

VARIATIONS

Broiled Salmon with Mango Salsa

Follow the recipe for Broiled Salmon with Pineapple Salsa, substituting 1 mango, peeled and chopped medium, for the pineapple.

PER SERVING (WILD SALMON): Cal 310; Fat 12g; Sat fat 1.5g; Chol 95mg; Carb 17g; Protein 34g; Fiber 1g; Sodium 220mg

PER SERVING (FARMED SALMON): Cal 380; Fat 19g; Sat fat 3.5g; Chol 100mg; Carb 17g; Protein 34g; Fiber 1g; Sodium 250mg

Broiled Salmon with Honeydew and Radish Salsa

You can substitute cantaloupe for the honeydew melon.

Follow the recipe for Broiled Salmon with Pineapple Salsa, substituting 1¼ cups chopped honeydew melon for the pineapple, 3 chopped radishes for the jalapeño, and 4 teaspoons fresh lemon juice for the lime juice.

PER SERVING (WILD SALMON): Cal 290; Fat 11g; Sat fat 1.5g; Chol 95mg; Carb 13g; Protein 34g; Fiber 1g; Sodium 230mg

PER SERVING (FARMED SALMON): Cal 360; Fat 19g; Sat fat 3.5g; Chol 100mg; Carb 13g; Protein 34g; Fiber 1g; Sodium 260mg

NOTES FROM THE TEST KITCHEN

HOW TO SKIN A SALMON FILLET

1. Using the tip of a boning knife (or sharp chef's knife), begin to cut the skin away from the fish at one corner of the fillet.

2. When there is enough skin exposed, grasp the skin firmly with a paper towel, hold it taut, and carefully cut the flesh off the skin.

CUTTING PINEAPPLE FOR FRUIT SALSA

1. After trimming off the bottom and top of the pineapple, set the fruit on its bottom and cut off the skin in strips, top to bottom, with a sharp knife.

2. Quarter the pineapple lengthwise, then cut the tough core from each quarter. The pineapple can then be chopped.

FISH EN COCOTTE

WE LIKE TO PREPARE FISH IN A VARIETY OF WAYS, from baking and steaming to pan-searing, grilling, and oven-roasting. While the best method might depend on the variety of fish, they all have one trait in common: they tend to cook fairly quickly. And fish cooked for an extended period of time usually winds up dry. That said, we have had a lot of recent success in the test kitchen cooking chicken, lamb, beef, even eggs, *en cocotte* (roasting in a covered pot in a low oven), and we wondered if the method might work well for fish.

Cooking en cocotte is a classic French method similar to braising. The meat (or eggs) is cooked in a covered pot low and slow, but unlike in a braise, it cooks in its own juice rather than in liquid that has been added to the pot. The method results in ultra-tender meat with concentrated, undiluted flavor. Adding a few choice ingredients to the pot with the meat means an entrée and accompanying sauce or relish can be ready at the same time. As a bonus, cooking en cocotte requires only a minimum of added fat, and it's a fairly simple and mostly hands-off cooking process. We were skeptical this technique would translate to fish, but given all its positive attributes, we decided to head into the kitchen to find out just how far we could push the limits of cooking en cocotte.

We decided to focus our attention on two meaty fish with promise for our slow-cooking method: halibut and swordfish. We started testing with halibut, and we settled on steaks rather than fillets, assuming a thicker cut would fare better over the long haul in the oven. Since the steaks we came across varied considerably in size (depending on the weight of the particular fish), we made sure to inspect the steaks in the fish case and choose two that were closest in size. This ensured that our steaks would cook at the same rate. Cutting off the cartilage and small bones found at the end of the halibut steaks ensured they would fit neatly in the pot (and lowered the chances of bones ending up on our dinner plate).

Test kitchen experience with cooking meat en cocotte had taught us to sear the meat first to develop flavor and seal in the juice, so we did the same for our halibut steaks. After searing them quickly in a Dutch oven, just until they got some color, we set them aside and added our aromatics and a few other ingredients that would infuse the fish steaks with flavor and serve as an accompaniment to the fish. Tasters agreed that a simple combination of olive oil, garlic, and tomatoes would best complement the lean, mildly flavored halibut. After removing the halibut from the pot, we pan-roasted sliced garlic in extra-virgin olive oil to draw out its flavor, and once the garlic was golden brown, we stirred in some cherry tomatoes and placed the halibut on top. We then put the covered pot in a 250-degree oven, where the fish took about 40 minutes to cook through. As the fish cooked, the tomatoes began to break down, releasing their juice and helping to build a flavorful sauce, just as we'd hoped.

When we uncovered the pot, we were happy to find that the combination of the low oven temperature, the moist-heat environment, and the right cut of fish gave us results that were juicy and tender and infused with flavor with a minimum of work. A few additional tests proved that the ideal size of the steaks was between 10 and 12 inches in length and roughly 1¼ inches thick, and pressing a large piece of foil over the pot before covering it further ensured a tight seal in the oven.

But still, we wondered if we could improve on and streamline the process even further: Was it really necessary to sear the fish steaks? For our next test we skipped the searing and proceeded as we had before. Happily, we got just what we wanted: perfectly cooked halibut that flaked apart into large moist chunks. By not searing the fish, we were able to cut the amount of oil, giving us the flexibility to stir a tablespoon of oil into the sauce before serving. This went a long way toward enriching the flavor of our finished dish. For a final hit of bold flavor, we added some capers, thyme, and red pepper flakes.

Next we turned our attention to the swordfish. Swordfish has a relatively strong flavor, so we knew it could stand up to a boldly flavored sauce. Chermoula, a traditional Moroccan sauce or paste used as a marinade for fish, seemed like a good choice. Chermoula typically consists of generous amounts of cilantro, lemon, garlic, and olive oil, so we started there. Since carrots work well with those flavors, we decided to incorporate some into our dish. After sautéing a couple of shredded carrots, we added the chermoula ingredients to the pot and nestled the swordfish on top. When the fish was done, we transferred it to a platter and spooned the sauce on top. This recipe went over as well as the halibut, so we went further and came up with a couple more variations, one for the halibut and another for the swordfish.

Elegant enough for a dinner party, yet simple enough for a weeknight meal, these dishes were so flavorful and easy (not to mention healthy), we knew they'd become a regular addition to our cooking repertoire.

SWORDFISH EN COCOTTE WITH CARROTS AND CHERMOULA

Halibut en Cocotte with Cherry Tomatoes

SERVES 4

Make sure your halibut steaks are of equal size to ensure even cooking; if your steaks are thicker or thinner than 1¼ inches, adjust the cooking time as needed. We prefer to use 2 full halibut steaks (see below), which we trim before cooking; if you can find only belly steaks, you will need 4 steaks. If using full steaks, see photos below about removing the skin and serving.

 2 tablespoons extra-virgin olive oil
 2 garlic cloves, sliced thin
 ⅛ teaspoon red pepper flakes
 12 ounces cherry tomatoes (about 2 cups), quartered
 1 tablespoon drained capers, rinsed
 1 teaspoon minced fresh thyme
 2 (1¼-pound) halibut steaks, each about 1¼ inches thick and 10 to 12 inches long, trimmed of cartilage at both ends (see photos)
    Salt and pepper

1. Adjust an oven rack to the lowest position and heat the oven to 250 degrees. Cook 1 tablespoon of the oil, garlic, and pepper flakes in a large Dutch oven over medium-low heat until the garlic is light golden brown, 2 to 4 minutes. Off the heat, stir in the tomatoes, capers, and thyme.

2. Pat the halibut steaks dry with paper towels and season with ⅛ teaspoon salt and ⅛ teaspoon pepper. Lay the halibut on top of the tomatoes. Press a large sheet of foil over the pot to seal, then cover tightly with the lid. Transfer the pot to the oven and cook until the fish flakes apart when gently prodded with a paring knife, 35 to 40 minutes.

3. Gently transfer the halibut to a platter and tent loosely with foil. Simmer the tomato mixture over medium-high heat until thickened slightly, about 2 minutes. Off the heat, stir in the remaining 1 tablespoon oil and season with salt and pepper to taste. Spoon the sauce over the halibut and serve.

PER SERVING: Cal 300; Fat 12g; Sat fat 1.5g; Chol 65mg; Carb 4g; Protein 42g; Fiber 1g; Sodium 260mg

VARIATION

Halibut en Cocotte with Fennel and Saffron

Pernod is a French anise-flavored liqueur available at most liquor stores. You can substitute dry sherry for the Pernod; however, the flavor of the sauce will be quite different.

Follow the recipe for Halibut en Cocotte with Cherry Tomatoes, adding 1 thinly sliced fennel bulb and a pinch

---

NOTES FROM THE TEST KITCHEN

THREE KINDS OF HALIBUT STEAKS

Most halibut steaks consist of four pieces of meat attached to a central bone (left). It is not uncommon, however, to encounter a steak with just two pieces, both located on the same side of the center bone (center). These steaks were cut from the center of the halibut, adjacent to the belly cavity. The belly, in effect, separates the two halves. We slightly prefer full steaks with four meat sections; each full steak serves two people. If you can find only the belly steaks, you will have to purchase four steaks instead of two to make the recipe. Avoid very small, boneless steaks (right) cut entirely free from the bone and each other. Most boneless steaks won't serve even one person.

| **FULL STEAK** | **BELLY CUT** | **BONELESS STEAK** |
| 4 sections | 2 sections | 1 section |

TRIMMING AND SERVING FULL HALIBUT STEAKS

1. Before cooking, cut off the cartilage at each end of the steaks to ensure they fit neatly in the pot and to diminish the chances that the small bones located there will end up on your dinner plate.

2. Before serving, remove the skin from the cooked steaks and separate the quadrants of meat from the bone by slipping a spatula or knife gently between them.

saffron to the pot after the garlic has lightly browned in step 1; cover and cook until the fennel is tender, 8 to 10 minutes, then continue with step 2. Stir in 1 tablespoon Pernod when simmering the tomato mixture in step 3.

PER SERVING: Cal 320; Fat 12g; Sat fat 1.5g; Chol 65mg; Carb 8g; Protein 43g; Fiber 3g; Sodium 290mg

Swordfish en Cocotte with Carrots and Chermoula

SERVES 4

Chermoula is a traditional Moroccan sauce made by pureeing generous amounts of cilantro, garlic, and lemon. Make sure your swordfish steaks are of equal size to ensure even cooking; if your steaks are thicker or thinner than 1¼ inches, be sure to adjust the cooking time as needed.

¾ cup packed fresh cilantro leaves

2 tablespoons extra-virgin olive oil

2 tablespoons fresh lemon juice

4 garlic cloves, minced

1 teaspoon ground cumin

1 teaspoon sweet paprika

¼ teaspoon cayenne pepper

Salt

2 carrots, peeled and shredded

4 (6-ounce) swordfish steaks, about 1¼ inches thick

Black pepper

1. Adjust an oven rack to the lowest position and heat the oven to 250 degrees. Process the cilantro, 1 tablespoon of the oil, lemon juice, garlic, cumin, paprika, cayenne, and ¼ teaspoon salt in a food processor until smooth, about 20 seconds.

2. Heat the remaining 1 tablespoon oil in a large Dutch oven over medium-low heat until shimmering. Add the carrots, cover, and cook, stirring occasionally, until softened, 4 to 6 minutes. Off the heat, stir in the cilantro mixture.

3. Pat the swordfish steaks dry with paper towels and season with ⅛ teaspoon salt and ⅛ teaspoon black pepper. Lay the swordfish on top of the carrot mixture. Press a large sheet of foil over the pot to seal, then cover tightly with the lid. Transfer the pot to the oven and cook until the swordfish flakes apart when gently prodded with a paring knife, 35 to 40 minutes.

4. Gently transfer the swordfish to a platter. Season the carrot mixture with salt and black pepper to taste, spoon it over the swordfish, and serve.

PER SERVING: Cal 300; Fat 14g; Sat fat 3g; Chol 65mg; Carb 6g; Protein 34g; Fiber 2g; Sodium 400mg

VARIATION

Swordfish en Cocotte with Shallots, Cucumber, and Mint

Follow the recipe for Swordfish en Cocotte with Carrots and Chermoula, substituting ¾ cup packed fresh mint leaves and ¼ cup packed fresh parsley leaves for the cilantro and 3 thinly sliced shallots for the carrots. Omit the paprika and add 1 peeled, seeded, and thinly sliced cucumber to the pot with the herb mixture in step 2.

PER SERVING: Cal 300; Fat 14g; Sat fat 3g; Chol 65mg; Carb 8g; Protein 35g; Fiber 1g; Sodium 380mg

EASY BAKED COD AND POTATOES

WE HAD JUST DEVELOPED A HANDFUL OF RECIPES FOR fish en cocotte (see pages 110–111), which allowed us to prepare fish and an accompanying sauce in one pot, but we wondered if we could go a step further and develop a recipe that would give us fish and side dish at once. We were after flavorful results from only a handful of ingredients and an easy one-pot method. After a little research, we discovered a few dishes from the northern Italian coast, where there is an abundance of fresh fish, herbs, and vegetables. These recipes all called for simple preparations and allowed the handful of fresh ingredients to speak for themselves. One dish in particular caught our attention. Fresh fish is cooked over a bed of thinly sliced potatoes and seasoned simply with salt, pepper, fresh parsley, and lemon—and, unfortunately for our light and healthy cooking, a copious ⅓ cup of oil. We gave a few of these recipes a test run and loved how just a few ingredients came together to produce a final dish that was far more than the sum of its parts. We had to wonder if we could achieve similar results without all that extra fat. Since we were in New England, we quickly settled on cod, an easy-to-find local favorite. We wanted moist, flaky cod fillets on a bed of perfectly cooked potatoes, and both would need to be complemented by a simple yet discriminating combination of flavors and seasoning, all the while keeping calories and fat in check.

Starting from the bottom up, our first question was what variety of potato would work best in this situation. Over the years we have learned that choosing the right potato can make or break a recipe. There are three basic types: high-starch/low-moisture potatoes (like russet and Idaho), medium-starch potatoes (Yukon Gold, Yellow Finn, and purple Peruvian), and low-starch/high-moisture potatoes (red-skinned potatoes). Because of their low-starch/high-moisture makeup, we settled on red potatoes since they would hold their shape well and also retain a good amount of moisture throughout cooking, which kept them tender.

As with our fish en cocotte recipes, we knew that choosing fish fillets of equal size and thickness would be crucial here as well, so we carefully surveyed the options in the fish case before making our selections. Because this was a one-dish meal cooked in the oven, we needed all four pieces to cook evenly and at the same rate.

With fish and potatoes in hand, we turned our attention to our cooking method. Layering the raw potato slices in a casserole dish, topping them with the fish fillets, and sliding the dish into the oven until the fish cooked through, however, was an out-and-out failure—the potatoes were far from tender and clearly needed a head start. For our next test we started by layering the potatoes in the dish as we had before, but this time we let them roast for 30 minutes on their own, just until they were tender, before adding the fish. After placing the fish on top of the potatoes and returning the dish to the oven, we continued to cook until the potatoes were completely tender and the fish flaked apart, which took about 20 to 25 minutes more.

This method worked far better, and tasters particularly liked the textural variation in the potatoes, with their combination of crispy edges where the potatoes had been exposed directly to the heat of the oven and tender, moist interiors where they had cooked underneath other potatoes or tucked under the fish.

Up to this point we had been working with potatoes cut ¼ inch thick. We tested potatoes cut to varying thicknesses to see if we could improve the texture further and, if possible, minimize cooking time. We tried potatoes cut ⅛ inch thick, ¼ inch thick, and ½ inch thick. The potatoes cut ½ inch thick did not crisp well on the edges, sacrificing the appealing texture that tasters had liked so much, and the thinnest potatoes crisped

too much. We decided to stick with ¼ inch.

It was time to add a few key flavors. We started with the basics, tossing the potatoes with shallots, garlic, and olive oil (just 2 tablespoons) before cooking, and then simply squeezed fresh lemon juice over the fish just before serving. Tasters noted that while the potatoes had gained some flavor from the garlic and shallots, they still needed another boost, and the fish was fairly bland. For our next test, we reserved some of the garlic to make a *gremolata*, a traditional Italian garnish combining lemon zest, parley, olive oil, and garlic that is often paired with veal and sometimes seafood. We spooned it over the fish just before serving, but the idea didn't win any fans—though it might have worked with a more boldly flavored fish, the raw garlic was too harsh for the delicate cod. However, all was not lost; everyone approved the idea of a fresh herb mixture sprinkled on the fish before serving. After testing a variety of combinations, we ended up with a simple mixture of parsley, lemon juice, lemon zest, and extra-virgin olive oil. This gave the fish just the bright, fresh flavor it needed without much work.

Our recipe was almost there, but something was still missing. Keeping with the Mediterranean theme, we found that tossing a few tablespoons of chopped kalamata olives with the potatoes (and garlic and shallots) punched up flavor and gave the potatoes some character. With that, we knew we had a one-dish, no-fuss meal that was sure to become a weeknight favorite.

Easy Baked Cod and Potatoes

SERVES 4

You can substitute haddock or halibut for the cod. Prepare and assemble all of the ingredients before slicing the potatoes or the potatoes will begin to turn brown (do not store the sliced potatoes in water).

2 tablespoons extra-virgin olive oil
2 tablespoons minced fresh parsley
1 teaspoon grated lemon zest plus 1 teaspoon fresh lemon juice
4 (6-ounce) skinless cod fillets, 1 to 1½ inches thick
  Salt and pepper
1½ pounds large red potatoes (about 3 to 4), sliced ¼ inch thick
4 garlic cloves, minced
2 shallots, sliced thin
2 tablespoons kalamata olives, pitted and chopped

1. Adjust an oven rack to the middle position and heat the oven to 400 degrees. Stir 1 tablespoon of the oil, the parsley, lemon zest, and lemon juice together in a bowl and set aside.

2. Pat the cod fillets dry with paper towels and season with ⅛ teaspoon salt and ⅛ teaspoon pepper. Cover with plastic wrap and refrigerate while preparing the potatoes.

3. Toss the remaining 1 tablespoon oil, potatoes, garlic, shallots, olives, ¼ teaspoon salt, and ⅛ teaspoon pepper together in a large bowl and spread in an even layer in a 13 by 9-inch baking dish. Bake the potatoes until just tender and a paring knife can be slipped into a potato with little resistance, about 30 minutes.

4. Place the cod fillets, skinned side down, on top of the potatoes and bake until the cod flakes apart when gently prodded with a paring knife, 20 to 25 minutes. Spoon the lemon-parsley mixture over the fish and serve.

PER SERVING: Cal 360; Fat 10g; Sat fat 1.5g; Chol 75mg; Carb 32g; Protein 34g; Fiber 3g; Sodium 440 mg

FISH CAKES

MARYLANDERS MAY RAVE ABOUT THEIR CRAB CAKES, but here in New England we love a good cod cake. There is certainly no shortage of recipes, but most we've tried make more of a bread patty or potato cake than fish cake. They are laden with binders that not only mask the flavor of the fish but also pack on unnecessary fat and calories. We set out to develop a recipe for fish cakes that would make a New Englander proud: They would need to be moist, delicate, and tender yet still cohesive, and with seasoning and binding that complemented the clean, subtle flavor of the cod without drowning out the fish or weighing down the cakes.

Initial research turned up two basic approaches to making fish cakes: using cooked cod (usually bound by mashed potatoes) and using raw cod (bound by bread crumbs). After a few tests, tasters agreed that the cakes made with cooked cod and potatoes were heavy and the fish was overwhelmed by the potato flavor—not the clean, light cakes we were after. They were also much more time-consuming to prepare since we had to pre-cook the cod and potatoes separately before forming and browning the cakes. The few recipes we found that used raw cod showed more promise—they were light and cleaner-tasting, but still, they were not without faults,

including the fact that they tended to fall apart in the pan (and those that didn't fall apart relied on far too much binder). But at least it was a starting point.

The next issue was how to prepare the raw cod before forming the cakes. Early tests told us a combination of textures was best. Finely chopped cod helped bind the cakes (and kept the fish flavor at the forefront), and larger, bite-size chunks added heartiness and visual appeal. We started with 1 pound of skinless cod fillets and cut half of it into 1-inch chunks, then tossed them into the food processor and pulsed them until finely minced. We chopped the other half by hand. This worked well, but then we realized we could eliminate a step and pulse it all in the food processor for just four pulses and get similar results, since so few pulses produced an inconsistent texture anyway—annoying for some applications but exactly what we were looking for in this recipe.

As for a binder, we wanted to use as little as possible. We had already ruled out mashed potatoes, as they created a pasty, heavy cake and required precooking. The other usual suspects didn't win fans either. Saltines were a pain to smash into small enough crumbs, and fresh bread crumbs absorbed too much moisture and created doughy, wet pockets in and around the cod—we wanted fish cakes, not dough balls. We settled on finely ground dry bread crumbs. They didn't have an overwhelming flavor, they were easy to mix in, and they didn't mask the texture of the mild cod. The trickiest part was knowing when to stop. Fish cakes need just enough binder to hold together, but not so much that the filler takes over the flavor. We started with 1 cup of dry bread crumbs and eventually worked our way down to just ¼ cup. This gave us tender cakes with the cod flavor taking center stage. Any less and the cakes could not hold their shape.

Because cod is a lean, flaky fish, we knew we would need some moisture to supplement the bread crumbs and keep the cakes from falling apart. We tried a range of low-fat options. Low-fat yogurt and buttermilk were too wet and added too much moisture, and light sour cream and cream cheese added unwanted tang. Finally we tried light mayonnaise, which provided the right amount of moisture but came across as somewhat sweet. Some Dijon mustard provided just the right sharpness to balance it out. Two tablespoons of mayonnaise combined with 4 teaspoons of mustard worked perfectly. To further help the binding, instead of the whole egg that most recipes call for, we added a single egg white and found that's all it took to keep our cod cakes together.

FISH CAKES

Careful mixing proved a must to avoid a pasty, mushy cake. We found a rubber spatula worked best, and we used it in a folding, rather than stirring, motion. Handling the mixture as little as possible was also key in keeping our cakes tender and light yet cohesive.

When it came time to cook our cakes, we still had some trouble making them hold together. We didn't want to add more binder, so we tried chilling the cakes before cooking, a technique we've used successfully for crab and shrimp cakes. Just half an hour in the refrigerator made a huge difference. We also tried different cooking methods. After baking, pan-frying, and broiling, we settled on sautéing our cod cakes in a nonstick skillet over medium-high heat. It was fast but still gave us complete control over how brown and crisp the cakes got. Dredging them lightly in flour before putting them in the pan helped create a crust and prevented sticking.

For seasonings, tasters preferred simplicity—some minced shallot and parsley, as well as lemon juice, accented the delicate cod and brought out its fresh flavor. Served with our lightened-up Tartar Sauce, these fish cakes we would happily put head-to-head against the best of the crab cakes.

Fish Cakes

SERVES 4

Be sure to use raw cod here; do not substitute cooked cod. Don't overprocess the cod in step 1 or the cakes will have a pasty texture. Serve with Tartar Sauce (recipe follows), if desired.

- 1 **pound skinless cod fillets, cut into 1-inch pieces**
- ¼ **cup plain dry bread crumbs**
- 1 **large egg white**
- 1 **shallot, minced (about 3 tablespoons)**
- 3 **tablespoons minced fresh parsley**
- 2 **tablespoons light mayonnaise**
- 4 **teaspoons Dijon mustard**
- 1 **tablespoon fresh lemon juice**
- ¼ **teaspoon salt**
- ⅛ **teaspoon pepper**
- ¼ **cup unbleached all-purpose flour**
- 2 **tablespoons canola oil**
  Lemon wedges, for serving

1. Pulse half of the cod fillets in a food processor until there is an even mix of finely minced and coarsely chopped pieces, about 4 pulses. Transfer the processed cod to a large bowl and repeat with the remaining cod. Sprinkle the bread crumbs over the cod.

2. Whisk the egg white, shallot, parsley, mayonnaise, mustard, lemon juice, salt, and pepper together in a bowl until combined. Using a rubber spatula, gently fold the mixture into the cod and bread crumbs until the cod mixture just holds together.

3. Divide the cod mixture into 4 equal portions and shape each into a round cake, about 3 inches across and 1½ inches high. Transfer to a plate, cover with plastic wrap, and refrigerate for at least 30 minutes or up to 24 hours.

4. Spread the flour in a shallow dish. Dredge the fish cakes in the flour and shake off the excess. Heat the oil in a 12-inch nonstick skillet over medium-high heat until shimmering. Carefully lay the chilled fish cakes in the skillet and cook until well browned on both sides, 8 to 10 minutes, flipping them halfway through. Carefully transfer the fish cakes to a platter and serve with the lemon wedges.

PER SERVING: Cal 240; Fat 10g; Sat fat 1g; Chol 50mg; Carb 13g; Protein 23g; Fiber 1g; Sodium 460mg

Tartar Sauce

MAKES ABOUT ½ CUP

This is a lighter version of the classic sauce for fried seafood. If cornichons are not available, substitute dill pickles.

- ¼ **cup light mayonnaise**
- 2 **tablespoons low-fat sour cream**
- 4 **large cornichons, minced (about 2 tablespoons), plus 2 teaspoons cornichon juice**
- 2 **tablespoons minced red onion**
- 1 **tablespoon drained capers, rinsed and minced**
- ⅛ **teaspoon pepper**
  Water

Mix the mayonnaise, sour cream, cornichons, cornichon juice, onion, capers, and pepper together in a bowl, adding water as needed to thin the sauce. Cover and refrigerate until the flavors blend, about 30 minutes. (The sauce will keep in an airtight container in the refrigerator for up to 1 day.)

PER 2-TABLESPOON SERVING: Cal 50; Fat 4g; Sat fat 0.5g; Chol 5mg; Carb 3g; Protein 0g; Fiber 0g; Sodium 210mg

FISH STICKS

TEST KITCHEN
MAKEOVER

FRIED FISH STICKS HAVE A LOT OF APPEAL NO MATTER how old you are. A crunchy coating surrounding light, flaky fingers of fish has great textural contrast, and the mild, toasty flavor of the fried coating wins over just about everyone. But just because it's fish, it doesn't make it good for you. A plate of typical (deep-fried) fish sticks can tally nearly 560 calories and 30 grams of fat, and that's not including any tartar sauce. Meanwhile, the baked fish sticks we've had, whether homemade or from the supermarket freezer section, are usually a combination of overcooked fish surrounded by a soggy coating sorely lacking in flavor. We wanted to develop a recipe for fish sticks that had a crispy, fresh-tasting coating surrounding tender and flaky fish and was good enough to make anyone put down unhealthy fried fish sticks in favor of our just-as-good and better-for-you version.

Our first task was to select the best fish for the job. After we ran a few tests following a working recipe, tasters immediately ruled out dense varieties such as swordfish since its firm flesh didn't offer the right flaky contrast to the crust. Thin fillets such as flounder and sole were out—they ended up overcooked long before the coating was done and they had a tendency to break apart. Flaky cod, haddock, and halibut were perfectly tender after baking, and they required enough time in the oven that we would have a fighting chance to develop a crisp crust. We cut the fish fillets into sticks that measured about ¾ inch thick and 3 to 4 inches long, the perfect size for finger food and easy dipping.

With the fish settled, we turned our attention to the coating. We started out by trying the classic breading process—a dip in flour, then egg (in this case egg whites), then bread crumbs—and baking the fish sticks on a baking sheet in a hot oven. This method was a no-go. The breading never turned brown or crisp, the bottoms turned soggy, and the breading tasted stale. We decided to focus on the issue of oven temperature first. Coating aside, we found that baking fish sticks for 8 to 10 minutes at 475 degrees produced the most tender and juicy fish. To encourage browning on the underside of the sticks, we tried coating the baking sheet with a thin film of oil and heating it in the oven before adding the breaded fish, but the bread crumbs merely soaked up the oil and turned greasy. Baking the coated fish sticks on a wire rack set over a baking sheet solved the soggy bottom issue, but what about the top sides? Looking to a trick we'd used successfully for our Easy Chicken Cordon Bleu (page 71), we tried spraying the tops of the sticks lightly with vegetable oil spray. Bingo! Now the top portion of the breading crisped up nicely and had just enough moisture to avoid turning dusty and dry.

Now we were getting the texture we were after, but we still had issues with bland flavor, and the crumbs were still not as golden brown as we would have liked. Then it hit us—why didn't we toast the bread crumbs before breading the fish? We toasted the crumbs in a dry skillet over medium heat until golden (this took less than 10 minutes), then breaded the fish, sprayed the tops with vegetable oil, and baked the sticks on the rack. These fish sticks were a big improvement, with an even golden color and crisp fried texture.

The flavor of the breading still needed help. Adding 2 tablespoons of canola oil to the crumbs gave them a nice "fried" flavor without turning them greasy or adding too many calories. We also tested changing the coating. Store-bought dried bread crumbs were fine as a binder in our Fish Cakes (page 115), but for a coating for our fish sticks they didn't offer much flavor and were too finely ground. Tasters liked both the fresh bread crumbs and Japanese-style panko. In the end we settled on the panko, for its neutral flavor and ultra-crisp texture.

Finally, we focused on fine-tuning the flavor. A combination of garlic powder and cayenne stirred into the flour lent a nice kick. Following the lead of our Cordon Bleu recipe again, we added some Dijon mustard to the egg whites for a little acidity. Thyme helped boost the flavor and added just the right depth. For our dipping sauce, we turned to our lightened Tartar Sauce (page 115) that we had just developed for our Fish Cakes. Now that we had a recipe for easy oven-baked fish sticks, with a perfect crunchy coating and flaky fresh fish within, that tallied only 380 calories and 9 grams of fat per serving, we were confident our days of restaurant fried fish and boxed sticks from the grocer's freezer aisle were over.

MAKEOVER SPOTLIGHT: FISH STICKS

	CALORIES	FAT	SAT FAT	CHOLESTEROL
BEFORE	560	30g	6g	70mg
AFTER	380	9g	0.5g	75mg

Fish Sticks

SERVES 4

Panko, Japanese-style bread crumbs, can be found in the international aisle of the supermarket. You can substitute haddock or halibut for the cod. Serve with Tartar Sauce (page 115), if desired.

- 2 cups panko
- 2 tablespoons canola oil
- ½ cup unbleached all-purpose flour
- 1 teaspoon garlic powder
- ⅛ teaspoon cayenne pepper
- 3 large egg whites
- 1 tablespoon water
- 1 tablespoon Dijon mustard
- 1 teaspoon minced fresh thyme or ¼ teaspoon dried
  Vegetable oil spray
- 1½ pounds skinless cod fillets, cut into ¾-inch-wide
  fingers (see photo)
- ¼ teaspoon salt
- ⅛ teaspoon black pepper

1. Adjust an oven rack to the middle position and heat the oven to 475 degrees. Combine the panko and oil in a 12-inch skillet and, following the photo below,

NOTES FROM THE TEST KITCHEN

TOASTING PANKO

To give panko the crisp crunch of fried crumbs, combine the panko and oil in a skillet and toast over medium heat until deeply golden brown, 8 to 10 minutes.

CUTTING FISH FILLETS INTO STICKS

Fish fillets can vary dramatically in terms of thickness and shape, but do your best to cut them into evenly sized sticks. Using a chef's knife, slice each fillet on the diagonal into strips measuring about ¾ inch thick and 3 to 4 inches long.

toast over medium heat, stirring often, until golden, 8 to 10 minutes. Transfer the crumbs to a shallow dish and let cool slightly.

2. Combine the flour, garlic powder, and cayenne in a second shallow dish. In a third shallow dish, whisk the egg whites, water, mustard, and thyme together.

3. Lightly coat a wire rack with vegetable oil spray and place over a foil-lined rimmed baking sheet. Pat the cod fillets dry with paper towels and season with the salt and black pepper. Working with a few pieces of fish at a time, dredge in the flour and shake off the excess. Coat the fish with the egg white mixture, allowing the excess to drip off. Coat all sides with the toasted crumbs, pressing to help the crumbs adhere.

4. Lay the breaded fish on the prepared wire rack. Lightly coat the fish with vegetable oil spray. Bake until the fish flakes apart when gently prodded with a paring knife, 10 to 12 minutes. Serve.

PER SERVING: **Cal** 380; **Fat** 9g; **Sat fat** 0.5g; **Chol** 75mg; **Carb** 32g; **Protein** 39g; **Fiber** 2g; **Sodium** 450mg

SEARED SHRIMP WITH TOMATO AND AVOCADO

WHEN WE ARE AFTER LIGHTER, HEALTHIER FARE, shrimp are a must-have. They are low in fat, they're easy to find year-round in the grocery's freezer section, and they cook quickly, making them a great weeknight option. Looking for inspiration for a shrimp recipe that would boast fresh, bold flavors without much added fat or calories, we came across a coastal Mexican dish known as *camarones a la plancha*. Fresh shrimp are seared on a hot griddle (the plancha) and topped with a mixture of tomatoes, chiles, cilantro, and lime juice. We wondered if we could capture the flavor of the authentic version here in the test kitchen.

Searing shrimp on a hot griddle produces a well-caramelized exterior and moist, tender interior. This cooking method also preserves the shrimp's plumpness and trademark briny sweetness. In the absence of a plancha, our next-best option was a 12-inch skillet; its large surface area would keep the shrimp from crowding in the pan and steaming, which is a surefire way to prevent caramelization. Using a nonstick pan rather than a traditional one would allow us to cut back on the amount of oil we needed to sear the shrimp.

SEARED SHRIMP WITH TOMATO AND AVOCADO

As for the shrimp themselves, we typically prefer to buy shrimp that are still in their shells. We knew we'd need to peel the shrimp before putting them in the pan; if we left the shells on during cooking, the shrimp would never achieve the proper caramelization. For this simple and light recipe, 1½ pounds of extra-large shrimp seemed just right for serving four people.

Experience had taught us that to achieve the perfect sear, no matter what we were cooking, we would have to add at least a little fat to the pan. Butter was likely to burn and would add a nutty flavor we didn't want in the final dish, so we opted to use oil. To further increase the caramelization of the shrimp, we seasoned them with sugar in addition to salt and pepper before placing them in the pan, a trick we had used with great success when grilling shrimp. Just ⅛ teaspoon of sugar would promote browning and accentuate the shrimp's natural sweetness.

We quickly learned that even in a 12-inch skillet, 1½ pounds of shrimp had to be cooked in two batches or they steamed instead of seared. A few tests proved two minutes was all it took for each batch to achieve a good sear. Once they were cooked, we set the shrimp aside in a bowl covered with foil and moved on to the sauce.

For our sauce, we began with the classic camarones a la plancha components—chopped fresh tomatoes, onions, garlic, jalapeño, lime juice, and cilantro. We knew the sauce would need to come together quickly to ensure that our seared shrimp didn't turn cold. We added our chosen sauce ingredients to the pan and cooked them until the tomatoes broke down slightly, which was just enough time for the flavors to meld. Unfortunately, we ended up with a sauce that was too loose, and tasters complained of the raw texture of the onions. Tasters also agreed that for a dish that should have pizzazz it needed a more assertive flavor.

For an easy fix to the onion issue, we switched to soft-textured scallions. The scallions had an added benefit in that their whites could replace the onion in the sauce and their green tops could serve as a colorful garnish that also lent a fresh hint of onion flavor at the end. To give our sauce the smokiness that typifies foods prepared on a hot plancha, we replaced the fresh jalapeño with canned chipotle chiles in adobo sauce. This gave us the deeper flavor we were after as well as a hint of spiciness.

To reduce the amount of liquid in our sauce, we tested seeding the tomatoes as well as seeding and draining the tomatoes in a colander to further reduce their liquid content. Tasters vastly preferred the sauce with tomatoes that were only seeded; the seeded and drained tomatoes made a sauce that was too dry. We also adjusted the length of time that we cooked the sauce. Instead of giving the tomatoes a chance to release their liquid, we simply warmed the sauce through in the hot pan for a mere minute. Then all we had to do was stir in the shrimp until they were coated in the sauce before transferring it all to a platter to serve. Since our recipe was incredibly lean at this point, we opted to add a touch of richness with the help of a little diced avocado, which we added just before serving. This made for the perfect finishing touch. These shrimp were terrific on their own with a squeeze of lime, and even better served over steamed rice to catch the juice.

Seared Shrimp with Tomato and Avocado
SERVES 4

The cooking times below are for extra-large shrimp. If using smaller or larger shrimp, adjust the cooking time as needed. This dish is fairly spicy; to make it milder, use less chipotle. Serve over steamed rice, if desired.

- 1 pound tomatoes (2 to 3 medium), cored, seeded, and cut into ½-inch pieces
- 6 scallions, white and green parts separated and sliced thin
- ¼ cup minced fresh cilantro
- 3 garlic cloves, minced
- 1 tablespoon fresh lime juice
- 1 teaspoon minced canned chipotle chiles in adobo sauce
  Salt
- 1½ pounds extra-large shrimp (21 to 25 per pound), peeled and deveined (see page 120)
  Pepper
- ⅛ teaspoon sugar
- 4 teaspoons canola oil
- 1 avocado, pitted, peeled, and cut into ½-inch pieces
  Lime wedges, for serving

1. Combine the tomatoes, scallion whites, cilantro, garlic, lime juice, chipotle, and ¼ teaspoon salt in a bowl.

2. Pat the shrimp dry with paper towels and season with ¼ teaspoon salt, ⅛ teaspoon pepper, and sugar. Heat 2 teaspoons of the oil in a 12-inch nonstick skillet over high heat until just smoking. Add half of the shrimp and cook until curled and lightly browned, about 2 minutes.

DEVEINING SHRIMP

Although the vein running along the back of shrimp has no adverse effect on flavor or texture (except especially large, gritty veins), removing it can improve the appearance of the shrimp.

1. After removing the shell, use a paring knife to make a shallow cut along the back of the shrimp so that the vein is exposed.

2. Use the tip of the knife to lift the vein out of the shrimp. Discard the vein by wiping the blade against a paper towel.

3. Transfer the shrimp to a bowl and cover with foil. Repeat with the remaining 2 teaspoons oil and shrimp and transfer to the bowl with the other shrimp.

4. Return the skillet to high heat, add the tomato mixture, and cook until the tomatoes soften slightly, about 1 minute. Off the heat, return the shrimp to the skillet and toss to coat. Transfer the shrimp to a platter, season with salt and pepper to taste, and sprinkle with the scallion greens and avocado. Serve with the lime wedges.

PER SERVING: **Cal** 340; **Fat** 15g; **Sat fat** 2g; **Chol** 260mg; **Carb** 13g; **Protein** 37g; **Fiber** 5g; **Sodium** 560mg

BAKED SCALLOPS

HERE IN THE TEST KITCHEN WE FAVOR PAN-SEARED scallops served with a relish or pan sauce for its ease of preparation and fresh flavor. But we admit, for an indulgent treat, we love scallops baked in a cream sauce. It is a comforting yet indulgent New England dish reminiscent of the classic French *coquilles St. Jacques*, scallops baked with cheese, cream, and buttery bread crumbs. And while easy to make, it is also laden with fat and calories; it is so rich that we usually have to put our forks down after a few bites. We wanted to develop a recipe for perfectly cooked, tender baked scallops prepared in a creamy sauce that tasted indulgent and hinted at richness but didn't weigh us down.

We began our testing by lightening up a basic cream sauce, swapping in low-fat milk for the cream. We added our low-fat milk, leeks, garlic, thyme, and white wine to the baking dish, followed by the scallops, then popped the whole thing into the oven. After a few tests, we knew we had our work cut out for us. While we were encouraged by the tender texture and sweet flavor of the scallops, the sauce was another story. It was thin, watery, and flavorless.

For our next test we precooked our sauce on the stovetop so it could partially reduce; we assumed it would continue to reduce in the oven and reach the proper consistency by the time the scallops were done. After a few minutes on the stovetop, we poured the sauce over the scallops set in an 8-inch casserole dish and baked them in a 450-degree oven for about 15 minutes. The scallops once again looked good, but still, our sauce was too thin.

Maybe using a thickener was a better bet. For our next test, we added a few teaspoons of flour to the pan after sautéing the garlic and thyme, then slowly whisked in the wine and milk. After about a minute our sauce was nicely thickened, so we poured it over the scallops and moved the dish to the oven. By the time the scallops had finished cooking, the sauce wasn't nearly as thin and watery as it had been previously, but it was still a far cry from the thickened sauce that had gone into the oven.

Clearly the issue wasn't just the sauce. The scallops were releasing water as they cooked. For our next test, we made a batch of sauce as usual, but this time we also pressed the scallops dry before placing them in the dish. Once again, our sauce was too thin. We then tried letting the scallops drain for 30 minutes on kitchen towels, but this didn't work much better. We obviously couldn't control how much water the scallops released, so we went back to tweaking our sauce.

Back at the stovetop, for our next test we tried taking thickening the sauce a step too far, overthickening it before we poured it over the scallops. Before going into the oven it didn't look at all like the light yet creamy sauce we were after, but a short stint in the oven and eureka! As the scallops released their moisture, the sauce thinned out to just the right consistency by the time the scallops were cooked through. All it needed before serving was a quick whip with a whisk to incorporate the water the scallops had released. To fine-tune the ratios, a few more tests proved that ¾ cup of milk, ¼ cup of wine, and 1 tablespoon of flour was just right. The length of time we cooked the sauce to overthicken it was crucial as well. Two to three minutes did the trick.

It was time to focus on finessing the flavors of the sauce. Lemon zest and lemon juice added a needed brightness and balance, and a little parsley rounded out the flavors of the dish. Finally, we had a foolproof method for baked scallops that were infused with flavor and perfectly cooked every time, not to mention that they had a smooth, luxurious sauce ready to go.

Baked Scallops with Lemon and Herbs

SERVES 4

For this recipe, we prefer using large sea scallops. Depending on the size of your scallops, the cooking time may vary slightly. Try to buy "dry" scallops for this dish but if you cannot find them, see our quick soak solution at right. Dry scallops will look ivory or pinkish and feel sticky or flabby, while processed are bright white, slippery, and swollen.

- 8 ounces leeks, white and light green parts only, halved lengthwise, sliced ¼ inch thick, and washed thoroughly (see page 44)
- 2 teaspoons canola oil
  Salt
- 2 garlic cloves, minced
- 1 teaspoon minced fresh thyme or ¼ teaspoon dried
- 1 tablespoon unbleached all-purpose flour
- ¼ cup dry white wine
- ¾ cup 1 percent low-fat milk
- ¼ teaspoon grated lemon zest plus 1 tablespoon fresh lemon juice
  Pepper
- 1½ pounds large sea scallops (about 16 scallops), muscle removed (see photo)
- 2 teaspoons minced fresh parsley

1. Adjust an oven rack to the middle position and heat the oven to 450 degrees. Combine the leeks, oil, and ⅛ teaspoon salt in a medium saucepan. Cover and cook over medium-low heat, stirring occasionally, until softened, 8 to 10 minutes.

2. Stir in the garlic and thyme and cook until fragrant, about 30 seconds. Stir in the flour and cook for 30 seconds. Slowly whisk in the wine, then the milk. Bring to a simmer and cook until the sauce is thickened, 2 to 3 minutes. Off the heat, stir in the lemon zest and season with salt and pepper to taste.

3. Pat the scallops dry with paper towels and season with ⅛ teaspoon salt and ⅛ teaspoon pepper. Arrange the scallops in a single layer in an 8-inch square baking dish and pour the sauce over the top. Bake until the scallops are cooked through and their sides feel firm, 15 to 20 minutes.

4. Carefully transfer the scallops to a platter, leaving the sauce behind in the dish. Whisk the lemon juice and parsley into the sauce, pour it over the scallops, and serve.

PER SERVING: **Cal** 250; **Fat** 4.5g; **Sat fat** 0.5g; **Chol** 60mg; **Carb** 17g; **Protein** 31g; **Fiber** 1g; **Sodium** 450mg

VARIATION

Baked Scallops with Leeks and Saffron

Follow the recipe for Baked Scallops with Lemon and Herbs, adding ⅛ teaspoon saffron threads, crumbled, with the garlic. Omit the lemon zest and reduce the amount of lemon juice to 1½ teaspoons.

PER SERVING: **Cal** 250; **Fat** 4.5g; **Sat fat** 0.5g; **Chol** 60mg; **Carb** 17g; **Protein** 31g; **Fiber** 1g; **Sodium** 450mg

---

NOTES FROM THE TEST KITCHEN

PREPPING SCALLOPS

The small, crescent-shaped muscle that is sometimes attached to the scallop will be incredibly tough when cooked. Use your fingers to peel this muscle away from the side of each scallop before cooking.

QUICK SOAK FOR WET SCALLOPS

We prefer untreated "dry" scallops to treated, or "wet," scallops, but if you cannot find them, a simple soaking in a solution of 1 quart cold water, ¼ cup lemon juice, and 2 tablespoons table salt for 30 minutes will mask the off-putting taste of the chemicals that have been added to these scallops to increase their shelf life.

WHOLE WHEAT SPAGHETTI WITH ITALIAN SAUSAGE AND FENNEL

CHAPTER 6

PIZZA & PASTA

MULTIGRAIN
FLATBREAD PIZZAS

WITH ITS THIN, CRISP CRUST AND A SMATTERING OF well-chosen toppings, flatbread pizza has grown in popularity to become more than just a first-course offering at nicer restaurants. Now you can find these pizzas everywhere from casual family restaurants to fast-food joints, and even in the supermarket's freezer aisle. It's no surprise they have caught on. When prepared well, flatbread pizzas offer a lighter, and often more refined, alternative to pizza, making them satisfying without weighing you down and a great choice for a summer meal or casual entertaining. They struck us as a dish that offered great potential as a light and healthy dinner option. However, we soon learned, after testing a few existing recipes, that that's not always the case. Many versions produced a crust that was thick, chewy, and too bready, resembling pizza more than flatbread, and the toppings often seemed mismatched, overloaded (too much cheese!), or out of balance. We set out to create a healthy flatbread pizza recipe that could hold its own against the best restaurant versions, one with a crisp-tender crust and an appealing assortment of judiciously chosen toppings.

As it is for pizza, the crust is probably the trickiest part of making flatbread at home. The successful recipes we found started with a basic pizza dough, which was divided and rolled thin before toppings were added. The test kitchen had already developed a whole wheat pizza crust, so we started there; but then we decided that for our healthy recipe we would take it a step further and turn it into a multigrain crust that packed a bigger nutritional punch. This dough needed to be easy to shape and stretch thin, and it needed to bake up crisp and chewy, full of multigrain flavor. The existing whole wheat dough recipe was pretty straightforward: bread flour, whole wheat flour, yeast, water, salt, and oil blended in a food processor. It produced a crust that was fairly thin, crispy on the bottom, and had good chew. It also held up well under the weight of different toppings.

So now we just needed to introduce more grains into this dough. But simply adding more grains—we tested a combination of rye, bran, barley, and flaxseeds—resulted in a tough, dense crust. Substituting the grains for some of the bread flour was better, but we found that the grains were too crunchy in the final pizza; they didn't soften in the time it took to make and cook the pizza. We

needed a way to soften the grains before adding them to the dough, so we brought the water in the recipe to a simmer and let the grains soak and soften. This was a big step in the right direction, but because the grains absorbed a fair amount of the liquid, we needed to go up from the 1½ cups of water in our original whole wheat crust recipe to 1¾ cups.

At this point our crust was very good, but we were a little frustrated with collecting and measuring the various grains. Then a fellow test cook suggested swapping out the various grains for a product called hot cereal mix. Usually located in the supermarket health-food aisle, it is essentially a blend of whole grains (our favorite brand, Bob's Red Mill, includes wheat, rye, oats, oat bran, barley, rice, and flaxseeds). We gave it a test, and once steeped in the warm water, this mix became soft like a porridge. It easily blended into the dough, and when baked, it tasted comparable to the custom mix we had put together, but without all the fuss. This crust was a winner all the way around. One recipe of pizza dough usually gives us two 12-inch pizza crusts, so for our flatbread we divided the dough instead into thirds and rolled each one out into a thin 16 by 8-inch crust. With three flatbread crusts, we would have the perfect amount for serving a small group of friends or the family.

With the dough settled, we turned our attention to the toppings. To keep our recipe healthy, we decided to stick with all-vegetable toppings accented with cheese. For one version, we started with cherry tomatoes, corn, and shallots. A full 6 cups of tomatoes divided up nicely among the three crusts and allowed for good coverage, and 2 cups of corn for the group added just the right color and touch of summery sweetness. We found that tossing the vegetables with 2 tablespoons of oil was key to keeping them moist during cooking. Tasters liked this veggie combination, but they all agreed they wanted a deeper, richer flavor. Roasting the mixture briefly in the oven, just until the tomatoes started to shrivel and the edges of the shallots began to brown, before adding them to the pizza concentrated the vegetables' sweetness and gave them the depth they were missing. For the cheese, we chose salty, tangy feta, which paired well with the sweet vegetables and nutty crust. Eight ounces of cheese divided among the three flatbreads added flavor and creaminess without taking over.

Our tomato, corn, and feta recipe was a winner, so we came up with another version, substituting meaty, sweet eggplant for the corn, and a third one using mushrooms

MULTIGRAIN FLATBREAD WITH ROASTED TOMATOES, CORN, AND FETA

instead of the corn. We found that the earthy qualities of both vegetables gave the flatbread a heartiness and richness that were plenty satisfying; no one even missed the meat or gobs of cheese. This was a healthy flatbread we could feel good about eating, and it was elegant enough to serve to company—and perhaps best of all, we could enjoy it without leaving the comfort of our own home.

MAKING FLATBREAD PIZZA

1. To soften the dry cereal, combine the boiling water and cereal mix, cover, and let stand, stirring occasionally, until the mixture resembles a thick porridge and is just warm (about 110 degrees), about 30 minutes.

2. Turn out the risen dough onto a lightly floured counter. Press and roll the dough into a 16 by 8-inch oval, then transfer to a parchment paper–lined rimless (or inverted) baking sheet.

3. Brush the dough with 1 tablespoon of oil, then scatter one-third of the roasted vegetables and ⅔ cup of the crumbled feta evenly over the dough, leaving a ½-inch border around the edge.

4. Using the parchment paper, carefully slide the flatbread onto the hot baking stone.

Multigrain Flatbread with Roasted Tomatoes, Corn, and Feta

MAKES 3 (16 BY 8-INCH) FLATBREADS, SERVES 9

For an accurate measurement of boiling water, bring a full kettle of water to a boil, then measure out the desired amount. You can substitute unbleached all-purpose flour for the bread and/or whole wheat flour; however, the resulting crust will be a little less chewy.

DOUGH

1¾	cups boiling water (see note)
1	cup (5 ounces) seven-grain hot cereal mix (see at left)
2–2¼	cups (11 to 12⅔ ounces) bread flour
1	cup (5½ ounces) whole wheat flour
2¼	teaspoons (about 1 envelope) instant or rapid-rise yeast
1½	teaspoons salt
3	tablespoons olive oil

TOPPING

2¼	pounds cherry tomatoes (about 6 cups), halved
2	cups frozen corn (8 ounces)
5	tablespoons olive oil
2	shallots, halved and sliced thin
3	garlic cloves, sliced thin
1	teaspoon sugar
⅛	teaspoon red pepper flakes
½	teaspoon salt
¼	teaspoon pepper
8	ounces feta cheese, crumbled (about 2 cups)
2	scallions, sliced thin

1. FOR THE DOUGH: Stir the boiling water and cereal mix together in a bowl, cover, and let sit, stirring occasionally, until the mixture resembles thick porridge and is just warm (about 110 degrees), about 30 minutes.

2. Pulse 2 cups of the bread flour, whole wheat flour, yeast, and salt together in a food processor to combine. Dollop the porridge mixture evenly over the top and drizzle in the oil. Process the mixture until a rough ball forms, 30 to 40 seconds. Let the dough rest for 2 minutes, then process for 30 seconds longer. If the dough is sticky and clings to the blade, add the remaining ¼ cup bread flour, 1 tablespoon at a time, and pulse to incorporate.

3. Turn out the dough onto a lightly floured counter and knead it into a smooth, round ball. Place the dough in a large, lightly greased bowl and cover with greased plastic wrap. Let rise in a warm place until nearly doubled in size, 1 to 1½ hours.

4. FOR THE TOPPING: Adjust the oven racks to the lower-middle and upper-middle positions and heat the oven to 350 degrees. Toss the tomatoes, corn, 2 tablespoons of the oil, shallots, garlic, sugar, pepper flakes, salt, and pepper together in a bowl.

5. Spread the vegetables on two rimmed baking sheets. Roast, without stirring, until the tomato skins have shriveled slightly but the tomatoes still retain their shape, and the shallot edges are beginning to brown, 35 to 40 minutes, switching and rotating the baking sheets halfway through. Let the vegetables cool slightly.

6. TO MAKE THE FLATBREAD: Place a baking stone on the lower-middle rack and increase the oven temperature to 500 degrees. Let the baking stone heat for at least 30 minutes (but no longer than 1 hour). Line a rimless (or inverted) baking sheet with parchment paper.

7. Following the photos on page 126, turn out the dough onto a lightly floured counter, divide it into 3 equal pieces, and cover with greased plastic wrap. Working with 1 piece of dough at a time (keep the other pieces covered), press and roll the dough into a 16 by 8-inch oval, flouring the counter as needed. Transfer the dough to the prepared baking sheet and reshape as needed.

8. Lightly brush the dough with 1 tablespoon more oil. Scatter one-third of the roasted vegetables evenly over the dough and sprinkle with ⅔ cup of the feta, leaving a ½-inch border at the edge.

9. Slide the parchment paper and flatbread onto the hot baking stone. Bake until the edges are brown and crisp, 8 to 13 minutes. (Assemble the remaining flatbreads while the first bakes.)

10. Remove the flatbread from the oven by sliding the parchment paper back onto the baking sheet. Slide the flatbread onto a cutting board and discard the parchment paper. Sprinkle with one-third of the scallions, slice into 6 pieces, and serve. Let the stone reheat for 5 minutes before baking the other flatbreads.

PER SERVING (2 SLICES): **Cal** 470; **Fat** 19g; **Sat fat** 6g; **Chol** 20mg; **Carb** 63g; **Protein** 16g; **Fiber** 7g; **Sodium** 810mg

VARIATIONS

Multigrain Flatbread with Roasted Tomatoes, Eggplant, and Feta

We like to leave the skin on the eggplant in this recipe so that it holds its shape.

Follow the recipe for Multigrain Flatbread with Roasted Tomatoes, Corn, and Feta, substituting 1 eggplant, cut into ½-inch pieces, for the corn and 1 tablespoon minced fresh mint for the scallions (use 1 teaspoon mint per flatbread).

PER SERVING (2 SLICES): **Cal** 450; **Fat** 19g; **Sat fat** 6g; **Chol** 20mg; **Carb** 59g; **Protein** 15g; **Fiber** 9g; **Sodium** 810mg

Multigrain Flatbread with Roasted Tomatoes, Mushrooms, and Feta

Follow the recipe for Multigrain Flatbread with Roasted Tomatoes, Corn, and Feta, substituting 1 pound white mushrooms, quartered, for the corn and 3 tablespoons chopped fresh basil for the scallions.

PER SERVING (2 SLICES): **Cal** 450; **Fat** 19g; **Sat fat** 6g; **Chol** 20mg; **Carb** 57g; **Protein** 15g; **Fiber** 7g; **Sodium** 810mg

PASTA WITH ROASTED VEGETABLES

COMBINING CARAMELIZED ROASTED VEGETABLES with pasta sounds like a winning proposition for a simple yet satisfying light meal that doesn't require much work. After all, there are just a minimum of ingredients to deal with. But anyone who's tried to make such a dish knows that it's not that cut-and-dried. The problem doesn't stem so much from the vegetables as from the lack of a true sauce. A minimalist sauce is appealing in its simplicity, but all too often these super-simple sauces can leave you with a meal that feels unfinished. Most recipes attempt to unify the vegetables and pasta with nothing more than olive oil and a little cheese. Although oil helps make the dish more cohesive, it also makes it greasy, not to mention high-fat and high-calorie. Using less oil solves those problems, of course, but is likely to leave you with a dry and uninspired dish. Could we create a simple, subtle sauce that would succeed in uniting the pasta and perfectly roasted vegetables without packing on the fat and calories?

PASTA WITH ROASTED CAULIFLOWER

At the outset, we decided to develop multiple recipes on this theme, each focused on getting the best from a single vegetable. We settled on cauliflower for its sweet and nutty flavor when roasted; broccoli, which browns nicely; and portobello mushrooms for their intense, meaty taste. To prepare them, we used the test kitchen's proven method for roasting vegetables: cutting them into slices or pieces to maximize the surface area available for browning; tossing them with a modest 1 tablespoon of olive oil, salt, pepper, and a little sugar to jump-start caramelization; and finally roasting them on a preheated baking sheet. The key to perfectly roasted vegetables is preheating the baking sheet, which cuts the cooking time nearly in half and boosts browning dramatically.

So with the vegetables settled, we were ready to face the main hurdle: the sauce. Aiming to keep things light, we eliminated cream sauces right off the bat (these would also drown out the flavor of the vegetables). We tried both vegetable-based sauces and vinaigrettes similar to those found on pasta salads. Vegetable-based sauces weren't much of an improvement: A puree of roasted red peppers overwhelmed the roasted veggies, and a puree of roasted onions turned the pasta an unappetizing gray. Only a garlicky vinaigrette was a step in the right direction. We liked the way the garlic bumped up the overall flavor of the dish, but tasters agreed the vinegar was too harsh. Cutting back on vinegar meant upping the oil, and then we were back where we started. What we needed was an ingredient that could replace some of the oil, adding body and complementary flavor without overt richness.

We found a solution right in front of us: garlic. When roasted, garlic turns sweet and buttery-soft. We wrapped two whole garlic heads in foil, roasted them, then squeezed the roasted cloves from their skins and mashed them with extra-virgin olive oil and a little lemon juice. A few tests of various oil amounts proved that ¼ cup of oil was the happy medium, giving our sauce the ability to coat without making the pasta greasy. Just ¼ teaspoon of red pepper flakes added the bite our pasta needed. This smooth puree worked beautifully as a sauce, adding an earthy sweetness that complemented all three vegetables.

We were almost there, but we still wanted a bit more flavor in each dish. The answer was to supplement the robust flavors of the vegetables with fresh herbs and 2 ounces of cheese for each recipe. We matched the cauliflower with parsley and sharp Parmesan, the broccoli with basil and nutty Manchego, and the mushrooms with rosemary and tangy Pecorino. While not a must, we also liked the flavor and texture that a handful of toasted nuts—walnuts, almonds, or pine nuts—added to each one. These vegetable and pasta dishes were light yet flavorful, with nicely roasted vegetables taking center stage and perfectly married to the pasta by our sauce. Clearly, simple dishes can become more than the sum of their parts with the right recipe.

Pasta with Roasted Cauliflower

SERVES 6

Prepare the cauliflower for roasting after you put the garlic in the oven so that both will finish roasting at about the same time.

  2 heads garlic, papery skins removed, top quarter of heads cut off and discarded (see page 130)
  2 tablespoons water
  2 tablespoons fresh lemon juice
  ¼ teaspoon red pepper flakes
  5 tablespoons extra-virgin olive oil
  1 head cauliflower (about 2 pounds), cut into 8 wedges (see page 130)
     Salt and pepper
  ¼ teaspoon sugar
  1 pound fusilli, campanelle, or orecchiette
  2 ounces Parmesan cheese, grated (about 1 cup)
  1 tablespoon minced fresh parsley
  ¼ cup walnuts, toasted and chopped coarse (optional)

1. Adjust the oven racks to the middle and upper-middle positions, place a large rimmed baking sheet on the middle rack, and heat the oven to 500 degrees.

2. Place the garlic heads, cut side up, in the center of a sheet of foil. Drizzle 1 tablespoon of the water over each head and seal the foil to make a packet. Place the packet on the upper-middle rack and roast until the garlic is very tender, about 30 minutes. Open the packet and set aside to cool to room temperature.

3. When cool enough to handle, squeeze the roasted garlic cloves from their skins into a small bowl. Using a fork, mash the garlic to a smooth paste, then stir in the lemon juice and pepper flakes. Slowly whisk in ¼ cup of the oil.

4. While the garlic roasts, toss the cauliflower with the remaining 1 tablespoon oil, ½ teaspoon salt, pinch pepper, and sugar. Remove the baking sheet from the oven and carefully arrange the cauliflower, cut side down, in an even layer on the sheet. Return the baking sheet to the oven and roast until the cauliflower is well browned, 20 to 25 minutes. Transfer the cauliflower to a cutting board. When cool enough to handle, chop the cauliflower into ½-inch pieces.

5. Meanwhile, bring 4 quarts water to a boil in a large pot. Add the pasta and 1 tablespoon salt and cook, stirring often, until al dente. Reserve 1 cup of the cooking water, then drain the pasta and return it to the pot.

6. Add ¼ cup of the pasta cooking water, garlic mixture, cauliflower, ½ cup of the Parmesan, and parsley and toss to combine, adjusting the sauce consistency with additional cooking water as desired. Season with salt and pepper to taste. Sprinkle with the remaining ½ cup Parmesan and toasted nuts (if using) and serve.

PER 2-CUP SERVING (WITHOUT WALNUTS): Cal 480; Fat 16g; Sat fat 3.5g; Chol 5mg; Carb 70g; Protein 18g; Fiber 7g; Sodium 610mg

PER 2-CUP SERVING (WITH WALNUTS): Cal 510; Fat 18g; Sat fat 3.5g; Chol 5mg; Carb 71g; Protein 19g; Fiber 7g; Sodium 610mg

VARIATIONS

Pasta with Roasted Broccoli

Cut 1 bunch broccoli (about 1½ pounds) at the juncture of the crowns and stems. Trim the stems, then cut into 2-inch lengths, each ½ inch thick. Cut the crowns into 4 wedges if 3 to 4 inches in diameter or 6 wedges if 4 to 5 inches in diameter.

Follow the recipe for Pasta with Roasted Cauliflower, substituting the prepared broccoli for the cauliflower and reducing the roasting time in step 4 to 10 to 15 minutes. Substitute ¼ cup chopped fresh basil for the parsley, Manchego cheese for the Parmesan, and slivered almonds for the walnuts (optional).

PER 2-CUP SERVING (WITHOUT ALMONDS): Cal 480; Fat 16g; Sat fat 3.5g; Chol 5mg; Carb 69g; Protein 19g; Fiber 6g; Sodium 600mg

PER 2-CUP SERVING (WITH ALMONDS): Cal 510; Fat 18g; Sat fat 3.5g; Chol 5mg; Carb 70g; Protein 20g; Fiber 6g; Sodium 600mg

Pasta with Roasted Mushrooms

Follow the recipe for Pasta with Roasted Cauliflower, substituting 8 portobello mushroom caps (each 3 to 4 inches in diameter), sliced ¾ inch thick, for the cauliflower, minced fresh rosemary for the parsley, Pecorino Romano cheese for the Parmesan, and toasted pine nuts for the walnuts (optional).

PER 2-CUP SERVING (WITHOUT PINE NUTS): Cal 470; Fat 16g; Sat fat 3.5g; Chol 5mg; Carb 68g; Protein 17g; Fiber 5g; Sodium 530mg

PER 2-CUP SERVING (WITH PINE NUTS): Cal 510; Fat 20g; Sat fat 3.5g; Chol 5mg; Carb 69g; Protein 17g; Fiber 5g; Sodium 530mg

---

NOTES FROM THE TEST KITCHEN

CUTTING CAULIFLOWER FOR ROASTING

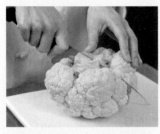

1. Trim the base of the stalk, then place the head upside down and cut the cauliflower crown in half through the stalk.

2. Cut each half of the crown in half to make 4 wedges, and each of those in half again to make 8 equal wedges.

PREPPING GARLIC FOR ROASTING

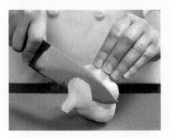

Rinse the garlic heads and remove the outer papery skin. Cut the top quarter off each head of garlic and discard.

WHOLE WHEAT PASTA SAUCES

WHOLE WHEAT PASTA HAS A LOT GOING FOR IT. IT HAS an appealingly distinctive, rustic, and nutty flavor you won't find in traditional white pasta, and it is also nutritionally higher in fiber and a host of other nutrients than regular pasta. But because of its distinctive flavor, it lacks the versatile, blank-slate quality that makes white pasta so easy to sauce. Still, while this whole grain product may not take well to just any sauce (particularly acidic tomato), its profile becomes a real advantage when combined with the right ingredients. The test kitchen had recently designed a few sauces that provided just the right complement to the hearty flavor and firm texture of the best whole wheat pastas. These sauces relied on *aglio e olio*, Italy's bold garlic and red pepper flake–infused olive oil sauce, as a base, to which we added sausage and vegetables such as zucchini, fennel, and sun-dried tomatoes, before capping it all off with some pine nuts. While these sauces elevated the flavor of the whole wheat pasta, they also bumped up the fat and calories higher than we like for a light and healthy recipe. Could we keep the flavors of the recipe we'd created but cut the fat?

Our original master recipe began with browning the sausage, then cooking some fennel in the rendered fat. Next the garlic–olive oil sauce was stirred in, the sausage was returned to the pan along with the pine nuts and final seasonings, and finally the cooked pasta was tossed with the mixture until combined. The flavor was great, but unfortunately, the recipe incorporated ¼ cup extra-virgin olive oil in addition to the rendered fat. To lighten things up, our first step was to switch from fatty Italian sausage to lighter but still flavorful turkey sausage. The next obvious step was to cut oil. We started our testing by reducing the amount of oil incrementally and replacing it with an equal amount of pasta water. We quickly learned all that oil was doing more than adding flavor and body to our sauce: It was coating the noodles, lubricating them and keeping them from absorbing all of the pasta water. With less oil, tasters quickly noticed the gluey texture of the pasta, which had been caused by all the moisture from both the sauce and the pasta water it had absorbed. Tasters agreed that less than ¼ cup

of oil would be unacceptable in this situation, so it was clear we were going to have to rethink our strategy. An olive oil–based sauce was simply not going to work for a light recipe.

As we brainstormed various options that could keep the integrity of our original recipe without the oil, a fellow test cook suggested thinking outside the pasta box, so to speak. What about trying a pan sauce, which we rely on frequently when making quick sauces for chicken breasts or pork chops? Pan sauces are a simple way to make a flavorful sauce without much fat; we could cook down a liquid component until it reached the right consistency, then toss the sauce with the pasta. It seemed worth a try. We started by browning the sausage, fennel, and aromatics, just as we would for a pan sauce. We then deglazed the pan with 3 cups of chicken broth and simmered the liquid about 20 minutes until it had reduced and thickened slightly. Once this sauce was tossed with our pasta, tasters agreed that we were on the right track, but everyone concurred that the sauce seemed a little thin and not very silky, as the olive oil version had been. We often use flour as a thickener, so it seemed like our best bet, but we would have to be careful about just how much we used. Four teaspoons proved to be the magic number, thickening the sauce to a velvety consistency; any more and our sauce became unappealingly gluey and overly starchy.

Now that our sausage and fennel sauce was on track, we needed to fine-tune our variation, which swapped out the fennel in favor of zucchini. While the fennel required about 10 minutes of precooking before the liquid was even added to the pan, and then held up well during the 20-minute simmer of the sauce, zucchini would turn to mush in that amount of time. Our solution was simple. We built the sauce in the pan, reduced it partially, and added the zucchini for only the last 5 minutes of cooking. This gave us perfectly cooked zucchini every time.

The final tweak to our original recipe was to reduce the pine nuts from ½ cup to ⅓ cup. Tasters agreed there was still plenty of texture and subtle pine nut flavor in the final dish. Now we had sauces that not only highlighted the unique flavor of the whole wheat spaghetti as in our original, but they also kept the fat and calories in check.

NOTES FROM THE TEST KITCHEN

PREPARING FENNEL

1. Cut off the stems and feathery fronds.

2. Trim a very thin slice from the base and remove any tough or blemished outer layers from the bulb.

3. Cut the bulb in half through the base, then use a small, sharp knife to remove the pyramid-shaped core. Slice each half into thin strips, and if called for in the recipe, chop strips crosswise.

WHOLE WHEAT PASTA STEPS UP

Given the push lately toward whole grains, it's no surprise that supermarkets carry whole wheat or multigrain noodles from just about every major pasta manufacturer. We recently bought 18 nationally distributed brands of whole wheat and multigrain spaghettis and sampled them plain with olive oil, rating them on flavor and texture. We narrowed the field to 10 and tested these with homemade marinara and pesto. So what did our tasting panel find? First, most of the 100 percent whole wheat and 100 percent whole grain pastas fell quickly to the bottom of the rankings, garnering descriptions like "mushy," "doughy," "sour," and "fishy." But there was one dark horse in the bunch: Italian-made **Bionaturae Organic 100% Whole Wheat Spaghetti**, made entirely of whole wheat but with an appealingly chewy and firm texture like the pastas with little or no whole grains. Some tasters even deemed it "more flavorful than white pasta." The manufacturer's secret? Custom milling (which ensures good flavor); extrusion through a bronze, not Teflon, die (which helps build gluten in the dough); and a slower drying process at low temperatures (which yields sturdier pasta).

Whole Wheat Spaghetti with Italian Sausage and Fennel

SERVES 6

There are big discrepancies from brand to brand in the flavor of whole wheat spaghetti; the test kitchen's favorite is Bionaturae Organic 100% Whole Wheat Spaghetti (see at left for more information about whole wheat spaghetti).

- 2 **teaspoons olive oil**
- 8 **ounces sweet Italian turkey sausage, casings removed**
- 1 **fennel bulb (about 12 ounces), stalks removed, bulb halved, cored, and cut into ¼-inch-thick strips (see photos)**
- 1 **onion, minced (about 1 cup)**
   Salt
- 6 **garlic cloves, minced**
- ½ **teaspoon red pepper flakes**
- 4 **teaspoons unbleached all-purpose flour**
- 3 **cups low-sodium chicken broth**
- 1 **cup dry white wine**
- ½ **cup chopped fresh basil**
- ⅓ **cup pine nuts, toasted and coarsely chopped**
- 2 **tablespoons fresh lemon juice**
- 1 **pound whole wheat spaghetti**
   Pepper
- 1 **ounce Pecorino Romano cheese, grated (about ½ cup)**

1. Heat 1 teaspoon of the oil in a 12-inch nonstick skillet over medium-high heat until just smoking. Add the sausage and cook, breaking up the meat with a wooden spoon, until browned, about 5 minutes. Transfer the sausage to a paper towel–lined plate.

2. Add the remaining 1 teaspoon oil, fennel, onion, and ⅛ teaspoon salt to the skillet and return to medium-low heat. Cover and cook, stirring occasionally, until the vegetables are softened, 8 to 10 minutes. Uncover, stir in the garlic and pepper flakes, and cook until fragrant, about 30 seconds.

3. Stir in the flour and cook for 1 minute. Slowly whisk in the broth and wine and bring to a simmer, scraping up any browned bits. Cook, stirring occasionally, until the sauce is thickened and reduced to 3 cups, 15 to 20 minutes. Remove the skillet from the heat and stir in the sausage, basil, pine nuts, and lemon juice and set aside.

4. Meanwhile, bring 4 quarts water to a boil in a large pot. Add the pasta and 1 tablespoon salt and cook, stirring often, until al dente. Reserve ½ cup of the cooking water, then drain the pasta and return it to the pot.

5. Add the sauce to the pasta and toss to coat, adjusting the sauce consistency with the reserved cooking water as desired. Season with salt and pepper to taste. Sprinkle with the cheese and serve.

PER 1¾-CUP SERVING: Cal 450; Fat 14g; Sat fat 2.5g; Chol 25mg; Carb 57g; Protein 20g; Fiber 10g; Sodium 760mg

VARIATION

Whole Wheat Spaghetti with Italian Sausage, Zucchini, and Sun-Dried Tomatoes

Follow the recipe for Whole Wheat Spaghetti with Italian Sausage and Fennel, omitting the fennel and adding 2 medium zucchini, cut into ½-inch pieces, to the sauce for the last 5 minutes of simmering in step 3. Substitute ⅓ cup oil-packed sun-dried tomatoes, rinsed, patted dry, and chopped coarse, for the lemon juice in step 3.

PER 1¾-CUP SERVING: Cal 460; Fat 15g; Sat fat 3g; Chol 25mg; Carb 57g; Protein 20g; Fiber 10g; Sodium 760mg

CREAMY ORZO WITH CHICKEN

ORZO IS OFTEN PIGEONHOLED IN ITS CULINARY roles: It's typically served as either a cold pasta salad or a quick side dish. While both have their merits, we wondered if we couldn't promote this quick-cooking, ricelike pasta from supporting player to star of the show for an easy weeknight dinner. In the past we have had success cooking orzo like risotto, gently but quickly so that the grains are coated in a creamy sauce that develops from the grains' own starch. With the simple additions of tender poached chicken and fresh vegetables to this style of orzo, we felt we could have the makings of an elegant yet quick-to-prepare meal. We wanted tender, flavorful chicken and carefully selected, perfectly cooked vegetables—all married with our perfectly cooked orzo risotto. We set out to see what we could do.

First up was the chicken. Similar to how we would incorporate a protein into a traditional rice-based risotto, our plan for this recipe was to cook the chicken separately, then shred it and stir it into the orzo once the orzo was done. Quick-cooking boneless, skinless breasts were the obvious choice, and for the cooking

method, we considered broiling, sautéing, and poaching. Broiling was an appealing low-fat method, but it gave the chicken a leathery exterior that tasters rejected. We liked the color and deeper flavor of the sautéed chicken, but at the same time tasters preferred the tender, juicy meat of the poached chicken. We decided our best route was to merge the two techniques, so we began by browning both sides of the chicken breasts in a skillet, then moved them to a saucepan to cook through (this freed up the skillet to start cooking aromatics for the orzo). We knew from our testing for Spa Chicken (page 66) that the best way to ensure perfectly poached chicken is to add the meat to room-temperature liquid, slowly bring the liquid up to a low simmer, and then cook the meat through. Cooking the chicken in chicken broth rather than water gave the meat another boost of flavor. Once the chicken was cooked, we let it cool a bit and then shredded it into bite-size pieces. Now it was ready for the orzo.

The test kitchen had previously developed a reliable procedure for cooking orzo that is very much like the method for making the traditional rice-based version. We started by sautéing aromatics, then added the orzo to the skillet to toast, giving it a deeper flavor. We then deglazed the skillet with wine, added liquid to the skillet with the pasta, and cooked, stirring frequently, until it was creamy and tender. It was key here (just as it is when making risotto) to determine the correct ratio of liquid to orzo. We had found in the previous testing that a ratio of roughly 3 to 1 gave us orzo that after about 25 minutes was perfectly tender and swathed in a creamy sauce that was neither gluey nor watered-down. For the liquid, water would have been an easy choice, but we realized that using the broth from poaching the chicken would give our pasta another boost of chicken-y flavor and help to unify the dish even more.

It was time to move on to the vegetables and other final additions. We sampled a number of vegetable combinations, and while everyone liked the duo of artichokes and peas, as well as summer squash and tomatoes, tasters were quick to put the pairing of fresh, clean-tasting asparagus and rich, sweet sun-dried tomatoes at the top of their lists. We sliced the asparagus on the bias into ¼-inch pieces, and rather than deal with cooking the asparagus separately, we found we could simply stir it into the pot with the orzo. Adding it halfway through the orzo's cooking time ensured that the asparagus was tender yet crisp by the end. Stirring in the sun-dried tomatoes at the end, along with the chicken, was easy enough. Tasters also wanted a little more richness and depth, and looking to traditional risotto recipes, we thought Parmesan might do the trick. A few ounces amplified the creaminess of our recipe and added just the right nutty flavor it needed.

At this point our recipe was close, but tasters noted that the shredded chicken seemed unappealingly long and stringy when matched with the short, stubby orzo. We found that by cutting the cooked chicken breasts in half crosswise before shredding, we got smaller shreds of chicken that were much better matched to the pasta. After stirring in a few tablespoons of fresh basil, we had an elegant skillet meal that took weeknight cooking to the next level.

Creamy Orzo with Chicken, Asparagus, and Sun-Dried Tomatoes

SERVES 4

The orzo in this dish cooks until tender and will take on a creamy texture similar to that of risotto.

2	**(6-ounce) boneless, skinless chicken breasts, trimmed**
	Salt and pepper
1	**tablespoon olive oil**
4	**cups low-sodium chicken broth**
1	**onion, minced (about 1 cup)**
1¼	**cups orzo**
4	**garlic cloves, minced**
½	**cup dry white wine**
1	**bunch asparagus (about 1 pound), tough ends trimmed, cut on the bias into ¼-inch pieces**
¼	**cup oil-packed sun-dried tomatoes, rinsed, patted dry, and chopped fine**
2	**ounces Parmesan cheese, grated (about 1 cup)**
2	**tablespoons chopped fresh basil**

1. Pat the chicken breasts dry with paper towels and season with ⅛ teaspoon salt and ⅛ teaspoon pepper. Heat 2 teaspoons of the oil in a 12-inch nonstick skillet over medium-high heat until shimmering. Carefully lay the chicken breasts in the skillet and cook until golden brown on the first side, about 5 minutes. Flip the breasts and continue to cook until lightly browned on the second side, about 3 minutes longer. Transfer the chicken to a medium saucepan.

2. Pour the broth over the chicken, bring to a simmer, and cook over medium-low heat until the chicken registers 160 to 165 degrees on an instant-read thermometer, 18 to 25 minutes. Transfer the chicken to a plate, reserving the broth. When cool enough to handle, cut the chicken breasts in half crosswise and shred the meat into bite-size pieces. Set aside.

3. Combine the remaining 1 teaspoon oil, onion, and ⅛ teaspoon salt in the skillet. Cover and cook over medium-low heat until softened, 8 to 10 minutes. Uncover, increase the heat to medium-high, and continue to cook, stirring occasionally, until the onion is lightly browned, 4 to 6 minutes longer.

4. Stir in the orzo and cook over medium heat until lightly golden, 2 to 3 minutes. Stir in the garlic and cook until fragrant, about 30 seconds. Stir in the wine, scraping up any browned bits, and cook until evaporated.

5. Add the reserved broth to the skillet, bring to a simmer, and cook over medium heat, stirring frequently, until the liquid is almost absorbed and the orzo is almost tender, 12 to 15 minutes. Add the asparagus and continue to cook, stirring frequently, until the asparagus is crisp-tender and the orzo is creamy, about 10 minutes longer.

6. Off the heat, stir the shredded chicken, sun-dried tomatoes, Parmesan, and basil into the orzo. Season with salt and pepper to taste and serve.

PER 1½-CUP SERVING: Cal 480; Fat 11g; Sat fat 3g; Chol 60mg; Carb 52g; Protein 37g; Fiber 5g; Sodium 980mg

MEATY SKILLET LASAGNA

WITH ITS UNIVERSAL COMFORT-FOOD APPEAL, A lasagna with tender noodles, gooey cheese, and plenty of hearty meat is a classic. Our recently developed method for preparing lasagna in a skillet turns this otherwise labor-intensive dish into a weeknight option, but with its combination of a full pound of meatloaf mix (a mix of ground beef, veal, and pork) and whole-milk mozzarella, ricotta, and Parmesan cheeses, this lasagna isn't exactly the epitome of light dining. Could we make our easy-to-prepare recipe a little easier on the waistline?

For starters, we knew that the pound of meatloaf mix in our original recipe was going to have to go, since it was contributing 12 grams of fat per serving. We had had success substituting ground poultry for ground meat in recipes like our Tomato Soup with Meatballs and Pasta (page 34) and our French Pork and White Bean Casserole (page 95), so it seemed like a natural substitution here as well. Ground turkey comes in three forms: ground dark meat (labeled 80 to 85 percent lean), ground white meat (98 to 99 percent lean), and a combination of the two (simply labeled "ground turkey"). While tasters liked the juiciness of the ground dark meat, the calorie savings were so insignificant that we might as well have used ground beef. Conversely, ground white meat was tough and dry. The combination of the two was the perfect middle ground; it was both tender and low-fat. Nevertheless, tasters still complained about a lack of flavor. A few more tests proved Italian turkey sausage was the answer. A combination of both white and dark meat, this sausage is flavored with garlic and herbs. It added the needed extra zip to our skillet meal along with significant nutritional savings, cutting 5 grams of fat per serving.

Following our full-fat method, we browned the sausage, then scattered lasagna noodles, broken into 2-inch lengths, on top. Next came the simple tomato sauce, which we made by processing three cans of whole tomatoes in the food processor. We cooked our lasagna until the noodles were tender. So far, so good. Next up was the cheese. The original recipe called for stirring mozzarella and Parmesan into the skillet and dotting ricotta cheese over the top to finish. These cheeses contributed both flavor and richness to the final dish, but also some fat. Starting with the mozzarella, we tested low-calorie substitutes. Tasters panned fat-free mozzarella, noting its bland flavor and rubbery texture. However, part-skim mozzarella worked well, as it melted nicely and offered flavor much like its fattier cousin. Next we tried substituting both part-skim and fat-free ricotta for the full-fat. Tasters disliked the grainy texture of the fat-free ricotta, but like the part-skim mozzarella, the part-skim ricotta worked impressively well. When it came time to test adjusting the Parmesan, tasters weren't so forgiving. We tested cutting back incrementally on the original recipe's ¼ cup, but tasters were adamant that any less than the

original amount was insufficient. The Parmesan contributed a complexity and bolder flavor that our lasagna needed, and since it's a relatively low-fat cheese, we left it as is. After the pasta was tender, all we had to do was add our cheese, cover the skillet, and let it sit off the heat for just a few minutes until the cheese had melted. This was a gooey, satisfyingly meaty lasagna, and no one could guess that we had cut any of the calories or fat from the original.

Meaty Skillet Lasagna
SERVES 6

Do not substitute no-boil lasagna noodles for the traditional, curly-edged lasagna noodles here. We like the flavor and creaminess of part-skim ricotta here; do not use fat-free ricotta. The tomatoes and sausage are the primary sources of sodium in this recipe; if you are concerned about sodium intake, substitute low-sodium or salt-free canned tomatoes.

3   (14.5-ounce) cans whole peeled tomatoes
1   teaspoon olive oil
1   pound sweet Italian turkey sausage, casings removed
1   onion, minced (about 1 cup)
    Salt
3   garlic cloves, minced
⅛   teaspoon red pepper flakes
10 curly-edged lasagna noodles (about 8½ ounces), broken into 2-inch lengths (see note)
2   ounces part-skim mozzarella cheese, shredded (about ½ cup)
¼   cup grated Parmesan cheese
    Pepper
¾   cup part-skim ricotta cheese
3   tablespoons chopped fresh basil

1. Pulse the tomatoes with their juice in a food processor until coarsely ground and no large pieces remain, about 12 pulses, and set aside.

2. Heat the oil in a 12-inch nonstick skillet over medium-high heat until just smoking. Add the sausage and cook, breaking up the meat with a wooden spoon, until browned, about 5 minutes. Transfer the sausage to a paper towel–lined plate.

3. Add the onion and ⅛ teaspoon salt to the fat left in the skillet and return to medium-low heat. Cover and cook, stirring occasionally, until softened, 8 to 10 minutes. Uncover, stir in the garlic and pepper flakes, and cook until fragrant, about 30 seconds.

BUILDING SKILLET LASAGNA

1. After the onion, garlic, pepper flakes, and browned sausage have been added to the skillet, scatter the pasta over the top. Top with the processed tomatoes, then cover and cook.

2. Once the pasta is tender, stir in half of the mozzarella and Parmesan and dollop the ricotta over the top. Sprinkle with the remaining mozzarella and Parmesan, then cover and let sit off the heat until the cheese is melted.

THE BEST INEXPENSIVE NONSTICK SKILLET

A nonstick skillet's surface inevitably becomes marred by scratches, rough and stained, and it may even pill or flake. Nevertheless, we rely on nonstick skillets for cooking fragile foods and for making stir-fries, and since these pans have to be replaced frequently, we prefer not to spend a lot of money on them. We tested seven contenders under $50 against our longtime favorite, the All-Clad Stainless 12-Inch Nonstick Frying Pan, $159.99, and our former best buy, the Calphalon Simply Nonstick Omelette Pan, $55. We tested the nonstick effectiveness of each pan by frying eggs and stir-frying beef and vegetables. To see which pans cooked food evenly and had good size and heft but were comfortable to maneuver, we made crepes in each. We also ran them through a number of durability tests. We'd like to say our new favorite pan, the **T-Fal Professional Total 12.5-inch Nonstick Fry Pan**, aced every test, but a loose handle that resulted from the durability testing was a sign that it's not high-end cookware. Still, at $34.99, it's a bargain, and it was the only pan in the lineup to give us the best of both worlds: an exceptionally slick, durable nonstick coating and top performance in cooking. As for the All-Clad, it boasts a lifetime warranty, so we still recommend it. But we'll be buying the T-Fal from now on for our own kitchens.

4. Return the sausage to the pan, then scatter the pasta over the top. Pour the processed tomatoes over the pasta. Cover, increase the heat to medium-high, and cook, stirring often and adjusting the heat to maintain a vigorous simmer, until the pasta is tender, about 20 minutes.

5. Off the heat, stir in half of the mozzarella and half of the Parmesan. Season with salt and pepper to taste. Dot heaping tablespoons of the ricotta over the top, then sprinkle with the remaining mozzarella and Parmesan. Cover and let sit off the heat until the cheese melts, 2 to 4 minutes. Sprinkle with the basil and serve.

PER SERVING: Cal 410; Fat 14g; Sat fat 6g; Chol 65mg; Carb 43g; Protein 26g; Fiber 3g; Sodium 1100mg

SPICY SPAGHETTI PIE

A SPAGHETTI SUPPER IS A QUICK, SATISFYING MEAL, but dishing it up and eating it can be a messy endeavor. Enter spaghetti pie. Essentially, it's baked pasta, but with a hook: The sauced, cheesy pasta is packed into a pie plate, then baked until browned, bubbly, and sliceable. In the test kitchen we recently developed our own version of this homey casserole with a zesty tomato sauce (which was not only baked with the noodles but also served alongside at the table), Mexican cheese blend, and pepperoni that everyone loved, but the heavy cream, 2 cups of cheese, and pepperoni made this crowd-pleaser a scale-tipper as well. We set out to lighten our recipe and make a pie that had the same satisfying flavor as our original but without all that fat.

There are three main components of spaghetti pie: the sauce, the cheese, and the noodles. Our first task was to rework the sauce, which is what lent the spicy flavor that gave our pie its name. The sauce started with slices of spicy deli pepperoni, which were fried crisp and then simmered in a simple combination of canned diced tomatoes, onion, and red pepper flakes. The pepperoni provided both deep flavor and a chewy texture to the pie, but it seemed like a good place to begin lightening the recipe. Luckily, we found an easy substitute in turkey pepperoni, which packs a similar spicy, meaty flavor but with nearly half the fat, so we could keep the full 4 ounces called for in our original recipe.

In most spaghetti pie recipes the sauce is enriched with cream, and our full-fat version was no different, calling for ½ cup of heavy cream. We wanted to maintain

SPICY SPAGHETTI PIE

this creaminess (it also helped the pie to brown) but cut back on the fat, so we tried pies made with half-and-half, whole milk, 2 percent milk, and skim milk in lieu of the heavy cream. The versions made with milk, especially those with the 2 percent milk and skim milk, were immediately dismissed, since they made pies that tasted dry and too lean, far from the comfort food we were after. Whole milk fared slightly better, but the real winner was the half-and-half. It lent not only creaminess but also a critical richness without all the fat.

Next we moved on to the cheese. Most versions we found in cookbooks and online used shredded mozzarella, but when developing our original recipe, the test kitchen had felt it was too one-dimensional. After experimenting with store-bought cheese blends, we landed on Mexican cheese blend (which is typically a mix of Monterey Jack, cheddar, queso quesadilla, and asadero cheeses). Two cups mixed into our pie had melted smoothly and added an appealing robust flavor. Happily, in our search for lower-fat alternatives, we found reduced-fat Mexican cheese blend, made from 2 percent milk. We found that it melted well and offered the same flavor as its full-fat counterpart. Wondering if we could cut even more calories by reducing the amount of cheese, we tested lesser increments of the original 2 cups. Tasters agreed that anything less than 1½ cups of cheese caused the pie's gooey appeal to suffer, and the noodles did not hold together well enough, so we stopped there.

As for the noodles, our earlier testing taught us the choice was not as obvious as you would think. Even though the name of the dish is "spaghetti pie," we had found that spaghetti is actually too thick, as the strands don't really stick together well and create a cohesive pie. Thinner vermicelli worked much better and yielded near-perfect slices.

After combining our cooked pasta and prepared sauce in a pie plate and baking for 15 minutes, we had a golden brown and bubbling spaghetti pie. Served with extra sauce on the side, our new version had all the spicy kick and appeal of the original. As people lined up for seconds, they never would have guessed it was light.

Spicy Spaghetti Pie

SERVES 6

For a bold flavor, be sure to use low-fat Mexican cheese blend, which is a combination of Monterey Jack, cheddar, queso quesadilla, and asadero cheeses. Don't substitute another pasta for the vermicelli in this recipe. To measure vermicelli without a scale, bundle the noodles into a tight, round bunch and measure the diameter with a ruler; 12 ounces of vermicelli should measure 1¾ inches. The tomatoes and pepperoni are the primary sources of sodium in this recipe; if you are concerned about sodium intake, substitute low-sodium or salt-free canned tomatoes. This dish is best served the day it is made.

4   ounces sliced turkey pepperoni, chopped fine
1   onion, minced (about 1 cup)
3   (14.5-ounce) cans diced tomatoes
¼   teaspoon red pepper flakes
12 ounces vermicelli (see note)
1   tablespoon salt
6   ounces shredded reduced-fat Mexican cheese blend
    (about 1½ cups)
½   cup half-and-half
½   cup chopped fresh basil

1. Adjust an oven rack to the upper-middle position and heat the oven to 475 degrees. Lightly coat a 9-inch pie plate with vegetable oil spray.

2. Cook the pepperoni in a 12-inch skillet over medium-high heat until crisp, about 2 minutes. Add the onion, reduce the heat to medium, and cook until softened, 5 to 7 minutes.

3. Stir in the tomatoes, with their juice, and pepper flakes and bring to a simmer. Reduce the heat to medium and cook until the sauce is thickened and reduced to about 4 cups, about 10 minutes. Cover and set aside off the heat to keep warm.

4. Meanwhile, bring 4 quarts water to a boil in a large pot. Add the pasta and salt and cook, stirring often, until nearly tender, about 5 minutes. Drain the pasta and return it to the pot.

5. Add 2 cups of the tomato sauce, cheese, half-and-half, and basil to the pasta and toss to combine. Transfer the mixture to the prepared pie plate and press with a spatula to flatten the surface. Bake until golden brown and bubbling, 10 to 15 minutes. Let cool for 5 minutes. Cut into 6 wedges and serve, passing the remaining 2 cups sauce separately.

PER SERVING: **Cal** 410; **Fat** 12g; **Sat fat** 5g; **Chol** 50mg; **Carb** 55g; **Protein** 24g; **Fiber** 2g; **Sodium** 1220mg

PEANUT NOODLE SALAD

WITH CHILLED NOODLES, CRISP RAW VEGETABLES (often red bell peppers and cucumbers), and chopped roasted peanuts tossed in a light coating of velvety, mildly spicy peanut sauce, the concept of a chilled peanut noodle salad struck us as a great change of pace that was at once light, savory, and satisfying. But after testing a number of existing recipes, we found that the concept of peanut noodle salad rarely delivers on its promise. Some recipes skimped on the sauce, leaving us with a boring bowl of noodles and add-ins that lacked cohesion, but most included so much peanut butter that the salad was nothing but a gluey mess, with vegetables that sank in the mucky sauce as if in quicksand, not to mention that they were a nutritional nightmare. Could we develop a cohesive sauce and vegetable combination that was light and healthy and didn't sacrifice the peanut flavor we love?

We started our testing with the sauce, with a focus on the peanut butter in particular. Drawing from a number of existing recipes, we cobbled together a working sauce that combined peanut butter, soy sauce, rice vinegar, toasted sesame oil, sugar, and red pepper flakes. From here, we made a few batches, each with a different type of peanut butter: one with chunky, one with creamy, and we also tested a few all-natural brands. Of all the options, tasters preferred chunky peanut butter for its lack of grittiness, gentle sweetness, and crunch (and it eliminated the need to add chopped peanuts). While many of the recipes we found called for up to 1 cup of peanut butter, it was obvious that this made for an excessively stodgy sauce. Tasters agreed that ⅓ cup of peanut butter per pound of pasta was more than

enough to impart distinct peanut flavor without adding excess calories.

With the peanut butter in line, we were ready to fine-tune the other components of the sauce. Swapping out regular granulated sugar in favor of brown sugar added a hint of maple flavor that everyone approved. Five tablespoons of soy sauce seasoned the sauce nicely, and 2 tablespoons of rice vinegar cut through the peanut butter and added a welcome brightness. The vinegar led us to wonder, in turn, if it wouldn't be an improvement to swap out the pepper flakes for bottled hot sauce, which is vinegar-based. Our hunch was right; everyone loved the hot sauce's one-two punch of acidity and heat. As for the toasted sesame oil, although it added fat to our recipe, one test confirmed that without it the salad lacked an essential toasty, nutty flavor. Many recipes call for 2 or 3 tablespoons of sesame oil, but we found that just 1 tablespoon was enough to impart the flavor we wanted without adding too much fat. And finally, grated ginger added the right finishing touch with its note of freshness.

For the vegetables, thinly sliced red peppers and cucumbers are common inclusions in peanut noodle salads, and we liked both for the sweet taste and crisp texture they added. We found numerous recipes that also included onions, jalapeños, snow peas, cabbage, and carrots, and we gave them all a try. Tasters unanimously disliked the strong flavor of onions, noting that they added an overwhelming sharpness. Jalapeños added too much heat and threw the salad out of balance. Tasters liked the snow peas, but because they had to be blanched first, they added an extra step to our recipe, so we ruled them out to keep things simple. Cabbage was cut from the list

as well; it became slimy when coated with the sauce. However, carrots, quickly shredded on a box grater, were a winner. Tasters liked the slightly sweet flavor and color they lent to the salad.

The final component of our salad was also a central one: the noodles. We tried both thick and thin varieties and quickly eliminated thin noodles like angel hair and super-skinny rice noodles. They matted under the thick sauce and made it almost impossible to incorporate the vegetables. Thicker noodles, like the wide rice noodles used in dishes such as pad thai, worked well. But in the end we settled on spaghetti. It worked great and is something we always have on hand, so it was also a convenient choice. In previous test kitchen experience with cold noodle salads, we knew it would be imperative to rinse the cooked noodles with cold water to keep them from overcooking and to remove some of the starch from the noodles, which would otherwise make them pasty. Tossing the noodles with the sesame oil, instead of whisking it into the dressing, helped keep our noodles separated and prevented them from absorbing liquid once tossed with the dressing.

After adding a little cilantro just before serving, we had a light peanut noodle salad that was ready for the picnic table.

Peanut Noodle Salad

SERVES 6

Use a milder hot sauce, such as the test kitchen's favorite, Frank's RedHot, in this recipe. If using a hotter sauce, such as Tabasco, reduce the amount to ½ teaspoon.

- 1 **pound spaghetti**
- **Salt**
- 1 **tablespoon toasted sesame oil**
- ⅓ **cup chunky peanut butter**
- 5 **tablespoons low-sodium soy sauce**
- 2 **tablespoons rice vinegar**
- 2 **tablespoons light brown sugar**
- 1 **tablespoon grated or minced fresh ginger**
- 2 **garlic cloves, minced**
- 1 **teaspoon hot sauce (see note)**
- 2 **red bell peppers, stemmed, seeded, and sliced thin**
- 2 **carrots, peeled and shredded**
- 1 **cucumber, peeled, halved lengthwise, seeded, and sliced thin (see page 22)**
- ⅓ **cup minced fresh cilantro**

1. Bring 4 quarts water to a boil in a large pot. Add the pasta and 1 tablespoon salt and cook, stirring often, until tender. Reserve ¾ cup of the cooking water, then drain the pasta in a colander and rinse with cold water until cool. Drain the pasta well and transfer to a large bowl. Add the sesame oil and toss to coat.

2. Whisk the peanut butter, soy sauce, vinegar, sugar, ginger, garlic, and hot sauce together in a bowl until smooth.

3. Add the dressing, bell peppers, carrots, cucumber, and cilantro to the pasta and toss to combine, adjusting the sauce consistency with the reserved cooking water as desired. Season with salt to taste and serve.

PER 1¾-CUP SERVING: Cal 430; Fat 11g; Sat fat 2g; Chol 0mg; Carb 71g; Protein 16g; Fiber 6g; Sodium 660mg

VIETNAMESE NOODLE SALAD

THE VIETNAMESE DISH KNOWN AS *BUN* IS A naturally light multilayered noodle salad that starts with shredded lettuce, followed by pickled carrots and daikon radish, fresh herbs, and then rice noodles. The salad is then topped with marinated, grilled meat or seafood, garnished with a sprinkle of chopped roasted peanuts, and finally dressed with a sweet-tart and mildly spicy sauce. A few tests of existing recipes quickly revealed why homemade versions haven't caught on. These recipes yielded tough, dry meat or overcooked seafood, gummy noodles, a hodgepodge of vegetables, and saccharine sauces. Could we develop a simple and successful recipe that would bring this restaurant favorite home?

We began by choosing among shrimp, beef, and pork, all of which we saw in existing recipes, used either alone or in combination. To keep our version simple, we settled on pork, and we tested various lean cuts to find the best one for the job: chops, loin, and tenderloin. The pork chops offered great flavor, but the meat was a little tough for this dish. The loin and the tenderloin were both winning options, but the tenderloin proved to be our top pick—at about 1 pound, a tenderloin would give us just the right amount of meat for our recipe.

Next we turned our attention to the marinade, which traditionally gives the meat a signature salty-sweet flavor. All of the marinades we came across consisted of the

VIETNAMESE RICE NOODLE SALAD WITH PORK

same basic foundation of fish sauce, vegetable oil, and sugar. From there they deviated, with some also calling for soy sauce, Vietnamese-style caramel sauce (a simple sugar-water mixture cooked until just slightly bitter), and chili paste. Beginning with the sugar, we tested the caramel sauce, dark brown sugar, light brown sugar, and granulated white sugar. Light brown and granulated white sugar both failed to caramelize in the short time it took for the meat to cook. Tasters found no discernible difference between the caramel and dark brown sugar and liked both for their deep nutty flavors, so we opted for the less fussy addition of dark brown sugar. Then we tested fish sauce amounts, and 2 tablespoons added just the right amount of saltiness to balance the sugar. Finally, a modest 1 tablespoon of oil was just enough to keep the lean meat of the tenderloin moist without adding too much fat.

Traditionally, the meat for this salad is thinly sliced, marinated, and grilled to create crispy, browned edges. We loved that grilled flavor but quickly tired of firing up the coals or burners for our early tests. So instead, we turned to our broiler, which offered a high direct heat that could mimic the char we were after. We sliced the meat thin, about ⅛ inch, and gave it a run under the broiler. This yielded lackluster results. By the time the meat had the browned, caramelized edges we wanted, it was also overcooked and dry on the interior. For the next test, we sliced the pork ¼ inch thick. This did the trick, allowing the inside of the pork to stay moist while the outside browned.

Bun usually contains a mixture of pickled carrots and daikon radish. However, since daikon can be difficult to find, we opted to leave it out. We tried adding other vegetables like red peppers, onions, and bean sprouts. Tasters ultimately liked the simple combination of carrots and cucumbers with a chile added for heat (Thai, serrano, and jalapeño all worked fine). For the greens we tried red and green leaf lettuce, Bibb lettuce, and iceberg. Tasters thought that the iceberg lacked flavor and got lost in the noodles. While the Bibb lettuce was an acceptable option, tasters preferred red or green leaf for the way it held the dressing and for its soft yet crunchy texture. In addition, an abundance of fresh herbs is traditional; we liked mint, Thai basil, and cilantro in any combination.

Having used delicate rice noodles in other recipes like our Vietnamese Spring Rolls with Hoisin-Peanut Dipping Sauce (page 22), we already had a preferred cooking technique for them. We dropped the noodles into boiling water that had just been removed from the heat and let them soften for 10 minutes before draining them. Unsure what width noodle would be best in this instance, we tested all four sizes: small, medium, large, and extra-large. We settled on the smallest (aka rice vermicelli) as the best for our salad—the dressing easily coated the thinner noodles, and we got more even proportions of noodles, meat, and vegetables in every bite.

All we needed now was the dressing. Our researched recipes told us that the fundamental ingredients are traditionally lime juice, fish sauce, sugar, garlic, and chiles, a combination that provides a careful balance of tart, sweet, salty, and spicy flavors. We liked the distinct flavor fish sauce added, and we were surprised that we settled on a full ⅔ cup for six servings to get the right bold, salty flavor that complemented the pork. This amount was nicely tempered by 5 tablespoons of granulated sugar. For heat we opted for some minced chiles, and tasters confirmed that three was the magic number. A few recipes we found called for rice vinegar, but we preferred the citrusy acidity provided by lime juice. Because tasters kept requesting more and more dressing, we decided to use half of it to dress the salad and save the other half for serving.

Our recipe was really good, but then a fellow test cook suggested one more improvement. Some recipes had called for pickling the vegetables, but we had ruled it out early on as too fussy. What if we soaked the vegetables in the dressing, just while we cooked the noodles and pork, to mimic the pickling? This worked like a charm, yielding vegetables with a distinct pickled taste without much extra effort or additional ingredients.

With each component ready to go, we assembled our salad and dug in. It was so packed with flavor and appealing texture, we didn't even think about the fact that it was good for us, too.

NOTES FROM THE TEST KITCHEN

TRIMMING CILANTRO QUICKLY

Picking cilantro leaf by leaf off the stems can be a pain. To trim the leaves quickly, simply wash and dry a bunch of cilantro, then hold it at an angle by the stems. Shave off the leaves with a sharp chef's knife and you're done.

Vietnamese Rice Noodle Salad with Pork

SERVES 6

Freezing the pork for 15 minutes before slicing makes it easier to cut thin slices. To make this dish spicier, add the chile seeds. Italian basil can be substituted for the Thai basil.

PORK

- 2 tablespoons fish sauce
- 2 tablespoons dark brown sugar
- 1 tablespoon canola oil
- 1 (1-pound) pork tenderloin, trimmed of all visible fat and sliced crosswise into ¼-inch-thick medallions

DRESSING

- ⅔ cup fish sauce
- ½ cup warm water
- 6 tablespoons fresh lime juice (about 3 limes)
- 5 tablespoons granulated sugar
- 3 fresh Thai, serrano, or jalapeño chiles, seeded and minced
- 2 garlic cloves, minced

SALAD

- 3 large carrots, peeled and shredded
- 1 large cucumber, peeled, halved lengthwise, seeded, and cut into 2-inch-long matchsticks (see page 22)
- ¼ cup chopped unsalted roasted peanuts
- 1 fresh Thai, serrano, or jalapeño chile, seeded and minced
- 8 ounces dried rice vermicelli (see page 31)
- 4 ounces red or green leaf lettuce, sliced thin (about 4 cups)
- ½ cup loosely packed fresh Thai basil leaves
- ½ cup loosely packed fresh cilantro or mint leaves

1. FOR THE PORK: Whisk the fish sauce, brown sugar, and oil together in a medium bowl until the sugar dissolves. Add the pork and toss to coat evenly. Cover and refrigerate for at least 30 minutes or up to 24 hours.

2. FOR THE DRESSING: Whisk the fish sauce, water, lime juice, granulated sugar, chiles, and garlic together in a bowl until the sugar dissolves; set aside.

3. FOR THE SALAD: Toss the carrots, cucumber, peanuts, and chile with ¼ cup of the dressing in a bowl and set aside to marinate while cooking the noodles and pork.

4. Bring 4 quarts water to a boil in a large pot. Remove from the heat, add the rice vermicelli, and let sit, stirring occasionally, until the noodles are tender, about 10 minutes. Drain the noodles and transfer to a large bowl. Layer the carrot-cucumber mixture, lettuce, basil, and cilantro on top of the noodles (do not toss) and set aside.

5. Position an oven rack 6 inches from the heating element and heat the broiler. Line a broiler pan bottom with foil and top with a broiler pan top. Remove the pork from the marinade and spread it out on the broiler pan top. Broil the pork until golden on both sides with crisp edges, about 10 minutes, flipping the slices halfway through.

6. Pour half of the remaining dressing over the noodles, carrot-cucumber mixture, lettuce, and herbs and toss to combine. Divide the noodles evenly among 4 large individual serving bowls and top with the broiled pork. Serve, passing the remaining dressing separately.

PER 1½-CUP SERVING: Cal 410; Fat 7g; Sat fat 1g; Chol 50mg; Carb 59g; Protein 26g; Fiber 3g; Sodium 1530mg

SPANISH-STYLE NOODLES WITH SEAFOOD

IN SPAIN, *FIDEOS* ARE VERY SHORT NOODLES SIMILAR to vermicelli, but the word also refers to a classic Valencian dish in which these noodles are toasted to a golden brown and simmered in a flavorful, saffron-spiked broth until they have soaked up most of the broth and are tender and only lightly sauced. With the addition of chorizo and shellfish, it becomes a hearty meal that is similar to paella but with noodles instead of rice. It's an elegant yet satisfying one-pot meal, but it isn't without its challenges. Labor-intensive homemade stock and oil-slicked noodles plagued many of the recipes we found. And then there were the issues with timing the noodles and seafood so they were properly cooked simultaneously and ending up with just the perfect amount of sauce to coat the noodles. We headed to the kitchen to see if we could create a light, streamlined fideos with each component perfectly cooked.

Our first hurdle was the noodles. Traditional fideos are very thin noodles that are about 2 inches long. Because we couldn't find them in our neighborhood grocery store, we were going to have to come up with an alternative. We settled on similarly thin vermicelli, which we could easily and tidily break into 2-inch lengths by placing them in a zipper-lock bag and breaking them over the edge of the counter.

Just as toasting the rice is key to paella, toasting the noodles is an integral part of what gives fideos its signature flavor. Traditionally, the uncooked noodles are tossed with several tablespoons of oil and toasted in a skillet until golden brown. We found that we could achieve acceptable browning with just 2 teaspoons of oil, and it took just five minutes over medium heat for the noodles to turn the right deep golden color.

After toasting the noodles, we set them aside so we could focus on the noodles' cooking liquid. Homemade fish stock was common to many of the recipes we had found, but we wanted a dish we could make any night of the week. We turned to clam juice, an ingredient we often use in the test kitchen when looking for an easy alternative to stock. To round out the flavor of our cooking liquid, we looked to our paella recipe for inspiration. We began by sautéing the chorizo, which, though not always included in fideos recipes, we felt was key for adding smoky flavor and complexity to the dish. If we cut the sausage into small ¼-inch pieces, just 2 ounces was enough to infuse its smoky flavor throughout. After it had browned, we set it aside and sautéed our aromatics, a mixture of garlic and onion. Once they were softened, the clam juice went into the skillet along with some crushed saffron, a signature ingredient (just as in paella) for adding grassy, flowery notes, and we also stirred in a combination of diced tomatoes and white wine, both of which gave the dish an acidic brightness. Then we added the noodles and chorizo to the mixture, gave it all a stir, covered the skillet, and let it simmer until the noodles were tender. Unfortunately, by the time they were done (it took about 15 minutes), our skillet was completely dry and all we had were gummy noodles. We had started with 2 cups of clam juice, so for our next test we tried upping the amount to 3 cups. This produced the tender noodles we were after, but now the flavor was too salty. Using water rather than clam juice for the additional

cup of liquid was an easy fix. These noodles were tender, nicely flavored, and just slightly saucy.

When it comes to fish and shellfish, fideos can contain anything and everything from shrimp, clams, and mussels to calamari, monkfish, and octopus. Keeping in mind our simple and streamlined goal, we limited ourselves to clams and shrimp. But because both are quick-cooking, we gave the noodles a five-minute head start before adding the clams and shrimp to the pan. However, one test proved the shrimp needed even less time. Adding the clams five minutes into the noodles' cooking time and the shrimp three minutes after that did the trick. Now every component was perfectly cooked.

Tasters liked everything about the recipe, but still, we felt it was missing something. Traditionally fideos is served with a garlicky aïoli, but we didn't want to fuss with another recipe at this point. We tried adding extra olive oil to boost the richness, but everyone agreed it fell a little flat. Though not traditional, we found our solution in a tablespoon of butter. It added not just richness but also a sweetness that echoed that of an aïoli. A sprinkling of parsley added a bright, fresh flavor and a pop of color. With that, we had a Spanish-style noodles recipe that was festive enough for company but easy enough for a fun family dinner, no trip to Spain required.

Spanish-Style Noodles with Seafood
SERVES 4

You can substitute andouille or linguiça for the chorizo if preferred. Be sure to discard any clams that are open or have broken shells prior to cooking.

1   **pound extra-large shrimp (21 to 25 per pound), peeled and deveined (see page 120)**
    Salt and pepper
1   **tablespoon olive oil**
12   **ounces vermicelli, broken into 2-inch pieces**
2   **ounces chorizo sausage, cut into ¼-inch pieces**
1   **onion, minced (about 1 cup)**
3   **garlic cloves, minced**

1   (14.5-ounce) can diced tomatoes

2   (8-ounce) bottles clam juice

1   cup water

½   cup dry white wine

½   teaspoon saffron threads, crumbled

1   pound littleneck clams (about 12 clams), scrubbed

1   tablespoon unsalted butter

2   tablespoons minced fresh parsley

    Lemon wedges, for serving

1. Toss the shrimp with ¼ teaspoon salt and ⅛ teaspoon pepper in a bowl and set aside.

2. Heat 2 teaspoons of the oil in a 12-inch nonstick skillet over medium heat. Add the vermicelli and cook, stirring frequently, until golden, 4 to 6 minutes. Transfer the noodles to a large plate.

3. Add the remaining 1 teaspoon oil to the skillet and return to medium-high heat until just smoking. Add the chorizo and cook, stirring occasionally, until lightly browned, 2 to 4 minutes. Transfer the chorizo to a paper towel–lined plate.

4. Add the onion and ⅛ teaspoon salt to the oil left in the skillet and return to medium-low heat. Cover and cook, stirring occasionally, until the onion is softened, 8 to 10 minutes. Uncover, stir in the garlic, and cook until fragrant, about 30 seconds. Stir in the tomatoes with their juice, clam juice, water, wine, and saffron and bring to a simmer.

5. Return the vermicelli and chorizo to the skillet. Cover, increase the heat to medium-high, and cook for 5 minutes, stirring often and adjusting the heat to maintain a vigorous simmer. Nestle the clams, hinge side down, into the vermicelli. Cover and simmer for 3 minutes. Sprinkle the shrimp over the top, cover, and cook until the shrimp are translucent and the clams have opened, 5 to 7 minutes.

6. Gently stir in the butter, sprinkle with the parsley, and season with salt and pepper to taste. Serve with the lemon wedges.

PER SERVING: Cal 630; Fat 15g; Sat fat 5g; Chol 205mg; Carb 75g; Protein 44g; Fiber 4g; Sodium 1110mg

NOTES FROM THE TEST KITCHEN

BREAKING NOODLES

To break the noodles evenly and keep them from going all over the kitchen, put them in a zipper-lock bag (or wrap them in a clean kitchen towel), then press against the corner of the counter.

THE BEST CLAM JUICE

When there's no time to shuck fresh little-necks and cherrystones for a homemade seafood base, we reach for a jug of their juice. Clam juice is made by briefly steaming fresh clams in salted water and filtering the resulting broth before bottling. Of the three brands we tried in a basic seafood pasta dish, only one sample garnered criticism for tasting "too strong" and "too clammy"—perhaps because its sodium content was more than double that of the other brands. Our top brand, **Bar Harbor**, hails from the shores of clam country in Maine, is available nationwide, and brings a "bright" and "mineral-y" flavor to seafood dishes.

SAFFRON: DOES BRAND MAKE A DIFFERENCE?

Saffron threads are the world's most expensive spice. So how important is brand? The answer: not very, if your recipe has other strong flavors. When we tasted four brands (two mail-order, two supermarket, all high-grade red Spanish threads) in spicy, garlicky mayonnaise, we couldn't distinguish one from another. Only when we sampled the spices in plain chicken broth, with no other competing flavors, did the grassy, hay-like taste of our winner, **Morton & Bassett Saffron Threads**, $10.99 for 0.01 ounce, stand out. Despite being sold in the supermarket, this brand was the most expensive in the lineup. Unless saffron is the main flavoring in your recipe, you'll likely be fine with any brand of red threads.

CHICKPEA CAKES WITH CUCUMBER-YOGURT SAUCE

VEGETARIAN ENTRÉES

M   = TEST KITCHEN MAKEOVER

CHICKPEA CAKES

A HEALTHY STAPLE WITH A GREAT NUTTY FLAVOR, chickpeas appear in cuisines throughout the world, particularly the Mediterranean, Middle East, and India, gracing tables in everything from hearty soups and salads to spicy curries, creamy hummus, and crispy falafel. Looking for a new way to use this healthy bean in a vegetarian entrée, we came across several recipes for chickpea cakes in modern Indian cookbooks. We loved the idea of a dish featuring the buttery, nutty flavor of chickpeas that would be satisfying but not too heavy. We knew that our biggest challenge would be creating cakes that were tender but at the same time would hold together, all without going overboard on binders that would take away from the chickpea flavor. We wanted to develop a chickpea cake that was infused with the subtle flavor of Indian spices and had an appealing texture that was neither pasty nor too chunky.

We started with the chickpeas themselves. We prefer dried beans in most applications for their superior texture, but since these beans were going to be at least partially mashed, dried beans weren't as critical. Using canned beans was a great time-saver since it would eliminate the steps of soaking and precooking the beans, and two cans of beans would provide the right amount of bulk to make six cakes.

We found there were two main camps when it came to preparing the cakes: Some mash some of the beans and leave some whole; others mash all of the beans. We tried both, combining the chickpeas with some shallot, olive oil, and an egg (for binding), forming them into cakes, and pan-searing them on each side (we found we had more control over the cakes in a skillet rather than the oven). We weren't surprised when tasters declared the texture of the all-mashed style to be pasty and unappealing. However, leaving some chickpeas whole did come with problems; the cakes did not hold together well. For our next test, we tried using the food processor to create a blend of small and larger pieces, which avoided the problem of whole beans without making cakes that were pasty. Tasters gave the texture of these cakes the thumbs-up, but even with the texture worked out, we had trouble keeping the cakes from falling apart in the skillet.

We wondered if more eggs would keep our cakes together, so we made two more batches using two and three eggs. The cakes made with three eggs turned out too moist, closer to a dippable hummus than a firm cake, but those with two held together perfectly and were still tender.

With our cakes in good shape, we could turn our attention to giving them a flavor boost. Typical additions include minced vegetables, spices, herbs, and yogurt. We started by testing vegetables: onions, garlic, scallions, shallot, and red bell pepper. Tasters disliked the bell pepper; its sweet flavor competed with the chickpeas, and both the raw garlic and onion were too potent for the mild beans. A mix of scallion and shallot provided the right amount of subtle bite and herbal flavor, and a touch of cilantro lent just the right freshness.

For the spices, we started by testing cumin, coriander, cayenne, and cardamom, alone and in various combinations. They all worked fine, but to simplify our ingredient list we opted for garam masala—an Indian spice blend of warm spices such as black pepper, cardamom, cinnamon, cloves, cumin, and coriander—and a bit of cayenne for heat.

These cakes were close, but they tasted lean. To round out the flavor, a little olive oil (for richness) and Greek yogurt (for creaminess and tang) did the trick.

But now an old problem reared its ugly head: Once again our cakes did not hold together well because the olive oil and yogurt were adding too much moisture. Borrowing a classic method from meatballs and meatloaf, we added fresh bread crumbs to our mixture. Unfortunately, the crumbs turned our cakes gummy. We found that pretoasting the crumbs fixed the problem, drying them out so their texture—and the cakes'—wouldn't suffer. After a few minutes in the skillet on each side, these chickpea cakes browned nicely and tasted great, but tasters agreed the dish felt unfinished. In many of the recipes we had found the chickpea cakes were served with a sauce, which we agreed would do the job nicely.

We came across two types of sauces served with Indian-style chickpea cakes: a tahini-based sauce (tahini is a sesame paste) and *raita*, which is a cucumber and yogurt sauce. Side by side, tasters preferred the cucumber and yogurt option, which combined diced cucumber with yogurt, cilantro, salt, and pepper. Its fresh and cooling flavor helped brighten the dish, but its texture wasn't quite right; chunks of cucumber were surrounded by a thin pool of yogurt. Switching to thicker Greek yogurt helped, but not enough. Instead of using diced cucumber, for our next test we tried shredding it. Tasters agreed this sauce was more cohesive. Watery cucumber is notorious for releasing its liquid and diluting sauces and dressings, so we made sure to salt and drain the shredded cucumber before combining it with the yogurt. With a dollop of cucumber-yogurt sauce on top of each chickpea cake, we had a winning healthy entrée that was light yet flavorful and satisfying, a perfect summertime meal.

Chickpea Cakes with Cucumber-Yogurt Sauce

SERVES 6

You can substitute ½ teaspoon ground coriander, ¼ teaspoon black pepper, ⅛ teaspoon ground cardamom, and ⅛ teaspoon ground cinnamon for the garam masala if preferred. Avoid overmixing the bean mixture in step 3 or the cakes will have a mealy texture.

- 2 slices high-quality white sandwich bread, torn into pieces
- 1 cucumber, peeled, halved lengthwise, seeded (see page 22), and shredded
  Salt
- 1¼ cups 2 percent Greek yogurt
- 6 scallions, sliced thin
- ¼ cup minced fresh cilantro
  Black pepper
- 2 (15-ounce) cans chickpeas, drained and rinsed
- 2 large eggs
- 3 tablespoons plus 1 teaspoon olive oil
- 1 teaspoon garam masala
- ⅛ teaspoon cayenne pepper
- 1 shallot, minced (about 3 tablespoons)
  Lime wedges, for serving

1. Adjust an oven rack to the middle position and heat the oven to 350 degrees. Pulse the bread in a food processor to coarse crumbs, about 10 pulses. (Do not wash the food processor bowl.) Spread the crumbs on a rimmed baking sheet and bake, stirring occasionally, until golden brown and dry, 10 to 12 minutes. Let the crumbs cool to room temperature.

2. Meanwhile, toss the cucumber with ½ teaspoon salt in a colander and let drain for 20 minutes. Combine the drained cucumber, ¾ cup of the yogurt, 2 tablespoons of the scallions, and 1 tablespoon of the cilantro in a bowl and season with salt and black pepper to taste.

3. Pulse the chickpeas in the food processor to a coarse puree with large pieces remaining, about 8 pulses. In a medium bowl, whisk the eggs, 2 tablespoons of the oil, garam masala, cayenne, and ⅛ teaspoon salt together. Stir in the toasted bread crumbs, remaining ½ cup yogurt, remaining scallions, remaining 3 tablespoons cilantro, processed chickpeas, and shallot until just combined. Divide the chickpea mixture into 6 equal portions, about ½ cup each, and lightly pack into 1-inch-thick cakes.

4. Heat 2 teaspoons more oil in a 12-inch nonstick skillet over medium heat until shimmering. Carefully lay half of the cakes in the skillet and cook until well browned on both sides, 8 to 10 minutes, flipping them halfway through.

5. Transfer the cakes to a plate and tent loosely with foil. Return the skillet to medium heat and repeat with the remaining 2 teaspoons oil and remaining cakes. Serve with the cucumber-yogurt sauce and lime wedges.

PER SERVING (1 CAKE PLUS ¼ CUP SAUCE): Cal 240; Fat 12g; Sat fat 2.5g; Chol 75mg; Carb 23g; Protein 12g; Fiber 5g; Sodium 610mg

---

NOTES FROM THE TEST KITCHEN

GREEK YOGURT

Greek yogurt is thicker and creamier than American-style yogurts. Much of the whey (the watery liquid that separates from the solids) is strained out of Greek yogurt, giving it a rich, smooth texture that is slightly thicker than that of sour cream. (A close cousin to Greek yogurt, *labne*, or yogurt cheese, is strained of all its whey.) In terms of flavor, Greek yogurt is fairly mild, with a slight tang. These qualities make it ideal for dips and spreads such as Cucumber-Yogurt Sauce. Note that FAGE Total Classic Greek Yogurt (the most widely available brand in the United States) contains 23 grams of fat. However, this brand is also available in 2 percent and nonfat varieties. To make our own version of Greek yogurt, we strained plain low-fat yogurt in a fine-mesh strainer lined with a coffee filter and set over a bowl to catch the whey. After an hour (in the refrigerator, covered with plastic wrap), the yogurt had reduced in volume by one third, achieving a thick, rich consistency closely resembling that of Greek yogurt. Its taste was pretty close as well.

TEMPEH TACOS

AFFORDABLE, EASY TO MAKE, AND FUN TO EAT, HARD-shell tacos are an all-time Tex-Mex favorite. But while recipes for homemade beef or chicken tacos are easy to come by, vegetarian versions are not quite so ubiquitous. Those that do exist usually rely on beans or grilled vegetables as the stand-in for the meat, which are fine but can sometimes seem like tacos that are just missing the meat. We're particularly fond of the classic ground beef taco, and with all the options for vegetarian meat substitutes available these days, we felt confident we could develop a taco recipe that had a filling with great savory flavor and texture comparable to ground beef tacos—but was 100 percent vegetarian friendly.

First we set our sights on finding the best meat substitute. Soy products are a staple vegetarian protein source and were a logical starting point. We gathered tofu, tempeh, and textured vegetable protein (TVP, a soy product sold in dehydrated flake form) and cooked up three basic batches, sautéing onion and garlic, then stirring in the protein and simmering with basic seasonings until done. Tofu was an out-and-out failure. Silken and soft tofus disintegrated in the skillet as expected, and the extra-firm tofu crumbled into unappealing bits. TVP became swollen when cooked, with a spongy texture that won over no one. However, tasters were pleased by the tacos made with tempeh. A tender but firm soybean cake made from fermented whole soybeans, tempeh can taste slightly sour or yeasty on its own, but here it came across as mildly nutty when mixed with the bolder taco flavors. Also, the texture of these tacos was actually "meaty."

With our protein chosen, we moved on to seasoning our filling beyond the simple onion and garlic combination. The classic choice for beef tacos is of course the packet of supermarket seasoning mix. But the labels on these packets indicate a hodgepodge of ingredients, including dehydrated onion and/or garlic, MSG, mysterious "spices," and even soy sauce, and their flavor is dusty. In the test kitchen we usually season beef tacos with chili powder, cumin, coriander, oregano, and cayenne. We started there. Since we weren't using ground beef, we knew we would probably have to alter these seasonings to better complement the tempeh. Tasters agreed that cumin was too strong and smoky here, and coriander too mild. For the chili powder, we began with 2 tablespoons but quickly increased it to 3 tablespoons for the right kick. One teaspoon of dried oregano provided herbal notes. This simple combination added the right depth without overpowering the tempeh. To make their flavor fuller and rounder, we bloomed the spices by heating them briefly in a skillet. This simple step gave the filling a rich, deep flavor that was markedly better than stirring them in raw.

Taco fillings are usually made cohesive by a light sauce, which also helps carry the flavors of the spices. Many taco recipes call only for water, but water produced a hollow-tasting mixture for these tacos. We tried making one batch with canned vegetable broth and another with canned plain tomato sauce. Made with all vegetable broth, the filling took on a sweet flavor and the sauce did not thicken enough. On the other hand, made with only tomato sauce, the sauce was too thick and tomatoey, overshadowing the flavor of the spices. A combination of the two was perfect, with a nice acidity from the tomato sauce but not so much as to mask the spices, and together they reduced into just the right consistency.

The last adjustments to the filling came in the form of sweet and sour. A teaspoon of brown sugar complemented the spices and 1 tablespoon of lime juice picked up where the tomato sauce left off, adding just enough acidity to brighten it up. We moved on to the shells.

We crunched the numbers and determined that homemade deep-fried taco shells wouldn't make the cut because of all the oil they absorbed. We liked the idea of baked tortilla shells, but they were a pain to make. For

NOTES FROM THE TEST KITCHEN

TEMPEH

While tofu has hit the mainstream, its soy-based cousin, tempeh, might not be as familiar. Tempeh is made by fermenting cooked soybeans and then forming the mixture into a firm, dense cake. (Some versions of tempeh also contain beans, grains, and flavorings.) Because it's better than tofu at holding its shape when cooked, it serves as a good meat substitute and is a mainstay of many vegetarian diets. It has a strong, almost nutty flavor, and it tends to absorb the flavors of any foods or sauces to which it is added, making it a versatile choice for all sorts of dishes, from chilis and stews to sandwiches and tacos. It is also a healthy choice since it's high in protein (depending on the variety, a 4-ounce portion provides 18 to 20 grams of protein), contains many essential vitamins and minerals, is cholesterol-free, and is very low in fat. Tempeh is sold in most supermarkets and can be found with different grain combinations and flavorings. We prefer to use low-fat five-grain tempeh in our recipes but any tempeh variety will work.

the sake of convenience we decided store-bought shells would be best. These crunchy premade shells complemented our tasty tempeh filling well, and they didn't add much fat. Served with any combination of low-fat cheddar, shredded lettuce, diced tomato, avocado, onion, low-fat sour cream, or hot sauce, these healthy vegetarian tacos could hold their own against the beef versions any day—and with a lot less fat and calories.

Tempeh Tacos

SERVES 6

Any type of tempeh will work well in these tacos; for more information on tempeh, see page 150. Feel free to top these tacos with low-fat cheese, lettuce, and tomatoes. Avocado, onion, low-fat sour cream, and hot sauce are also worthy garnishes.

- 1 tablespoon canola oil
- 1 onion, minced (about 1 cup)
  Salt
- 3 tablespoons chili powder
- 4 garlic cloves, minced
- 1 teaspoon dried oregano
- 2 (8-ounce) packages low-fat 5-grain tempeh, crumbled into ¼-inch pieces
- 1 (8-ounce) can plain tomato sauce
- 1 cup vegetable broth
- 1 teaspoon light brown sugar
- 2 tablespoons minced fresh cilantro
- 1 tablespoon fresh lime juice
  Pepper
- 12 store-bought taco shells, warmed

1. Heat the oil in a 12-inch nonstick skillet over medium heat until shimmering. Add the onion and ⅛ teaspoon salt and cook, stirring occasionally, until softened, 5 to 7 minutes. Stir in the chili powder, garlic, and oregano and cook until fragrant, about 30 seconds.

2. Add the tempeh to the skillet and cook until lightly browned, about 5 minutes. Stir in the tomato sauce, broth, and sugar. Bring to a simmer and cook until thickened, about 2 minutes.

3. Off the heat, stir in the cilantro and lime juice and season with salt and pepper to taste. Divide the filling evenly among the taco shells and serve.

PER SERVING: Cal 300; Fat 11g; Sat fat 2g; Chol 0mg; Carb 42g; Protein 13g; Fiber 6g; Sodium 620mg

STUFFED EGGPLANTS

WHETHER GRILLED, ROASTED, OR FRIED, EGGPLANT'S flesh is transformed from mildly bitter to rich and complex when cooked, making it a versatile, satisfying vegetable. Each preparation has its merits, but the idea of marrying the creamy, rich eggplant with a texturally contrasting filling offers great potential as a hearty meal. Unfortunately, many recipes for stuffed eggplant that we tried featured oil-saturated eggplant and bland, watery fillings. We wanted stuffed eggplant with a perfectly cooked creamy shell and a hearty, flavorful filling that would make a satisfying vegetarian main course.

We began our testing by picking our variety of eggplant. We quickly found that the long, slender Japanese or Asian eggplants did not have enough flesh, which made stuffing them difficult, and they weren't large enough to make a substantial entrée. Large (sometimes called globe) eggplants, on the other hand, were too big. The smaller variety of eggplant—sometimes labeled Italian—was just right. Smaller than the globes but not as thin as the Japanese eggplants, these were ideal for stuffing.

With the type of eggplant resolved, we were ready to determine the best cooking method. Our basic method for stuffed vegetable recipes calls for precooking the vegetable, then stuffing it with a prepared filling, and finally heating it through. We immediately ruled out cooking our eggplants on the stovetop because they were too big to fit in the skillet all at once, and we didn't want to deal with cooking in batches. Instead, we turned to the oven. We cut the eggplants in half, scored the flesh (we knew from past experience that this would allow the eggplants to release liquid more quickly and concentrate the flavor faster), then brushed them with oil and seasoned them with salt and pepper. We arranged them cut side down on a preheated baking sheet so that we could maximize the amount of caramelized flesh. After less than an hour in a 400-degree oven, the eggplant emerged golden brown and tender. The cut sides of the eggplants caramelized beautifully, which further intensified the flavor. We could turn our attention to the filling.

We needed a filling that would transform the eggplant into a hearty meal, and one that could be easily prepared while the eggplant was in the oven. To start, we tested fillings made with toasted bread crumbs and a few whole grains. For the grains, we tried barley, bulgur wheat, and brown rice since they all offered a heartiness that would lend a rustic feel to the dish. The fillings made with bread crumbs, not surprisingly, had a mushy texture. Those that were grain-based, however, were substantial and complemented the eggplant well. Since both barley and brown rice would require lengthy precooking and we wanted to keep this simple, we eliminated both. Bulgur (wheat kernels that have been steamed, dried, and crushed, a familiar ingredient from our Middle Eastern Tabbouleh Salad; see page 202) requires only soaking before it's ready. Tasters approved both its texture and the nutty flavor it lent to the filling.

While we liked the flavor of the bulgur, our filling was still a bit one-dimensional. The addition of onion was a good start, as well as a touch of Pecorino cheese. Looking to add even more depth, as well as texture, we turned to other vegetables we thought might add complexity. We tried batches made with green bell peppers, fresh tomatoes, and zucchini. Tasters thought the green bell peppers were too bitter and the zucchini too mild to make enough of an impact. However, the chopped fresh tomatoes lent a nice bright flavor and a bit of moisture without making the filling mushy, and their subtle sweetness was a perfect complement to the eggplant.

To round out the flavor, we seasoned the filling with oregano for an herbal note, cinnamon for warmth, and a little cayenne for heat. To further boost the filling's flavor, just 2 tablespoons of pine nuts divided among the filling for eight eggplant halves imparted richness and flavor and also added a pleasant, lightly crunchy texture. After stirring in some red wine vinegar to brighten the overall flavor and balance the sweetness of the onions, we were ready to stuff the eggplants.

We simply made a pocket for the filling in each eggplant by pushing the soft flesh to the sides using two forks. We then mounded about ½ cup of filling into each opening and sprinkled a small amount of grated cheese over the top of each eggplant half for a nice finishing touch. After a few minutes in the oven, a sprinkling of fresh parsley for color and freshness was all it took to finish things off. Now we had a recipe for stuffed eggplant that tastes so good and is so satisfying, even a carnivore would enjoy it.

Stuffed Eggplants with Bulgur

SERVES 4

Do not use coarse-grain bulgur or cracked wheat in this recipe; for more information on buying bulgur, see page 203. Remember to rinse the bulgur before soaking. The time it takes for the bulgur to become tender and fluffy in step 3 will depend on the age and type of the bulgur.

- 4   Italian eggplants (10 ounces each), halved lengthwise
- 2   tablespoons extra-virgin olive oil
     Salt and black pepper
- ½   cup fine- or medium-grain bulgur wheat, rinsed and drained
- ¼   cup water
- 1   onion, minced (about 1 cup)
- 3   garlic cloves, minced
- 2   teaspoons minced fresh oregano or ½ teaspoon dried
- ¼   teaspoon ground cinnamon
     Pinch cayenne pepper
- 1   pound plum tomatoes (3 to 4 tomatoes), cored, seeded, and chopped medium
- 2   ounces Pecorino Romano cheese, grated (about 1 cup)
- 2   tablespoons pine nuts, toasted
- 2   teaspoons red wine vinegar
- 2   tablespoons minced fresh parsley

1. Adjust the oven racks to the upper-middle and lowest positions, place a rimmed baking sheet lined with foil on the lower rack, and heat the oven to 400 degrees.

NOTES FROM THE TEST KITCHEN

SCORING AN EGGPLANT

Using the tip of a chef's knife (or paring knife), score each eggplant half in a 1-inch diamond pattern, making cuts about 1 inch deep. This allows the eggplant to release liquid more quickly and concentrate its flavor faster.

PREPARING EGGPLANT FOR STUFFING

Using two forks, gently push the flesh to the sides of each baked eggplant half to make room for the filling.

2. Following the photo on page 152, score the cut sides of the eggplants, then brush with 1 tablespoon of the oil and season with ⅛ teaspoon salt and ⅛ teaspoon black pepper. Carefully lay the eggplants, cut side down, on the preheated baking sheet. Roast until the flesh is tender, 40 to 50 minutes. Carefully transfer the eggplants to a paper towel–lined baking sheet and let drain.

3. Meanwhile, toss the bulgur with the water in a bowl and let sit until the grains are tender and fluffy, 20 to 40 minutes.

4. Combine the remaining tablespoon oil, onion, and ⅛ teaspoon salt in a 12-inch skillet. Cover and cook over medium-low heat, stirring occasionally, until softened, 8 to 10 minutes. Stir in the garlic, oregano, cinnamon, and cayenne and cook until fragrant, about 30 seconds. Stir in the soaked bulgur, tomatoes, ¾ cup of the cheese, pine nuts, and vinegar and cook until warmed through, about 1 minute. Season with salt and black pepper to taste.

5. Return the roasted eggplants, cut side up, to the foil-lined baking sheet. Following the photo on page 152, use two forks to gently push the eggplant flesh to the sides to make room for the filling. Mound the bulgur mixture into the eggplant shells (about ½ cup of filling per eggplant half).

6. Sprinkle the remaining ¼ cup cheese over the top of the stuffed eggplants and bake on the upper-middle rack until the cheese is melted, 5 to 10 minutes. Sprinkle with the parsley and serve.

PER SERVING: **Cal** 310; **Fat** 15g; **Sat fat** 3.5g; **Chol** 10mg; **Carb** 39g; **Protein** 11g; **Fiber** 15g; **Sodium** 500mg

VEGETABLE AND BEAN TOSTADAS

AFTER MAKING A BIG HIT IN THE TEST KITCHEN WITH our vegetarian Tempeh Tacos (page 151), we decided to transform another Tex-Mex favorite, the tostada, into a healthy vegetarian entrée. Since some people might find tempeh a little too off the beaten path, we decided that for this recipe we would feature beans as the protein. Ideally, we envisioned a vegetable tostada composed of a crisp tortilla topped with creamy beans, flavorful vegetables, and complementary garnishes. Most recipes we tried failed in a number of ways: limp tortillas, bland beans, and soggy vegetables. It wasn't hard for us to imagine a better version. We were after a quick, streamlined, and healthy vegetable tostada that would bring out the best flavor and texture from the vegetables and highlight the creamy, rich texture of the beans.

We began building our tostada from the ground up. As for all tostadas, our foundation would be a crispy tortilla. We knew that deep-frying was out; these tortillas would have to be oven-baked, and we'd already determined the best method when developing our Spicy Mexican Shredded Pork Tostadas (page 97). We arranged corn tortillas on a baking sheet, lightly sprayed them with vegetable oil spray, and baked them for about 10 minutes in a 450-degree oven until they were lightly browned and crispy. This method would work just as well for our Vegetable and Bean Tostadas, so we moved on to our next component, the beans.

Mashed beans are commonly used in tostadas—vegetarian or otherwise—not just for flavor and texture but also to serve as the "cement" that holds other components to the crisped tortilla. To keep this recipe from being too time-consuming, we decided to work with canned beans (since these beans were going to be mashed, the superior texture of the dried beans was not much of an issue). We narrowed the field to pinto beans, black beans, and kidney beans. We rinsed the beans, mashed each, then cooked them with a little oil and water until they thickened to a consistency similar to that of refried beans. Tasters unanimously chose pinto beans for their mild flavor and creamy texture. But they agreed they wanted the consistency to be even creamier and the flavor more complex. We tried whirling the beans in the blender before cooking, but they turned gummy and pasty. Adding vegetable broth instead of water helped the flavor, but then someone suggested using the canning liquid. This took care of both problems at once, as cooking them in their own starchy juice upped the level of creaminess noticeably and amplified the beans' flavor.

With the texture just right, it was time to adjust the seasoning of the beans. Many recipes call for cumin or coriander, and most bring some sort of heat in the form of fresh or pickled jalapeños or cayenne. Tasters thought both the cumin and the coriander were too potent. For the heat, everyone favored the briny flavor of the pickled jalapeños over both cayenne and fresh jalapeños. They liked it so much they wanted even more briny flavor, and the addition of 1 tablespoon of the jalapeño brine did the trick. These beans were ready for our tostadas.

It was time to move on to the vegetables. To keep

VEGETABLE AND BEAN TOSTADAS

our recipe easy and quick, we decided to simply sauté the vegetables for our tostadas, forgoing the more time-consuming methods of grilling or roasting. We made four batches of tostadas, topping each with a different sautéed vegetable—onion, sliced portobello mushrooms, yellow squash, and bell peppers—to find our favorites. The squash was immediately dismissed for its mushy texture. We thought portobello mushrooms would be nice because of their meaty texture, but tasters thought the beans muted their flavor too much. Ultimately, we liked a mix of sliced onions and bell peppers, a combination that brought a hint of sweetness that complemented the slight spiciness of the beans. To brighten them up and add a hit of freshness, we tossed the vegetables with 1 tablespoon of lime juice after they were cooked.

Many versions of tostadas we had come across were topped off with a spicy cabbage slaw. We thought it could provide a nice crunchy contrast to the beans and vegetables, so we decided to follow suit. Instead of dealing with making a dressing, we opted to simply toss the cabbage with some more of the jalapeño brine. We tested slaws made from green cabbage, red cabbage, and bagged coleslaw mix. The red cabbage leached reddish liquid everywhere, turning our tostadas an unappealing pink color. While the green cabbage was better, the ease of using bagged coleslaw mix pushed it into the winner's circle.

We had built a great-tasting vegetable tostada, but adding garnishes of *queso fresco*, low-fat sour cream, and minced cilantro really sealed the deal.

Vegetable and Bean Tostadas

SERVES 6

If you can't find queso fresco, feta makes a fine substitute. Make sure not to drain the canned pinto beans, as the canning liquid is part of the recipe.

TOSTADAS

12 (6-inch) corn tortillas
   Vegetable oil spray

VEGETABLES

3 green bell peppers, stemmed, seeded, and sliced thin
2 onions, halved and sliced thin
2 tablespoons canola oil
   Salt and pepper

3 garlic cloves, minced
3 tablespoons fresh lime juice
2 (15-ounce) cans pinto beans (see note)
1 tablespoon finely chopped jarred pickled jalapeños plus ¼ cup jalapeño brine
1 (10-ounce) bag coleslaw mix
4 ounces queso fresco, crumbled (about 1 cup) (see page 76)
½ cup low-fat sour cream
2 tablespoons minced fresh cilantro

1. FOR THE TOSTADAS: Adjust the oven racks to the upper-middle and lower-middle positions and heat the oven to 450 degrees. Spread the tortillas on 2 rimmed baking sheets. Lightly coat both sides of the tortillas with vegetable oil spray.

2. Bake until lightly browned and crisp, 8 to 10 minutes, switching and rotating the baking sheets halfway through. Set the tostadas aside.

3. FOR THE VEGETABLES: Meanwhile, combine the bell peppers, onions, 1 tablespoon of the oil, and ¼ teaspoon salt in a 12-inch skillet. Cover and cook over medium-low heat until softened, 8 to 10 minutes. Uncover, increase the heat to medium-high, and continue to cook, stirring occasionally, until lightly browned, 4 to 6 minutes longer.

4. Stir in the garlic and cook until fragrant, about 30 seconds. Off the heat, stir in 1 tablespoon of the lime juice and season with salt and pepper to taste. Transfer the vegetables to a bowl and cover to keep warm.

5. Add the remaining 1 tablespoon oil to the skillet and heat over medium heat until shimmering. Add the beans with their canning liquid, pickled jalapeños, and 1 tablespoon of the jalapeño brine. Cook, mashing the beans with a potato masher, until the mixture is thickened, about 5 minutes. Season with salt and pepper to taste. Transfer the beans to a bowl and cover to keep warm.

6. Toss the coleslaw mix with the remaining 3 tablespoons jalapeño brine in a bowl and season with salt and pepper to taste.

7. TO ASSEMBLE THE TOSTADAS: Spread the bean mixture evenly over the crisp tortillas, then top with the cheese, vegetables, and slaw. Whisk the sour cream and remaining 2 tablespoons lime juice together in a bowl, then drizzle over the top. Sprinkle with the cilantro and serve.

PER SERVING: Cal 400; Fat 10g; Sat fat 1.5g; Chol 10mg; Carb 60g; Protein 14g; Fiber 13g; Sodium 580mg

TOFU SALAD

ALL TOO OFTEN TOFU IS A SUPPORTING PLAYER AND not the star of the show—witness pad thai, where the tofu is often greasy and buried under mounds of noodles and sauce, or a curry or stir-fry where the sauce and vegetables really shine but the tofu is just thrown in to appease the health-conscious. We wanted to develop a recipe that was all about the tofu and where its most admirable qualities would really stand out. After all, it's a great source of protein, creamy but low in fat, and it marries well with lots of different flavors. Could we develop a satisfying salad that put the tofu front and center?

We began our testing with the tofu. We cut extra-firm, firm, and soft tofu into ¾-inch pieces and dressed them with a basic working dressing. Tasters all agreed that the extra-firm and firm tofus were too firm, almost rubbery, in this context. They unanimously chose soft tofu for its creamy, custard-like texture. To drain the tofu of excess moisture, we simply cut it into cubes and placed them on multiple layers of paper towels to drain.

While tofu would be the star, we needed other vegetables to fill out our salad. We wanted the vegetables to be crisp and bright, a nice counterpoint to the creamy texture of the tofu, so we knew they would remain raw. Without any cooking involved, we found that vegetables like broccoli and green beans lent an unappealing toughness, and mild vegetables like zucchini and squash did not offer enough flavor. Tasters liked carrots, snow peas, and bell peppers for both their crisp textures and bright colors, so all three made the cut. Bean sprouts, which are often used in Asian cooking, added a nice crunch and clean flavor that everyone approved.

It was time to move on to the dressing. We limited our scope to creating a boldly flavored Asian-inspired dressing and started by testing three basic flavor profiles: peanut butter, sesame paste (tahini), and soy sauce. The soy sauce made for a dressing that didn't coat the tofu well, and the sesame dressing was a little overpowering. However, the peanut butter flavor held its own with the tofu and vegetables, adding just the right sweetness and nutty flavor. To balance out the dressing and bring in some Asian flavors, we favored a blend of peanut butter, hoisin sauce, lime juice, sesame oil, and garlic, a combination that created the right balance of salty, acidic, and savory. A little chili-garlic sauce added a touch of heat. To achieve the consistency we wanted, we found that 3 tablespoons of hot water thinned the dressing out perfectly for coating the tofu and vegetables. This bold dressing tasted great, but once it was tossed with the tofu and vegetables, the tofu seemed washed out.

In the test kitchen, we have developed ways to boost the flavor of tofu, including glazing, marinating, and broiling. We immediately eliminated the glazing technique since it requires oil to create a crisp coating on the tofu (so that the glaze can cling), and we wanted to avoid any additional fat. To compare the other two methods, we marinated one batch in half of the dressing for an hour; we brushed the other batch with some of the dressing and broiled it until it turned spotty brown. Tasters barely noticed a benefit from the marinating; even after one hour the flavors had barely penetrated the tofu. But the broiled tofu emerged lightly charred and flavorful. We had our winner.

Our tofu now had great flavor and gave the salad more of an identity. After broiling the tofu, we gently tossed it with our crisp and colorful vegetables and the remaining dressing. Thinly sliced scallion, minced cilantro, and toasted sesame seeds gave our salad just the right finishing touches.

Tofu Salad with Vegetables

SERVES 6

We prefer the texture of soft tofu in this recipe; however, firm tofu may be substituted.

DRESSING

- 3 tablespoons creamy peanut butter
- 3 tablespoons hot water
- ¼ cup hoisin sauce
- 4 teaspoons fresh lime juice
- 2 teaspoons toasted sesame oil
- 1 garlic clove, minced
- ¾ teaspoon Asian chili-garlic sauce
- ½ teaspoon salt

SALAD

- 28 ounces soft tofu, cut into ¾-inch pieces and drained
- 8 ounces snow peas (about 4 cups), trimmed and cut into ½-inch-wide pieces
- 1 red or yellow bell pepper, stemmed, seeded, and cut into ½-inch pieces

2 cups bean sprouts

2 carrots, peeled and shredded

2 scallions, sliced thin on the bias

3 tablespoons minced fresh cilantro

1 tablespoon sesame seeds, toasted

Salt and pepper

1. FOR THE DRESSING: Whisk the peanut butter and water together in a bowl until smooth, then whisk in the hoisin, lime juice, sesame oil, garlic, chili-garlic sauce, and salt until combined; set aside.

2. FOR THE SALAD: Position an oven rack 6 inches from the broiler element and heat the broiler. Line a rimmed baking sheet with foil.

3. Toss the tofu pieces with half of the dressing and spread them on the prepared baking sheet. Broil the tofu until spotty brown, 5 to 6 minutes.

4. Meanwhile, toss the snow peas, bell pepper, bean sprouts, carrots, and scallions with the remaining dressing in a large bowl until well combined. Gently fold in the broiled tofu, cilantro, and sesame seeds. Season with salt and pepper to taste and let sit until the flavors have blended, about 15 minutes, before serving.

PER 1½-CUP SERVING: Cal 220; Fat 12g; Sat fat 1g; Chol 0mg; Carb 13g; Protein 15g; Fiber 4g; Sodium 300mg

VEGETARIAN STIR-FRIES

FOR A FAST AND EASY WEEKNIGHT DINNER, IT'S HARD to beat a stir-fry: a medley most often of vegetables and meat or shrimp that are sliced or chopped, cooked quickly over high heat, then tossed with a bold-flavored sauce and served (usually over rice). However, most of the all-vegetable stir-fries we've had, while they offered plenty of pleasing flavor and textural contrast, lacked the substance of the meat-based stir-fries. They had nothing substantial enough to anchor the dish firmly in entrée territory. It wasn't necessarily the meat that was missing from these healthy all-veggie stir-fries, but the *meatiness*. We were convinced that with a few strategically chosen vegetables, there was a way to make a healthy, satisfying, and hearty meal out of nothing but stir-fried vegetables.

We needed a focal point for our stir-fry, and it wasn't hard to figure out where to start. If it was meaty heft and texture we were after, mushrooms were the obvious choice. From test kitchen experience, we knew hearty portobellos would fill the role better than any other variety. To capitalize on their bulk and meatiness, we cut them into wedges, rather than the smaller pieces we would normally call for if they were simply a supporting player. These larger pieces ensured that they would stand out from the other vegetables. For our first test, we tried treating them as we would "meat" in a stir-fry, searing the mushrooms on both sides with the goal of deepening their flavor, then incorporating a basic sauce (we would deal with other ingredients and fine-tuning the sauce later). But it wasn't so simple; the gills broke off and muddied the sauce. We tried cooking the mushrooms on the top sides only to keep the gills intact, but this technique made them leathery. The best solution, which didn't require much additional prep work on our part, was to scrape the gills off the mushrooms with a spoon before cutting them up to cook.

We were off to a good start, but we thought the portobellos could still offer a deeper flavor. Taking another cue from meat stir-fries, we experimented with marinades and coatings, but to no avail. Soaking the mushrooms in a soy sauce–based marinade left them soggy, slimy, and difficult to sear. Dipping them in different combinations of egg and cornstarch created a nice crust initially, but the mushrooms' high moisture content eventually made the crust unappetizingly chewy and wet. A simple sear proved best after all, but we wondered if a glaze (made from our existing sauce ingredients) might help. Adding low-sodium soy sauce, vegetable broth, and sugar as the mushrooms finished cooking yielded a shiny, flavorful glaze that provided just the boost they had been lacking.

After the portobellos were glazed, we removed them from the skillet and moved on to our other vegetables. We found the vegetable combinations to be almost endless but in the end chose to pair the portobellos with carrots, snow peas, and bok choy. Since the carrots needed a little more time to cook through than the other two, we browned them, then added a bit of broth to the pan, put on the cover, and let them steam. Once they were crisp-tender, the lid came off and the liquid was allowed to evaporate. Then we set them aside and cooked the snow peas and bok choy. Just a few minutes in the pan was all it took. Working in stages like this ensured that each of our vegetables was cooked perfectly.

We were ready for the aromatics. In most stir-fry recipes the aromatics are added at the outset, when the pan is empty, and they are saturated with as much as ¼ cup of oil (which, in essence, fries them). By the time the stir-fry is done, the aromatics have burned, and all that unnecessary oil just makes the stir-fry greasy. We knew from experience with other stir-fries that we could avoid these problems by waiting to cook the aromatics until after we had cooked the vegetables. When the bok choy and snow peas were done, we pushed them to the sides of the pan, added the aromatics and 1 teaspoon of oil to the center, and cooked until they were just fragrant, about 30 seconds.

All we needed now was to bind the whole dish together with a sauce. In our meat-based stir-fries, chicken broth serves as the best base for the sauce because it is not too overpowering. To keep our recipe vegetarian, vegetable broth was the best option. Low-sodium soy sauce, oyster sauce, and sesame oil boosted its flavor and contributed an appealing salty flavor that worked nicely with the mushrooms. The flavor of our sauce was good, but its consistency was too thin and it did not cling to the vegetables properly. The solution was as simple as adding a little cornstarch, as we do with many of our other stir-fry sauces.

Our components and method were set: We made the glaze and sauce, cooked and glazed the portobellos, and then cooked the vegetables and aromatics. We then added the mushrooms back to the pan and cooked the whole dish just until the sauce thickened. With everything so quick and simple, it was not hard to develop a variation on this dish. We followed the same method, swapping in red bell peppers and napa cabbage for the snow peas and bok choy and pairing them with a sweet and spicy chili-garlic sauce. These quick portobello stir-fries offered all the heartiness we could have hoped for.

NOTES FROM THE TEST KITCHEN

REMOVING GILLS FROM PORTOBELLO MUSHROOMS

We found it was necessary to remove the black gills from the portobello mushrooms because they made our stir-fry muddy. Using a soup spoon, scrape and discard the dark-colored gills from the underside of each mushroom.

Stir-Fried Portobellos with Ginger and Oyster Sauce

SERVES 4

This stir-fry cooks quickly, so have everything chopped and ready before you begin cooking. Serve with steamed white rice.

GLAZE

- ¼ cup vegetable broth
- 2 tablespoons low-sodium soy sauce
- 2 tablespoons sugar

SAUCE

- 1 cup vegetable broth
- 3 tablespoons oyster-flavored sauce
- 1 tablespoon low-sodium soy sauce
- 1 tablespoon cornstarch
- 2 teaspoons toasted sesame oil

STIR-FRY

- 2 tablespoons canola oil
- 4 teaspoons grated or minced fresh ginger
- 2 garlic cloves, minced
- 1½ pounds portobello mushroom caps (about 6 medium), gills removed (see photo), cut into 2-inch wedges
- 3 carrots, peeled and sliced thin on the bias
- ½ cup vegetable broth
- 2 ounces snow peas (about 1 cup), trimmed
- 1 small head bok choy (about 1 pound), stalks and greens separated, stalks sliced thin on the bias and greens sliced thin

1. FOR THE GLAZE: Whisk the broth, soy sauce, and sugar together in a bowl and set aside.

2. FOR THE SAUCE: Whisk the broth, oyster-flavored sauce, soy sauce, cornstarch, and sesame oil together in a bowl and set aside.

3. FOR THE STIR-FRY: Mix 1 teaspoon of the oil, ginger, and garlic together in a bowl. Heat 1 tablespoon more oil in a 12-inch nonstick skillet over medium-high heat until shimmering. Carefully lay the mushrooms in the skillet and cook until browned on the first side, 2 to 3 minutes. Flip the mushrooms, reduce the heat to medium, and continue to cook until the second side is browned and the mushrooms are tender, about 5 minutes longer.

4. Increase the heat to medium-high, add the glaze, and cook, stirring frequently, until the glaze is thick and the mushrooms are coated, 1 to 2 minutes. Transfer the mushrooms to a plate. Rinse the skillet clean and dry with paper towels.

5. Heat 1 teaspoon more oil in the skillet over medium-high heat until shimmering. Add the carrots and cook, stirring occasionally, until lightly browned, 1 to 2 minutes. Add the broth, cover, and cook until the carrots are just tender, 2 to 3 minutes. Uncover and cook until the liquid evaporates, about 30 seconds. Transfer the carrots to the plate with the mushrooms.

6. Heat the remaining 1 teaspoon oil in the skillet over medium-high heat until shimmering. Add the snow peas and bok choy stalks and cook, stirring occasionally, until the vegetables are lightly browned and softened, 1 to 2 minutes. Add the bok choy greens and cook, stirring frequently, until wilted, about 1 minute.

7. Push the vegetables to the sides of the skillet to clear the center. Add the ginger-garlic mixture to the clearing and cook, mashing the mixture with a spoon or spatula, until fragrant, about 15 seconds, then stir the mixture into the vegetables.

8. Stir the mushrooms, carrots, and sauce into the skillet and cook until the sauce is thickened, 2 to 3 minutes. Transfer to a platter and serve.

PER SERVING: Cal 260; Fat 10g; Sat fat 1g; Chol 0mg; Carb 34g; Protein 10g; Fiber 6g, Sodium 1290mg

VARIATION

Stir-Fried Portobellos with Sweet Chili-Garlic Sauce

SERVES 4

This stir-fry cooks quickly, so have everything chopped and ready before you begin cooking. To make this dish less spicy, cut the amount of Asian chili-garlic sauce by half. Serve with steamed white rice.

GLAZE

¼ **cup vegetable broth**
2 **tablespoons low-sodium soy sauce**
2 **tablespoons sugar**

SAUCE

¼ **cup water**
¼ **cup rice vinegar**
2 **tablespoons sugar**
2 **tablespoons low-sodium soy sauce**
1 **tablespoon cornstarch**
1 **tablespoon Asian chili-garlic sauce**

STIR-FRY

2 **tablespoons plus 1 teaspoon canola oil**
4 **teaspoons grated or minced fresh ginger**
2 **garlic cloves, minced**
1½ **pounds portobello mushroom caps (about 6 medium), gills removed (see page 158), cut into 2-inch wedges**
3 **carrots, peeled and sliced thin on the bias**
½ **cup vegetable broth**
1 **red bell pepper, stemmed, seeded, and cut into ¼-inch-wide strips**
1 **pound napa cabbage (about ½ medium head), cored and cut into 1-inch strips**

1. FOR THE GLAZE: Whisk the broth, soy sauce, and sugar together in a bowl and set aside.

2. FOR THE SAUCE: Whisk the water, vinegar, sugar, soy sauce, cornstarch, and chili-garlic sauce together in a bowl and set aside.

3. FOR THE STIR-FRY: Mix 1 teaspoon of the oil, ginger, and garlic together in a bowl. Heat 1 tablespoon more oil in a 12-inch nonstick skillet over medium-high heat until shimmering. Carefully lay the mushrooms in the skillet and cook until browned on the first side, 2 to 3 minutes. Flip the mushrooms, reduce the heat to medium, and continue to cook until the second side is browned and the mushrooms are tender, about 5 minutes longer.

4. Increase the heat to medium-high, add the glaze, and cook, stirring frequently, until the glaze is thick and the mushrooms are coated, 1 to 2 minutes. Transfer the mushrooms to a plate. Rinse the skillet clean and dry with paper towels.

5. Heat 1 teaspoon more oil in the skillet over medium-high heat until shimmering. Add the carrots and cook, stirring occasionally, until lightly browned, 1 to 2 minutes. Add the broth, cover, and cook until the carrots are just tender, 2 to 3 minutes. Uncover and cook until the liquid evaporates, about 30 seconds. Transfer the carrots to the plate with the mushrooms.

6. Heat 1 teaspoon more oil in the skillet over medium-high heat until shimmering. Add the bell pepper and cook, stirring occasionally, until lightly browned and softened, 1 to 2 minutes. Add half of the cabbage and cook, stirring frequently, until wilted, about 1 minute. Transfer the bell pepper and cabbage to a bowl and set aside.

7. Add the remaining 1 teaspoon oil and remaining cabbage to the skillet and cook until wilted, about

1 minute. Return the bell pepper and cabbage to the skillet.

8. Push the vegetables to the sides of the skillet to clear the center. Add the ginger-garlic mixture to the clearing and cook, mashing the mixture with a spoon or spatula, until fragrant, about 15 seconds, then stir the mixture into the vegetables.

9. Stir the mushrooms, carrots, and sauce into the skillet and cook until the sauce is thickened, 2 to 3 minutes. Transfer to a platter and serve.

PER SERVING: **Cal** 260; **Fat** 9g; **Sat fat** 0.5g; **Chol** 0mg; **Carb** 37g; **Protein** 7g; **Fiber** 6g; **Sodium** 750mg

TAMALE PIE

TEST KITCHEN
MAKEOVER

TAMALE PIE IS THE SOUTHWEST'S ANSWER TO shepherd's pie. The dish is inspired by Mexican tamales, with their masa coating surrounding a filling of meat, cheese, or vegetables topped with a tomato or chili sauce, but in an easier-to-make, casserole-style version. Typically, a chili-like mixture of ground meat and vegetables is topped with cheese and a cornmeal crust of cornbread or polenta. Tasty and satisfying, yes. Good for you, not so much. Meat- and cheese-heavy pies rank high in flavor but heavy on fat and calories, often pushing 27 grams of fat and 530 calories per serving. All-vegetable tamale pie recipes exist, but those we tested were anything but impressive. The vegetables were a hodgepodge, the filling lacked cohesion, and the tomato-based sauce was muddy-tasting and watery. A heavy hand with ground spices vastly overcompensated for the lack of meat and fat in an attempt to boost flavor. Could we lighten it up and create a tasty vegetarian version while we were at it? Our goal was to create a killer combination of vegetables, beans, and cheese bound together with a flavorful sauce that would satisfy even the most confirmed carnivore—a vegetable-*full*, rather than meat-*less*, tamale pie.

The defining ingredient in tamales is the surrounding masa dough exterior, with its soft yet sturdy texture and toasty corn flavor. For tamale pie, the stand-in is most often a polenta-like cornmeal mush, though you'll also find tamale pies topped with a cornbread crust. In a side-by-side tasting, tasters agreed the polenta topping was too soft. They strongly preferred the slightly crunchy, subtle sweetness of the cornbread crust, knowing it would provide a nice textural contrast to the saucy vegetable filling.

Our topping settled, we moved on to creating a base, or sauce, for our pie with just the right consistency. Since we were going the cornbread topping route, we needed a filling thick enough to adhere to and support the crust and also hold the vegetables and beans together (we used zucchini and black beans for now) as a unified whole, rather than a medley of juicy vegetables topped with some cornbread. The meatless tamale pie recipes we had tested early on simply relied on the juice in canned tomatoes to moisten and bind the ingredients, which left us with a wet, watery filling. We talked about pureeing tomatoes for a thicker texture, which seemed like a good route to take, but then someone suggested, while we were at it, that swapping out the usual red sauce in favor of a brighter-tasting tomatillo-based green sauce might help give our tamale pie a fresh lift. While it's common to see a green (or *verde*) sauce paired with enchiladas, we knew it was a little unorthodox for tamale pie, but that didn't cause us to hesitate.

For our next test we tried convenient canned tomatillos but they were too acidic; fresh tomatillos, which we would precook to mellow their flavor, were a must. We tried both boiling the tomatillos and roasting them under the broiler, then pureeing each. Roasting softened the acidity of the tomatillos without the waterlogging effect of boiling, so we settled on the former. To smooth out the texture of the pureed tomatillos, we added small amounts of vegetable broth and olive oil, and a teaspoon of sugar nicely balanced the sauce's acidity. The final ingredient, cilantro, provided a bright, herbal burst of freshness and deepened the sauce's already vibrant color.

Now we needed to pick beans and vegetables to complement our sauce. Tasters were united in their preference for white cannellini beans over black beans. The white beans' creamy, mild flavor provided good contrast to the tangy green sauce. When it came to the vegetables, the surprise star turned out to be poblanos, as they added a great smoky flavor and hit of spice that worked perfectly with the sauce. They became the anchor of our filling, followed by corn since it nicely echoed the sweet flavor in our cornbread crust. We considered both butternut squash and zucchini, but the dense winter squash seemed out of place texturally, not to mention it would require precooking before being added to the other vegetables. We kept the zucchini, approved in our preliminary tests

VEGETABLE TAMALE PIE

for its fresh flavor and chunky texture, adding it at the end of cooking to keep it from turning mushy.

To leave no vegetable unearthed, we also experimented with hearty greens. Swiss chard, though not usually found in tamale pie, is a popular green in Mexican cooking, and we thought it might work well here. However, while we liked its flavor, the texture just didn't work with the other vegetables, no matter how big or small we sliced it. The chard came across as slimy, and it muddied the other flavors. Other greens like kale and spinach fared no better. We all agreed that for our recipe, less is more: It wasn't about how many kinds of vegetables we mixed together; it was finding the right combination. With the addition of a little cumin, cayenne, garlic, and onion, we felt confident our filling hit the mark.

We then turned to the final ingredient: cheese. Though not an essential component of traditional tamales (unless it's the tamale's filling), cheese typically makes an appearance in tamale pie as a thin, melted layer beneath the crust. We didn't want to give up its gooey appeal in our lighter version. We wondered if adding our cheese to the filling would help fully incorporate it into the dish, so we tried mixing *queso fresco*, a fresh, crumbly Mexican cheese, into the filling. Because this cheese does not melt well, it dispersed in unappealing chunks, and the flavor was lost amid the stronger flavors of the vegetables and sauce. We next tried our favorite low-fat cheddar to see how it would perform. Mixed into the sauce, it gave the sauce a thick, gloppy texture we disliked. Also, we noticed that the cornbread topping was slightly soggy without the typical barrier of cheese. Maybe tradition is best after all. When we sprinkled the low-fat cheddar on top of the filling before adding the crust, the final pie had good cheese flavor in every bite and an appealing gooey layer that kept our topping from getting waterlogged.

After 15 minutes in the oven, the cornbread topping was cooked through and golden brown, sealing the filling and melting cheese inside. The result? A hearty tamale pie that was chock full of vegetables and full of fresh, bright flavor, clocking in at just 13 grams of fat and 390 calories. We'd take it over the meaty versions any day.

MAKEOVER SPOTLIGHT: TAMALE PIE

	CALORIES	FAT	SAT FAT	CHOLESTEROL
BEFORE	530	27g	13g	120mg
AFTER	390	13g	4.5g	50mg

Vegetable Tamale Pie

SERVES 6

Purchase tomatillos with dry outer husks, bright green skin, and a fresh, fruity smell. We prefer to make our own cornbread topping, but you can substitute 1 (6.5- to 8.5-ounce) package of your favorite cornbread mix if desired; follow the package instructions to make the cornbread batter, then dollop the batter over the filling and bake as directed in step 6. Don't try this recipe with a standard pie plate; substitute a 2-quart casserole dish if you don't have a deep-dish pie plate.

- 1 pound tomatillos (about 12), husks removed, washed
  Vegetable oil spray
- ½ cup packed fresh cilantro leaves
- ¼ cup vegetable broth
- 2 tablespoons olive oil
- 1 teaspoon sugar
- 2 poblano peppers, stemmed, seeded, and chopped medium
- 1 red bell pepper, stemmed, seeded, and chopped medium
- 1 onion, minced (about 1 cup)
  Salt
- 3 garlic cloves, minced
- ¼ teaspoon ground cumin
- ⅛ teaspoon cayenne pepper
- 1 (15-ounce) can cannellini beans, drained and rinsed
- 1 medium zucchini, halved lengthwise, seeded, and chopped medium
- 1 cup fresh or frozen corn kernels (about 4 ounces)
  Black pepper
- 4 ounces 50 percent light cheddar cheese, shredded (about 1 cup)
- 1 recipe Homemade Cornbread Topping (recipe follows)

1. Position an oven rack 6 inches from the heating element and heat the broiler. Line a rimmed baking sheet with foil. Arrange the tomatillos on the prepared baking sheet and lightly coat with vegetable oil spray. Broil until the tomatillos blacken and begin to soften, 5 to 10 minutes, rotating the baking sheet halfway through.

2. Remove the tomatillos from the oven and let cool slightly. Adjust an oven rack to the middle position and heat the oven to 450 degrees.

3. Process the broiled tomatillos, cilantro, broth, 4 teaspoons of the oil, and sugar together in a food processor until almost smooth, 30 to 60 seconds; set aside.

4. Combine the remaining 2 teaspoons oil, poblanos, bell pepper, onion, and ¼ teaspoon salt in a large Dutch oven. Cover and cook over medium-low heat until the vegetables are softened, 8 to 10 minutes. Uncover, increase the heat to medium-high, and continue to cook, stirring occasionally, until the vegetables are lightly browned, 4 to 6 minutes longer.

5. Stir in the garlic, cumin, and cayenne and cook until fragrant, about 30 seconds. Stir in the tomatillo sauce, beans, zucchini, and corn. Bring to a simmer over medium-high heat and season with salt and black pepper to taste.

6. Transfer the mixture to a 9-inch deep-dish pie plate. Sprinkle the cheese evenly over the top. Dollop the cornbread topping evenly over the filling, then spread it into an even layer, covering the filling completely. Bake until the topping is golden and set, 15 to 20 minutes. Let the pie cool for 10 minutes before serving.

PER SERVING: Cal 390; Fat 13g; Sat fat 4.5g; Chol 50mg; Carb 57g; Protein 15g; Fiber 7g; Sodium 510mg

---

Homemade Cornbread Topping
MAKES ENOUGH TO TOP ONE 9-INCH PIE

- ¾ cup (3¾ ounces) unbleached all-purpose flour
- ¾ cup (3¾ ounces) yellow cornmeal
- 3 tablespoons sugar
- ¾ teaspoon baking powder
- ¼ teaspoon baking soda
- ½ teaspoon salt
- ¾ cup buttermilk
- 1 large egg
- 1 tablespoon unsalted butter, melted and cooled

Whisk the flour, cornmeal, sugar, baking powder, baking soda, and salt together in a large bowl. In a separate bowl, whisk the buttermilk and egg together. Stir the buttermilk mixture into the flour mixture until uniform, then stir in the melted butter until just combined. Use as directed.

SAVORY CRÊPES

WHAT'S NOT TO LOVE ABOUT A THIN CRÊPE WRAPPED around a savory, simple, yet flavorful filling? The richness and heaviness of most recipes, for one. While these fillings often start with chicken or a mix of vegetables—a healthy way to begin—with hefty amounts of cheese and butter they wind up high in fat. To top it off, crêpes are often covered with a heavy cream sauce. These rich crêpes are anything but light fare. We wondered if we could reinterpret this classic dish, updating it into a healthy vegetarian entrée that would highlight a simple yet flavorful vegetable filling and wouldn't weigh us down.

We began with the crêpes themselves. The test kitchen had previously developed an easy crêpe batter recipe and we saw no reason to reinvent the wheel. In this simple recipe all the ingredients—eggs, milk, water, flour, salt, and melted butter—are combined in a food processor, forming a smooth batter after a few seconds. Many recipes call for resting the batter, but our previous testing had found that rested crêpe batter yields crêpes that are difficult to roll around a robust filling. Unrested batter was the way to go, yielding sturdier crêpes that were easier to roll, not to mention that skipping the step saved time.

To see if we could cut some fat from our full-fat crêpe recipe, we swapped in skim milk for the whole and were happy that these crêpes turned out well. However, for the butter, we found we didn't have as much leeway; the original recipe used 5 tablespoons, and we found that any less than 4 tablespoons for a batch made texture and flavor suffer.

Turning our attention to the filling, we narrowed our options quickly to a few of the typical choices: ricotta, spinach, and mushrooms, testing each one alone and in combination with another. Tasters preferred the combination of spinach and mushrooms because it was the most substantial. But sautéing ½ pound of white mushrooms, then wilting some baby spinach in the pan, made for a fairly bland filling. Since browning mushrooms deepens their flavor, our first adjustment was to give them more time in the pan to develop more color, and for more impact we upped the amount to a full pound. Adding some onion to the pan with the mushrooms contributed sweetness, and a couple of cloves of minced garlic added depth. To incorporate all the highly flavorful fond from browning the mushrooms into the filling, we deglazed the pan with sherry, a classic match for mushrooms that added a nice complementary flavor. Then the spinach was stirred in. This filling had great mushroom flavor but tasters wanted more spinach; unfortunately, there simply wasn't enough room in the pan to wilt a sufficient amount of baby spinach to make everyone happy. The solution was simple; we switched from fresh spinach to frozen, which allowed us to pack more spinach into the pan since it is already cooked.

We had hoped we could skip making a sauce entirely, but our crêpes felt unfinished and slightly dry. A sauce, we realized, was a must. The most common types we found paired with crêpes were béchamel (a sauce of milk thickened with a roux made of butter and flour) and Mornay (béchamel with a rich cheese added), neither of which is traditionally light. Though not as frequently seen, we also came across tomato sauces. We started with the tomato sauce since it was our leanest candidate. While tasters liked the moisture that the tomato sauce added to the dish, they felt the acidic flavor competed too much with the filling. So we went back to the béchamel and Mornay sauces. Of the two, béchamel was the lighter choice since the Mornay also includes cheese. But to keep this healthy, we couldn't pour on a sauce made of butter and milk as you normally would. We tried cutting down on the amount of sauce, but the results were disappointing. It acted more like a garnish and didn't add enough creaminess. We were stumped about what to do until one of our fellow test cooks suggested incorporating a small amount of the béchamel with the spinach and mushrooms, just enough to add the right moisture and creaminess to the filling. Theoretically, we would get more mileage this way and hoped these crêpes wouldn't even need a sauce to top them off.

For our next test, we made a small batch of béchamel, substituting skim milk for the usual whole, and incorporated it into the filling before stuffing and baking our crêpes. Just as we'd hoped, the lightened béchamel worked wonders, adding the moisture and richness we had missed and turning the filling from slightly dry to creamy and satisfying. To simplify our cooking process, we eliminated the extra saucepan used to make the béchamel and instead built it right in the pan with our filling. After adding the garlic, all we had to do was sprinkle a few teaspoons of flour over the vegetables and allow the flour to combine with the butter left in the skillet from sautéing the vegetables. Then, after we had added the sherry and it had evaporated, the milk went into the skillet and we allowed the sauce to thicken. We realized now we actually had some leeway to add more fat and calories without tipping our recipe over the edge, and stirring in a few ounces of grated Parmesan cheese (and a pinch of nutmeg) took this filling from good to great.

With our crêpes made and our filling set, all that was left was to stuff the crêpes and heat them in the oven. We placed 3 tablespoons of filling on each crêpe and rolled them into cylinders, sprinkled them with some more Parmesan cheese, and baked them, covered with foil, for about 15 minutes. Running them under the broiler, uncovered, browned the cheese and gave our healthy crêpes just the right finishing touch.

Mushroom and Spinach Crêpes

SERVES 6

It takes a few crêpes to get the heat of the pan right; your first two or three will almost inevitably be unusable. (To allow for practice, the recipe yields about 16 crêpes; only 12 are needed for the dish.) A dry measuring cup with a ¼-cup capacity is useful for portioning the crêpe batter.

CRÊPES

1½ cups (7½ ounces) unbleached all-purpose flour
1½ cups skim milk
½ cup plus 2 tablespoons water
3 large eggs
4 tablespoons (½ stick) unsalted butter, melted
½ teaspoon salt

FILLING

1 pound white mushrooms, sliced thin
1 onion, minced (about 1 cup)
2 tablespoons unsalted butter
Salt and pepper
2 garlic cloves, minced
4 teaspoons unbleached all-purpose flour
¼ cup dry sherry
1 cup skim milk
1 (10-ounce) package frozen chopped spinach, thawed and squeezed dry
3 ounces Parmesan cheese, grated (1½ cups)
Pinch ground nutmeg

1. **FOR THE CRÊPES:** Process the flour, milk, water, eggs, melted butter, and salt together in a food processor until a smooth batter forms, 3 to 4 seconds. Transfer the batter to a bowl.

2. Lightly coat the bottom and sides of a 10-inch non-stick skillet with vegetable oil spray. Heat the skillet over medium heat until hot, about 3 minutes. Following the photos, remove the skillet from the heat, add ¼ cup of the batter, and quickly swirl the pan to create a smooth, even coating. Return the skillet to the heat and cook until the bottom of the crêpe is a spotty golden brown, 30 to 60 seconds.

3. Using a heatproof rubber spatula, loosen the crepe, then grasp the edge with your fingers and flip the crêpe. Continue to cook until the second side is a spotty golden brown, about 30 seconds longer. Transfer the crêpe to a paper towel–lined plate. Repeat with the vegetable oil spray and remaining crêpe batter, stacking the cooked crêpes on top of one another.

4. **FOR THE FILLING:** Combine the mushrooms, onion, butter, and ⅛ teaspoon salt in a 12-inch skillet over medium-low heat. Cover and cook until the vegetables are softened, 8 to 10 minutes. Uncover, increase the heat to medium-high, and continue to cook, stirring occasionally, until the vegetables are well browned, 8 to 12 minutes longer.

5. Stir in the garlic and cook until fragrant, about 30 seconds. Stir in the flour and cook for 1 minute. Stir in the sherry, scraping up any browned bits, and cook until the liquid has almost evaporated, about 30 seconds. Stir in the milk, bring to a simmer, and cook until thickened, 2 to 3 minutes. Transfer the mixture to a medium bowl and stir in the spinach, 1 cup of the Parmesan, and nutmeg. Season with salt and pepper to taste.

6. **TO ASSEMBLE THE CRÊPES:** Adjust an oven rack to the upper-middle position and heat the oven to 425 degrees. Lightly coat a 13 by 9-inch broiler-safe baking pan with vegetable oil spray.

7. Place 3 tablespoons of the filling on each crêpe and roll into a cylinder. Place the rolled crêpes in the prepared baking pan and sprinkle with the remaining ½ cup Parmesan. Cover with foil and bake until heated through, about 15 minutes. Uncover, turn the oven to broil, and broil until the cheese is browned, about 5 minutes. Serve.

PER SERVING (2 CRÊPES): Cal 330; Fat 15g; Sat fat 9g; Chol 115mg; Carb 28g; Protein 16g; Fiber 2g; Sodium 590mg

MAKING MUSHROOM AND SPINACH CRÊPES

1. Pour ¼ cup of the crêpe batter into the pan and gently tip and swirl the skillet so that the batter covers the skillet bottom. Cook the crêpe until it is spotty light golden brown on the bottom, 30 to 60 seconds.

2. Using a heatproof rubber spatula, loosen the edges of the crêpe and grasp it gently with your fingertips. Quickly flip the crêpe and continue to cook until the second side is dry, about 30 seconds.

3. After preparing the filling, place 3 tablespoons of the filling on each crêpe, about 1½ inches from the bottom. Fold the sides over the filling, then fold up the crêpe bottom and continue to roll the crêpe into a tidy cylinder.

4. Place the crêpes, seam side down, in a 13 by 9-inch broiler-safe baking dish, sprinkle with the remaining cheese, and bake, covered, for 15 minutes. Uncover and move it to the broiler. Cook until the cheese is just brown.

GRILLED SHRIMP TACOS WITH PINEAPPLE-JÍCAMA SALSA

BARBECUED CHICKEN

BARBECUED CHICKEN IS THE EPITOME OF BACKYARD summertime fare. Succulent meat and a zesty sauce make for not only a satisfying meal but one that is also a healthy choice. But don't let the everyday nature of this grilled favorite fool you: This dish isn't that easy to get right. Before you know it the chicken can dry out and the sauce can burn, leaving you with a lackluster dinner. We set out to eliminate the guesswork so we could get perfect barbecued chicken to the table every time.

For the chicken, we started our testing with breasts since they are the leanest choice. Knowing that the big barbecue flavor we were after takes time to develop on the grill, we eliminated boneless, skinless chicken breasts because they would cook too quickly. Plus, we knew from test kitchen experience that bone-in chicken breasts retain their moisture when grilled better than their boneless counterparts. To eliminate calories, we removed the skin before we started cooking. However, with the skin gone, one test proved what we suspected would happen: The delicate white meat, exposed to the high heat of the grill, dried out. To fix the problem, we turned to a favorite test kitchen technique, brining, to ensure that our chicken remained juicy (and well seasoned). After a quick one-hour soak in a saltwater solution, our chicken was ready for the fire.

Many recipes recommend grilling chicken over high heat and a single-level fire (where the heat is even across the grill). In the test kitchen, we've learned this approach doesn't work for bone-in breasts. By the time the chicken is cooked through, the outside is scorched. Building a modified two-level fire was a more promising technique. On a gas grill the primary burner is left on high while the other burners are turned off. On a charcoal grill all the coals are pushed to one side of the grill to create a hot area and a cooler area. These hot and cool zones allowed us greater control when cooking the chicken.

We started by placing the chicken on the cooler part of the grill, where we allowed it to stay until it just started to brown, which took about 25 minutes. We then moved the chicken closer to the hotter part of the grill. Here, the exteriors of the breasts gradually browned as the chicken finished cooking, which took about 25 minutes more. With our method down, we turned to how best to apply the sauce.

Timing was the key issue when it came to the sauce. Added too soon and we had a scorched, dry exterior with an unmistakable burned flavor; added too late and our chicken was unappealingly slimy. We had the most success when we brushed the sauce on while the chicken was closer to the hot side of the grill. But one good slathering wasn't enough; tasters said this barbecued chicken had weak flavor. We found that basting every five minutes helped develop not only layers of flavor, but also that characteristic sticky and slightly charred exterior that makes barbecued chicken so appealing. This was a meal the whole family could enjoy.

Barbecued Chicken Breasts

SERVES 4

If using kosher chicken, do not brine; if brining the chicken, omit the salt in the spice mixture in step 1. We prefer to use a homemade sauce here, but your favorite store-bought sauce will also work.

- ¼ teaspoon salt
- ¼ teaspoon black pepper
- ¼ teaspoon cayenne pepper
- 4 (10-ounce) bone-in split chicken breasts, skin removed, brined if desired (see page 61)
- 1 tablespoon canola oil
- 1 (13 by 9-inch) disposable aluminum roasting pan (if using charcoal)
- 2 cups Easy Pantry Barbecue Sauce (recipe follows)

1. Combine the salt, black pepper, and cayenne in a bowl. Pat the chicken breasts dry with paper towels, rub with the oil, then thoroughly coat with the spice mixture.

2A. FOR A CHARCOAL GRILL: Open the bottom grill vents completely and place the roasting pan on one side of the grill. Light a large chimney starter filled with charcoal briquettes (100 briquettes; 6 quarts). When the coals are hot, pour them in an even layer over half the grill, opposite the roasting pan. Set the cooking grate in place, cover, and open the lid vents completely. Heat the grill until hot, about 5 minutes.

2B. FOR A GAS GRILL: Turn all the burners to high, cover, and heat the grill until hot, about 15 minutes. Leave the primary burner on high and turn off the other burner(s). (Adjust the primary burner as needed to maintain the grill temperature around 350 degrees.)

3. Clean and oil the cooking grate. Place the chicken, bone side down, on the cooler part of the grill. Cover and cook until the chicken begins to brown, 25 to 30 minutes.

4. Slide the chicken into a single line between the hotter and cooler parts of the grill and cook, uncovered, turning the chicken and brushing with some of the barbecue sauce every 5 minutes, until sticky, about 20 minutes.

5. Slide the chicken to the hotter part of the grill and cook, uncovered, turning and brushing the chicken with the remaining barbecue sauce, until well glazed and the breasts register 160 to 165 degrees on an instant-read thermometer, about 5 minutes.

6. Transfer the chicken to a platter, tent loosely with foil, and let rest for 10 minutes before serving.

PER SERVING: Cal 440; Fat 6g; Sat fat 1g; Chol 105mg; Carb 53g; Protein 44g; Fiber 0g; Sodium 1280mg

Easy Pantry Barbecue Sauce

MAKES ABOUT 2 CUPS

For a fiery change of pace to this no-cook sauce, stir in 1 stemmed, seeded, and minced jalapeño chile and 2 tablespoons minced canned chipotle chiles in adobo sauce, and increase the amount of hot sauce to taste.

1½ cups ketchup

½ cup molasses

2 tablespoons cider vinegar

1½ teaspoons hot sauce

½ teaspoon liquid smoke

Salt and pepper

Whisk the ketchup, molasses, vinegar, hot sauce, and liquid smoke together in a bowl. Season with salt and pepper to taste before serving.

CHICKEN FAJITAS

WITH SMOKY CHICKEN AND VEGETABLES WRAPPED UP in warm tortillas, fajitas are an all-in-one meal that can be a great light-eating choice (assuming you use low-fat toppings). But what passes for chicken fajitas these days is usually far from perfect, with dry, stringy chicken and limp and flavorless vegetables. We wanted to go back to the fajita basics, a simple combination of smoky grilled vegetables and chicken strips in toasty flour tortillas.

Some meats, a well-marbled steak for instance, don't have to rely on a marinade for juiciness or flavor, but boneless chicken breasts, while a healthy choice, need some help, so a marinade was a must in our minds. We started with a mixture made with plenty of lime juice, plus oil, garlic, salt, and pepper. This combination gave us the right unadulterated tang. Because this was a high-acid marinade, we had to be careful and watch the clock. The chicken could handle only a quick 15 minutes of marinating time—any longer and the meat became mushy because it essentially started to cook in the acid (like ceviche).

Although we were moving in the right direction, tasters agreed that our marinade lacked depth. We tried numerous additions and finally hit upon Worcestershire sauce, an unlikely candidate for chicken but one that has some of the characteristics of umami, an overused and little-understood culinary term that refers to a fifth taste sensation beyond the familiar sweet, sour, bitter, and salty. A mere tablespoon of Worcestershire was plenty to add another layer of saltiness and smoke without standing out. A bit of brown sugar helped round out the salty flavors in our marinade, and minced jalapeño and cilantro added freshness. Once the chicken was finished with its 15-minute marinade, we cooked it over a hot fire. After about 10 minutes, this chicken was juicy, flavorful, and ready for the tortillas. We just needed some vegetables to go with it.

Both green and red bell peppers would give the fajitas some needed contrast, in terms of both color and flavor. Quartering the peppers allowed them to lie flat on the grill and cook evenly on both sides, and cutting an onion into rounds proved both pretty and most practical. We quickly discovered that while the chicken needed a blazing-hot grill, the vegetables were more prone to burning and required more moderate heat. To allow the chicken and vegetables to cook side by side, we created a two-level fire with a hotter and a cooler side.

We also turned to the grill to rid the tortillas of their raw, gummy texture, heating them for 40 seconds on the grill's cooler side. With everything ready to go, including the requisite toppings—which could now be used to complement, not overshadow, our fajitas—we gave our fajitas a try. Something was still missing. Next time around, just before serving we tossed the chicken strips and vegetables with a small amount of marinade we had set aside, which gave them a burst of fresh flavor. These fajitas were so good we didn't even need the toppings.

Grilled Chicken Fajitas

SERVES 4

Do not marinate the chicken for longer than 15 minutes; any longer and the lime juice will turn the meat mushy. To make this dish spicier, add the chile seeds. Bring a clean kitchen towel or a large piece of foil out to the grill to wrap up the tortillas and keep them warm as they come off the grill. Serve with salsa, low-fat shredded cheese, low-fat sour cream, and lime wedges if desired.

- ¼ cup fresh lime juice (about 2 limes)
- 3 tablespoons canola oil
- 2 tablespoons minced fresh cilantro
- 3 garlic cloves, minced
- 1 tablespoon Worcestershire sauce
- 1½ teaspoons brown sugar
- 1 jalapeño chile, stemmed, seeded, and minced
  Salt and pepper
- 4 (6-ounce) boneless, skinless chicken breasts, trimmed
- 1 red onion, cut into ½-inch-thick rounds (do not separate the rings)
- 1 red bell pepper, stemmed, seeded, and quartered
- 1 green bell pepper, stemmed, seeded, and quartered
  Vegetable oil spray
- 8 (6-inch) flour tortillas

1. Combine the lime juice, oil, cilantro, garlic, Worcestershire, sugar, jalapeño, 1 teaspoon salt, and ¾ teaspoon pepper in a bowl. Measure out and reserve 3 tablespoons of the marinade for serving. Add ½ teaspoon more salt to the remaining marinade, transfer to a large zipper-lock bag, and add the chicken breasts. Seal the bag tightly, toss to coat the chicken, and let the chicken marinate in the refrigerator for 15 minutes.

2. Lightly coat both sides of the onion rings and the bell peppers with vegetable oil spray and season with a pinch of salt and a pinch of pepper. Following the photo on page 192, thread the onion rounds onto skewers. Remove the chicken from the marinade.

3A. FOR A CHARCOAL GRILL: Open the bottom grill vents completely. Light a large chimney starter filled with charcoal briquettes (100 briquettes; 6 quarts). When the coals are hot, spread two-thirds of them evenly over the grill, then pour the remaining coals over half of the grill. Set the cooking grate in place, cover, and heat the grill until hot, about 5 minutes.

3B. FOR A GAS GRILL: Turn all the burners to high, cover, and heat the grill until hot, about 15 minutes. Leave the primary burner on high and turn the other burners to medium. (Adjust the burners as needed to maintain a hot fire and a medium fire on separate sides of the grill; see page 182.)

4. Clean and oil the cooking grate. Place the chicken on the hotter part of the grill and cook until well browned and the breasts register 160 to 165 degrees on an instant-read thermometer, 8 to 12 minutes, flipping them halfway through. Transfer the chicken to a carving board, tent loosely with foil, and let rest for 5 minutes.

5. While the chicken cooks, place the onion rings and bell peppers on the cooler part of the grill and cook until spottily charred, 8 to 12 minutes, turning as needed. Transfer the vegetables to the carving board with the chicken and tent loosely with foil.

6. Working in batches, place a few of the tortillas in a single layer on the cooler part of the grill and cook until warm and lightly browned, about 20 seconds per side. As the tortillas are done, wrap them in a kitchen towel or a large piece of foil.

7. Separate the onion rings, slice the bell peppers into ¼-inch strips, then toss together in a bowl with half of the reserved marinade. Slice the chicken into ¼-inch strips and toss with the remaining reserved marinade in a separate bowl. Arrange the chicken and vegetables on a large platter and serve with the warmed tortillas.

PER SERVING: Cal 510; Fat 17g; Sat fat 2.5g; Chol 100mg; Carb 42g; Protein 45g; Fiber 4g; Sodium 1410mg

GRILLED CHICKEN CAESAR SALAD

NOTHING IS MORE CONVENIENT THAN AN ENTIRE dinner cooked right on the grill. Usually when we're looking for such a meal, we think of recipes like tacos or our Grilled Chicken Fajitas (see at left). But a salad? Sure, salad is an obvious choice for eating healthy, but why would anyone want to grill one, lettuce and all? Nevertheless, we've seen a few grilled salads prepared on TV cooking shows and listed on restaurant menus, so obviously the idea is catching on. We were more than a little skeptical at first, thinking it was more of a gimmick than anything, but after a few preliminary tests we discovered that one grilled salad in particular stood out from the pack for its potential: chicken Caesar salad. The grill could take its ordinary components—plain romaine lettuce, bread (for the croutons), and chicken—and make them extraordinary with the simple addition of a slightly smoky, charred flavor. Of course, we'd have to perfect a method to get perfectly charred but not soggy lettuce, tender meat, and perfect toasts, all tossed in a dressing with the trademark Caesar flavor, but keeping it all light in the process.

We knew the grilled chicken would be a snap. Test kitchen experience had taught us a hot grill is best for cooking boneless, skinless chicken breasts. Because they are thin and low in fat, cooking them quickly over high heat is essential to getting a nice char without overcooking the interior. Brining the chicken gave us more insurance that the meat wouldn't dry out.

We were ready to tackle the lettuce. Grilling requires a sturdy, robust lettuce, as anything too dainty or leafy would wilt and become unappealingly slimy under the heat. Luckily, romaine hearts, the lettuce of choice for Caesar salad, filled the bill nicely. The grilling process took more than a few tries to iron out, but we learned some key things along the way.

High heat left the outer leaves of the lettuce burned while the inner leaves were completely untouched, with no real smoky grilled flavor. If we were going to grill the lettuce, we wanted it to be obvious in each bite that the lettuce had been grilled. Low heat allowed more grilled flavor to penetrate the lettuce, but it also wilted the romaine into a soggy mess before it browned. It turned out that medium heat is crucial to the success of the lettuce. Over a medium-hot fire, the outside of the lettuce was nicely charred and many of the inner leaves had that nice grill flavor we after. Still, we wanted more grill flavor throughout. A colleague suggested cutting the hearts in half to increase the surface contact with the grill. This worked like a charm. The outside of each half was uniformly charred, while the interior was crisp but with a smoky grilled flavor throughout.

Next, we set our sights on the croutons. As the previous two components were already naturally low in fat, this was our first opportunity to shed some calories. In a traditional Caesar salad the croutons are at best baked with lots of oil, or at worst fried. By spraying the bread lightly with olive oil and grilling it, we managed to avoid a lot of unnecessary added fat. But chasing bite-size pieces of bread around a grill seemed impractical, so we settled on grilling slices of bread, which we would cut into smaller pieces after they were cooked. After testing a few different bread varieties, including sandwich bread, rustic Italian

loaves, and focaccia, we crowned French baguette the winner. Because of its sturdy texture, it held up perfectly on the grill. We found that cutting it on an extreme bias made the pieces easier to handle and increased the surface area, allowing for more charred flavor.

The dressing was another area where we knew we could cut calories. Most existing low-fat versions fall short because they omit the egg yolk and most of the oil; this removes the creamy character of the dressing and doesn't leave enough body to cling to the romaine. We started by looking for a way to omit the egg and reduce the oil without compromising taste or richness. We found that sour cream and yogurt were too tart and dairy-rich. Soft tofu added a nice creamy texture but was too bland. Tasters, however, were impressed with buttermilk's tang and its silkiness. Some complained that the dressing was still missing richness, so we added 3 tablespoons of light mayonnaise. This did the trick, and it also allowed us to decrease the amount of olive oil to 2 tablespoons from the ⅓ cup called for in the classic recipe.

Next we looked at finessing the dressing's flavor. Tasters liked 2 tablespoons of lemon juice, a modest teaspoon of Worcestershire sauce, and 2 teaspoons of minced garlic. Three anchovy fillets contributed a classic flavor, and Dijon mustard—an untraditional ingredient—added depth and helped further emulsify the ingredients. And instead of sprinkling the salad with grated Parmesan (the traditional method), we found that stirring the Parmesan into the dressing itself spread the flavor of the cheese further. With only ½ cup of cheese (many recipes called for twice that), our dressing now had big Parmesan flavor without unnecessary fat and calories.

With all of the components figured out we thought we were home free. But as we set up the grill for a final run-through from start to finish, we quickly realized that between the chicken, romaine hearts, and bread, we were quickly running out of space on the grill. We knew that for everything to cook properly, we would need to work in batches. We started with the chicken; when it was almost done we added the bread, which cooked quickly. We then set aside the chicken and bread, thereby freeing up the grill for the romaine. With all of the components perfectly cooked, we cut the lettuce and bread into bite-size pieces, sliced the chicken, and tossed the salad with the dressing. This took the typical Caesar salad to the next level, as the smoky charred flavor of the lettuce perfectly tempered the tang of the buttermilk and the garlic in the dressing. With all that flavor, no one could have guessed it was light.

Grilled Chicken Caesar Salad

SERVES 4

If using kosher chicken, do not brine; if brining the chicken, do not season with salt in step 2. Make sure to cut the bread on an extreme bias so that it is easy to handle on the grill.

DRESSING

⅓   cup nonfat buttermilk

3   tablespoons light mayonnaise

2   tablespoons fresh lemon juice

2   tablespoons water

2   teaspoons Dijon mustard

1   teaspoon Worcestershire sauce

3   anchovy fillets, rinsed, patted dry, and minced

2   garlic cloves, minced

2   tablespoons extra-virgin olive oil

1   ounce Parmesan cheese, grated (about ½ cup)

    Salt and pepper

SALAD

4   (6-ounce) boneless, skinless chicken breasts, trimmed, brined if desired (see page 61)

    Olive oil spray

⅛   teaspoon salt

⅛   teaspoon pepper

3   romaine lettuce hearts (about 1 pound), halved lengthwise

3   ounces baguette, sliced 1 inch thick on the bias

1. FOR THE DRESSING: Process the buttermilk, mayonnaise, lemon juice, water, mustard, Worcestershire, anchovies, and garlic together in a blender until smooth, about 30 seconds. With the motor running, add the oil in a steady stream until incorporated. Transfer the dressing to a bowl and stir in all but 1 tablespoon of the Parmesan. Season with salt and pepper to taste and set aside.

2. FOR THE SALAD: Pat the chicken breasts dry with paper towels, lightly coat with olive oil spray, and season with the salt and pepper. Lightly coat the romaine hearts and bread with olive oil spray.

3A. FOR A CHARCOAL GRILL: Open the bottom grill vents completely. Light a large chimney starter filled with charcoal briquettes (100 briquettes; 6 quarts). When the coals are hot, spread two-thirds of them evenly over the grill, then pour the remaining coals over half of the grill. Set the cooking grate in place, cover, and heat the grill until hot, about 5 minutes.

3B. FOR A GAS GRILL: Turn all the burners to high, cover, and heat the grill until hot, about 15 minutes. Leave the primary burner on high and turn the other burners to medium. (Adjust the burners as needed to maintain a hot fire and a medium fire on separate sides of the grill; see page 182.)

4. Clean and oil the cooking grate. Place the chicken on the hotter part of the grill and cook until well browned and the breasts register 160 to 165 degrees on an instant-read thermometer, 8 to 12 minutes, flipping the chicken halfway through. Transfer the chicken to a carving board and tent loosely with foil.

5. While the chicken cooks, place the bread on the cooler part of the grill and cook until golden brown, 4 to 6 minutes, flipping the slices halfway through. Transfer the bread to the carving board with the chicken. Place the romaine halves on the cooler part of the grill and cook until lightly charred on all sides, 3 to 5 minutes, turning as needed.

6. Slice the chicken breasts crosswise into ½-inch-thick strips. Cut the bread into 1-inch chunks and chop the romaine hearts into 1-inch pieces.

7. TO ASSEMBLE THE SALAD: Whisk the dressing to recombine. In a large bowl, toss the chicken and lettuce with the dressing to coat. Divide the salad evenly among 4 plates. Sprinkle the bread cubes and the remaining 1 tablespoon Parmesan evenly over the top and serve.

PER SERVING: Cal 400; Fat 14g; Sat fat 3g; Chol 110mg; Carb 18g; Protein 47g; Fiber 2g; Sodium 750mg

SAUSAGES WITH PEPPERS AND ONIONS

GRILLED SAUSAGES WITH PEPPERS AND ONIONS FROM a street vendor are a summer staple, and the very scent of them cooking is hard to resist. But Italian pork sausages—the classic choice—are hardly light and healthy fare. We wondered if we could achieve the appeal of the classic version but cut the fat.

In the past, we have used leaner Italian turkey sausage in lieu of fattier pork sausages with great success. Few things sound easier than grilling up a few sausages— all you need is meat and a fire. But we know from experience that nicely browned links with juicy interiors can be an elusive goal, especially if you're choosing low-fat meat. The outside can scorch before the center cooks through.

Or worse, the sausage becomes dry and overcooked. Throw onions and peppers into the mix and things just get worse; they usually wind up raw with a few charred spots. We wanted to lose the fat, keep the flavor, and create a foolproof method that re-created the best street vendor sausages, with each component cooked to perfection.

The common technique among vendors is to precook the meat with the onions and peppers on a griddle that sits on the cooking grate of the grill. The onions and peppers are sliced, spread over the griddle, topped with the sausages, and then placed over the fire. Once the vegetables are nearly done and full of flavor from the cooking meat's released juice, the partially cooked sausages are put directly over the flames. In just a few minutes, their exteriors can crisp and they can finish cooking through without risk of scorching.

So how could we re-create the method of the professionals? The closest thing we had to a griddle was a skillet, and we really didn't want to put it on top of a searing-hot grill. However, we often use a disposable aluminum roasting pan on the grill—would that work here in lieu of the griddle? We layered the sliced onions and peppers in the pan, topped them with the sausages, and then placed the pan over a single-level fire. After 15 minutes the sausages were nearly cooked through, so we removed them from the pan and placed them directly over the fire. Six minutes later, we had nicely browned links infused with lots of onion and pepper flavor.

Tasters were happy with the sausages; the vegetables left something to be desired. Some were tender but others were crunchy, and they needed a flavor boost. What if we gave the peppers and onions a head start on the grill? Taking a cue from our Grilled Chicken Fajitas (page 170), we sliced the onions and quartered the peppers so they wouldn't slip through the cooking grate, then lightly charred them on all sides before adding them to the pan with the raw sausages. The vegetables were evenly charred and more flavorful than ever, but the pendulum had swung too far. Since we weren't adding excess oil, in the time it took the sausages to cook through and brown, the vegetables were starting to burn on the bottom of the pan. A cup of water added when the vegetables went into the roasting pan solved the problem. The steam ensured even cooking and prevented scorching without diluting the flavor.

After toasting a few hot dog buns and nestling the sausages, peppers, and onions inside, we knew we had a winner. Tasters confirmed we had a recipe that would do any street vendor proud.

Grilled Turkey Sausages with Peppers and Onions

SERVES 6

Make sure to cut the onions ½ inch thick. Cutting them any thinner will make them difficult to skewer.

- 3 red bell peppers, stemmed, seeded, and quartered
- 2 onions, cut into ½-inch-thick rounds (do not separate the rings)
  Vegetable oil spray
- ⅛ teaspoon salt
- ⅛ teaspoon pepper
- 1 (13 by 9-inch) disposable aluminum roasting pan
- 1 cup water
- 6 (4-ounce) sweet or hot Italian turkey sausage links
- 6 hot dog buns, toasted

1. Lightly coat the bell peppers and onions with vegetable oil spray and season with the salt and pepper. Following the photo on page 192, thread the onion rounds onto skewers.

2A. FOR A CHARCOAL GRILL: Open the bottom grill vents completely. Light a large chimney starter filled with charcoal briquettes (100 briquettes; 6 quarts). When the coals are hot, pour them in an even layer over the grill. Set the cooking grate in place, cover, and open the lid vents completely. Heat the grill until hot, about 5 minutes.

2B. FOR A GAS GRILL: Turn all the burners to high, cover, and heat the grill until hot, about 15 minutes. (Adjust the burners as needed to maintain a hot fire; see page 182.)

3. Clean and oil the cooking grate. Place the bell peppers and onions on the grill and cook until lightly charred on both sides, 6 to 10 minutes, turning as needed. Transfer the vegetables to the roasting pan and pour the water over the top. Lay the sausages in a single layer on top of the vegetables. Place the roasting pan in the center of the grill, cover, and cook 18 minutes.

4. Move the roasting pan to one side of the grill. Transfer the sausages directly to the cooking grate and cook until well browned on all sides, about 5 minutes, turning as needed. Transfer the sausages to a platter and tent loosely with foil. Continue to cook the peppers and onions in the roasting pan until softened and no longer wet, about 5 minutes longer. Slice the bell peppers into strips, separate the onion rings, and serve with the sausages in the buns.

PER SERVING: Cal 280; Fat 10g; Sat fat 2g; Chol 50mg; Carb 31g; Protein 19g; Fiber 3g; Sodium 880mg

GRILL-ROASTED BEEF

WE LOVE THE IDEA OF A SUNDAY-NIGHT SUMMERTIME supper of perfectly pink grill-roasted beef. Unfortunately, the reality is that the beef usually comes off the grill with spots of perfection mixed with areas that are fibrous, chewy, and woefully dry—in other words, it's tricky to evenly grill a beef roast. Though we use a thermometer to ensure a perfectly medium-rare center, the roast's tapered end always ends up an overcooked storm-cloud gray. And typically, even the more uniform, thicker sections develop a wide band of overcooked meat around the edges. We wanted a recipe that would consistently give us grill-roasted beef that was juicy, perfectly pink, and with a substantial, well-seasoned crust.

We knew the cut of meat needn't be anything fancy—an inexpensive leg or shoulder portion could probably do the job just fine. First, we surveyed the "cheap" ($5.99 per pound or less) beef roast options at our local market. By the end of the trip down the meat aisle, our cart was filled with the best lean options we could find: top and bottom round, eye round, and top sirloin. Each of these then sat through a 24-hour salt rub—a step we discovered in previous testings as worthwhile for improving flavor and texture—before hitting the fire. For practicality and flexibility, we wanted our technique to work with any of these beef cuts, but we focused our testing on the winner of this preliminary tasting: top sirloin, a beefy, relatively tender cut from the back half of the steer that is also relatively lean.

Our usual method for grilling large cuts of meat is to use indirect heat, but for this large beef roast, we wanted to achieve a well-developed crust on the outside comparable to a steak, and we knew indirect heat alone wouldn't get the job done. Our already established technique for cooking thick-cut steaks to achieve evenly cooked interiors and well-developed crusts dictates two stages of heat exposure: first, low and slow for a rosy interior, followed by a fast, hard sear for a nicely charred exterior. It's in this order because during that initial phase, the surface of the meat dries out, allowing for more efficient searing in the second phase. Figuring the same method would work for our 3-pound roast, we set up a modified two-level fire, with all the coals banked to one side. This divided the grill into hot and cool zones, for searing and gentler indirect cooking, respectively. But the slow-roast-then-sear approach didn't translate well from smaller steaks to a big roast; by the time the

center of this larger cut had cooked through, there wasn't enough firepower left in the coals to sear the meat and develop a crust. Adding a second chimney of coals to the grill partway through might have worked if the timing hadn't been impossible to nail down. (Plus, it was more hassle than we were willing to deal with.) This meant we needed to sear the meat first while the fire was still blazing. With this adjustment, our roast developed a thick, dark crust in 10 minutes.

Unfortunately, that initial blast of heat cycled us right back to our initial conundrum: This roast was unevenly cooked and tough. The hot fire meant the outer edge and thinner sections overcooked before the center was done. What's more, our science editor explained, beef contains enzymes that break down muscle fibers and act as natural tenderizers. These enzymes work faster as the temperature of the meat rises—but only until it reaches 122 degrees, at which point all action by the enzymes stops. The bottom line: For more tender results, we needed to keep the meat's interior below this point for as long as possible. (See "Secrets to Perfect Grill-Roasted Beef," page 176.)

Our only alternative was to try tinkering with the temperature of the grill (and, in turn, the cooking time): A full 6-quart chimney put out too much heat too fast, cooking our roast through in under 30 minutes, before the enzymes had a chance to work effectively. We started taking away briquettes, incrementally lowering the amount until we arrived at a half-chimney—the absolute minimum we could get away with while still maintaining a good sear. But even then the meat cooked too quickly. To make this technique work, we'd need to find a way to protect the meat from excess heat as soon as it came off the initial sear. In other words, we needed a meat shield.

When grilling and barbecuing, we keep a supply of disposable aluminum pans at the ready. Could they also function as protective walls against the heat? We started experimenting with them: covering the coals (this time to repel their heat), shielding the meat from the top, and sandwiching the meat between two pans to deflect the heat. (We even tried cutting off the air supply to the grill, causing the coals to die, but this left a sooty taste on the meat.) The most promising method turned out to be searing the roast over the coals, then placing it directly inside the aluminum pan on the cooler side of the grill; this technique slowed the cooking time by about 20 minutes (for a total of just over an hour) and

GRILL-ROASTED BEEF WITH GARLIC AND ROSEMARY

delivered meat that was as tender as any we'd tasted, not to mention uniformly rosy throughout. But it wasn't a perfect solution: As the juice exuded from the meat, it pooled around the roast and turned its underside boiled and gray, ruining any crust we'd achieved from searing. No problem—nothing a little hole punching couldn't fix. The addition of a dozen or so small escape channels in the bottom of the pan allowed the liquid to drain away and left the meat perfectly pink with a crisp, flavorful crust. For a little added flavor, we threw a healthy dose of garlic and rosemary into the salt rub; the flavors made their way deep into the meat by the time we lit the grill.

As the carving knife peeled off wafer-thin slices of rosy meat (another trick for making the roast seem even more tender), we knew we had achieved our goal.

Grill-Roasted Beef with Garlic and Rosemary

SERVES 8

A pair of kitchen shears works well for punching the holes in the aluminum pan. Start this recipe the day before you plan to grill so the salt rub has time to flavor and tenderize the meat. We prefer this roast cooked to medium-rare, but if you prefer your meat more or less done, see our guidelines in "Testing Meat for Doneness" on page 91. Open the grill lid as little as possible in step 4.

- 6 garlic cloves, minced
- 2 tablespoons minced fresh rosemary
- 4 teaspoons kosher salt
- 1 tablespoon pepper
- 1 (3-pound) top sirloin roast, trimmed of all visible fat
- 1 (13 by 9-inch) disposable aluminum roasting pan

1. Combine the garlic, rosemary, salt, and pepper in a bowl. Pat the roast dry with paper towels and sprinkle evenly with the salt mixture. Wrap the roast with plastic wrap and refrigerate for 18 to 24 hours. Punch fifteen ¼-inch holes in the center of the roasting pan, about the size of the roast, and set aside.

2A. FOR A CHARCOAL GRILL: Open the bottom grill vents completely. Light a large chimney starter half full with charcoal briquettes (50 briquettes; 3 quarts). When the coals are hot, spread them in an even layer over one-third of the grill. Set the cooking grate in place, cover, and open the lid vents halfway. Heat the grill until hot, about 5 minutes.

2B. FOR A GAS GRILL: Turn all the burners to high, cover, and heat the grill until hot, about 15 minutes. Turn the primary burner to medium and turn off the other burner(s). (Adjust the primary burner as needed to maintain the grill temperature around 325 degrees.)

3. Clean and oil the cooking grate. Place the roast on the hotter part of the grill and cook (covered if using gas) until well browned on all sides, about 10 minutes, turning as needed. Place the roast in the pan over the holes and transfer the pan to the cooler part of the grill.

4. Cover (positioning the lid vents over the meat if using charcoal) and cook until the roast registers 125 degrees on an instant-read thermometer (for medium-rare), 40 to 60 minutes, rotating the pan halfway through.

5. Transfer the roast to a wire rack set over a rimmed baking sheet, tent loosely with foil, and let rest for 20 minutes. Transfer the roast to a carving board and cut across the grain into thin slices. Serve.

PER SERVING: Cal 230; Fat 7g; Sat fat 2.5g; Chol 70mg; Carb 1g; Protein 38g; Fiber 0g; Sodium 660mg

NOTES FROM THE TEST KITCHEN

SECRETS TO PERFECT GRILL-ROASTED BEEF

In traditional recipes for grill-roasting, the meat is seared first over high heat, then cooked through more slowly and gently over lower heat. To ensure an evenly cooked, rosy-pink interior for our Grill-Roasted Beef, we adjust that approach in two ways. Our goal in doing so was to keep the roast below 122 degrees for as long as possible. Past this temperature, the enzymes that tenderize meat are inactivated, and the more time meat has to break down, the more tender the results.

1. We minimize the overall heat by using a half-chimney of coals—just enough to give the meat a good sear. (To replicate this effect on a gas grill, we turn one burner to medium and the other burners off.)

2. When it is time to cook it through over gentler heat, we shield the seared roast from excess heat by placing it in a disposable aluminum pan. Cutting holes in the pan's bottom ensures juices won't pool and ruin the meat's crust.

CUBAN-STYLE ROAST PORK

CITRUSY, GARLICKY ROASTED MEATS ARE POPULAR in the Caribbean, and one such dish hailing from Cuba achieves the trademark flavor with pork marinated in a mixture of citrus, garlic, olive oil, and spices. Tradition calls for a whole pig cooked on a spit over a wood fire, but in many modern versions a suckling pig, fresh ham, or pork shoulder is grilled instead. And while these recipes are successful, with tender meat and a bracing, flavorful sauce known as mojo, they also rely on fattier cuts that won't pass muster for a light and healthy meal. Could we use a leaner cut of pork and still create a foolproof version of this classic dish?

Identifying the right cut of lean pork was easy. Boneless pork loin roasts are large, tender, widely available, relatively quick to cook, and easy to carve. But because this cut is so lean, it can easily dry out if overcooked, so we'd have to be careful. Loin roasts come with a thin layer of fat on the surface, and while we were watching our fat content, a few preliminary tests told us our tasters much preferred the added moisture and flavor that resulted from leaving at least some of it intact. We settled on trimming it down to a ⅛-inch-thick layer.

The test kitchen's method for grilling large cuts of meat is to use indirect heat, which allows the meat to cook through without the exterior burning. Indirect heat is easy to set up; simply isolate the fire on one part of the grill and place the meat on the cooler part, opposite the coals and flames. We did find, however, that the meat was moister, with better grill flavor, when we cooked the roast on the cooler part of the grill until it was almost done (130 to 135 degrees), then moved it to the hot side to brown the exterior and finish cooking (140 to 145 degrees).

With the cut of pork and the cooking method settled, we turned our attention to getting the characteristic Cuban flavor into the meat. We started by trying marinades that took as long as 24 hours, as tradition dictates, but tasters were less than satisfied with the weak flavor they contributed. In the past we'd had success with getting big flavor from a spice rub on the grill, which as a bonus adds negligible fat and calories, so we thought we would give it a try here. A simple mix of ground cumin, dried oregano, garlic powder, salt, and pepper complemented the lean, mild-tasting pork without overwhelming it. To make sure the spice rub penetrated the meat, we rubbed it over our roast and let it sit at room temperature for an hour before grilling.

All the pork needed now was a final splash of mojo sauce, which could be quickly mixed and cooled to room temperature before we cooked the pork. Made with garlic, olive oil, oregano, cumin, orange juice, salt, pepper, and a shot of white vinegar, the mojo provided a bright, fresh hit of flavor to our healthy grilled pork.

Cuban-Style Grill-Roasted Pork Loin

SERVES 8

We found that leaving a ⅛-inch-thick layer of fat on top of the roast is ideal; if your roast has a thicker fat cap, trim it back to be about ⅛ inch thick. If the pork is enhanced (see page 101), do not brine. If brining the pork, do not add salt to the spice rub in step 3. Note that the length and diameter of boneless pork roasts can vary dramatically; short, wide roasts will take longer to cook through than long, thin roasts.

SAUCE

2 garlic cloves, minced
¼ teaspoon salt
¼ cup olive oil
¼ teaspoon ground cumin
2 tablespoons white vinegar
2 tablespoons orange juice
⅛ teaspoon dried oregano
Pinch pepper

PORK

2 teaspoons ground cumin
2 teaspoons dried oregano
1 teaspoon garlic powder
½ teaspoon salt
½ teaspoon pepper
1 (3-pound) boneless center-cut pork loin roast, trimmed, brined if desired (see page 61)

1. FOR THE SAUCE: Place the minced garlic on a cutting board and sprinkle with the salt. Using the flat side of a chef's knife, scrape the garlic and salt together against the cutting board until the garlic is ground into a smooth paste.

2. Heat the oil in a medium saucepan over medium heat until shimmering. Stir in the garlic paste and cumin and cook until fragrant, about 30 seconds. Off the heat, whisk in the vinegar, orange juice, oregano, and pepper and cool to room temperature.

3. FOR THE PORK: Combine the cumin, oregano, garlic powder, salt, and pepper in a bowl. Following the photos, score the fat on top of the roast in a crosshatch pattern at ½-inch intervals, then tie the roast crosswise at 1½-inch intervals. Pat the pork loin dry with paper towels and coat with the spice mixture. Let sit at room temperature for 1 hour.

4A. FOR A CHARCOAL GRILL: Open the bottom grill vents halfway. Light a large chimney starter filled with charcoal briquettes (100 briquettes; 6 quarts). When the coals are hot, pour them in an even layer over half the grill. Set the cooking grate in place, cover, and open the lid vents halfway. Heat the grill until hot, about 5 minutes.

4B. FOR A GAS GRILL: Turn all the burners to high, cover, and heat the grill until hot, about 15 minutes. Leave the primary burner on high and turn off the other burner(s). (Adjust the primary burner as needed to maintain the grill temperature around 350 degrees.)

5. Clean and oil the cooking grate. Place the pork, fat side up, on the cooler part of the grill. Cover and cook until the pork registers 130 to 135 degrees on an instant-read thermometer, 45 to 60 minutes.

6. Slide the pork to the hotter part of the grill. Cook (covered if using gas) until well browned on all sides and the pork registers 140 to 145 degrees, 5 to 10 minutes longer, turning as needed.

7. Transfer the pork to a carving board, tent loosely with foil, and let rest for 20 minutes. Remove the kitchen twine, slice the pork thin, and serve, passing the sauce separately.

PER SERVING: **Cal** 360; **Fat** 23g; **Sat fat** 6g; **Chol** 115mg; **Carb** 1g; **Protein** 36g; **Fiber** 0g; **Sodium** 310mg

SPICE-CRUSTED PORK TENDERLOIN

WHETHER YOU'RE THUMBING THROUGH A COOKbook or searching online, it's hard to find a recipe for grilled pork tenderloin that doesn't involve a spice crust. It makes sense, and it's a healthy choice since such a crust adds minimal fat and calories to an already lowfat cut. These spice crusts promise to add texture and flavor to the lean, mild tenderloin, but though it may deliver the latter, the typical coating does nothing for the texture. Even in the best versions, ground spices leave the pork with a sandy exterior that's more spice dusted than crusted. We vowed to come up with our own version that would have a flavorful crunch.

Pork tenderloin is easy to grill: Plunk it onto the grate over a hot fire and turn it every few minutes until the meat reaches 145 degrees, which takes about 15 minutes. But how could we build a substantial spice crust? Since ground spices didn't cut it and only left us with a dusty coating, we decided to try whole. We brushed a pair of pork tenderloins (to serve six) with olive oil and sprinkled them with a mixture of black peppercorns, coriander seeds, and mustard seeds (a flavor combination we'd liked in ground form in our earlier tests). But we immediately had problems, as most of the spices tumbled off the tenderloins when the meat hit the grill. However, the few odd seeds that managed to stay put were crunchy and charged with flavor. We were at least on the right track.

Clearly, unlike ground spices, which stick to the meat's surface moisture, the whole spices needed some assistance. Thinking "sticky," we tried brushing tenderloins with a light coating of honey, maple syrup, and even corn syrup before sprinkling on the spices. Each helped the spices stick, but they also caused the pork to stick to the grate. Next we tried mayonnaise, then mustard, to anchor

NOTES FROM THE TEST KITCHEN

SCORING AND TYING PORK LOIN

1. To encourage the fat to render so it can baste the meat as it cooks, use a sharp knife to cut a shallow crosshatch pattern into the fat. Avoid cutting through the fat and into the meat, as this may result in moisture loss.

2. Tying the roast tightly with kitchen twine at 1½-inch intervals gives it an even shape, promoting even cooking on the grill.

SPICE-CRUSTED GRILLED PORK TENDERLOIN

the spices. The meat didn't stick to the grill for either of these, but the spices didn't stick to the meat. Stumped, we went back to basics and tried what chefs call "bound breading," which is typically used for pan-fried foods. We dredged the tenderloins in a light coating of flour, dipped them in beaten egg, and then coated them with the spices instead of the usual bread crumbs. This gave us the best crust so far, but the egg coating was spongy and tough. Losing the egg yolks solved that problem and lost some fat along the way, too. Finally, we pitted flour

---

NOTES FROM THE TEST KITCHEN

REMOVING SILVER SKIN FROM PORK TENDERLOIN

The silver skin is a thin, tough membrane covering parts of the tenderloin and should be removed before cooking. Slip a knife under the silver skin, angle it slightly upward, and use a gentle back-and-forth motion to remove it.

MAKING SPICE-CRUSTED PORK TENDERLOIN

1. Roll each tenderloin in cornstarch to help the egg whites adhere.

2. Dip the cornstarch-coated tenderloins in lightly beaten egg whites, which will help the spices adhere.

3. Gently press the spices onto the pork to ensure the crust stays put.

---

against cornstarch as a dredge for the meat. Tasters preferred the lightness and cling of cornstarch to the slightly gummy flour. A spritz of vegetable oil spray right before grilling ensured adhesion.

Now our pork was definitely crusty—to a fault. The egg white coating glued the spices so successfully, each bite tasted like potpourri. If we used fewer spices, the pork was sparsely coated. To stretch the crust, we cracked the whole spices, which retained plenty of crunch and better covered the meat. At the same time, we augmented the spices in a series of tests with small amounts of bread crumbs, flour, cornstarch, and cornmeal. In the end, 1 tablespoon of cornmeal gave the crust more coverage, more texture, and a subtle toasty flavor. A modest teaspoon each of coarse sugar and kosher salt added balance and further crunch. And to keep the coating from burning, we started the cooking on the hotter part of the grill to ensure the crust adhered, then finished cooking the pork on the cooler part of the grill.

Spice-Crusted Grilled Pork Tenderloin
SERVES 6

We prefer Demerara sugar (such as Sugar in the Raw) in this recipe, but plain brown sugar works, too. If you don't have kosher salt, use ½ teaspoon table salt.

- 3 tablespoons mustard seeds
- 1 tablespoon cornmeal
- 1 tablespoon coriander seeds, cracked
- 1 teaspoon peppercorns, cracked
- 1 teaspoon Demerara sugar
- 1 teaspoon kosher salt
- 2 (1-pound) pork tenderloins, silver skin removed (see photo), trimmed of all visible fat
- ½ cup cornstarch
- 2 large egg whites
  Vegetable oil spray

1A. FOR A CHARCOAL GRILL: Open the bottom grill vents completely. Light a large chimney starter filled with charcoal briquettes (100 briquettes; 6 quarts). When the coals are hot, pour them in an even layer over half the grill. Set the cooking grate in place, cover, and open the lid vents completely. Heat the grill until hot, about 5 minutes.

1B. FOR A GAS GRILL: Turn all the burners to high, cover, and heat the grill until hot, about 15 minutes. Leave the primary burner on high and turn off the other burner(s). (Adjust the primary burner as needed to maintain the grill temperature around 350 degrees.)

2. Meanwhile, combine the mustard seeds, cornmeal, coriander seeds, peppercorns, sugar, and salt in a bowl. Pat the pork tenderloins dry with paper towels. Place the cornstarch in a shallow dish. In a second shallow dish, whisk the egg whites together until foamy. Working with one tenderloin at a time, lightly coat with the cornstarch, dip in the egg whites, and sprinkle evenly with the spice mixture, pressing gently to adhere. Transfer the tenderloins to a plate and lightly coat with vegetable oil spray.

3. Clean and oil the cooking grate. Place the tenderloins on the hotter part of the grill and cook until browned on all sides, 6 to 8 minutes, turning as needed. Slide the tenderloins to the cooler part of the grill and continue to cook, covered, until the meat registers 140 to 145 degrees on an instant-read thermometer, 6 to 12 minutes longer.

4. Transfer the pork to a carving board and let rest for 5 minutes. Cut into ¼-inch-thick slices and serve.

PER SERVING: Cal 220; Fat 5g; Sat fat 1g; Chol 100mg; Carb 9g; Protein 34g; Fiber 1g; Sodium 280mg

THAI-STYLE GRILLED PORK

IN OUR FAVORITE THAI RESTAURANT, WE LOVE TO order the salty-sweet grilled pork, usually served with a spicy, slightly tangy sauce. The caramelized, crispy-charred edges and juicy interior of each thinly sliced piece make this dish almost addictive. But unfortunately, what you get at a number of restaurants is greasy pork (they usually rely on fatty shoulder cuts) and a sauce chock-full of sodium. Since cooking on the grill is easy to do without adding a lot of fat, we thought this recipe was an ideal candidate for making our own homemade version. We wanted to develop a lean recipe for this restaurant favorite, one with well-seasoned, flavorful pork that had crispy edges and a moist interior.

We started our testing with the cut of pork. We knew it had to be a lean cut, so fatty options like pork shoulder and country spareribs were out. Pork chops offered great flavor, but the meat was a little tough for this dish. The loin and tenderloin were both winning options, but the tenderloin proved to be our top pick, as two 1-pound tenderloins gave us just the right amount of meat for the recipe.

Having settled on the meat, we focused next on infusing it with flavor with the help of a marinade. After a little research, we found that most of the marinades were based on a combination of fish sauce, sugar, and oil, while some recipes included additional ingredients like aromatics, soy sauce, coconut milk, or chili paste. We began our testing with the fish sauce. Although most recipes don't call for much, we knew nonetheless that it was an important ingredient since its salty makeup would work in a way like a quick brine, helping to ensure moist meat. After a few incremental tests, we found that 2 tablespoons of fish sauce was perfect. When we used any more, tasters thought the potent flavor of the fish sauce overwhelmed the meat. Two tablespoons of soy sauce added just the right amount of depth and seasoning to balance the fish sauce.

Next, we tested additional flavorings in our marinade base. For aromatics, we tested ginger, garlic, and lemon grass, but tasters preferred just the simple addition of three cloves of minced garlic. For the sugar, we tried granulated sugar, light brown sugar, and dark brown sugar. Tasters liked both the light and dark brown sugars for the deep caramel-y flavor they contributed, and a mere tablespoon added just the right amount of sweetness. Two tablespoons of canola oil kept the meat from drying out from the intense heat of the grill without adding too much fat to the recipe. With that, our simple but flavorful marinade was set.

The next challenge was grilling the pork. We knew the pork had to be sliced thin before it hit the grill to get the crispy edges we were after. But we quickly realized the thin slices were difficult to deal with on the grates. Several recipes we came across in our research worked around this by using skewers, so we gave them a try. We sliced the pork tenderloins into 3 by ¼-inch strips and threaded them onto skewers. The skewers made easy work of maneuvering the pork on and off the grill. Twelve-inch-long metal skewers worked best. We were able to thread two pieces of pork onto each. In order to get the caramelized edges we were after, we found a hot fire did the best job; thin slices of pork cook so quickly that over lower heat they were done before any browning occurred. Just 7 to 10 minutes was all the time it took for the pork to cook through and turn beautifully browned.

NOTES FROM THE TEST KITCHEN

CUTTING AND SKEWERING PORK

1. Cut the partially frozen pork tenderloin into 3-inch lengths, then cut each piece lengthwise into ¼-inch-thick strips.

2. After marinating the pork, weave two pieces of the pork onto each skewer.

OUR FAVORITE SKEWERS

Over the years we've learned a lot about which skewers are best—and worst—for grilling. Wooden skewers are generally our least favorite since they can burn and break over the high heat of the grill. Instead we rely on long metal skewers, particularly those that are flat rather than round (shrimp perpetually spin and flop around on the latter). Our favorite skewers are **Norpro's 12-Inch Stainless Steel Skewers** ($8 for a set of six), which are ³⁄₁₆ inch thick, never burn, last forever, and hold food in place.

HOW HOT IS YOUR FIRE?

To determine the heat level of the cooking grate itself, heat up the grill and hold your hand 5 inches above the cooking grate, counting how long you can comfortably keep it there. Note that this works with both charcoal and gas grills.

Hot fire	2 seconds
Medium-hot fire	3 to 4 seconds
Medium fire	5 to 6 seconds
Medium-low fire	7 seconds
Low fire	10 seconds

Tasters were happy with our recipe, but a few wanted the pork to have some acidity. We didn't want to add acid to the marinade for fear of making the slices of meat mushy, but we recalled a few recipes from our research where the meat was tossed with a pungent sauce before serving. We combined sugar, vinegar, lime juice, fish sauce, garlic, and red pepper flakes to make a sauce to serve with the meat at the table; this gave our crispy, juicy pork the right final hit of salty-sweet and spicy-tart flavors. As a finishing touch, we added a sprinkling of fresh cilantro leaves for color and brightness.

Thai-Style Grilled Pork

SERVES 6

Freezing the meat for 30 minutes makes it easier to slice. Serve with steamed white rice.

SAUCE

⅓ cup granulated sugar

¼ cup white vinegar

¼ cup fresh lime juice (about 2 limes)

2 tablespoons fish sauce

2 garlic cloves, minced

1 teaspoon red pepper flakes

PORK

2 tablespoons canola oil

2 tablespoons fish sauce

2 tablespoons low-sodium soy sauce

1 tablespoon brown sugar

3 garlic cloves, minced

½ teaspoon pepper

2 (1-pound) pork tenderloins, silver skin removed (see page 180), trimmed of all visible fat, and cut into 3 by ¼-inch strips (see photo)

½ cup lightly packed fresh cilantro leaves

1. FOR THE SAUCE: Whisk the granulated sugar, vinegar, lime juice, fish sauce, garlic, and red pepper flakes together in a bowl; set aside for serving.

2. FOR THE PORK: Combine the oil, fish sauce, soy sauce, brown sugar, garlic, and pepper in a bowl. Combine the marinade and pork in a large zipper-lock bag. Seal the bag tightly, toss to coat the pork, and let the pork marinate in the refrigerator for 1 hour.

3. Following the photo on page 182, weave 2 pieces of the pork onto each skewer.

4A. FOR A CHARCOAL GRILL: Open the bottom grill vents completely. Light a large chimney starter filled with charcoal briquettes (100 briquettes; 6 quarts). When the coals are hot, pour them in an even layer over the grill. Set the cooking grate in place, cover, and heat the grill until hot, about 5 minutes.

4B. FOR A GAS GRILL: Turn all the burners to high, cover, and heat the grill until hot, about 15 minutes. (Adjust the burners as needed to maintain a hot fire; see page 182.)

5. Clean and oil the cooking grate. Place the skewers on the grill and cook until the meat is cooked through and lightly charred around the edges, 7 to 10 minutes, flipping the skewers halfway through.

6. Transfer the skewers to a platter and let rest for 5 minutes. Remove the meat from the skewers, sprinkle the cilantro leaves over the top, and serve, passing the sauce separately.

PER SERVING (2 SKEWERS WITH 2 TABLESPOONS SAUCE): **Cal** 280; **Fat** 8g; **Sat fat** 1.5g; **Chol** 100mg; **Carb** 18g; **Protein** 34g; **Fiber** 0g; **Sodium** 720mg

BLACKENED FISH FILLETS

EVER SINCE FAMED CAJUN CHEF PAUL PRUDHOMME popularized blackened redfish in the 1980s, blackened anything has become synonymous with nouvelle Cajun cookery. With their crusty, sweet-smoky, toasted-spice exteriors surrounding moist, mild-flavored fish, blackened redfish fillets offer unique flavor and texture, not to mention simple preparation. Though Prudhomme first blackened fish in a white-hot cast-iron skillet, he later moved it to the grill because his recipe created a fair amount of smoke. It seemed like a perfect recipe to add to our grilling repertoire, but we had one problem. In addition to all the spices, Prudhomme's other key ingredient is butter. His original recipe calls for dipping the fish in the equivalent of 1 cup of butter for four fillets, far too much for our light-cooking repertoire. Could we lighten it up and still achieve the classic flavor?

Because redfish is found primarily near the Gulf Coast, our first step was switching to the similar but more readily available red snapper. During our early attempts the fish almost always stuck to the cooking grate and either burned on the outside by the time the flesh cooked through or failed to get dark and crusty enough. Also, because the skin on these thin fillets shrank as they cooked, they were curling midway through, leading to burned edges and arched, barely blackened centers. We found that our issue with even cooking could be taken care of by using a half-grill fire that had a hotter and a cooler side (cooking on the hot side promoted blackening, while the cooler side could be used to finish cooking through thicker fillets). Addressing the curling problem was a quick fix—we simply scored the skin, which ensured that the fillets stayed flat as the skin shrank during cooking.

But even when we had our grilling technique down, the fillets were still sticking to the cooking grate. Because preheating the grate is what keeps food from sticking, we realized that what we needed to do was get it super-hot and super-clean. Placing a piece of heavy-duty foil on the cooking grate while it preheated allowed the grate to reach almost 200 degrees hotter than normal, incinerating any nasty gunk left from previous grilling. Now we could cook our fillets without any fear of sticking.

Prudhomme's original recipe called for dipping the fillets in butter, then coating them in the spices. To cut fat, we'd been using a basic dry rub made from paprika, black and white pepper, cayenne, and salt up to this point, but its unexciting flavor was less than ideal, not to mention it was burning. To fix the flavor, we added coriander, which could take the heat and gave the rub a needed bright floral note. Prudhomme's recipe calls for garlic powder and onion powder, and adding both to our rub gave it a robust boost. But we still wanted more flavor, so we decided we needed to add back at least some of the butter. We tried sautéing, or blooming, the spices in melted butter to help release their flavors. We found we needed only 3 tablespoons of butter to get the job done. Once the spice mixture cooled, we broke up any large clumps and applied it to the fish in a thin layer. This not only brought the flavor up to the level we were after but also kept the spices from burning.

One more test proved we had it right. By the time the fillets were fully cooked, they were also well blackened (but not burned), and the spice crust had finally acquired the depth and richness we were after. At last, we had blackened fish that brought New Orleans right into our backyard, and with a fraction of the fat.

Grilled Blackened Red Snapper

SERVES 4

If your fish fillets are thicker or thinner, adjust the cooking time accordingly. Move thicker fillets to the cooler side of the grill to finish cooking them through on the second side. We typically cook with the lid down on a gas grill; however, you need to keep a constant eye on the spices to ensure that they don't burn, so we recommend leaving the lid open for this recipe. Be sure to use heavy-duty foil when pre-heating the grill in step 3 and leave a few inches of the grill grate uncovered around the edges for ventilation.

- 2   **tablespoons paprika**
- 2   **teaspoons onion powder**
- 2   **teaspoons garlic powder**
- ¾   **teaspoon ground coriander**
- ¾   **teaspoon salt**
- ¼   **teaspoon black pepper**
- ¼   **teaspoon white pepper**
- ¼   **teaspoon cayenne pepper**
- 3   **tablespoons unsalted butter**
- 4   **(6-ounce) skin-on red snapper fillets, about ¾ inch thick**

1. Combine the paprika, onion powder, garlic powder, coriander, salt, black pepper, white pepper, and cayenne in a bowl. Melt the butter in an 8-inch skillet over medium heat. Stir in the spice mixture and cook, stirring constantly, until fragrant and the spices turn a dark rust color, 2 to 3 minutes. Transfer the mixture to a pie plate and cool to room temperature, about 10 minutes. Once the mixture has cooled, use a fork to break up any large clumps.

2. Pat the fish fillets dry with paper towels. Using a serrated knife, score the skin of the fish with 3 or 4 parallel slashes, being careful not to cut into the flesh. Rub the spice mixture evenly over both sides of the fillets.

3A. FOR A CHARCOAL GRILL: Open the bottom grill vents completely. Light a large chimney starter three-quarters full with charcoal briquettes (75 briquettes; 4½ quarts). When the coals are hot, pour them in an even layer over half the grill. Set the cooking grate in place and loosely cover the grate with a large piece of heavy-duty aluminum foil, positioning it directly over the coals. Cover and heat the grill until hot, about 5 minutes.

3B. FOR A GAS GRILL: Turn all the burners to high and loosely cover the grate with a large piece of heavy-duty aluminum foil, positioning it directly over the coals.

Cover and heat the grill until hot, about 15 minutes. Leave all the burners on high. (Adjust the burners as needed to maintain a hot fire; see page 182.)

4. Remove the foil and clean and oil the cooking grate. Following the photos, place the fish directly where the foil was, skin side down and perpendicular to the bars of the cooking grate. Cook until the fish is opaque and flakes apart when gently prodded with a paring knife, 10 to 14 minutes, gently turning the fish halfway through with two spatulas.

5. Transfer the fish to a wire rack, tent loosely with aluminum foil, and let rest for 5 minutes before serving.

PER SERVING: Cal 270; Fat 11g; Sat fat 6g; Chol 85mg; Carb 4g; Protein 36g; Fiber 1g; Sodium 550mg

GRILLED STUFFED TROUT

COOKING A WHOLE FISH ON THE GRILL ALWAYS MAKES for an impressive meal. And although we sometimes opt for more manageable fillets when faced with large fish, cooking a smaller fish, like trout, whole is absolutely feasible. In fact, it is a much simpler feat than you might think. Sure, it might be a little extra work for you or your diners to fillet the fish, but the flavorful, juicy results of cooking a fish on the bone make it well worth the effort. Of all the fish you can cook whole, rainbow trout is a variety that is underappreciated and readily available, and it offers a sweet, mild flavor that makes it attractive for any number of preparations. Each weighs about 7 ounces, making it a perfect serving for one. One of our favorites is trout stuffed with a simple filling prior to grilling.

But before we could tackle the filling, we needed to figure out the best method for grilling the fish. Fresh-water rainbow trout have thin, delicate skin and fine flesh. It isn't terribly oily, so flare-ups are not really a concern, and the small size of each fish means that the flesh can cook through quickly, before the skin has a chance to char. Oiling the fish in addition to the cooking grate helped us avoid any sticking issues. We had the best results grilling our trout over a hot fire. Though making slits in the sides of thicker fish can help with even cooking or to avoid curling fillets, we found it wasn't necessary to make them here since each fish was so thin, and we didn't want to encourage any tearing of the trout's skin or unnecessary release of juice.

Now it was time to focus on the filling. We immediately decided to step off the beaten path from standard bread-based stuffings and create a vegetable stuffing. Spinach and red bell pepper offered a combination of mild bitterness and sweetness that was a great starting point. Bacon and trout are a classic pairing, and the bacon's smoky flavor and hint of richness were just what the filling needed to give it some depth. To keep the fat and calories down, we used just two slices. A little onion rounded out the flavors.

Because the fish would cook quickly on the grill, and because we didn't want the spinach to turn soggy as it wilted, we knew we would need to precook our stuffing before it went into the fish. We began with the bacon, which we chopped before adding it to the skillet for speed and simplicity. Once it was browned, we set it aside, waiting to stir it into the cooked spinach-pepper mixture until right before we stuffed the fish. This kept the bacon bits from becoming chewy. For a full, smoky flavor, we sautéed the pepper and onion in the fat rendered from the bacon before tossing the spinach into the skillet to wilt. We tried several styles of spinach, and although flavor differences were slight, the differences in preparation were not. Baby spinach was by far the easiest to deal with since it can be purchased already cleaned. Letting it drain in a colander for 10 minutes after cooking was enough to get rid of any excess moisture. This filling tasted good, but it was still missing something. A shot of cider vinegar

was just what it needed to brighten the flavors.

All we had to do was stuff each fish's cavity with some of the stuffing and put them on the grill. In less than 15 minutes, we had perfectly browned trout with flaky, moist flesh and a smoky-sweet stuffing.

Grilled Stuffed Trout

SERVES 4

The filling can be made up to a day ahead of time, but the fish should be stuffed just before grilling.

- 2 slices bacon, cut into ¼-inch pieces
- 1 onion, halved and sliced thin
- 1 red bell pepper, stemmed, seeded, and chopped medium
  Salt
- 10 ounces baby spinach (about 10 cups)
- 2 teaspoons cider vinegar
  Pepper
- 4 (10-ounce) whole rainbow trout, gutted and cleaned
- 1 tablespoon vegetable oil
- 1 lemon, cut into wedges, for serving

1. Cook the bacon in a 12-inch skillet over medium-low heat until browned and crisp, about 10 minutes. Using a slotted spoon, transfer the bacon to a paper towel lined plate, leaving the fat in the skillet. Return the skillet to medium-high heat, add the onion, bell pepper, and ½ teaspoon salt, and cook until the vegetables are softened and beginning to brown, 5 to 7 minutes.

2. Stir in the spinach and vinegar, and cook until the spinach is wilted and all extra moisture has evaporated, about 5 minutes. Transfer the mixture to a colander and let drain for 10 minutes. Stir in the cooked bacon and season with salt and pepper to taste.

3. Meanwhile, pat the fish dry with paper towels and rub the exteriors with the oil. Season the exteriors and cavities of the fish with salt and pepper. Divide the spinach mixture evenly among the cavities, about a generous ¼ cup per fish.

4A. FOR A CHARCOAL GRILL: Open the bottom grill vents completely. Light a large chimney starter filled with charcoal briquettes (100 briquettes; 6 quarts). When the coals are hot, pour them in an even layer over the grill. Set the cooking grate in place, cover, and heat the grill until hot, about 5 minutes.

4B. FOR A GAS GRILL: Turn all the burners to high, cover, and heat the grill until hot, about 15 minutes. (Adjust the burners as needed to maintain a hot fire; see page 182.)

5. Clean and oil the cooking grate. Lay the trout on the grill, perpendicular to the bars of the cooking grate. Cook (covered if using gas) until the sides of the fish are browned and crisp, the flesh is opaque, and the filling is hot, 10 to 14 minutes, gently flipping the fish halfway through with two spatulas.

6. Transfer the fish to a wire rack, tent loosely with foil, and let rest for 5 minutes. Serve with the lemon wedges.

PER SERVING: Cal 380; Fat 19g; Sat fat 5g; Chol 110mg; Carb 12g; Protein 39g; Fiber 5g; Sodium 580mg

FISH SKEWERS

HERE IN THE TEST KITCHEN, WE HAVE TRIED SKEWERING and grilling everything from the basics like beef, chicken, and vegetables to shrimp and even tofu. So we were surprised when we realized we didn't have a recipe for skewered fish in our repertoire. We wondered if this was simply an oversight, or if preliminary tests had revealed that fish is simply too delicate to hold together on a skewer and testing had never gotten past step 1. But given how healthy, easy, and quick kebabs can be, we felt now was the time to run fish kebabs through some serious testing. We had a hunch that if we chose the right fish, we could produce a successful recipe, one with moist, well-seasoned chunks of fish and a vegetable or two to skewer along with them.

We started with finding the right fish for the job. We knew we needed one that wouldn't flake apart on the skewer and could hold up to the grill's high heat. We tested a range of firm-fleshed fish, including tuna, swordfish, mahi-mahi, and halibut. The tuna was always overcooked and dry—we like tuna grilled to medium-rare, and that proved nearly impossible to achieve on a skewer because the skewers themselves heat up on the grill and end up cooking the small pieces of fish from the inside out. Though mahi-mahi and halibut worked fine, meaty-textured swordfish was the favorite. Its firm, steaklike flesh held up well on the skewer, and its mild flavor was complemented by the flavor it picked up on the grill.

We found that cutting the swordfish into 1¼-inch pieces before skewering was ideal. The exterior of larger pieces charred before the inside cooked through, and smaller pieces dried out. Testing a range of heat levels, we found that a medium-hot fire was best for cooking the skewers. At this heat, the swordfish chunks picked up some nice grill flavor and were lightly browned in the time that the interiors took to be perfectly cooked through and juicy.

To add flavor to the fish, we first tried a basic marinade with olive oil, basil, shallot, and lemon juice, but even after just a short soak, the swordfish had absorbed enough moisture that it didn't brown well on the grill, and its texture suffered because the acid from the lemon juice had caused the fish to essentially cook. Adding a spice rub was our next idea. We rubbed the fish with a simple mix of ground cumin, coriander, paprika, cayenne pepper, and black pepper. Tasters liked the idea of the spice rub, but they agreed this combination came on a little strong when paired with the mild-tasting fish. We singled out warm, citrusy coriander and rubbed it on the fish with just a little salt and pepper. To protect the fish on the grill and ensure that it didn't stick, we lightly sprayed the kebabs with vegetable oil spray before cooking.

For the other kebab components, tasters agreed that red onion was a classic and essential kebab choice. After a few test runs, we found that if we cut the onion into 1-inch squares, the pieces cooked through at the same rate as the fish. We also tried bell peppers, mushrooms, cherry tomatoes, and zucchini, but none was a good match, so we opted to stop where we were and keep things simple.

Our recipe was close, but our skewers needed a little more flavor. Thinking back to the marinade idea, we realized we could brush the kebabs with the mixture after they came off the grill. This gave our kebabs a great boost and added the brightness they were missing. We thought we were finished when someone suggested that we could get even richer, deeper flavor if we grilled the lemons instead of simply adding the juice to the oil mixture. We halved, then quartered a few lemons, then put them on the skewers with the swordfish and onion. After the kebabs came off the grill, we brushed them with the oil mixture (this time minus the lemon juice) and squeezed the grilled lemons over the kebabs at the table once we'd taken everything off the skewers. These

GRILLED SWORDFISH SKEWERS

lemons had caramelized nicely, adding a sweetness that really took these kebabs to the next level. With that, we finally had a great recipe for skewered fish to add to our grilling rotation.

Grilled Swordfish Skewers

SERVES 4

We like the flavor of swordfish here but you can substitute other sturdy, firm-fleshed fish such as mahi-mahi or halibut.

- 1 (1½-pound) skinless swordfish steak, cut into 1¼-inch pieces
- 4 teaspoons ground coriander
  Salt and pepper
- 3 lemons, halved, each half quartered
- 1 large red onion, cut into 1-inch squares (see photos)
  Vegetable oil spray
- 2 tablespoons extra-virgin olive oil
- 2 tablespoons chopped fresh basil
- 1½ teaspoons minced shallot

1. Pat the swordfish dry with paper towels, rub with the coriander, and season with ⅛ teaspoon salt and ⅛ teaspoon pepper. Thread the fish, lemons, and onion evenly onto the skewers, in an alternating pattern, then lightly coat with vegetable oil spray.

2A. FOR A CHARCOAL GRILL: Open the bottom grill vents completely. Light a large chimney starter three-quarters full with charcoal briquettes (75 briquettes; 4½ quarts). When the coals are hot, pour them in an even layer over the grill. Set the cooking grate in place, cover, and heat the grill until hot, about 5 minutes.

2B. FOR A GAS GRILL: Turn all the burners to high, cover, and heat the grill until hot, about 15 minutes. Turn all the burners to medium-high. (Adjust the burners as needed to maintain a medium-hot fire; see page 182.)

3. Clean and oil the cooking grate. Place the skewers on the grill and cook (covered if using gas) until the fish is opaque and flakes apart when gently prodded with a paring knife, 5 to 8 minutes, turning as needed.

4. Transfer the skewers to a platter, tent loosely with foil, and let rest for 5 minutes. Combine the oil, basil, and shallot in a bowl and season with salt and pepper to taste. Brush the skewers with the oil mixture before serving.

PER SERVING (1 SKEWER): Cal 290; Fat 14g; Sat fat 3g; Chol 65mg; Carb 4g; Protein 34g; Fiber 1g; Sodium 230mg

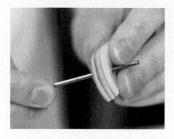
SHRIMP TACOS

IF IT'S A HEALTHY AND FLAVORFUL DINNER OFF the grill you're looking for, you can't go wrong with a shrimp taco paired with a fruit salsa. Easy, refreshing, and quick to make, this dish should be in everyone's light recipe repertoire. But after trying a few existing recipes, we discovered that most out there are riddled with problems. Underseasoned, overcooked shrimp paired with a salsa that was either watery or cloyingly sweet was not something we wanted to have for dinner, light or not. We headed to the test kitchen to see what we could do.

Based on past experience, we already knew the best way to tackle the overcooked shrimp issue. Small shrimp on a hot grill cook so quickly that it is tricky to keep them from becoming tough and dry. We have found that threading the shrimp tightly on skewers helps slow down the cooking process enough to let the outside develop a slight char while the inside remains tender. Sprinkling a small amount of sugar over one side of the skewered shrimp promotes browning and complements their briny sweetness. We also knew we'd need the grill set up with a hot side for a quick sear and a cooler side for cooking the shrimp through gently. We grilled our shrimp, sugared side down, over the hot side for a few minutes. When a nice crust had developed, we flipped the skewers and moved them to the cool part of the grill to finish up. This method left us with perfect results. The shrimp had a smoky crust on the outside and were tender and moist on the inside.

With our technique settled, we began working on the flavor of the shrimp. Borrowing again from proven test kitchen techniques, we knew that butterflying and marinating the shrimp would boost their flavor considerably. We tested a number of different marinade ingredients, but tasters settled on a combination of fresh garlic, cayenne, chili powder, cumin, and coriander as their favorite for a taco recipe. A colleague suggested quickly cooking the spices in a small amount of oil before tossing them with the shrimp to marinate. This bloomed the spices and helped deepen the flavor of the shrimp even more.

With the shrimp ready to go, it was time to work on the fresh fruit salsa. We chopped up all the fruits we could get our hands on that we thought might work in a salsa: oranges, papayas, mangoes, and kiwi, to name a few. We liked a number of combinations, but ultimately the duo of pineapple and jícama (a refreshing, slightly sweet root vegetable with white crunchy flesh that is grown in Mexico and South America) won the day. Minced jalapeño gave our salsa a touch of heat to cut the sweetness, and cilantro and lime juice added the right tang and herbal flavors.

Excited to try our creation, we fired up the grill. We wrapped our shrimp in a lightly charred tortilla and topped it with the salsa. It took only one bite to realize something was missing. The tacos were flavorful, no doubt, but something was amiss with the texture. Tasters wanted something smooth to balance all of the crunch.

We lightly mashed an avocado with some lime juice and salt to make a quick guacamole. After topping each taco with a tablespoon of the avocado mixture we knew we had done it. Tasters agreed; these tacos were so good and full of flavor, they'd make them again and again.

Grilled Shrimp Tacos with Pineapple-Jícama Salsa
SERVES 6

Don't let the shrimp marinate for longer than 15 minutes or the acid marinade will begin to "cook" the shrimp and turn them rubbery. We find it easiest to buy fresh pineapple that has already been peeled and cored, but you can also buy a whole medium pineapple and prep it yourself. To make this dish spicier, add the chile seeds.

  1 medium ripe avocado, pitted and peeled
  ¼ cup fresh lime juice (about 2 limes)
     Salt
 10 ounces jícama, peeled and cut into ¼-inch pieces
 10 ounces cored and peeled fresh pineapple, cut into ¼-inch pieces (see page 107)
  2 tablespoons minced fresh cilantro
  1 jalapeño chile, stemmed, seeded, and minced
  2 tablespoons canola oil
  3 garlic cloves, minced
  2 teaspoons chili powder
  1 teaspoon ground coriander
  1 teaspoon ground cumin
  ¼ teaspoon cayenne pepper
 1½ pounds extra-large shrimp (21 to 25 per pound), peeled, deveined, butterflied (see page 190), and tails removed
  ½ teaspoon sugar
 12 (6-inch) corn tortillas

1. Using a fork or potato masher, mash the avocado with 1 tablespoon of the lime juice until some small chunks remain. Season with salt to taste. Cover and refrigerate until ready to serve.

2. Combine 2 tablespoons more lime juice, jícama, pineapple, cilantro, and jalapeño in a bowl. Season with salt to taste. Cover and refrigerate until ready to serve.

3. Heat the oil in a small skillet over medium heat. Add the garlic, chili powder, coriander, cumin, and cayenne and cook until fragrant, about 1 minute. Scrape the mixture into a medium bowl and cool to room temperature, then stir in the remaining 1 tablespoon lime juice and ½ teaspoon salt.

4. Add the shrimp to the spice mixture and toss to coat. Cover and refrigerate for 15 minutes. Following the photo, thread the shrimp onto the skewers, then sprinkle one side of the shrimp with the sugar.

5A. FOR A CHARCOAL GRILL: Open the bottom grill vents completely. Light a large chimney starter filled with charcoal briquettes (100 briquettes; 6 quarts). When the coals are hot, pour them in an even layer over half the grill. Set the cooking grate in place, cover, and open the lid vents completely. Heat the grill until hot, about 5 minutes.

5B. FOR A GAS GRILL: Turn all the burners to high, cover, and heat the grill until hot, about 15 minutes. (Adjust the burners as needed to maintain a hot fire; see page 182.)

6. Clean and oil the cooking grate. Place the shrimp, sugared side down, on the grill (over the coals if using charcoal) and cook (covered if using gas) until lightly charred on the first side, 3 to 4 minutes.

7. Flip the shrimp and slide them to the cooler part of the grill, away from the coals if using charcoal, or if using gas, turn all the burners to low. Cover and continue to cook the shrimp until the second side is no longer translucent, 1 to 2 minutes longer. Transfer the shrimp to a platter and remove the shrimp from the skewers.

NOTES FROM THE TEST KITCHEN

BUTTERFLYING AND SKEWERING SHRIMP

1. Using a paring knife, make a shallow cut down the outside curve of the shrimp to open up the flesh.

2. Alternate the direction of the shrimp as you pack them tightly on the skewer. This allows you to fit about a dozen shrimp snugly on each skewer.

8. If using gas, turn the burners to medium. Working in batches, place a few of the tortillas in a single layer on the grill and cook until warm, about 10 seconds per side. As the tortillas are done, wrap them in a kitchen towel or a large sheet of foil.

9. To serve, place 3 shrimp in a warm tortilla and top with 1 tablespoon of the avocado mixture and ¼ cup of the pineapple-jícama salsa.

PER SERVING: **Cal** 410; **Fat** 14g; **Sat fat** 1.5g; **Chol** 170mg; **Carb** 45g; **Protein** 27g; **Fiber** 8g; **Sodium** 450mg

PORTOBELLO BURGERS

BURGERS HAVE CHANGED A LOT SINCE THEY FIRST hit the mainstream in the early 1900s. Back then, and really until recent decades, "burger" meant "hamburger," a cooked ground beef patty served on a bun with all the garnishes. But burgers these days are being made out of everything from turkey, to chicken, to black beans. We already had great recipes for poultry burgers and black bean burgers under our belt, but another one of our favorites we hadn't explored is the portobello burger. Infused with smoky flavor from the grill, portobello mushrooms develop a rich, meaty taste and have a hearty texture that makes them satisfying. But making a portobello burger isn't as easy as throwing a few mushroom caps on the grill, waiting until they brown, then sandwiching them in a bun. Our initial tests brought up a variety of problems. Some mushrooms were the perfect size before cooking, but shrank so much during cooking they were insignificant on the bun. All the mushrooms oozed moisture and made our buns soggy. And frankly, they were bland as can be. With these challenges ahead, we fired up the grill and set out to create a hearty portobello burger that was ideally cooked, packed with flavor, and a perfect match for the bun.

Clearly, picking the right size of portobello cap was imperative. We needed a cap that would fill up a bun—after it had been cooked. Because of their high moisture content, mushrooms shrink considerably when cooked, so we needed to start with caps that seemed a little oversized for them to end up just right. We grilled up 4- and 6-ounce portobello caps. Once cooked, the 4-ounce caps, which were about 2 to 3 inches in diameter, were much too small for a regular-size bun. The 6-ounce caps, which were about 4 to 5 inches in diameter, looked much too big in the raw state but were the perfect size after grilling.

With the size squared away, we could turn to the next problem: soggy buns. The mushrooms were leaching so much water that they inevitably made our buns a mushy mess. If we grilled the mushrooms until their moisture was gone, the buns certainly remained dry, but the mushrooms were also leathery, overcooked, and inedible. Drawing on past test kitchen experience from recipes like our Stuffed Eggplants with Bulgur (page 152), we knew that scoring the flesh of certain vegetables can help draw out excess moisture, and we had a hunch it would help out here as well. Using the tip of a sharp knife, we scored a shallow diamond pattern into each cap before placing the mushrooms on the grill. This worked like a charm. In less than 10 minutes, the mushrooms were tender yet still moist, and they were no longer leaching liquid all over the buns. We had the best of both worlds.

These mushrooms had picked up good smoky flavor, but our burgers still needed a boost. We settled on a two-pronged attack: infusing the mushrooms themselves with flavor, and picking the right toppings to take these burgers from ordinary to extraordinary. Starting with the mushrooms, we tried brushing them with a basic vinaigrette before grilling, but the vinaigrette's flavors mellowed too much during cooking, and the mushrooms didn't brown properly. Tossing the mushrooms with the vinaigrette after they were cooked was more promising, but the mushrooms absorbed the dressing like a sponge. In the end, we found that brushing the vinaigrette on halfway through cooking gave us the best flavor boost and control. Tasters preferred a simple blend of oil, garlic, and thyme, noting that the woodsy flavor of the thyme heightened the earthiness of the mushrooms.

With the mushrooms complete, we began experimenting with toppings. Tasters eliminated raw onions off the bat, noting that they overpowered the mushrooms. However, grilled onions were another story. They added a charred sweetness that complemented the earthy mushroom flavor. A favorite tip from the test kitchen helped make the grilled onion topping even easier to execute. Instead of chasing sliced onion rings around a grill, we simply skewered an entire slice of onion made up of several rings, making them easier to flip and cook more evenly. Tasters also wanted a fresh, crunchy element on the burger. Typical burger lettuces like iceberg couldn't stand up to the meatiness of the mushrooms, but arugula dressed with a bit of oil and balsamic vinegar brought out the sweetness in both the mushrooms and onions. The last crucial element was the cheese. In a side-by-side tasting of our portobello burger paired with various cheeses—including American, cheddar, blue cheese, fontina, goat cheese, and Parmesan—tasters liked the pungent, tangy taste of goat cheese most. A slice of tomato added a sweetness that paired well with the cheese and assertive arugula. Whole wheat buns (which we quickly toasted on the grill) completed our healthy, hearty grilled burgers. We felt confident they would be welcome at any barbecue.

Grilled Portobello Burgers
SERVES 4

We prefer to use portobello caps that measure 4 to 5 inches in diameter. If your mushrooms are larger or smaller, you may need to adjust the cooking time accordingly.

2 tablespoons plus 2 teaspoons olive oil
2 garlic cloves, minced
2 teaspoons minced fresh thyme
   Salt and pepper
4 medium portobello mushroom caps (about 1½ pounds)
1 large red onion, sliced into ½-inch-thick rounds (do not separate the rings)
   Olive oil spray
2 ounces goat cheese, crumbled (about ½ cup)
4 whole wheat hamburger buns
1 ounce baby arugula (about 1 cup)
¼ teaspoon balsamic vinegar
1 tomato, cored and sliced thin

1. Combine 7 teaspoons of the oil, garlic, thyme, ¼ teaspoon salt, and ¼ teaspoon pepper in a bowl. Following the photo on page 192, lightly score the mushroom caps with the tip of a sharp knife, then thread the onion rounds onto the skewers. Lightly coat the onions with olive oil spray, and season with salt and pepper.

2A. FOR A CHARCOAL GRILL: Open the bottom grill vents completely. Light a large chimney starter three-quarters full with charcoal briquettes (75 briquettes; 4½ quarts). When the coals are hot, pour them in an even layer over the grill. Set the cooking grate in place, cover, and heat the grill until hot, about 5 minutes.

2B. FOR A GAS GRILL: Turn all the burners to high, cover, and heat the grill until hot, about 15 minutes. Turn all the burners to medium-high. (Adjust the burners as needed to maintain a medium-hot fire; see page 182.)

3. Clean and oil the cooking grate. Place the mushrooms, gill side down, and the skewered onion on the grill. Cook the mushrooms (covered if using gas) until lightly charred and beginning to soften on the gill side, 4 to 6 minutes. Turn the mushrooms over, brush with the garlic-oil mixture, and cook until tender and browned on the second side, 4 to 6 minutes. Sprinkle the goat cheese over the mushrooms and cook until the cheese melts, about 2 minutes.

4. Meanwhile, cook the onion, turning the skewers as needed, until spottily charred on both sides, 8 to 12 minutes.

5. Transfer the mushrooms and onion skewers to a platter and tent loosely with foil. Split the hamburger buns and grill until warm and lightly charred, about 30 seconds. Transfer to the platter.

6. Toss the arugula with the vinegar and remaining 1 teaspoon oil in a bowl and season with salt and pepper to taste. Remove the onion from the skewers and separate the rings. Assemble the mushroom caps, arugula, tomato, and onion on the buns and serve.

PER SERVING: **Cal** 320; **Fat** 14g; **Sat fat** 3.5g; **Chol** 5mg; **Carb** 37g; **Protein** 12g; **Fiber** 7g; **Sodium** 490mg

---

NOTES FROM THE TEST KITCHEN

SCORING PORTOBELLO MUSHROOMS

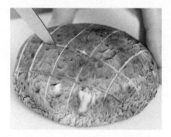

To help the mushrooms release their excess moisture on the grill, use the tip of a sharp knife to lightly score the cap of each mushroom on the diagonal in a crosshatch pattern.

SKEWERING ONIONS FOR GRILLING

After slicing the onion crosswise into ½-inch-thick rounds, slide a skewer all the way through each onion slice. You should be able to fit two slices on each skewer.

BARBECUED TOFU

WHEN YOU'RE TRYING TO EAT HEALTHY, TOFU IS AN excellent choice for a vegetarian main course. It's a good source of protein (as well as calcium and iron) and is relatively low in fat and calories. It is also convenient (since it is quick-cooking), will keep in the refrigerator for several days, and is an open canvas for pairing with a wide range of flavors. We already had a recipe for grilled tofu paired with a sweet, Asian-inspired glaze made with mirin, soy sauce, and ginger, so we wondered if we could develop a grilled tofu with a more all-American spin. If carnivores have their barbecued chicken, why not come up with a recipe for barbecued tofu? We had developed hundreds of recipes for a slew of barbecued meats in the test kitchen, so how hard could it be? There was only one way to find out. We set out to come up with a recipe for smoky tofu with a creamy interior and coated in a slathering of tangy barbecue sauce.

First, we settled on the best way to prepare tofu for the grill. We didn't see why the method we had developed for our Asian-glazed tofu recipe wouldn't work here as well. We had learned that strips of tofu and skewered cubes both were too hard to deal with on the grill. It was best to cut the tofu crosswise into six 1-inch-thick slabs. The shape maximized surface contact with the grill, and there weren't as many pieces of tofu to manage and flip. A quick brushing of olive oil before cooking helped prevent the tofu from sticking to the grates, and using two spatulas provided the best leverage for flipping the planks.

Next, we tested types of tofu. We grilled soft, medium-firm, firm, and extra-firm and had tasters try them side by side. The extra-firm tofu was the easiest to grill, but it had a dry, crumbly texture that most tasters found unappealing. The others were all well liked for their smooth, custardy texture. However, since the soft and medium-firm tofus had a higher tendency to stick to the grill, we settled on the firm variety.

We knew adding barbecue flavor to the mild-tasting tofu would be the key to making this a successful recipe. Spice rubs seemed promising, since they are traditional in barbecue recipes like brisket and pulled pork and could add a lot of flavor without much fat or calories. One test proved that the idea wasn't going to live up to its promise. The tofu cooked so quickly on the grill that the spices never had a chance to bloom and they tasted harsh and raw. A barbecue sauce was the next obvious choice. Back in the kitchen, we whipped up our favorite barbecue sauce recipe (see page 169) and brushed the sauce over the tofu as it finished cooking through (a technique we'd adapted from our Barbecued Chicken Breasts, page 168, to ensure that the sauce wouldn't burn).

We all agreed we were on the right track. But still, tasters thought something was missing. In the past we've boosted the flavor of not only large cuts of meat but also fish and even burgers on the grill by adding some smoke with the help of wood chips. We weren't sure if it would translate to tofu, but we felt it was worth a shot. We added a packet of soaked wood chips to the fire, grilled our tofu, and waited for the verdict from tasters. They all gave it the thumbs-up; the smoke had lightly permeated the tofu, leaving a subtle smoky flavor that added the depth it had been missing.

To prepare our tofu for the grill, we brushed it with oil and seasoned it with salt and pepper. We knew from past experience with grilling tofu and from our Barbecued Chicken Breasts that a two-level fire with two different heat zones was our best bet here as well. We grilled the tofu on the cooler part of the grill until browned on both sides, then moved it to the hotter part of the grill to finish cooking and brushed it with a layer of the sauce. This time the sauce caramelized beautifully and gave us the flavorful crust we were after. Another thick slather of sauce off the grill gave the tofu another flavor boost. The final touch was the addition of sliced scallions to add a little color and balance the sweetness of the sauce.

Sweet and Smoky Barbecued Tofu

SERVES 6

Be sure to handle the tofu gently or else it may break apart. You can use our Easy Pantry Barbecue Sauce (page 169) in this recipe or your favorite store-bought sauce.

- 2 (14-ounce) blocks firm tofu, cut lengthwise into 1-inch-thick slabs
- 2 cups wood chips, soaked, drained, and sealed in a foil packet (see photo)
- 2 tablespoons canola oil
- ⅛ teaspoon salt
- ⅛ teaspoon pepper
- ¾ cup barbecue sauce
- 2 scallions, sliced thin

1. Spread the tofu on several layers of paper towels and let sit for 20 minutes to drain slightly.

2A. FOR A CHARCOAL GRILL: Open the bottom grill vents halfway. Light a large chimney starter filled with charcoal briquettes (100 briquettes; 6 quarts). When the coals are hot, spread two-thirds of them evenly over the grill, then pour the remaining coals over half of the grill. Place the wood chip packet on top of the smaller coal pile. Set the cooking grate in place, cover, and open the lid vents halfway. Heat the grill until hot and the wood chips begin to smoke heavily, about 5 minutes.

2B. FOR A GAS GRILL: Place the wood chip packet directly on the primary burner. Turn all the burners to high, cover, and heat the grill until hot and the wood chips begin to smoke heavily, about 15 minutes. Turn all the burners to medium-low. (Adjust the burners as needed to maintain a medium-low fire; see page 182.)

3. Clean and oil the cooking grate. Pat the tofu dry with paper towels, brush with the oil, and season with the salt and pepper. Gently place the tofu on the grill (on the cooler part of the grill if using charcoal), cover, and cook until lightly charred, 8 to 10 minutes, gently flipping the tofu halfway through with two spatulas.

4. Slide the tofu to the hotter part of the grill if using charcoal, or turn all the burners to high (adjust the burners as needed to maintain a hot fire; see page 182) if using gas. Brush the tofu with some of the sauce and cook until well browned on both sides, 2 to 4 minutes, flipping and brushing the tofu with more sauce halfway through cooking.

5. Transfer the tofu to a platter and brush with the remaining sauce. Sprinkle with the scallions and serve.

PER SERVING: Cal 210; Fat 11g; Sat fat 1g; Chol 0mg; Carb 16g; Protein 12g; Fiber 2g; Sodium 370mg

---

NOTES FROM THE TEST KITCHEN

MAKING SMOKE WITH WOOD CHIPS
Wood chips add great smoky flavor to grilled foods; we prefer to use chips rather than chunks since they're easier to handle and don't take as long to soak before they are ready for the fire.

After soaking the wood chips in water for 15 minutes, drain and spread them in the center of a large piece of heavy-duty foil. Fold to seal the edges, then cut three or four slits in the foil packet to allow smoke to escape.

WILD RICE PILAF WITH PECANS AND CRANBERRIES

GREAT GRAINS & BEANS

M   = TEST KITCHEN MAKEOVER

EASY BAKED RISOTTO

RISOTTO MAY BE ONE OF THE HALLMARKS OF northern Italian cooking, but nobody ever said it was easy. Traditional risotto requires constant vigilance (and lots of stirring) for success, but that's not something we all have time for. Plus, it's hardly a light dish, as it's often finished with hefty amounts of butter and plenty of cheese. We wanted to rescue risotto from the list of oft-dismissed recipes by creating a more hands-off oven-baked version. We also wanted to lighten it up so it would earn a spot in the repertoire of those aiming to eat more healthfully.

The test kitchen has found methods for speeding up the stovetop risotto-making process, but the concept of moving risotto to the oven to bake has even greater appeal in terms of minimizing the labor. A lot of recipes for baked risotto exist, but oven temperatures and the ratios of grains to liquid vary dramatically, leading to drastically different results, with rice that ranges from inedibly crunchy to unappealingly gummy. The dump-and-bake method used in a few recipes—where rice, broth, wine, chopped onions, and flavorings get dumped into a 13 by 9-inch baking dish, covered with foil, and baked—was a nonstarter, as these recipes resulted in raw, crunchy onion, harsh wine flavor, and unevenly cooked rice.

So we went back to working with the test kitchen's traditional risotto recipe to see how (and if) it could be coaxed into an oven-baked version. We learned a few things quickly. To start, the onions and rice still needed their stovetop sauté in a Dutch oven or large saucepan to allow the onions to soften and the rice to start releasing its starch. We also found that we could trade in the usual butter (as much as 4 tablespoons in some recipes) for just 1 teaspoon of oil to cook the onions if we simply let them sweat in a covered pot until soft. We decided to also reduce the wine on the stovetop to rid it of its harsh alcohol flavor.

As in traditional stovetop recipes, we found that heating the broth before adding it to the other ingredients was necessary to jump-start the cooking process, so we brought it to a simmer in a separate pot—with a couple of bay leaves for flavor. We then combined everything in the baking dish, covered it with foil, and popped it into the oven. The risotto needed just 15 minutes to cook

through in the oven; the temperature was higher in a covered casserole dish than in an uncovered pot on the stove, shaving 5 to 10 minutes off the traditional recipe's cooking time.

However, "cook through" was an understatement—the risotto was as mushy as gruel. On the stove, we could have adjusted the amount of liquid as the rice simmered. But the amount of liquid that went into the oven version was a done deal. We were using 2 cups of rice to 8 cups of liquid, a ratio in line with our test kitchen stovetop recipe. The version baked in the oven, however, unlike the one cooked in an uncovered pot on the stove, allowed for no evaporation. We tried baking without the foil, but this left the top of the rice crunchy. So we reduced the amount of liquid, test by test, until we reached the right ratio—5 cups of broth combined with ½ cup of water (to lighten the chicken-y taste). No more mush.

Unfortunately, the rice grains were now distinct, not creamy, more similar to the texture of a pilaf. To fix that, we tried adding an obvious "creamy" component, half-and-half. However, it made the dish too heavy. Searching for other solutions, we tried grated russet potato (for its starch) and pulverized dried rice; these turned the risotto into gelatinous goo. We tried stirring in an egg after pulling the risotto from the oven. This version was surprisingly creamy and rich—for a few precious minutes until the egg made the risotto bind up like quick-drying cement.

Stumped, we took a second look at the shallow baking dish we had been using and decided to try something different. In the past the test kitchen has pressed a layer of foil directly onto the surface of foods such as rice and beans to trap the moisture right in the food (instead of letting it hover above). It seemed worth a shot here. For our next test we left the rice mixture in the deep Dutch oven, pressing a layer of foil directly onto the surface, then covered the pot with the lid. It worked! This risotto was finally creamy and perfectly cooked through. Now that we had our method in place, it was time to finish the dish.

Traditional risottos have butter and cheese stirred into the rice at the end of cooking for added richness, but obviously the usual 3 tablespoons of butter would add too much fat. Tasters agreed that our risotto needed *some* butter, as the creamy fat diminishes the subtle tacky character of the starchy sauce. We found that just 1 tablespoon did the trick. Next we tried to reduce the amount of Parmesan cheese called for in risotto recipes, but our tasters spoke loud and clear—nothing but a full 2 ounces (about 1 cup of grated cheese) would do. But even at this amount, our risotto's fat and calories didn't jump to an unreasonable range.

Maybe our oven-baked lighter version wasn't quite as plush as the classic stovetop version, but it was incredibly close—and stir-free!

Easy Baked Risotto

SERVES 8

Make sure you use a heavy pot with a tight-fitting lid for this recipe.

    5 cups low-sodium chicken broth
    ½ cup water
    2 bay leaves
    1 onion, minced (about 1 cup)
    1 teaspoon olive oil
       Salt
    3 garlic cloves, minced
    2 cups Arborio rice
    ½ cup dry white wine
    2 ounces Parmesan cheese, grated (about 1 cup)
    1 tablespoon unsalted butter
    1 tablespoon minced fresh parsley
       Pepper

1. Adjust an oven rack to the middle position and heat the oven to 400 degrees. Bring the broth, water, and bay leaves to a simmer in a medium saucepan, reduce the heat to low, and cover to keep warm.

2. Meanwhile, combine the onion, oil, and ⅛ teaspoon salt in a Dutch oven. Cover and cook over medium-low heat, stirring occasionally, until softened, 8 to 10 minutes. Uncover, stir in the garlic, and cook until fragrant, about 30 seconds.

3. Increase the heat to medium. Stir in the rice and cook, stirring often, until the ends of the rice grains are transparent, about 3 minutes. Stir in the wine and cook until it has been completely absorbed, about 1 minute.

4. Pour the warm broth mixture over the rice. Following the photos, place a large piece of foil flush

to the surface of the liquid. Cover the pot with the lid, transfer to the oven, and bake until the rice is tender and the liquid is almost completely absorbed, about 15 minutes.

5. Remove the pot from the oven, uncover, and remove and discard the bay leaves. Stir in the Parmesan, butter, and parsley. Season with salt and pepper to taste and serve.

PER ¾-CUP SERVING: Cal 160; Fat 4.5g; Sat fat 2g; Chol 10mg; Carb 21g; Protein 5g; Fiber 1g; Sodium 520mg

MEXICAN RICE

MEXICAN RICE

RED-HUED MEXICAN RICE, BRIGHTLY FLAVORED WITH a mixture of onions, garlic, tomatoes, spicy chiles, and fresh herbs, sounds like a wonderfully flavorful light side. But from our point of view, there was one catch. Mexican rice has a trademark complex, nutty flavor and richness that serve as a backdrop to all those fresh flavors. And it is achieved by cooking the rice grains first in oil—in some recipes the grains are essentially deep-fried. We wondered if we could achieve a full-flavored Mexican rice but at the same time make it an acceptable dish for our light and healthy table.

We started by putting a selection of recipes from respected Mexican cookbook authors to the test. Variable ingredient quantities and cooking techniques produced disparate results. Some of the recipes turned out soupy and greasy (no surprise given the copious amounts of oil). Others seemed misguided in terms of ingredient amounts; some had just a hint of garlic, others tasted of tomato and nothing else, and one was overtaken by pungent cilantro. To our thinking, the perfect version of this dish should exhibit clean, balanced flavors and tender, perfectly cooked rice. It should be rich but not oily, and moist but not watery.

The liquid traditionally used in this dish is a mixture of chicken broth and pureed fresh tomatoes; experiments with a variety of ratios helped us settle on 2 cups of broth and 12 ounces of tomatoes. With too much tomato puree, the rice tasted like warm gazpacho; with too little, its flavor waned. Each and every recipe we consulted called for fresh tomatoes, and when we pitted rice made with canned tomatoes against rice made with fresh, the reason for using the latter crystallized. Batches made with fresh tomatoes tasted, well, fresh. Those made with canned tomatoes tasted overcooked and too tomatoey. To capture the one benefit of canned tomatoes—an intense, tomato-red color—we stirred in an untraditional ingredient: tomato paste. It gave the rice an appealing red hue while adding a hint of deeper flavor at the same time.

The usual method for making Mexican rice is to sauté rinsed long-grain white rice in oil before adding the cooking liquid (rinsing helps produce more distinct, separate grains). While some recipes call for only a quick sauté, our initial testing proved that cooking the rice until it was golden brown was crucial for creating a mild,

toasted flavor and satisfying texture. As for the amount of oil used, we had our work cut out for us to lighten this dish but still maintain the trademark flavor. Deep-frying the rice in as much as 1¼ cups of oil, as some recipes required, was out of the question, so we experimented with increments ranging from 3 tablespoons up to ¾ cup. Insubstantial amounts of oil made rice that was dry and lacking richness; 3 tablespoons was too little. In the end, ¼ cup seemed just right—this rice was flavorful but not greasy.

We wondered whether sautéing the other components of the recipe, such as the aromatics and the tomatoes, would deepen the flavor. After testing all the options, we eventually settled on sautéing a generous amount of garlic and jalapeños, then mixing in raw pureed tomatoes and onion. This technique produced the deep yet fresh flavor we were after; it also conveniently allowed us to process the onion in the food processor along with the tomatoes rather than having to chop it by hand.

As for the cooking method, we had trouble achieving properly cooked rice on the stovetop. The grains inevitably scorched, then turned soupy when we attempted a rescue with extra broth. Clearly there was too much heat directed at the bottom of the pot. Inspired by our foolproof Easy Baked Risotto (page 197), we wondered if moving this recipe to the oven to bake in the even heat would solve the problem. A few tests proved our hunch right.

But still, as we baked batch after batch of rice, we were frustrated by inconsistency; most batches contained a smattering of crunchy grains mixed in with the tender ones. Prolonged cooking didn't solve the problem. Stirring the rice partway through cooking to reincorporate the moist tomato mixture, which had been settling on top of the pilaf, ended up being the solution. With this practice in place, every last grain—in every batch—cooked evenly.

While many traditional recipes consider fresh cilantro and minced jalapeño optional, our tasters deemed them mandatory. The raw herbs and a few pungent uncooked jalapeños stirred in at the end complemented the richer tones of the cooked tomatoes, garlic, jalapeños, and onions. When a little something still seemed missing from the rice, we added a squeeze of fresh lime juice—the acidity illuminated the flavor even further. This was a bright-tasting Mexican Rice that didn't have any fat to hide.

LONG-GRAIN WHITE RICE

Higher-quality white rice offers a pleasing "al dente" texture and a natural, slightly buttery flavor. While most of this subtle variation comes from the varietal of rice, processing also affects flavor. All rice starts out brown; to become white, it is milled, a process that removes the husk, bran, and germ, which contain flavor compounds as well as nutrients. The longer the rice is milled, the whiter it becomes. Many brands of rice (except organic rice) are then enriched to replace lost nutrients. Unlike medium- or short-grain white rice, cooked long-grain white rice remains fluffy and separate because it contains less of a starch called amylopectin that makes rice stick together. We tasted six national brands of long-grain white rice, plain (steamed in our favorite rice cooker) and in pilaf. **Lundberg Organic Long-Grain White Rice** stood out for its nutty, buttery flavor and distinct, smooth grains.

OUR FAVORITE TOMATO PASTE

Tomato paste provides deep, rich tomato flavor to many of our recipes. And because it's naturally full of glutamates, which stimulate tastebuds just like salt and sugar, it brings out subtle depths and savory notes, even in recipes where tomato flavor isn't at the forefront. So can a better-tasting brand have a bigger impact than others? We gathered 10 top-selling brands and sampled each uncooked, cooked plain, and in marinara sauce. **Goya Tomato Paste** earned top marks in both the uncooked and cooked tasting, and it came in second in our marinara test. Tasters praised Goya for its sweet-tart balance and lack of off-flavors; the latter dragged down other brands. But overall, scores were relatively close—the losers were not far behind top-ranked Goya. The bottom line? Any of these tomato pastes will supply reasonably good concentrated tomato flavor, but Goya has the edge.

STORING TOMATOES

We've heard storing a tomato with its stem end facing down can prolong shelf life. To test this, we placed one batch of tomatoes stem end up and another stem end down and stored them at room temperature. A week later, nearly all the stem end down tomatoes were in perfect condition, but the stem end up tomatoes had shriveled and started to mold. Why? We surmised that the scar left where the stem once grew provides both an escape for moisture and an entry point for mold and bacteria. Placing a tomato stem end down blocks air from entering and moisture from exiting the scar. To confirm this, we ran another test, this time comparing tomatoes stored stem end down with a batch stored stem end up, but with a piece of tape sealing off their scars. The taped, stem end up tomatoes survived just as well as the stem end down batch.

Mexican Rice

SERVES 10

Use an ovensafe pot about 12 inches in diameter so that the rice cooks evenly and in the time indicated. The pot's depth is less important than its diameter; we've successfully used both a straight-sided sauté pan and a Dutch oven. Whichever type of pot you use, it should have a tight-fitting, ovensafe lid. To make this dish spicier, add the chile seeds.

- 12 ounces tomatoes (about 2 tomatoes), cored and quartered
- 1 onion, root end trimmed, peeled and quartered
- ¼ cup canola oil
- 2 cups long-grain white rice, rinsed (see page 79)
- 4 garlic cloves, minced
- 3 jalapeño chiles, stemmed, seeded, and minced
- 2 cups low-sodium chicken broth
- 1 tablespoon tomato paste
  Salt
- ½ cup minced fresh cilantro
- 1 tablespoon fresh lime juice

1. Adjust an oven rack to the middle position and heat the oven to 350 degrees. Process the tomatoes and onion in a food processor until completely smooth, about 15 seconds, scraping down the bowl if necessary. Transfer the mixture to a liquid measuring cup; you should have 2 cups (if necessary, spoon off and discard any excess).

2. Heat the oil in a large Dutch oven over medium-high heat for 1 to 2 minutes. Drop 3 or 4 grains of the rinsed rice into the oil; if the grains sizzle, the oil is ready. Add the remaining rice and cook, stirring frequently, until light golden and translucent, 6 to 8 minutes. Reduce the heat to medium, stir in the garlic and two-thirds of the jalapeños, and cook until fragrant, about 30 seconds.

3. Stir in the pureed tomato mixture, broth, tomato paste, and 1 teaspoon salt and bring to a simmer over medium-high heat. Cover, transfer to the oven, and bake until the liquid is absorbed and the rice is tender, 25 to 30 minutes, stirring halfway through.

4. Remove the pot from the oven, uncover, and stir in the remaining jalapeños, cilantro, and lime juice. Season with salt to taste and serve.

PER ¾-CUP SERVING: Cal 190; Fat 6g; Sat fat 0g; Chol 0mg; Carb 32g; Protein 3g; Fiber 1g; Sodium 350mg

PERFECT WILD RICE

WILD RICE HAS A GREAT NUTTY FLAVOR AND CHEWY texture that makes it a nice change from white or brown rice, and it's a great option for a dressed-up side dish when serving company. But like many other grains, its success or failure relies heavily on how it is prepared. We wanted to come up with a recipe that produced distinct, flavorful grains of wild rice with just the right chew without becoming gluey. We also wanted to find what additions to our wild rice side dish would highlight and bring out the best in the rice's flavor and texture.

We started with the cooking method. We tested steaming, boiling, and simmering. Steaming produced grains that were unevenly cooked, and boiling too often caused some grains to become blown out, not to mention that much of the wild rice's flavor was lost to the cooking water. Slowly simmering the rice proved the best approach, but the timing varied from batch to batch. The key proved to be keeping a watchful eye so we could stop the cooking process at just the right moment; the texture could go from tough to gluey in a moment. We found that after the rice had simmered for 35 minutes, we needed to check it for doneness every couple of minutes. Once it was ready, we drained the rice to remove excess liquid and immediately stop the cooking.

Although it was now perfectly cooked, tasters found the rustic, toothy texture and strong flavor of the wild rice alone to be overwhelming. Perhaps it could be better appreciated if complemented by a mellower grain, such as brown or white rice. Tasters agreed that brown rice offered too little contrast, so we settled on white. Testing different proportions, we found that 1 cup of wild rice to 1½ cups of white rice gave our side dish balanced flavor and texture that still allowed the wild rice's best qualities to shine through.

But with a different kind of rice in the mix, our cooking method needed to be reevaluated. Cooking both rices in the same pot (we added the white rice midway through the wild rice's simmer since it requires less time) led to uneven cooking; we would have to cook them separately. To make the most of this second pan for the white rice, we decided to add a few ingredients and cook it in the style of a pilaf—a simple technique we already had down pat that guarantees flavorful, fluffy rice.

We sautéed our aromatics (onion and carrots—a combination that would add sweet, earthy undertones) in olive oil until softened. Then we toasted our rice in the skillet to deepen the grains' flavor before adding the liquid and simmering until the rice was tender. Because we were using the oil to not only sauté aromatics but also toast the rice, we knew from experience that using 1 tablespoon of oil was a necessity.

Once we combined our two rices, tasters agreed we were getting closer but the flavor needed some work. The wild rice was coming across as muddy. Up to this point we had been cooking it in water, so next we tested adding wine. This only worsened matters. Cooking the wild rice in beef broth was overwhelming, but chicken broth was a revelation. It tempered the rice's muddy flavor to a pleasant earthiness and affirmed its subdued nuttiness. Bay leaves and thyme added to the broth lent a nice finesse and complexity.

For contrasting texture and flavor, we tested various additions to the rice combination and eventually settled on sweet-tart dried cranberries, toasted pecans, and parsley. And finally, since we had some wiggle room in terms of fat, we tried drizzling in a tablespoon of olive oil at the end, just before serving. This touch pulled all the components together and lent a fresh richness that finished our wild rice pilaf perfectly.

NOTES FROM THE TEST KITCHEN

STEAMING RICE

After the rice is cooked, cover the pan with a clean kitchen towel, replace the lid, and allow the pan to sit for 10 minutes.

WILD RICE

Wild rice, like traditional cultivated rice, is a member of the grass family. Truly "wild" wild rice is native to the northern Great Lakes, where it is still harvested. But most so-called wild rice is now cultivated on farms in California. Cultivated wild rice grown in man-made paddies costs between $3 and $5 per pound, while hand-harvested rice from lakes and streams in Minnesota and Canada costs about $9 per pound. We prefer the cultivated variety for its more resilient texture, as well as its lower price tag.

Wild Rice Pilaf with Pecans and Cranberries

SERVES 12

Vegetable broth can be substituted for the chicken broth if desired. Wild rice goes from tough to pasty in a flash, so begin testing the rice at the 35-minute mark and drain it as soon as it is tender. Don't worry if the wild rice doesn't absorb all of the cooking liquid; just drain as directed in step 1. A nonstick saucepan works best for cooking the white rice in step 2, although a traditional saucepan will also work.

    2   cups low-sodium chicken broth
    8   sprigs fresh thyme
    2   bay leaves
    1   cup wild rice, rinsed (see page 79)
    2   tablespoons extra-virgin olive oil
    2   carrots, peeled and chopped fine
    1   onion, minced (about 1 cup)
        Salt
 1½   cups long-grain white rice, rinsed
        (see page 79)
 2¼   cups water
    ¾   cup dried cranberries
    ¾   cup pecans, toasted and chopped coarse
    2   tablespoons minced fresh parsley
        Pepper

1. Bring the broth, 4 of the thyme sprigs, and bay leaves to a boil in a medium saucepan. Add the wild rice and bring to a simmer. Reduce the heat to low, cover, and cook until the wild rice is tender and has absorbed most of the liquid, 35 to 40 minutes. Drain the rice, discarding the bay leaves and thyme sprigs. Return the wild rice to the pot and cover to keep warm.

2. While the wild rice cooks, heat 1 tablespoon of the oil in a large saucepan over medium heat until shimmering. Add the carrots, onion, and ½ teaspoon salt and cook, stirring occasionally, until the vegetables are softened, 5 to 7 minutes.

3. Stir in the white rice and cook, stirring often, until the edges of the grains begin to turn translucent, about 3 minutes. Stir in the remaining 4 thyme sprigs, water, and cranberries and bring to a simmer. Reduce the heat to low, cover, and cook until the white rice is tender and the water is absorbed, 16 to 18 minutes.

4. Remove the pot from the heat and, following the photo on page 201, lay a clean folded kitchen towel underneath the lid. Let sit for 10 minutes, then fluff the white rice with a fork. Remove and discard the thyme sprigs.

5. Combine the cooked wild rice and white rice, pecans, and parsley in a large bowl. Drizzle with the remaining 1 tablespoon oil and toss to combine. Season with salt and pepper to taste and serve. (The white rice and wild rice can be cooked through step 4, then combined and refrigerated in an airtight container for up to 1 day. Reheat the rice in a covered dish in the microwave on medium power until hot, then fluff thoroughly with a fork before continuing with step 5.)

PER ¾-CUP SERVING: Cal 250; Fat 8g; Sat fat 1g; Chol 0mg; Carb 41g; Protein 5g; Fiber 3g; Sodium 200mg

VARIATION

Wild Rice Pilaf with Scallions, Cilantro, and Almonds

Follow the recipe for Wild Rice Pilaf with Pecans and Cranberries, omitting the dried cranberries. Substitute ¾ cup toasted sliced almonds for the pecans and 2 tablespoons minced fresh cilantro for the parsley. Add 2 thinly sliced scallions and 1 teaspoon fresh lime juice with the almonds.

PER ¾-CUP SERVING: Cal 210; Fat 6g; Sat fat 0.5g; Chol 0mg; Carb 36g; Protein 6g; Fiber 2g; Sodium 200mg

TABBOULEH

TABBOULEH, A CLASSIC MIDDLE EASTERN SALAD, has become increasingly popular in the States in recent years. Featuring parsley, bulgur (which is a product of the wheat berry), fresh mint, and fresh tomato tossed in a bright lemon vinaigrette, this salad has refreshing flavors and a visual appeal that make it a cool, light side dish favorite, particularly in the summer. And while the principal ingredients typically remain the same, a variety of preparation techniques exist, each claiming to produce the finest version. We set out to determine the best method and develop a recipe featuring fluffy grains of bulgur with an appealing balance of parsley and tomatoes and a bright dressing that lent flavor but didn't weigh our salad down.

We began with the central ingredient, the bulgur itself. A product of the wheat berry, bulgur has been steamed, dried, and ground either fine, coarse, or medium. The result is an easily prepared, highly nutritious grain that is tender with a slight, appealing chew. Since coarse-grain is the only one of the three sizes that requires cooking—the other two can simply be soaked—we cut it from the running to keep our recipe simple. Between the medium- and fine-grain options, tasters slightly preferred the fine-grain bulgur as it is a bit more delicate.

When it came to the bulgur's preparation, we tested the five ways most commonly seen in tabbouleh recipes. For our first batch, we rinsed the grain, combined it with the chopped tomato, and set it aside to absorb the tomato juice. With this method, tasters agreed the bulgur remained unacceptably crunchy. Next we marinated the bulgur in the tabbouleh's lemon juice and olive oil dressing. This approach produced bulgur that was tasty but slightly greasy. The third method, soaking the grains in water, then squeezing out excess moisture, produced nutty-flavored—but heavy—wheat. We also tried soaking the bulgur in water for about five minutes, then draining the liquid and replacing it with the lemon–olive oil dressing. This bulgur's texture was good and the flavor was better than that of the other versions, but we had one more method to test, which turned out to be our winner. Using this method, we first rinsed the bulgur, then mixed it with some of the fresh lemon juice from the dressing and set the mixture aside to allow the juice to be absorbed. This bulgur acquired a fresh and intense flavor and just the right fluffy texture and distinct grains.

When it came to the dressing, we had already used some lemon juice for soaking the bulgur, so we needed just a touch more to bring together our dressing and lend the right finishing brightness; 4 teaspoons seemed about right. From there we would determine the balancing amount of oil. Wanting to save a few calories, we tested varying amounts of extra-virgin olive oil to see how much we really needed. After starting at ½ cup, we eventually tested all the way down to 3 tablespoons. We finally settled on ¼ cup—any less oil and our tabbouleh was simply too lean and lacking in richness and flavor. For a little zing, we opted to add some cayenne to our dressing, though we agreed it should remain optional.

Parsley is another starring component in tabbouleh. Although a number of recipes opt for a 9-to-1 ratio of parsley to bulgur, we felt that the bulgur was lost when it made up such a small proportion of the salad. We found that a finished dish with a ratio closer to 5 parts parsley to 3 or 4 parts wheat had the proper balance. Half a cup of dried bulgur bulked up to roughly 1½ cups once it was soaked, so 2 cups of parsley gave us just the proportion we were looking for.

NOTES FROM THE TEST KITCHEN

BUYING BULGUR
Adding recipes using bulgur to your repertoire is a great way to add fiber, protein, iron, and magnesium to your diet. But cooking with bulgur requires an understanding of what it is and how to buy it. A product of the wheat berry, bulgur has been steamed, dried, ground, and then sorted by size (fine-grain, medium-grain, and coarse-grain). The result of this process is a fast-cooking, highly nutritious grain that can be used in a variety of applications. In the test kitchen, we like fine-grain bulgur for our Tabbouleh because it requires little more than a soak to become tender and flavorful, but medium-grain bulgur will work as well (it just requires a longer soak). Cracked wheat, on the other hand, often sold alongside bulgur in the market, is not precooked and cannot be substituted for bulgur. Be sure to rinse bulgur, regardless of grain size, to remove excess starches that can turn the grain gluey.

FINE-GRAIN   MEDIUM-GRAIN

FLAT-LEAF VERSUS CURLY PARSLEY
We use a fair amount of parsley in our Tabbouleh, and you've probably noticed that your neighborhood grocer has two different varieties of this recognizable herb (though there are actually more than 30 varieties out there)—curly-leaf and flat-leaf (also called Italian). Curly-leaf parsley is more popular, but in the test kitchen flat-leaf is by far the favorite. We find flat-leaf parsley to have a sweet, bright flavor that's much preferable to the bitter, grassy tones of curly-leaf. Flat-leaf parsley is also much more fragrant than its curly cousin. While curly parsley might look nice alongside your steak, don't count on it to improve flavor if you use it in cooking. Reach for the flat variety in your supermarket, and your dinner guests will thank you. In a pinch, it's fine to substitute.

TABBOULEH

Now we just needed to bring it all together. We combined the lemon-soaked bulgur with the parsley, some finely chopped scallions, fresh mint, and tomatoes. Then we tossed it with the remaining dressing ingredients. We found that when we let the mixture sit for an hour or so, the flavors had a chance to blend before serving. But we quickly learned we couldn't let it sit for too long. After five or six hours the scallions' flavor permeated the dish and overpowered the other ingredients. But with this tabbouleh's bright, fresh flavor, it probably won't last that long anyway.

Tabbouleh

SERVES 6

Do not use coarse-grain bulgur or cracked wheat in this recipe; for more information on buying bulgur, see page 203. The time it takes for the bulgur to become tender and fluffy in step 1 will depend on the age and type of the bulgur.

- ½ cup fine- or medium-grain bulgur wheat
- ⅓ cup fresh lemon juice (about 2 lemons)
- 2 cups minced fresh parsley (about 2 bunches)
- 2 tomatoes, cored, seeded, and chopped medium
- 4 scallions, minced
- 2 tablespoons minced fresh mint
- ¼ cup extra-virgin olive oil
  Salt
- ⅛ teaspoon cayenne pepper (optional)
  Black pepper

1. Rinse the bulgur thoroughly in a fine-mesh strainer under running water, then set aside to drain, about 5 minutes. Toss the bulgur with ¼ cup of the lemon juice in a large bowl and let sit until the grains are tender and fluffy, 20 to 40 minutes.

2. Stir in the parsley, tomatoes, scallions, and mint. In a separate bowl, whisk the remaining 4 teaspoons lemon juice, oil, ¼ teaspoon salt, and cayenne (if using) together, then pour over the bulgur mixture and toss to coat. Cover and refrigerate to let the flavors blend, 1 to 2 hours. Season with salt and black pepper to taste and serve. (The tabbouleh can be refrigerated in an airtight container for up to 2 days; season with additional salt, pepper, and lemon juice to taste before serving.)

PER ¾-CUP SERVING: Cal 150; Fat 10g; Sat fat 1.5g; Chol 0mg; Carb 14g; Protein 3g; Fiber 4g; Sodium 115mg

QUINOA SALAD

WHEN STUDDED WITH VEGETABLES AND HERBS AND well dressed, a grain salad makes a flavorful, bright side dish. We had just developed a great Tabbouleh recipe (see at left) featuring bulgur and parsley, so we set out to find a grain that would serve as the foundation for another appealing grain-based salad. We eventually settled on quinoa, which, though it is generally treated as a grain, is actually a seed. It was a staple of the Inca civilization and is still a staple in Peru, and today quinoa is available in most supermarkets. Quinoa contains significantly more protein than most grains, and its protein is complete, which means it possesses all of the amino acids necessary for protein metabolism, unlike grains that have to be consumed in conjunction with other foodstuffs, such as beans, to unlock their nutritional benefits. But all these nutritional pluses aside, quinoa has a wholesome, hearty taste and "caviar-like texture" that make it an all-around winner.

The concept of making a quinoa salad seemed simple to us at first, yet we soon found after a few initial tests that two basic problems plague most recipes. For starters, quinoa has a unique, slightly earthy flavor, so a recipe must include complementary ingredients and flavors. We found some recipes that simply took a pasta or bean salad, then swapped out those starring ingredients in favor of the quinoa. While pasta and beans are a relatively mild backdrop, quinoa's stronger flavor simply didn't work in the same setting. Even more challenging than the delicate dance of flavors is the texture of the quinoa. When cooked, it all too often became dense and soggy, not appetizing when served cold as a salad. Our goals were twofold: First, come up with a dressing and combination of add-ins that would complement the flavor of the quinoa, and second, develop a cooking method for our quinoa that would preserve its texture and highlight individual grains when cooled.

Almost every recipe we found employed the same method for cooking: Rinse the quinoa well to rid the grains of a mildly toxic protective layer (called saponin), which is unpleasantly bitter; bring it to a boil in stock or water; and simmer over low heat, covered, for 15 minutes. In the test kitchen we found that this basic method worked pretty well for a warm side dish, but the results were too wet and dense for a salad. Next we tried simply simmering the quinoa, then draining and rinsing

RINSING AND DRYING QUINOA

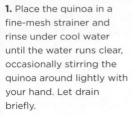

1. Place the quinoa in a fine-mesh strainer and rinse under cool water until the water runs clear, occasionally stirring the quinoa around lightly with your hand. Let drain briefly.

2. Line a rimmed baking sheet with a clean kitchen towel and spread the drained quinoa out to dry, about 15 minutes.

3. To remove the quinoa from the towel, use the corners of the towel to shake the quinoa into a bowl.

THE BEST LARGE SAUCEPAN

A few years ago we gave the All-Clad Stainless 4-Quart Saucepan top honors among large saucepans. At the time, this pot had a unique "fully clad" design that gave it a corner on the market. The others, without this design, were more likely to burn food. But now other manufacturers are producing multi-ply, fully clad pans, some at a price cheaper than our old favorite. We rounded up eight models priced from $49.97 to $384.95 to see how much we needed to spend to get a great fully clad saucepan. The real differences came down to design and maneuverability. We found a good-quality, fully clad, easy-to-maneuver pan in the Cuisinart MultiClad Unlimited 4-Quart Saucepan for just $69.99, but it did rate behind one other pan: the **All-Clad Stainless 4-Quart Saucepan with Lid and Loop**, $194.99, which gained top marks once again.

it. Texturally, this did not work either. The quinoa was waterlogged and the grains were too saturated to combine properly with the vinaigrette. We wondered whether the test kitchen's technique for cooking rice pilaf would give us the light, fluffy, dry quinoa we were after.

We toasted the rinsed quinoa in a saucepan (we found it was necessary to dry the rinsed grains on a towel to ensure proper toasting), then added liquid, brought it to a simmer, covered the pan, and cooked it over low heat until most of the water was absorbed. At this point, we removed the pan from the heat and allowed it to sit with the lid on for 10 minutes so that the warm grains could absorb the remaining water. Then we dressed the quinoa in a basic vinaigrette. This was leagues better than previous methods, but the salad was still a bit too soggy. We had a hunch our problem was the 10 minutes when the quinoa sat off the heat and soaked up the remaining water. When incorporated with the dressing, these grains were simply too moist.

So for our next test, instead of letting the grains sit in the pan once they were tender, we needed to cool off the quinoa quickly to stop the cooking and keep it from absorbing so much water. We immediately poured the grains onto a baking sheet so they would cool quickly. The texture of this quinoa was dramatically improved, but, of course, now there was some unabsorbed liquid left. Up to this point we had been using 1 cup of quinoa and 2 cups of water. Reducing the amount of water by ½ cup solved the problem, giving us perfect quinoa every time and no extra liquid. So with our cooking method under our belt, we moved on to creating a flavorful vinaigrette and adding the right vegetables, herbs, and seasonings to the mix.

Simplicity was the theme for adding flavor to our quinoa salad. We found that the earthy flavor of the grains paired well with jalapeño and cilantro (which is not surprising; both are common in traditional Peruvian quinoa recipes). Tasters felt that the zestiness of a lime vinaigrette made sense with the quinoa, jalapeño, and cilantro, and crisp red bell pepper added a nice sweetness and contrasting texture. Finally, cumin added warmth and rounded out the piquancy of the other ingredients.

With our method and ingredients down pat, we found that this healthy salad was quick to make and offered great texture and visual appeal that made it another crowd-pleasing dish for our repertoire.

Quinoa Salad with Red Bell Pepper and Cilantro

SERVES 4

To make this dish spicier, add the chile seeds. After 12 minutes of cooking, there will still be a little bit of water in the pan, but this will evaporate as the quinoa cools.

- 1 cup quinoa, rinsed and dried on a towel (see page 206)
- 1½ cups water
-   Salt
- ½ red bell pepper, stemmed, seeded, and chopped fine
- ½ jalapeño chile, stemmed, seeded, and minced
- 2 tablespoons minced red onion
- 1 tablespoon minced fresh cilantro
- 2 tablespoons fresh lime juice
- 1 tablespoon extra-virgin olive oil
- 2 teaspoons Dijon mustard
- 1 small garlic clove, minced
- ½ teaspoon ground cumin
-   Pepper

1. Toast the quinoa in a large saucepan over medium heat, stirring often, until lightly browned and aromatic, about 5 minutes. Stir in the water and ½ teaspoon salt and bring to a simmer. Reduce the heat to low, cover, and cook until the quinoa has absorbed most of the water and is nearly tender, about 12 minutes. Spread the quinoa on a rimmed baking sheet and set aside to cool to room temperature, about 20 minutes.

2. When the quinoa is cool, transfer to a large bowl. Stir in the bell pepper, jalapeño, onion, and cilantro. In a separate bowl, whisk the lime juice, oil, mustard, garlic, and cumin together, then pour over the quinoa mixture and toss to coat. Season with salt and pepper to taste and serve. (The quinoa salad can be refrigerated in an airtight container for up to 2 days; season with additional salt, pepper, and lime juice to taste before serving.)

PER ¾-CUP SERVING: Cal 200; Fat 6g; Sat fat 1g; Chol 0mg; Carb 30g; Protein 6g; Fiber 3g; Sodium 370mg

VARIATION

Quinoa Salad with Cucumber and Radish

Follow the recipe for Quinoa Salad with Red Bell Pepper and Cilantro, substituting ½ cucumber, halved lengthwise, seeded, and chopped fine, for the red bell pepper. Substitute 3 radishes, quartered and sliced thin, for the jalapeño, parsley for the cilantro, and lemon juice for the lime juice.

PER ¾-CUP SERVING: Cal 200; Fat 6g; Sat fat 1g; Chol 0mg; Carb 30g; Protein 7g; Fiber 4g; Sodium 360mg

EASY CUBAN-STYLE BLACK BEANS

A GREAT LOW-FAT SOURCE OF PROTEIN, BEANS ARE A worthwhile staple to add to your diet, and we love black beans in particular for their slightly earthy flavor, creamy texture, and bold presence on the plate. When looking for a black bean dish to add to our collection of light and healthy sides, we immediately looked to Latin American cuisine, where black beans are turned into a flavorful part of nearly every meal in dishes such as *frijoles negros*, or Cuban-style black beans. With the help of additions like onion, spicy chiles, ham hock, and warm spices such cumin, these beans are at once bright and richly seasoned, and eminently satisfying. But all that great flavor and texture usually come at a price, as most classic Cuban black bean recipes require half a day's work. We wanted to create a recipe for full-flavored, creamy Cuban-style black beans that could stand up by themselves as a side dish, or make a satisfying meal when served with white rice—but we didn't want to spend hours laboring over a slow-simmering pot of beans. We were after quick, easy, and streamlined, so we set out to develop a version that could be made in just one pot.

Since our goal was simplicity and ease (not to mention a recipe that would work well for weeknight cooking), canned beans were the obvious starting point, rather than working with dried beans that we'd have to soak and cook for a long time. We would just have to find a way to build complex flavor without drowning out the earthy flavor of the beans. We started by adding pork to our beans, a typical addition in many of the recipes we found, as meat lends the dish a necessary depth of flavor. We tested cooking beans with a ham hock, bacon, and ham. The ham hock (although traditional) was out. With our quick-style beans, there was not enough cooking time to extract the hock's flavor. Meanwhile, the ham seemed cumbersome for our small batch of beans. Bacon was the favorite, and just one slice gave our beans an undertone of smoky pork flavor without adding too much fat to the bottom line.

In many Latin recipes, a *sofrito* (the Latin American answer to the French *mirepoix* of carrots, onions, and celery), usually onion, garlic, and green bell pepper, is added to the cooked beans for flavor. The chopped vegetables are sautéed in generous quantities of olive oil until soft and then stirred into the beans. Looking to cut back on fat where we could, we traded in the oil for the lesser but more flavorful fat rendered from our slice of bacon, covered the pot, and allowed the vegetables to cook until soft. As predicted, this classic mixture added yet another layer of flavor to the beans.

With the basics in place, next we needed to focus on achieving the best texture. Most Cuban-style beans are a combination of whole beans coated in a slightly thickened "sauce." Some recipes suggest pureeing the sofrito with some of the beans to achieve the proper consistency, and others call for mashing some beans with the sofrito. We found that pureeing intensified the flavor of the vegetables too much, overwhelming the beans. Simply mashing some of the beans with the sofrito and 1 cup of water was a more promising route. We then added the remaining beans to the pot with another cup of water, brought the mixture to a simmer, and let it cook for about 15 minutes, until the liquid thickened and was creamy but not soupy.

Last, we ran several experiments to fine-tune additional flavorings. Some recipes include sugar, but tasters agreed they didn't like the added sweetness. Just 1 tablespoon of extra-virgin olive oil stirred in at the end went a long way toward enriching our beans and rounding out the flavors. For an acidic component, we tested red wine vinegar against balsamic and cider vinegars, as well as lime and lemon juices. Lime juice was the best fit, and when we paired it with a sprinkling of cilantro, we knew we finally had the taste of tradition—and in much less time.

Easy Cuban-Style Black Beans

SERVES 6

Our favorite brand of canned black beans is Bush's Best Black Beans (see page 11). Serve with low-fat sour cream, minced red onion, and hot sauce, if desired. Serve with steamed white rice to make it an authentic Cuban meal.

- 1 **slice bacon, minced**
- 1 **onion, minced (about 1 cup)**
- 1 **small green bell pepper, stemmed, seeded, and chopped fine**
  Salt
- 6 **garlic cloves, minced**
- 1½ **teaspoons dried oregano**
- 1 **teaspoon ground cumin**
  Pinch cayenne pepper (optional)
- 2 **(15-ounce) cans black beans, drained and rinsed**
- 2 **cups water**
- 1 **bay leaf**
- ¼ **cup minced fresh cilantro**
- 1 **tablespoon extra-virgin olive oil**
- 1 **tablespoon fresh lime juice**
  Black pepper

1. Cook the bacon in a large saucepan over medium-low heat, stirring often, until the fat is rendered and the bacon is crisp, 8 to 10 minutes. Add the onion, bell pepper, and ⅛ teaspoon salt, cover, and cook, stirring occasionally, until softened, 8 to 10 minutes. Uncover, stir in the garlic, oregano, cumin, and cayenne (if using), and cook until fragrant, about 30 seconds.

2. Stir in 1 cup of the beans and 1 cup of the water. Mash the beans with a potato masher or fork until the mixture is a coarse puree. Simmer over medium heat until the liquid is reduced and thickened, about 5 minutes.

3. Stir in the remaining beans, remaining 1 cup water, and bay leaf, bring to a simmer, and cook until the beans are creamy and the liquid thickens, 15 to 20 minutes. Remove and discard the bay leaf.

4. Stir in the cilantro, oil, and lime juice. Season with salt and black pepper to taste and serve. (The black beans can be refrigerated in an airtight container for up to 2 days. Reheat over medium-low heat before serving.)

PER ⅔-CUP SERVING: Cal 140; Fat 5g; Sat fat 1g; Chol 5mg; Carb 17g; Protein 6g; Fiber 6g; Sodium 380mg

REFRIED BEANS

TEST KITCHEN
MAKEOVER

REFRIED BEANS ARE A FAVORITE FOR BOTH YOUNG and old, great for topping tostadas or nachos, filling tacos, or serving alongside just about any Mexican-inspired entrée you can think of (not to mention all manner of barbecue). But in spite of their everyday, humble persona, refried beans do require some know-how when it comes to preparation if you want to achieve beans with just the right lush texture and rich, satisfying flavor. We've come across more than enough recipes for refried beans that are nothing more than gluey, flavorless spackle.

Successful authentic recipes for refried beans require soaking and cooking dried beans, then sautéing them with the other ingredients until they are soft enough to mash. So here was our first test kitchen challenge: We needed to create a streamlined method. Our second challenge? We'd need to turn this all-time favorite into a healthier recipe. The suave texture and rich flavor in authentic refried bean recipes are largely the result of cooking the beans in a more-than-generous amount of lard until they are soft enough to mash—hardly acceptable for everyday light cooking—and toppings like cheese and bacon only worsen the problem. With 19 grams of fat and 290 calories in a typical ⅔ cup serving, this side dish needed a serious overhaul to make it a regular on our healthier dinner plate. Nevertheless, we felt up to the challenge.

Our first step toward a streamlined recipe was obvious: We swapped out the dried beans for more convenient canned, which didn't need to be soaked or precooked. As for the type of bean to use, recipes typically call for either pinto or red kidney. In the end it was a close call, but tasters slightly favored the pinto beans.

With our beans in hand, we moved on to how best to prepare them. We came across various mashing procedures in our research. Most often, the beans and some liquid are mashed in the pan with a wooden spoon or potato masher, but we found this method was labor-intensive and yielded mediocre results. The chunky mash was punctuated with bits of tough, leathery bean skin. Clearly, we needed more force than that generated by a potato masher and an arm, and the food processor did an impressive job. We drained the beans, put a portion of them in the processor's workbowl with broth (which we favored over water for more flavor) to aid in pureeing, and processed the beans until smooth—about 30 seconds. The skins virtually disappeared, and the resulting puree was silky smooth. We then added the remaining beans and pulsed until the mixture was just slightly chunky. It was time to fry them.

Before the beans are added to the pan in traditional recipes, onions are sautéed (or fried) in lard. Putting a slab of lard in the pan was a nonstarter, so we looked to healthier alternatives. We pitted batches made with vegetable oil and olive oil against each other, and while the results were close, tasters favored the olive oil for its fuller flavor. We knew we would need to significantly cut back on the ½ cup of fat some recipes called for. We started testing at 2 tablespoons of oil, and while tasters approved the richness provided by even this small amount, we felt we could go lower still. We tried subsequent batches of beans, taking out 1 teaspoon of oil at a time. Tasters hit their limit at 1 tablespoon of oil, at which point they complained that the beans tasted too lean. In the end, we agreed 4 teaspoons of oil was as low as we could go and still achieve the rich-tasting beans we were after.

In an effort to maximize the olive oil's flavor, we found it was best to use just 1 teaspoon of the oil to sauté the onion and cook the beans, and then we stirred in the remaining 1 tablespoon of oil to finish the beans, which assured maximum flavor and complexity from the olive oil, and it boosted both the richness and the suave texture of our dish to a level that echoed those of the traditional recipes.

Now that we had a core technique for low-fat refried beans in place, we needed to focus on seasonings; these otherwise mild-tasting beans definitely needed deeper flavor. The sautéed onion had been a good start since it added both depth and body as well as sweetness. Jalapeño chiles brought a good hint of heat and a vegetal edge that tasters liked. Cumin, garlic, cilantro, and lime juice rounded out the seasonings, adding freshness, depth, and a warm spice flavor all at once. And with this full, well-rounded flavor combination and plenty of rich, creamy texture, we were confident no one would miss the old-fashioned versions.

MAKEOVER SPOTLIGHT: REFRIED BEANS

	CALORIES	FAT	SAT FAT	CHOLESTEROL
BEFORE	290	19g	6g	15mg
AFTER	160	4.5g	0g	0mg

Refried Beans

SERVES 6

To make this dish spicier, add the chile seeds. Though we think they are great as is, these refried beans can be served with a variety of garnishes, including warmed corn or flour tortillas, salsa, pickled jalapeño chiles (sold in cans or jars in most supermarkets), sliced scallions, shredded low-fat Monterey Jack or cheddar cheese, and low-fat sour cream.

3   (15-ounce) cans pinto beans, drained and rinsed
1   cup low-sodium chicken broth
1   onion, minced (about 1 cup)
1   large jalapeño chile, stemmed, seeded, and minced
4   teaspoons olive oil
    Salt
2   garlic cloves, minced
1   teaspoon ground cumin
2   tablespoons fresh lime juice
2   tablespoons minced fresh cilantro

1. Process 2 cups of the beans and broth in a food processor until smooth, 1 to 2 minutes, scraping down the bowl if necessary. Add the remaining beans and pulse until the mixture is slightly chunky, about 10 pulses, and set aside.

2. Combine the onion, jalapeño, 1 teaspoon of the oil, and ½ teaspoon salt in a medium saucepan. Cover and cook over medium-low heat, stirring occasionally, until the vegetables are softened, 8 to 10 minutes. Uncover, stir in the garlic and cumin, and cook until fragrant, about 30 seconds. Stir in the pureed beans until thoroughly combined.

3. Reduce the heat to low and cook, stirring frequently, until the beans have thickened and the flavors have blended, about 10 minutes. Stir in the remaining 1 tablespoon oil, lime juice, and cilantro. Season with salt to taste and serve. (The beans can be refrigerated in an airtight container for up to 2 days. Reheat in a pan over low heat until hot, adding water, 1 tablespoon at a time, as needed to adjust the consistency.)

PER ⅔-CUP SERVING: Cal 160; Fat 4.5g; Sat fat 0g; Chol 0mg; Carb 23g; Protein 8g; Fiber 8g; Sodium 580mg

HOPPIN' JOHN

IN THE LOW COUNTRY OF SOUTH CAROLINA AND Georgia, eating hoppin' John at the start of the new year is said to bring 365 days of good luck, but it tastes good any time of year. Traditional recipes for this homey one-pot meal call for simmering fresh black-eyed peas (which are beans, despite the name) with smoked ham hocks until creamy and infused with meaty flavor. Rice plumps in the broth toward the end of cooking. Hoppin' John's appeal was obvious to us, but could we come up with an easy-to-make light version that was just as satisfying and comforting as the old-fashioned Southern classic?

To find out what we were up against, we tested a handful of existing recipes. Since fresh black-eyed peas can be hard to find if you live outside the South, most modern recipes rely on their dried counterpart, which can take hours to achieve the perfect creamy—but not mushy—state. We found that while this extended cooking time helped infuse the dish with smoky, meaty flavor, it also made the results a bit starchy and gummy. We didn't want to cheat, as some recipes do, by cooking the rice and black-eyed peas separately (we tried it, and it just wasn't as flavorful), but we also didn't want our hoppin' John to sit like a rock in people's stomachs. Our goal was to perfect and streamline the method, shortening the cooking time considerably, and at the same time lighten this Southern favorite.

Our first challenge was cooking the beans faster, but not so fast as to eliminate the opportunity to meld all the flavors of the dish. Working from the most promising one-pot recipe we'd tried, we browned two slices of minced bacon (lightening things up from the usual six to eight slices) and sautéed onion, celery, garlic, and thyme in the rendered fat to boost their flavor. When it was time to add the beans, we tested two different options in our search for an easier and quicker-cooking route. To one batch we added 2 pounds of canned black-eyed peas, and to another an equal amount of frozen, and then we added water and a ham hock to both. The canned beans quickly blew apart, but the frozen ones held their shape and turned creamy after just 40 minutes.

Settled on frozen beans, we moved on to the rice. We followed the same method as before but added 1½ cups of rice at the 20-minute mark. After 40 minutes, both components were evenly cooked, but the dish was too starchy, and, without enough time to draw out the ham

HOPPIN' JOHN

hock's flavor, it lacked the smoky richness of slow-simmered versions.

We addressed the rice first. In the test kitchen we often rinse rice before cooking to remove excess starch, which in turn lightens the final texture. We saw that some existing hoppin' John recipes also used this technique, so we gave it a try. We put the rice in a strainer, opened the tap, and watched the milky starch run off the grains, then we proceeded as before. At the end of cooking, we removed the lid to find perfectly fluffy, tender rice amid creamy beans with no gumminess—the rinse made the difference.

Now we needed to address the ham hock. Smoked ham hocks require hours of simmering to extract their flavor. Looking for another smoked pork product that would give up its flavor more quickly (and with a little less fat), we grabbed a small boneless ham at the grocery store. We sliced it into steaks, browned the steaks in a little oil to deepen their flavor, removed them from the pot while we rendered the bacon, and then stirred them back in with the broth and beans. We added the rice as usual; when it was done, we removed the ham steaks, chopped them into bite-size pieces, and stirred them back into the pot. Tasters loved the meatiness of the ham and the smoky pork flavor it contributed, but the ham pieces were rubbery. To shorten their cooking time, we removed the steaks before adding the rice. We found that a 1-pound ham added the requisite meaty flavor without adding too much fat or too many calories.

NOTES FROM THE TEST KITCHEN

HURRYING HOPPIN' JOHN

Hoppin' John can take as long as four hours to make. We drastically reduce the cooking time by using boneless ham in place of a smoked ham hock and frozen peas instead of dried (which require long cooking).

BONELESS HAM
Brown and simmer boneless ham to add smoky depth and meatiness in a quarter of the time.

FROZEN BLACK-EYED PEAS
Use frozen black-eyed peas straight from the freezer, which will simmer to the perfect creamy consistency in less than one hour.

After a sprinkling of scallions for a hint of color, our quick, easy, and satisfying Hoppin' John was lightened up and ready to hop to the table.

Hoppin' John

SERVES 8 AS A MAIN COURSE

Small boneless hams are available in the meat case at most supermarkets. An equal weight of ham steak can be used. Make sure to use low-sodium chicken broth, or the dish will be too salty. Serve with hot sauce.

- 2 teaspoons canola oil
- 1 (1-pound) boneless ham, cut into ¾-inch-thick planks
- 2 slices bacon, minced
- 2 celery ribs, minced
- 1 onion, minced (about 1 cup)
- 4 garlic cloves, minced
- 1½ teaspoons minced fresh thyme or ½ teaspoon dried
- 4 cups low-sodium chicken broth
- 2 (16-ounce) bags frozen black-eyed peas
- 2 bay leaves
- 1½ cups long-grain white rice, rinsed (see page 79)
- 3 scallions, sliced thin

1. Heat the oil in a Dutch oven over medium heat until shimmering. Add the ham and cook until well browned on both sides, about 6 minutes, flipping the steaks halfway through. Transfer the ham to a plate and set aside. Reduce the heat to medium-low, add the bacon, and cook, stirring often, until the fat is rendered and the bacon is crisp, 8 to 10 minutes.

2. Add the celery and onion and cook, stirring occasionally, until softened, 5 to 7 minutes. Stir in the garlic and thyme and cook until fragrant, about 30 seconds. Add the browned ham, broth, peas, and bay leaves and bring to a simmer over medium-high heat. Reduce the heat to low, cover, and cook until the peas are just tender, about 20 minutes.

3. Transfer the ham to a carving board. When cool enough to handle, cut the ham into ½-inch pieces, cover, and set aside.

4. Stir the rice into the pot. Following the photos on page 197, place a large piece of foil flush to the surface of the liquid. Cover and continue to simmer until the liquid is absorbed and the rice is tender, about 20 minutes, stirring and replacing the foil twice during cooking. Remove the pot from the heat and let sit, covered, for 10 minutes.

5. Fluff the rice with a fork and remove and discard the bay leaves. Gently fold in the reserved ham and scallions and serve. (The Hoppin' John can be refrigerated in an airtight container for up to 2 days.)

PER 1½-CUP SERVING: Cal 400; Fat 8g; Sat fat 2g; Chol 30mg; Carb 59g; Protein 25g; Fiber 1g; Sodium 1090mg

MEATY BAKED BEANS

TEST KITCHEN
MAKEOVER

SMOKY, SAUCY BAKED BEANS ARE ABOUT AS All-American as it gets, perfect for pairing with dishes like Sloppy Joes (page 88) or Barbecued Chicken Breasts (page 168). And according to old-fashioned tradition, much of that flavor should come from meat— and a whole lot of it. For a single quart of beans, the great Fannie Farmer used to call for an entire pound of "mixed pork." (Apparently, 19th-century butchers didn't specialize in shrink-wrapped packages of just pork shoulder or ham hocks.) We wondered if we could develop a modern baked bean dish that still offered great meaty flavor like the old-fashioned version but didn't rely on copious amounts of pork (even modern takes on meaty baked beans can tally 440 calories and 19 grams of fat per serving). We imagined creamy, well-seasoned beans and tender pork simmered together in a thick, balanced sauce that was sweet and tangy, but with the fat and calories kept in check.

After trying out a few recipes to get our bearings, it was clear there were as many interpretations of this dish as beans in a bag, and just about as many pitfalls. Beans ended up overcooked and blown out—or as hard as raw peanuts. We tasted our way through cloying, syrupy sauces and stringy, chewy, flavorless meat. We had our work cut out for us.

We first focused our attention on the beans. In most recipes they are simmered for hours in the oven, but the details ran amok. To soak or not to soak? For how long and how hot? Times and temperatures varied from a 450-degree power sprint to a daylong, 250-degree affair. Starting with 1 pound of dried beans (we began with navy), 8 cups of water, a couple of ham hocks (an amount picked up from existing recipes, which we would obviously have to address later), and ½ cup each of molasses and barbecue sauce (for sweetness and zip), we made several batches, using every variety of technique and temperature. Just before serving, we stirred the meat pulled from the hocks into the saucy beans.

We got our best results when we cooked the beans in a 350-degree oven for three to four hours; these beans were creamy and evenly cooked. Regarding the soaking, tasters preferred beans that were soaked for several hours. It produced a bean with a more tender and creamy final texture and also pared down the cooking time. The tiny navy beans we had been using were perfectly tasty, but we wondered if a bigger bean might hold its own better and give our recipe a heartier, "meatier" profile. In a side-by-side comparison of navy beans, pink beans, pintos, and kidneys, our favorite turned out to be the meatier pinks (with pinto a close runner-up) for their luxuriously creamy interiors. We learned through more testing that the amount of water needed was variable, depending on the age of the beans and the pot used to cook the beans. Our solution was to start checking the beans after about two hours of uncovered cooking, and we added up to 2 cups more water as needed to keep them saucy.

Next, we turned to the pork. While ham hocks were providing decent flavor, given how big they were they comparatively didn't have much meat that we could actually pull off to include in the final dish. Even though we were creating a lighter recipe, we wanted at least a morsel of pork in every bite. Raising the number of ham hocks so we could get enough meat left hardly enough room in the pot for the beans and took the fat count too high anyway. We needed to look at other meaty options.

Tasters agreed a smoky taste was a must. Boneless smoked pork shoulder was a favorite in terms of flavor but was simply too fatty to make the cut, and smoked pork chops turned rubbery and bland. The winner proved to be not one pig product but two. A few slices of bacon delivered the smoky taste we wanted without adding too much fat per serving.

But since the bacon morsels simply melted into the sauce over the long cooking time, we also needed to include a cut that would lend some meaty substance. Lean ham steak was our answer. We cut a 1-pound ham steak into quarters and cooked the meat for about 45 minutes with the beans—after which point we removed it from the pot, shredded it, and stirred it in at the end—and it stayed nicely tender. If we left it in the pot any longer, the meat turned spongy. This ham steak–bacon duo ensured meat in every bite and smoky flavor throughout.

Next we turned our attention to the sauce. Ketchup beat out the smoky barbecue sauce we had been using, and dark brown sugar balanced the flavors better than molasses or light brown sugar. A quarter-cup of spicy brown mustard provided a welcome punch of heat, and sautéed onion and garlic added fragrant complexity. We gave the beans one more taste. Every forkful was packed with tender meat and perfectly creamy bean, and the sweet-smoky-tangy liquid reduced to a silky sauce that clung to the pork and beans perfectly. Finally, a recipe lived up to its meaty promise, and with just 260 calories and 4 grams fat per serving, it didn't tip the scales.

MAKEOVER SPOTLIGHT: MEATY BAKED BEANS

	CALORIES	FAT	SAT FAT	CHOLESTEROL
BEFORE	440	19g	7g	60mg
AFTER	260	4g	1.5g	20mg

Meaty Baked Beans

SERVES 12

Pink beans are smooth, reddish-brown beans particularly popular in the western United States; they can be found near the other dried beans in most supermarkets. Begin checking the beans after 2 hours of uncovered baking, adding more water as needed to adjust the consistency of the cooking liquid to ensure that the beans are not too dry and will be able to cook through completely.

    2   slices bacon, minced
    1   onion, minced (about 1 cup)
        Salt
    4   garlic cloves, minced
  8-10 cups water
    1   pound dried pink beans (about 2½ cups), rinsed, picked over, and soaked (see at right)
    1   cup ketchup
    ½   cup packed dark brown sugar
    ¼   cup spicy brown mustard
    1   pound ham steak, cut into quarters
        Pepper

1. Adjust an oven rack to the middle position and heat the oven to 350 degrees. Cook the bacon in a Dutch oven over medium-low heat, stirring often, until the fat is rendered and the bacon is crisp, 8 to 10 minutes. Add the onion and ⅛ teaspoon salt, cover, and cook, stirring occasionally, until the onion is softened, 8 to 10 minutes. Uncover, stir in the garlic, and cook until fragrant, about 30 seconds.

2. Stir in 8 cups of the water and the drained beans and bring to a simmer over medium-high heat. Cover, transfer to the oven, and bake until the beans are just beginning to soften, about 1 hour. Remove the pot from the oven, uncover, and stir in the ketchup, sugar, and mustard until well combined. Nestle the ham into the beans, return the pot to the oven, and continue to bake, uncovered, for 45 minutes. Transfer the ham to a plate. When cool enough to handle, shred the meat into bite-size pieces, cover, and set aside.

3. Continue to bake the beans, uncovered, until they are completely tender and the liquid has thickened, about 2 hours and 15 minutes longer, adding up to 2 cups more water as necessary to keep the beans saucy. Stir the reserved shredded ham into the beans, season with salt and pepper to taste, and serve. (The beans can be refrigerated in an airtight container for up to 2 days.)

PER ¾-CUP SERVING: Cal 260; Fat 4g; Sat fat 1.5g; Chol 20mg; Carb 40g; Protein 16g; Fiber 5g; Sodium 880mg

NOTES FROM THE TEST KITCHEN

SOAKING BEANS

Here in the test kitchen, we've found that many types of dried beans—such as the pink beans in our Meaty Baked Beans and the cannellini beans in our French Pork and White Bean Casserole (page 95)—benefit from being soaked before cooking. Soaking allows the dried beans to absorb water and hydrate evenly, resulting in a creamy, evenly cooked final texture when cooked. Don't worry if you don't have time to soak the beans (or forgot)—we've come up with a "quick-soak" method that works nearly as well (we still slightly prefer the overnight soak if given a choice).

Overnight Soaking Method: Pick through and rinse the beans, then place them in a large bowl or container and cover by several inches of water (about 5 cups of water for 1 pound of beans). Let the beans soak at room temperature for 12 to 24 hours. Drain the beans, discarding the soaking liquid, and cook as directed.

Quick Soaking Method: Pick through and rinse the beans, then place them in a saucepan and cover by 1 inch of water. Bring the beans to a boil and cook for 2 minutes. Remove the saucepan from the heat, cover, and let the beans steep for 1 hour. Drain the beans, discarding the cooking liquid, and cook as directed.

WHITE BEAN GRATIN

FROM REFRIED AND BAKED, TO CUBAN-STYLE AND Southern-inspired, the light yet satisfying bean side dishes we had developed thus far covered a lot of ground, but we wanted to come up with one more recipe to round out the group. We were after something a bit more upscale, a dish with comfort-food appeal that was worthy of a special occasion. Searching for a new flavor profile, we turned to the Mediterranean, and in particular to Tuscany. Beans play such a prominent role in this region's cuisine that the people of Tuscany are actually known as *mangiafagioli*, or "bean eaters," so we felt confident we would be inspired by their cuisine. Cannellini (white kidney beans) are the region's most famous legume, and Tuscan cooks go to great extremes to ensure that these beans are worthy of star status. Could we take this bean and some basic Mediterranean flavors and develop an easy yet sophisticated side dish that didn't require a lot of fuss?

During our initial research, we came across a few Tuscan-style recipes for white bean gratins, elegant yet homey casseroles with warm, saucy beans under a golden crust of bread crumbs or cheese. This sounded like just what we were looking for.

As with our other recently developed bean recipes, we wanted to keep things as easy as possible, so we opted for convenient canned beans over dried, knowing as such we'd have to focus on a method that would infuse the canned beans with flavor while preserving their texture. To make sure that the classic choice of cannellinis was indeed the best option, we tested three types of white beans in a basic gratin recipe: cannellini, navy, and great Northern. After extensive tasting, we sided with the Tuscans. The cannellinis won out for their creamy yet firm texture.

One thing we know about using canned beans is that they simply cannot withstand extended cooking times. And since traditional gratin recipes rely on longer cooking times to cook through not only the dried beans but some of the other ingredients as well, we were going to need to precook those components on the stovetop before combining them with the beans and placing the dish in the oven. So we sautéed some onions and a hefty dose of garlic, then combined them with the beans, a teaspoon of minced fresh rosemary, and some water to ensure that the beans stayed moist. We popped the dish into a 400-degree oven for 20 minutes, enough time to marry the flavors and get it piping hot. This method worked well for the beans' texture—they were creamy and remained intact; however, the flavors needed work.

Our first thought was to deeply caramelize the onions to add richness and depth. After years of making caramelized onions in the test kitchen, we had a head start on how best to get the job done. We started with three onions, sliced thin, and cooked them in 2 tablespoons of extra-virgin olive oil (with a little brown sugar and salt for added flavor) over medium-high heat to jump-start their release of moisture, which in turn begins the process of caramelization. We then turned the heat down and continued to cook the onions over moderate heat for 20 to 25 minutes, until they were dark golden and caramelized. We spread the caramelized onions in the bottom of the casserole dish, forming a flavorful base for our gratin.

Next, we swapped out the water for more flavorful chicken broth and briefly simmered the beans in the broth along with the rosemary to jump-start the cooking and start to infuse the rosemary's flavor into the dish since it wouldn't have much time to get the job done in the oven. We then poured our bean mixture on top of the onions. We agreed that Parmesan cheese was a logical fit for this Tuscan dish, and sprinkling just an ounce over the beans would add a nice nutty, salty flavor. We moved the casserole to the oven and baked it until it was bubbling and golden.

Tasters agreed we had made real progress, but we still needed to make a few more tweaks to transform our beans into a worthy side dish. We realized we were leaving a lot of flavor behind in the pan when caramelizing our onions, so before transferring the onions to the casserole dish, we deglazed the pot with a little white wine. A pinch of crushed red pepper flakes gave a faint hint of heat. Tasters liked the flavor the Parmesan added but not the crust it produced since it didn't melt well, so we stirred the Parmesan into the beans before adding them to the casserole dish. Finally, we added an extra tablespoon of olive oil to the beans along with the Parmesan, which bumped up the flavor and elevated these beans to star status.

Finally, with our beans in good form, we could move on to the topping. A true gratin crust is usually made with either copious amounts of cheese or buttery bread crumbs. We eventually settled on the cheese route, which struck us as another avenue for adding flavor and richness. But since we wanted to keep our side dish light, we needed a melting cheese with big impact. Gruyère fit the bill, and just ½ cup of grated cheese sprinkled over the top added a complex, earthy flavor that perfectly complemented the beans below. This white bean gratin was flavorful, elegant, and satisfying; no one could have imagined it was also light.

White Bean Gratin

SERVES 8

For the best flavor, make sure to cook the onions until they are well caramelized and darkly colored in step 1.

- 3   tablespoons extra-virgin olive oil
- 3   onions, halved and sliced thin
- ½   teaspoon brown sugar
-     Salt
- 6   garlic cloves, minced
- ⅛   teaspoon red pepper flakes
- ½   cup dry white wine
- 4   (15-ounce) cans cannellini beans, drained and rinsed
- 1   cup low-sodium chicken broth
- 1   teaspoon minced fresh rosemary or ¼ teaspoon dried
- 1   ounce Parmesan cheese, grated (about ½ cup)
-     Pepper
- 2   ounces Gruyère cheese, shredded (about ½ cup)
- 2   tablespoons minced fresh parsley

1. Adjust an oven rack to the middle position and heat the oven to 400 degrees. Heat 2 tablespoons of the oil in a Dutch oven over medium-high heat until shimmering. Add the onions, sugar, and ⅛ teaspoon salt and cook, stirring often, until softened, about 5 minutes. Reduce the heat to medium-low and continue to cook, stirring often, until the onions are dark golden and caramelized, 20 to 25 minutes.

2. Stir in the garlic and pepper flakes and cook until fragrant, about 30 seconds. Stir in the wine and cook until nearly evaporated, about 1 minute. Transfer the onion mixture to a 13 by 9-inch baking dish and spread into an even layer.

3. Add the beans, broth, and rosemary to the Dutch oven and bring to a brief simmer. Off the heat, gently stir in the remaining 1 tablespoon oil and Parmesan. Season with salt and pepper to taste and pour the beans evenly over the onions.

4. Sprinkle the Gruyère evenly over the top. Bake until the cheese is golden brown and the edges are bubbling, about 20 minutes. Sprinkle with the parsley and serve. (The gratin can be prepared through step 3, covered tightly with foil, and refrigerated for up to 1 day. Bring to room temperature before continuing with step 4.)

PER ⅔-CUP SERVING: Cal 230; Fat 9g; Sat fat 2.5g; Chol 10mg; Carb 26g; Protein 9g; Fiber 7g; Sodium 480mg

NOTES FROM THE TEST KITCHEN

OUR FAVORITE GRUYÈRE
Authentic versions of Gruyère, produced in both Switzerland and France, are made from raw cow's milk and aged for the better part of a year in government-designated regions. We have found that domestic cheeses labeled "Gruyère," which are aged for fewer months, have a rubbery texture and bland flavor and bear little resemblance to the real thing. In a blind taste test of nine brands, tasters overwhelmingly panned the two domestic versions, while imports received raves. The top picks were both reserve cheeses, aged 10 or more months to develop stronger flavor. The winner, Swiss-produced **Emmi Le Gruyère Reserve**, was described as "grassy," "salty," and "nicely dry" and won favor with most tasters, especially when melted.

WHITE BEAN GRATIN

SKILLET GREEN BEANS WITH SPICED WALNUTS

PERFECT VEGETABLES

 M = TEST KITCHEN MAKEOVER

STIR-FRIED BROCCOLI

WHEN WE'RE AFTER BROCCOLI WITH A CRISP-TENDER texture, we usually steam it, but we roast it in the oven if we want to highlight the vegetable's sweetness. But stir-frying promises both results from one method. The quick blast of high heat should coax out the vegetable's sweetness before it has a chance to overcook. However, Chinese takeout containers—and our own pans—too often contain one of two disappointments: limp florets weighed down by sauce, or broccoli so undercooked it's practically crunchy. What would it take to perfect this simple side and restore its fresh, light appeal?

For starters, we swapped the wok for a 12-inch non-stick skillet. (Round-bottomed woks were designed to rest in conical fire pits in China; a flat-bottomed pan works better on the flat surface of an American stovetop.) We proceeded with the simplest stir-fry method we came across, cutting 1½ pounds of broccoli into bite-size pieces, throwing them into the skillet with canola oil and a couple of cloves of minced garlic, and cooking everything over high heat for a few minutes. Yes, this method was simple—to a fault. Tossing everything into the pan at once rendered burned aromatics and florets that turned mushy before the stalks had time to cook through.

First, we recalled cardinal rule number one for successful stir-frying: timing. This refers not only to having all of your ingredients ready to go before you turn on the stove, but also to knowing when to add each component to the skillet. The garlic was spending too much time in the pan; we knew from experience that adding it toward the end of cooking would prevent it from burning.

Then there was rule number two: When it comes to knife work, pay attention to the details. The denser stems and more tender florets were cooking unevenly. We saw great improvement when we treated them as two separate components. Stems cut into ¼-inch-thick slices cooked at the same pace as larger ¾-inch florets. But follow-up tests revealed inconsistency. We kept getting batches of broccoli that were practically raw. Even as we meticulously extended the cooking time minute by minute, we couldn't consistently achieve the texture we wanted: The blistering heat was simply too hard to control.

Maybe the problem was outside the skillet. Traditional Chinese stir-fries call for blazing heat, but we were beginning to believe this method was better suited to quick-cooking vegetables like onions and snow peas than to

thick, stubby broccoli. Taking down the heat—from high to medium-high—turned out to be a dramatic turn for the better. A longer cooking time (roughly 10 minutes over a more moderate fire) slowed things down enough so that it was easy to cook the florets and stems just until they were perfectly crisp-tender and nicely browned. A little sugar sprinkled over the broccoli before stir-frying deepened the caramelization even further.

With our cooking technique settled, the broccoli just needed a few Asian-inspired sauces to dress it up. Our first attempt, made with chicken broth, spicy Asian chili-garlic sauce, sherry, and soy sauce, went overboard; even though we added it to the skillet at the last minute, all the liquid undid our hard work, rendering the broccoli soggy and drowning its flavor. The answer was a teaspoon of cornstarch, which thickened the sauce just enough to prevent it from bogging down the florets. In fact, chicken broth and cornstarch worked well as a base for a few more variations—one with oyster sauce, another with hoisin sauce, and a final one flavored with orange juice and fresh ginger. These options were so quick and flavorful, we wondered if our perfected broccoli stir-fry might all but eclipse the other dishes on the dinner table.

Stir-Fried Broccoli with Chili-Garlic Sauce
SERVES 4

Feel free to use 1 pound of broccoli florets and omit the stems if desired.

¼ cup low-sodium chicken broth
1 tablespoon dry sherry
2 teaspoons low-sodium soy sauce
2 teaspoons Asian chili-garlic sauce (see page 221)
1 teaspoon toasted sesame oil
1 teaspoon cornstarch
1 tablespoon canola oil
2 garlic cloves, minced
⅛ teaspoon red pepper flakes
1 bunch broccoli (about 1½ pounds), florets cut into ¾-inch pieces, stems trimmed and sliced ¼ inch thick (see page 221)
¼ teaspoon sugar

1. Whisk the broth, sherry, soy sauce, chili-garlic sauce, sesame oil, and cornstarch together in a bowl. In a separate bowl, combine 1 teaspoon of the canola oil, garlic, and pepper flakes.

2. Heat the remaining 2 teaspoons canola oil in a 12-inch nonstick skillet over medium-high heat until just smoking. Add the broccoli, sprinkle with the sugar, and cook, stirring frequently, until bright green and well browned, 8 to 10 minutes.

3. Clear the center of the skillet and add the garlic mixture. Cook, mashing the garlic mixture into the pan with the back of a spatula, until fragrant, about 1 minute. Stir the garlic mixture into the broccoli.

4. Whisk the broth mixture to recombine and add it to the skillet. Cook, stirring constantly, until the sauce is thickened, the florets are cooked through, and the stalks are crisp-tender, 30 to 45 seconds. Serve.

PER SERVING: Cal 110; Fat 5g; Sat fat 0g; Chol 0mg; Carb 14g; Protein 5g; Fiber 4g; Sodium 260mg

VARIATIONS

Stir-Fried Broccoli with Oyster Sauce

Follow the recipe for Stir-Fried Broccoli with Chili-Garlic Sauce, reducing the amount of broth to 3 tablespoons and substituting 3 tablespoons oyster-flavored sauce for the low-sodium soy sauce and 1 teaspoon brown sugar for the chili-garlic sauce. Reduce the amount of garlic to 1 clove.

PER SERVING: Cal 120; Fat 5g; Sat fat 0g; Chol 0mg; Carb 16g; Protein 6g; Fiber 4g; Sodium 590mg

Stir-Fried Broccoli with Hoisin and Five-Spice Powder

Follow the recipe for Stir-Fried Broccoli with Chili-Garlic Sauce, substituting 3 tablespoons hoisin sauce for the sherry and increasing the amount of low-sodium soy sauce to 1 tablespoon. Substitute ⅛ teaspoon Chinese five-spice powder for the chili-garlic sauce and reduce the amount of garlic to 1 clove.

PER SERVING: Cal 130; Fat 5g; Sat fat 0g; Chol 0mg; Carb 20g; Protein 5g; Fiber 4g; Sodium 630mg

Stir-Fried Broccoli with Orange and Ginger

Follow the recipe for Stir-Fried Broccoli with Chili-Garlic Sauce, substituting ¼ cup orange juice for the sherry and omitting the toasted sesame oil and chili-garlic sauce. Reduce the amount of garlic to 1 clove, increase the amount of red pepper flakes to ½ teaspoon, and add 1 tablespoon grated or minced fresh ginger to the garlic-oil mixture in step 1.

PER SERVING: Cal 100; Fat 4g; Sat fat 0g; Chol 0mg; Carb 15g; Protein 5g; Fiber 5g; Sodium 180mg

NOTES FROM THE TEST KITCHEN

PREPARING BROCCOLI FOR STIR-FRYING

1. Place the head of broccoli upside down on a cutting board. Trim the florets very close to their heads and cut into ¾-inch pieces.

2. Trim and square off the broccoli stalks, removing the tough outer ⅛-inch layer.

3. Slice the trimmed stalks crosswise into ¼-inch-thick pieces.

ASIAN CHILI SAUCES

Used in cooking and as a condiment, these chili-based sauces each have a slightly different character. Sriracha (left), the spiciest of the three, is made from garlic and chiles that are ground into a smooth paste. Chili-garlic sauce (middle) is similar but the chiles are coarsely ground, giving it a chunkier texture, and we have found it has a rounder flavor than sriracha. Sambal oelek (right) is made purely from ground chiles, without the addition of garlic or other spices, thus adding heat but not additional flavor.

SRIRACHA   CHILI-GARLIC SAUCE   SAMBAL OELEK

SAUTÉED PEAS

WE DON'T OFTEN REACH INTO THE FREEZER FOR vegetables here in the test kitchen, but peas are a different story. They're convenient and ready in minutes, and except for just-picked pods (which are almost impossible to obtain much of the year), frozen peas are sweeter and more tender than fresh peas. It may seem counterintuitive, but fresh peas turn starchy and bland within 24 hours of harvest, and what you find in the supermarket might be several days old. Meanwhile, frozen peas are picked, cleaned, sorted, and frozen within several hours of harvest. Frozen peas are a great side dish choice, and while our mothers may have simply dumped a box or bag of frozen peas into boiling water, drained, and served them, their clean sweetness can be easily gussied up with any number of flavorful embellishments. Numerous cream- and butter-based sauces exist for peas, but we were after something lighter. Our goal was to develop a repertoire of flavorful, lighter, easy side dishes of peas with fresh add-ins like herbs, aromatics, and quick-sautéed complementary vegetables.

We started by buying several bags of frozen baby peas, which we've found are even sweeter and more tender than regular-size frozen peas. Since all frozen peas have already been blanched, we quickly learned that the key was not overdoing it—five minutes of simmering to heat them through was all they needed. The peas didn't even need to be thawed; they went straight from freezer to skillet. And the less liquid the better; we settled on ¼ cup per pound of peas.

To build up their sweet, grassy taste, we turned to aromatics, sweating a minced shallot and garlic in the saucepan with 1 teaspoon of oil before adding the peas with a little water. This proved to be only a slight improvement; we realized that a good bit of flavor was being poured down the sink when we drained the peas. There wasn't that much cooking liquid as it was, so for our next go-round we treated the cooking liquid like a sauce and served it with the peas.

We were getting closer, but tasters complained that this sauce was too thin and bland. Swapping the water for chicken broth was a step in the right direction, adding depth without overwhelming the peas. A small amount of butter stirred in after the peas finished simmering (just 1 tablespoon—tasters wanted a little richness without drowning the peas in fat) contributed body, and a generous dose of chopped fresh mint provided a nice aromatic complement. Still, something was missing. A smidge of sugar added to the broth and a healthy squirt of lemon juice stirred into the peas just before serving were all it took to bring everything into balance.

We thought we were finished when a fellow test cook suggested switching from a saucepan to a skillet to ensure that the peas heated a tad more quickly and evenly across the larger surface area. Now our peas were ready in as little as three minutes.

With our method and first recipe established, we developed an easy variation that paired the peas with fresh, aromatic fennel. Both recipes were as easy as they could be, and so flavorful that no one would ever guess that these peas weren't fresh from the garden.

Sautéed Peas with Shallot and Mint
SERVES 4

Do not thaw the peas before cooking. Regular-size frozen peas can be used in place of baby peas; increase the cooking time in step 2 by 1 to 2 minutes. Make sure to add the lemon juice right before serving; otherwise the peas will turn brown.

- 1 teaspoon olive oil
- 1 small shallot, minced (about 1 tablespoon)
- Salt
- 1 garlic clove, minced
- 1 pound frozen baby peas (about 3 cups)
- ¼ cup low-sodium chicken broth
- ¼ teaspoon sugar
- ¼ cup minced fresh mint
- 1 tablespoon unsalted butter
- 2 teaspoons fresh lemon juice
- Pepper

1. Heat the oil in a 12-inch skillet over medium-high heat until shimmering. Add the shallot and ⅛ teaspoon salt and cook until softened, about 2 minutes. Stir in the garlic and cook until fragrant, about 30 seconds.

2. Stir in the peas, broth, and sugar. Cover and cook until the peas are bright green and just heated through, 3 to 5 minutes, stirring halfway through cooking.

3. Stir in the mint and butter until incorporated. Off the heat, stir in the lemon juice. Season with salt and pepper to taste and serve.

PER SERVING: Cal 130; Fat 4g; Sat fat 2g; Chol 10mg; Carb 17g; Protein 7g; Fiber 5g; Sodium 110mg

SAUTÉED PEAS WITH SHALLOT AND MINT

Sautéed Peas with Fennel

Follow the recipe for Sautéed Peas with Shallot and Mint, substituting ½ cup finely chopped fennel for the shallot and increasing the cooking time in step 1 to 3 to 5 minutes. Substitute 2 tablespoons minced fennel fronds for the mint.

PER SERVING: Cal 150; Fat 4g; Sat fat 2g; Chol 10mg; Carb 21g; Protein 7g; Fiber 7g; Sodium 140mg

SAUTÉED SPINACH

WE HEAR ALL THE TIME THAT WE NEED TO EAT MORE dark leafy greens. And spinach—unlike kale, collards, or Swiss chard—is conveniently easy to find year-round at the supermarket, so there's really no excuse for passing it over. The test kitchen typically reserves delicate baby spinach for salads, and we occasionally stir it into dishes like soups and stews off the heat just before serving. For a simple sautéed spinach side dish, we usually turn to bigger, mature flat-leaf spinach. The reason? Tender young baby spinach releases a lot of liquid when it hits a hot pan, so a large amount of it added right to a skillet is likely to turn into a waterlogged, mushy mess. But given how convenient baby spinach is (no stems to remove or grit to rinse out), we thought it was time to give it another try.

In the past, when working with mature spinach, we worked around the water-related issue by wilting the spinach first in a pan, squeezing it with tongs in a colander to remove liquid, and then returning it to the skillet. But this tactic failed when we tried it with baby spinach. As soon as the wilted and pressed baby spinach went into the pan, it exuded even more juice. We needed to find a way to remove more liquid from the baby spinach.

What if we began by microwaving the spinach? After all, that's the suggestion offered on the back of the spinach bag. We placed the leaves in a large glass bowl and covered it with a plate. Even after six minutes, the spinach was warm but still not sufficiently wilted. While we were loath to do it, we thought adding just a little water to the bowl might help speed things up. After three

minutes, the spinach had softened and shrunk to half its volume, thanks to the release of a great deal of liquid. Yet a nagging problem remained: How would we extract all the liquid from the leaves of spinach? We pressed the spinach against the inside of a colander, but that couldn't remove enough of the liquid without ruining its tissue-like texture.

At this point, a colleague told us about a recipe in which the wilted spinach was chopped as a way to remove liquid. For our next batch, we microwaved, pressed, and then roughly chopped the spinach on a cutting board before sautéing it as usual. The chopping had released even more of the excess water—the mushy texture was now gone.

Our sautéed baby spinach was on the right track, but we wondered if we could make a good thing even better. We decided to see if putting the greens back in the colander for a second squeeze after we had chopped them would make a difference. This chopped and double-pressed spinach needed only a couple of minutes in the skillet before it was just right. The leaves were tender and perfectly cooked, without even a drop of excess liquid weighing them down.

Now all our spinach needed was the right seasoning. A few cloves of garlic, sliced thin and added to the pan with some red pepper flakes before the chopped and double-drained spinach went in, lent just the right depth and bite. We enhanced the freshness of the spinach with a squeeze of lemon juice added off the heat just before serving.

We loved this spinach as is but decided to come up with a few variations with some add-ins to dress our side dish up a bit. Paired with almonds and raisins, or pecans and feta, our baby spinach was elevated from lowly salad green to delicious and fresh side dish, ready to take its place next to the main course.

Sautéed Spinach with Garlic and Lemon
SERVES 4

If you don't have a microwave-safe bowl large enough to accommodate the entire amount of spinach, cook it in a smaller bowl in two batches, reducing the amount of water to 2 tablespoons per batch and the cooking time for each batch to about 1½ minutes.

3 **(6-ounce) bags baby spinach (about 18 cups)**

¼ **cup water**

4 **teaspoons extra-virgin olive oil**

3 **garlic cloves, peeled and sliced thin**

¼ **teaspoon red pepper flakes**

Salt

1 **teaspoon fresh lemon juice**

Pepper

1. Place the spinach and water in a large microwave-safe bowl. Cover the bowl and microwave on high until the spinach is wilted and has decreased in volume by half, 3 to 5 minutes. Using potholders, remove the bowl from the microwave and keep covered for 1 minute.

2. Carefully uncover the spinach and transfer to a colander. Using the back of a rubber spatula, gently press the spinach against the colander to release the excess liquid. Transfer the spinach to a cutting board and roughly chop. Return the spinach to the colander and press a second time.

3. Cook 1 tablespoon of the oil, garlic, and pepper flakes in a 12-inch skillet over medium-high heat, stirring constantly, until the garlic is light golden and beginning to sizzle, 2 to 3 minutes. Add the drained spinach and ¼ teaspoon salt, toss with tongs to coat with the oil, and cook until uniformly wilted and glossy green, about 2 minutes.

4. Off the heat, stir in the lemon juice and season with salt and pepper to taste. Transfer to a serving dish, drizzle with the remaining 1 teaspoon oil, and serve.

PER SERVING: **Cal** 100; **Fat** 4.5g; **Sat fat** 0.5g; **Chol** 0mg; **Carb** 14g; **Protein** 3g; **Fiber** 6g; **Sodium** 350mg

VARIATIONS

Sautéed Spinach with Almonds and Golden Raisins

Follow the recipe for Sautéed Spinach with Garlic and Lemon, adding ½ cup golden raisins with the garlic and red pepper flakes in step 3. Substitute sherry vinegar for the lemon juice. Sprinkle 3 tablespoons toasted sliced almonds over the spinach before serving.

PER SERVING: **Cal** 190; **Fat** 7g; **Sat fat** 1g; **Chol** 0mg; **Carb** 31g; **Protein** 5g; **Fiber** 8g; **Sodium** 350mg

Sautéed Spinach with Pecans and Feta

Follow the recipe for Sautéed Spinach with Garlic and Lemon, omitting the red pepper flakes. Substitute 3 large shallots, sliced thin crosswise, for the garlic and red wine vinegar for the lemon juice. Sprinkle 3 tablespoons coarsely chopped toasted pecans and 1 ounce feta cheese, crumbled (about ¼ cup), over the spinach before serving.

PER SERVING: **Cal** 180; **Fat** 10g; **Sat fat** 2g; **Chol** 5mg; **Carb** 21g; **Protein** 5g; **Fiber** 7g; **Sodium** 430mg

NOTES FROM THE TEST KITCHEN

STORING BAGGED BABY SPINACH

We call for specific sizes of bags or packages of baby spinach when it works for a recipe, but sometimes you might not find that particular size. If you have leftover spinach, make sure to store it in its original bag, folding the opened end over and taping it shut. These specially designed breathable bags keep the spinach fresh as long as possible; if you transfer the spinach to a sealed airtight bag, it will spoil prematurely.

A CUT ABOVE

We want a chef's knife that's versatile enough to handle almost any cutting task, whether it's mincing delicate herbs, chopping spinach, or cutting through meat and bones. We want a sharp blade that slices easily, without requiring a lot of force, and a comfortable handle that doesn't get slippery when greasy. We tested nine chef's knives by butchering whole chickens, chopping butternut squash, chopping parsley, and dicing onions. We also evaluated their comfort and user-friendliness based on feedback from a variety of testers. We rated sharpness and edge retention by cutting ordinary sheets of paper before and after kitchen tests. We found plenty to admire among the top-rated innovative knives, but we remain hard-pressed to pay a premium—sometimes as much as $175—for their innovations. The very affordable **Victorinox Fibrox** (formerly **Victorinox Forschner) 8-inch Chef's Knife**, $24.95, is our favorite—lightweight and agile, it also has a comfortable nonslip handle.

SKILLET GREEN BEANS

STEAMED GREEN BEANS TOPPED WITH A JUST PAT OF butter are an easy weeknight staple, but it's a side dish that can get boring quickly. We wanted to come up with a healthy weeknight recipe for green beans that had more pizzazz in terms of both texture and flavor.

For our cooking method, we quickly settled on sautéing, knowing that it would be relatively fast (particularly compared to oven-roasting), and that the heat from the skillet would impart more flavor than steaming or boiling alone. Happily, a recently developed test kitchen recipe for sautéed green beans gave us a good jump start.

Standard recipes for sautéed green beans call for parboiling the beans, then shocking them in ice water, drying them with paper towels, and finally sautéing them, but the test kitchen has found a way around all those steps. After cooking our way through pounds of beans, we learned we could get the same results using only a single large skillet. We briefly sautéed the beans until they were spotty brown but not yet cooked through, stirred in some garlic, then added ¼ cup of water to the pan. As soon as the water hit the skillet, it turned to steam, and we quickly covered the pan. After a few minutes, the beans were bright green but still slightly undercooked.

To ensure that these beans didn't taste like ordinary steamed beans, we removed the lid, then gave the beans a blast of heat. This quickly evaporated what little water was left in the pan and allowed us to establish a second browning before the beans fully cooked through. With our beans perfectly cooked, it was time to turn our attention to the add-ins that would take our beans to the next level.

To lend both texture and flavor, we agreed nuts were a good choice. We eventually settled on a sprinkling of walnuts (these nuts are particularly high in heart-healthy omega-3 fatty acids), and just 1 tablespoon per person was enough to provide noticeable texture and flavor without adding too many calories or too much fat. But a mere sprinkling of raw nuts over our perfectly cooked green beans tasted like an afterthought.

For our next test, we tried toasting the nuts first to deepen their flavor. To keep our recipe streamlined, we opted to toast the walnuts in the skillet before cooking the beans. Then, once our beans were done, we stirred the toasted walnuts back into the pan. This was a step in the right direction, but the dish still fell short. These nuts needed more of a boost.

What if we added warm spices to season the nuts—almost like making spiced nuts—with flavors that would complement the beans? We started again, this time adding just 1 tablespoon of butter to the skillet after the nuts had toasted for five minutes. We let the butter brown for a few minutes, a technique that gives it a faintly nutty flavor. To help the spices adhere to the nuts (and add an appealing hint of sweetness to complement the beans), we then stirred in 1 teaspoon of brown sugar. We tried numerous batches, bringing together a few different spices. Tasters settled on ground ginger (for warmth and kick) and a combination of black pepper and cayenne for two layers of heat.

These walnut-studded sautéed beans were quick to make and so much more flavorful than plain old steamed beans, we knew they would have no trouble winning fans.

Skillet Green Beans with Spiced Walnuts
SERVES 4

Yellow wax beans can be used in place of some or all of the green beans.

- ¼ cup walnuts, chopped coarse
- 1 tablespoon unsalted butter
- 1 teaspoon brown sugar
- ¼ teaspoon ground ginger
- Pinch cayenne pepper
- Salt and black pepper
- 2 teaspoons olive oil
- 1 pound green beans, trimmed
- ¼ cup water

1. Toast the walnuts in a 12-inch skillet over medium-low heat until golden, about 5 minutes. Add the butter and cook, stirring constantly, until the butter is browned, about 2 minutes. Stir in the sugar, ginger, cayenne, ⅛ teaspoon salt, and ⅛ teaspoon black pepper and cook until fragrant, about 30 seconds. Transfer the walnut mixture to a bowl and set aside. Wipe out the skillet with paper towels.

2. Heat the oil in the skillet over medium heat until just smoking. Add the green beans and ⅛ teaspoon salt and cook, stirring occasionally, until spotty brown, 4 to 6 minutes.

3. Add the water, cover, and cook until the green beans are bright green but still crisp, 2 to 3 minutes. Uncover, increase the heat to high, and continue to cook until the water evaporates and the beans are crisp-tender and lightly browned, 3 to 5 minutes longer.

4. Off the heat, stir in the reserved walnut mixture. Season with salt and black pepper to taste and serve.

PER SERVING: Cal 130; Fat 9g; Sat fat 2.5g; Chol 10mg; Carb 10g; Protein 3g; Fiber 4g; Sodium 150mg

GLAZED CARROTS

ALMOST EVERYONE HAS A BAG OF CARROTS LINGERING in the vegetable bin, waiting for the moment when a few are needed for a soup or a stew. But unless it is a holiday, few of us turn to carrots as a side dish, which is a shame because they are cheap, sturdy, and long-lasting, and when cooked properly they are both healthy and delicious. One of our favorite ways to prepare carrots is to glaze them—it's super-easy and fast and a great way to infuse them with flavor.

All too often, however, glazed carrots turn into a saccharine-sweet nightmare, adrift in a sea of syrup. The carrots are either limp and soggy from overcooking or raw and fibrous from undercooking. The recipes we tried, many of which were hopelessly dated, never delivered what we hoped for: tender, well-seasoned carrots with a light coating of glossy, bright glaze. We headed into the kitchen with bunches of carrots in hand, ready to rejuvenate this tired side dish.

We began by preparing the carrots for cooking. Though some recipes call for carrots cut into matchstick-size pieces, we ruled out this technique from the get-go. We were after simplicity, not improving our knife skills. So instead, we peeled regular bagged carrots (just as flavorful as pricier slender bunch carrots sold with the tops on), then cut them on the bias into handsome oval pieces for visual appeal.

Most recipes suggest that the carrots need to be steamed, parboiled, or blanched prior to glazing, but this results in a battery of dirtied utensils. With the goal of minimizing the work and thus the cookware, we opted to try a different approach. We put the carrots, along with ½ cup of water, in a 12-inch skillet, then added some salt and 1 tablespoon of sugar for flavor, covered the skillet, and simmered away. Mission accomplished—these carrots were cooked through without much ado. But they were severely lacking in flavor.

We looked at two components of our recipe that we could utilize to boost the flavor of our carrots: the cooking liquid and the sweetener. We tried swapping out the water for wine, but this turned our carrots sour and astringent. Next we tried chicken broth. It was a winner; the broth lent the carrots a savory backbone and full, round flavor that tasters approved. As for the sugar, we tested using a more compelling sweetener instead. Maple syrup proved too assertive, but honey imparted a floral flavor that worked well with the carrots' earthy sweetness and won tasters over. Satisfied with the flavor of the chicken broth and honey combination, we moved on to finessing the glaze's consistency.

At this point, our glaze was a little too thin and watery. For our next test, when the carrots had simmered for a few minutes and were just on the verge of becoming tender, we lifted the lid from the skillet, stepped up the heat, and let the liquid reduce. To encourage glaze formation and increase the sweetness and richness, we also added a pat of butter and another tablespoon of honey when we removed the lid. These adjustments resulted in a light, clingy glaze that was just rich enough without being too heavy (or caloric), and with a few more minutes of high-heat cooking it took on a pale amber hue and a light caramel flavor, just as we had hoped. We found that adding all of the honey at this point, rather than half in the beginning, further helped the glaze cling to the carrots. A squirt of fresh lemon juice gave the dish brightness, and a touch of freshly ground pepper provided depth.

Inspired by the success of our simple recipe, we created a few variations: one with freshly grated ginger and sliced almonds, one with orange and thyme, and another with a pinch of cayenne pepper and toasted pecans. We were surprised—as were our tasters—that glazed carrots could be this good yet still so easy.

HONEY-GLAZED CARROTS WITH GINGER AND ALMONDS

Honey-Glazed Carrots

SERVES 4

Look for evenly sized carrots, which make uniform slicing easier. You will need a 12-inch nonstick skillet with a tight-fitting lid for this recipe.

1½ pounds carrots, peeled and sliced ¼ inch thick on the bias (see photo)
½ cup low-sodium chicken broth
Salt
2 tablespoons honey
1 tablespoon unsalted butter
2 teaspoons fresh lemon juice
Pepper

1. Bring the carrots, broth, and ¼ teaspoon salt to a simmer in a 12-inch nonstick skillet over medium-high heat. Cover, reduce the heat to medium, and cook until the carrots are almost tender, about 5 minutes.

2. Uncover, increase the heat to high, and simmer rapidly until the liquid measures about 2 tablespoons, 2 to 3 minutes. Stir in the honey and butter and continue to cook, stirring often, until the carrots are completely tender and the sauce has reduced to a light golden glaze, about 4 minutes longer.

3. Off the heat, stir in the lemon juice, season with salt and pepper to taste, and serve.

PER SERVING: Cal 120; Fat 3g; Sat fat 2g; Chol 10mg; Carb 24g; Protein 2g; Fiber 4g; Sodium 350mg

VARIATIONS

Honey-Glazed Carrots with Ginger and Almonds

Follow the recipe for Honey-Glazed Carrots, adding 2 teaspoons grated or minced fresh ginger to the skillet with the carrots. Stir in 2 tablespoons toasted sliced almonds with the lemon juice.

PER SERVING: Cal 140; Fat 4g; Sat fat 2g; Chol 10mg; Carb 25g; Protein 3g; Fiber 5g; Sodium 350mg

Honey-Glazed Carrots with Orange and Thyme

Follow the recipe for Honey-Glazed Carrots, adding 1 teaspoon minced fresh thyme and ½ teaspoon grated orange zest to the skillet with the carrots. Substitute ¼ cup orange juice for ¼ cup of the broth. Omit the lemon juice.

PER SERVING: Cal 130; Fat 3g; Sat fat 2g; Chol 10mg; Carb 26g; Protein 2g; Fiber 4g; Sodium 310mg

Spicy Honey-Glazed Carrots with Pecans

Follow the recipe for Honey-Glazed Carrots, adding a pinch cayenne pepper to the skillet with the carrots. Stir in 2 tablespoons coarsely chopped toasted pecans with the lemon juice.

PER SERVING: Cal 150; Fat 5g; Sat fat 2g; Chol 10mg; Carb 25g; Protein 3g; Fiber 5g; Sodium 350mg

---

NOTES FROM THE TEST KITCHEN

SLICING CARROTS ON THE BIAS

Cut the carrots on the bias into pieces that are ¼ inch thick and 2 inches long.

A PRO OF A PEELER

A recent survey of peelers on the market turned up more than 25 different styles. We set out to find the best of the best—a comfortable peeler that would make quick work of a wide variety of tasks. For the most part, vegetable peelers fall into two main categories: traditional peelers (whose blade is in line with the handle) and Y-shaped peelers (whose blade sits perpendicular to the handle). We found that these design variations made quite a difference. The traditional peelers were comfortable and slick, especially when used for delicate tasks such as peeling carrots. On the other hand, Y-shaped peelers proved their mettle by mowing over thick-skinned fruits and vegetables. In the end, the **Messermeister Pro-Touch Swivel Peeler**, $6.95, passed every peeling test with flying colors and had a comfortable grip, even after we'd peeled pounds of apples and potatoes. At 1.5 ounces, this sharp peeler is so light that hand strain is never a problem.

MAPLE-GLAZED BRUSSELS SPROUTS

MAPLE-GLAZED BRUSSELS SPROUTS

BRUSSELS SPROUTS GET A BAD RAP—BUT THAT'S NO surprise since they are almost always poorly prepared. Boiled to death, as is all too often their fate, they turn out limp and bitter. However, when properly cooked, Brussels sprouts are crisp, tender, and have a nutty flavor that can win over kids and adults alike. Wanting to rid this vegetable of its bad reputation, we set our sights on finding a simple method for cooking the sprouts and a light recipe that would appeal to the whole family. We quickly settled on developing a recipe for maple-glazed sprouts, which sounded like a guaranteed hit with all audiences and a great flavor profile for a fall or winter side dish. Of course, we'd have to find the right balance between savory and sweet and at the same time keep the calories in check.

There were a few basics about shopping for Brussels sprouts that we kept in mind from the get-go. The best Brussels sprouts are available in late fall through early winter, peaking in late November (they are often associated with the holidays because of their short season). When buying Brussels sprouts, choose those with small, tight heads, no more than 1½ inches in diameter, for the best flavor. Larger sprouts can often be trimmed of loose leaves along the stem and still be quite good. Look for firm, compact, bright green Brussels sprouts. Yellow or brown-tipped leaves usually indicate that they are older. Once purchased, sprouts can be stored in the refrigerator for four to five days but no longer.

With a few bags of perfect-looking Brussels sprouts in hand, it was time to get started. Fortunately, we had a jump-start on a winning method for cooking our sprouts. The test kitchen had recently developed a stovetop method for braising them, which offered the added bonus of creating a flavorful sauce from the cooking liquid to serve with the sprouts. Since poor cooking technique can turn Brussels sprouts mushy and sulfurous, we paid close attention to the details. Some recipes recommend cooking the sprouts whole, others halved, and many others with an X scored into the sprouts' stem end—that last, it's said, for even cooking. We put them all to the test both in a braising recipe and by simply boiling average-size sprouts (1 to 1½ inches in length) in salted water. The whole sprouts flunked. They took nearly 15 minutes to cook, and by the time the core was tender, the exterior was army green, mushy, and sulfurous. The halved sprouts not only cooked

faster (in 6 to 8 minutes) and more evenly, but the exposed interiors soaked up seasoning. Did X mark the spot? Not so much. While the scored sprouts cooked slightly faster (in about 13 minutes) than the whole sprouts, again the exterior overcooked before the inside was done.

In the end, when developing this basic braising method, we had found that braising 1 pound of sprouts, cut in half lengthwise, in a 12-inch skillet with ¼ cup of chicken broth (which tasters favored over both water and wine for a deeper flavor) until just tender proved best. We then removed the lid and reduced the cooking liquid to a sauce. Stirring in 1 tablespoon of butter and some sugar helped bring this sauce together and caramelize the sprouts. These Brussels sprouts were tender, nutty-flavored, and bright green. So for our maple-glazed version, we just needed to focus on incorporating the syrup.

We thought it would be a simple swap, but when we used maple syrup in place of sugar, the sweetness came through, but not the maple flavor. Increasing the volume of maple syrup turned the sprouts candy-sweet, and still without noticeably intensifying the maple flavor. We wondered if we would have better luck adding the maple syrup sooner by combining it with the braising liquid. Indeed we did—adding 2 tablespoons of syrup to the chicken broth (which we cut by the same amount) seasoned the Brussels sprouts from the inside out. The addition of butter at the end gave the sprouts the polished, glazed finish they needed.

The flavor was maple-y, but it also struck tasters as one-dimensional, in need of a component to balance the sweetness. We tested using orange and lemon juice,

---

NOTES FROM THE TEST KITCHEN

BUYING MAPLE SYRUP
The syrup options these days can be daunting. There are the imitation pancake syrups like Mrs. Butterworth's and Log Cabin (basically high-fructose corn syrup laced with maple flavoring), and there's real maple syrup, which is sold as grade A (in light, medium, and dark amber) and darker grade B, often called "cooking syrup." Tasters unanimously panned the imitation stuff. Among the real syrups, they preferred dark with intense maple flavor to the delicate, pricey grade A light amber. The favorite was **Maple Grove Farms Pure Maple Syrup**, a grade A dark amber, but our runner-up, Highland Sugarworks, a grade B syrup, is great for those looking for even bolder maple flavor.

as well as white and balsamic vinegars, in place of the chicken broth. All worked well, but in the end equal amounts of fruity cider vinegar and maple syrup fit together hand in glove. Fresh thyme and a dash of fiery cayenne pepper rounded out the flavors beautifully.

We thought we were finished, but several tasters commented that, while they liked the braising method, one thing they missed with these Brussels sprouts was the browned, caramelized edges you always get with roasted Brussels sprouts. In an effort to please everyone, for the next batch we browned the sprouts in just 2 teaspoons of olive oil at the outset before adding the liquid (and consequently we reduced the simmering time slightly). We found that taking a minute to arrange the Brussels sprouts cut side down went a long way toward encouraging browning. After we removed the lid and let the liquid reduce, we stirred in the finishing drizzle of vinegar and a tablespoon of butter for the glossy coating and final punch of flavor.

This recipe was so easy, so perfectly sweet and savory, that we felt confident that the reputation of Brussels sprouts was about to take a turn for the better.

Maple-Glazed Brussels Sprouts

SERVES 4

Choose Brussels sprouts with small, tight heads, no more than 1½ inches in diameter. Be careful not to cut too much off the stem end when trimming the sprouts, or the leaves will fall away from the core. Use pure maple syrup, not pancake syrup.

- 2 teaspoons olive oil
- 1 pound Brussels sprouts, trimmed, discolored leaves removed, and halved through the stems (see note)
- 2 tablespoons plus 1 teaspoon cider vinegar
- 2 tablespoons maple syrup
- 1 teaspoon minced fresh thyme
  Salt
  Pinch cayenne pepper
- 1 tablespoon unsalted butter
  Black pepper

1. Heat the oil in a 12-inch nonstick skillet over medium heat until shimmering. Add the Brussels sprouts, cut side down, and cook, stirring occasionally, until browned, 5 to 7 minutes. Stir in 2 tablespoons of the vinegar, maple syrup, thyme, ¼ teaspoon salt, and

cayenne. Reduce the heat to medium-low, cover, and cook until the Brussels sprouts are bright green and nearly tender, 6 to 8 minutes.

2. Uncover, increase the heat to medium-high, and continue to cook until the liquid is nearly evaporated, 3 to 5 minutes longer.

3. Off the heat, stir in the remaining 1 teaspoon vinegar and butter. Season with salt and black pepper to taste and serve.

PER SERVING: Cal 120; Fat 5g; Sat fat 2.5g; Chol 10mg; Carb 17g; Protein 4g; Fiber 4g; Sodium 180mg

ZUCCHINI AND TOMATO GRATIN

WHEN SUMMER'S BUMPER CROP OF ZUCCHINI AND tomatoes comes around each year, we inevitably end up looking for new ways to showcase the produce's fresh flavors. Making a simple, light vegetable gratin is a great option for an elegant yet simple dish that showcases the best of both ingredients. Though it is essentially a simple combination of vegetables layered in a casserole and baked with either a bread-crumb or cheese topping, many versions and variations of vegetable gratins exist. We are particularly fond of the Provençal-style version, in which the summer vegetables are perfumed with olive oil and thyme and finished off with a crust of Gruyère cheese. We knew the trick to a great vegetable gratin would be finding how to ensure perfectly cooked vegetables; mushy, watery, or undercooked vegetables would not do. We would also need to balance our ingredients carefully; we wanted to make the most of the flavorful olive oil and Gruyère yet avoid making our dish too fatty.

In our research, we found a couple of ways to prepare vegetable gratins. In one method, the vegetables are simply layered and baked. In the other, the dish is lined with caramelized onions (and sometimes garlic) and the vegetables placed on top. After trying both styles, tasters unanimously opted for the dish augmented with sweet caramelized onions.

The obvious starting point was the first layer, the onions. Using yellow onions (which we know from past test kitchen tests caramelize well and have great flavor), we tested both dicing and slicing. Tasters preferred the way the sliced onions looked, and since we didn't notice any difference in flavor between sliced and diced caramelized onions, we settled on the sliced since it was less work. As we had learned when making our White Bean Gratin (page 216), we cooked the sliced onions in olive oil with a little brown sugar and salt over medium-high heat to jump-start their release of moisture. We then turned the heat down and continued to cook the onions over moderate heat for 20 to 25 minutes until they were dark golden and caramelized. We also added some minced garlic toward the end of cooking to achieve a fuller, more aromatic flavor.

Next we focused on the tomatoes and squash. Size was important to evenly cooked and attractive rows of vegetables in the finished dish, so we chose plum tomatoes because their diameter most closely resembled that of the squash. We also sought out squash that were about the same size. Next we tested slicing the vegetables at various widths to find the right thickness for our gratin. Vegetables sliced ½ inch thick and ¼ inch thick simply took too long to cook. Slicing them ⅛ inch thick turned out to be just right. But after five minutes of precise cutting, we had barely accumulated enough slices to get the first row finished. Putting our knife aside, we turned to our mandoline, which allowed us to slice all the vegetables perfectly in seconds. (We found that a food processor fitted with the ⅛ inch slicing blade also worked reasonably well, although, because of the quickness of the machine, there was less control.)

With our vegetables ready to go, it was time for assembly. Alternating the slices and keeping them fairly tightly shingled proved to be an easier task than we had thought, and we managed to cover the entire baking dish quickly. We brushed 1 tablespoon of olive oil over the vegetables and sprinkled them with fresh thyme. Our gratin was ready for the oven.

Baking a layered vegetable gratin is usually a two-step process. First the assembled recipe (minus the cheese) goes into the oven until the vegetables are cooked. Then the gratin is sprinkled with shredded cheese and cooked again until the whole gratin is bubbling and the cheese has browned. In our first test, the vegetables were perfectly cooked after the first step, but by the time the cheese was done after the second round in the oven, the vegetables had overcooked and turned dull in color. Partially cooking the vegetables in step one didn't improve things—in fact, our gratin was even worse, as the vegetables turned dry and chewy after the second round in the oven.

Following the advice of a few recipes, we next tried covering the baking dish with foil for the first step. We worried about ending up with soggy vegetables, but surprisingly, it was the answer to our problem. The foil traps the heat and thus partially steams the vegetables. When the gratin emerged, the vegetables were only partially cooked, but they still contained moisture, which, it turns out, is key. Then we topped our gratin with cheese (a mere 2 ounces of Gruyère produced great flavor without packing on fat) and slid the dish back into the oven, uncovered. We checked the gratin every 5 minutes and found that 25 minutes produced a perfect vegetable gratin—soft, caramelized onions topped with bright, tender tomatoes and squash, and a browned and bubbling crust of cheese.

Zucchini and Tomato Gratin
SERVES 6

Try to buy vegetables that are roughly 2 inches in diameter. Slicing the vegetables ⅛ inch thick is crucial for the success of this dish; use a mandoline, V-slicer, or food processor fitted with a ⅛-inch slicing blade.

- 2 tablespoons extra-virgin olive oil
- 4 onions, halved and sliced thin
- 1 teaspoon brown sugar
  Salt
- 2 garlic cloves, minced
- 1 zucchini (about 8 ounces), ends trimmed, sliced crosswise into ⅛-inch-thick slices
- 1 yellow summer squash (about 8 ounces), ends trimmed, sliced crosswise into ⅛-inch-thick slices
- 1 pound plum tomatoes (4 to 6 tomatoes), cored and sliced ⅛ inch thick
- 1 teaspoon minced fresh thyme
  Pepper
- 2 ounces Gruyère cheese, shredded (about ½ cup)

1. Heat 1 tablespoon of the oil in a 12-inch nonstick skillet over medium-high heat until shimmering. Add the onions, sugar, and ¼ teaspoon salt and cook, stirring often, until softened, 5 to 7 minutes. Reduce the heat to medium-low and continue to cook, stirring often, until the onions are golden and caramelized, 20 to 25 minutes longer. Stir in the garlic and cook until fragrant, about 30 seconds; set aside off the heat.

2. Lightly coat a 13 by 9-inch baking dish with vegetable oil spray. Adjust an oven rack to the middle position and heat the oven to 375 degrees. Spread the

MAKING VEGETABLE GRATIN

Alternately shingle the vegetables—zucchini, yellow squash, and tomatoes—tightly on top of the onions in tidy, attractive rows.

onion mixture in the prepared baking dish. Following the photo, alternately shingle the sliced zucchini, yellow squash, and tomatoes on top of the onions.

3. Brush the tops of the vegetables with the remaining 1 tablespoon oil. Sprinkle with the thyme and season with salt and pepper to taste. Cover the dish tightly with foil and bake until the vegetables are almost tender, about 30 minutes.

4. Remove the foil, sprinkle with the cheese, and continue to bake until bubbling around the edges and lightly browned on top, 20 to 30 minutes longer. Let cool for 10 minutes before serving.

PER SERVING: Cal 140; Fat 9g; Sat fat 2.5g; Chol 10mg; Carb 13g; Protein 5g; Fiber 3g; Sodium 140mg

VARIATION

Zucchini, Tomato, and Potato Gratin

Follow the recipe for Zucchini and Tomato Gratin, substituting 1 pound russet potatoes (2 medium), peeled and sliced ⅛ inch thick, for the yellow squash.

PER SERVING: Cal 200; Fat 9g; Sat fat 2.5g; Chol 10mg; Carb 26g; Protein 6g; Fiber 4g; Sodium 140mg

CHEESY CAULIFLOWER BAKE

EVEN IF YOU'RE NOT A FAN OF CAULIFLOWER, YOU probably like cauliflower casserole. A rich, creamy white sauce with cheese bubbles and browns over the tender florets, and a cascade of toasty, crisp bread crumbs adds contrast and crunch. But all that saucy, cheesy, 1950s-style casserole appeal is (no surprise) a fat and calorie bomb—a single serving weighs in at 310 calories

TEST KITCHEN **MAKEOVER**

and 24 grams of fat. Could we lighten up this vegetable side dish without losing all its appeal?

A casserole may seem like a no-brainer sort of recipe, but in reality, getting a casserole right—cauliflower casserole included—takes some care. If you overcook the cauliflower, as in several recipes we tried, it tastes so waterlogged and sulfurous that no amount of sauce could disguise the problem. If you are heavy-handed with the cream (full-fat, low-fat, or otherwise), as many recipes are, the cauliflower virtually drowns. And if you neglect the bread crumbs, merely tossing them atop the casserole with scant thought given to seasoning, you'll taste the lack. We imagined a lighter casserole with fresh cauliflower flavor, seasoned bread crumbs, and a cheesy sauce with a sharp bite.

We decided to start by finding the best method to cook the cauliflower (we'd use full-fat recipes for now and tackle lightening the dish later). A fairly standard recipe we came across called for boiling and draining 12 cups of cauliflower florets, then stirring them into a sauce made from 2 tablespoons each of butter and flour, 2 cups of heavy cream, and 1 cup of mild cheddar cheese. In an attempt to keep things simple, we tried skipping the boiling and simply added raw cauliflower florets to the sauce. Although we baked the casserole for nearly an hour, the cauliflower never entirely lost its crunch. For our next test, we boiled the florets for about five minutes until they were not quite tender. We added the parboiled florets to the sauce with the idea that they'd finish cooking in the oven. This method did produce cauliflower with spot-on texture, but tasters found its flavor washed out.

The test kitchen has had success "boiling" potatoes for mashed potatoes directly in cream as a way to boost their flavor. We decided we should try that method with our cauliflower. We made the white sauce—sautéing the butter and flour, then gradually adding the cream. We stirred in the raw cauliflower florets, covered the pot, and simmered the mixture until the cauliflower was nearly tender. At that point we added the cheese, transferred the mixture to a casserole dish, topped it with bread crumbs (we'd perfect those later), and baked the whole thing for about 15 minutes. We were finally on target. But now a big question arose: Could we get the same appeal once we started lightening the recipe? It was time to find out.

We began with the rich sauce, and the cream in particular. We tried making it with half-and-half, whole milk, and evaporated milk, then various products in combination. But no matter what we did, tasters said the same thing: The sauce was one-dimensional. Maybe dairy wasn't the answer. On a hunch, we reached for a can of chicken broth. A few tests later, we'd landed on a combination of ¾ cup of broth and 1¼ cups of whole milk that worked well. The sauce lost some richness yet gained depth, and as a bonus, the cauliflower that simmered in it picked up even more flavor because of the broth.

But when we ran the nutritional numbers, we realized even whole milk was not going to make the cut. Looking for another way to knock down the fat, we tried to find a dairy substitute for the whole milk. Skim milk broke into a curdled mess; 2 percent milk fared better, but it still curdled. The latter seemed like our best hope if we could find a stabilizer to fix the curdling and if we could give the sauce some more body. One tablespoon of cornstarch helped immensely in stabilizing and thickening our sauce, but it still lacked the creamy richness tasters wanted. We then turned to an unlikely ingredient that the test kitchen has used successfully to add creamy richness to a lightened scalloped potato recipe we'd previously developed: light cream cheese. Once again, the cream cheese saved the day. Just 3 tablespoons added the right amount of silkiness to the sauce, giving the illusion of creaminess without all of the calories or fat. We rounded out the sauce with garlic, thyme, and dry mustard. Our light yet cheesy casserole was looking good.

Up until this point, we had been adding 1 cup of mild cheddar—but with this small amount, could we really call our cauliflower casserole "cheesy"? Even when we doubled the amount of cheese, its presence remained surprisingly faint, and it ratcheted up the calories and fat we had worked hard to knock down. We were curious to see if other, bolder cheese varieties might elevate the flavor in our recipe and at the same time allow us to use less. We tested several other cheeses in the casserole, alone and in combination. Ultimately, tasters voted for ¾ cup of extra-sharp cheddar for assertive bite plus 1 cup of Parmesan, which added a rich, nutty flavor. "Cheesy" accomplished.

We had been topping the casserole with a scattering of bread crumbs tossed with 2 teaspoons of olive oil. Aside from some crunch, they brought little to the table. But with a clove of minced garlic and a portion of the cheeses that we held back from the sauce mixed in, the bread crumbs became flavorful and ably shouldered

more responsibility. Our revamped cauliflower casserole had a mere 160 calories and 7 grams of fat per serving, and we finally had what the test kitchen expected from this retro comfort food, minus the guilt.

MAKEOVER SPOTLIGHT: CHEESY CAULIFLOWER BAKE

	CALORIES	FAT	SAT FAT	CHOLESTEROL
BEFORE	310	24g	15g	75mg
AFTER	160	7g	4g	20mg

Cheesy Cauliflower Bake

SERVES 10

Make sure to gently simmer the cauliflower, partially covered, so the milk does not boil over and separate.

    3   slices high-quality white sandwich bread, torn
        into pieces
    2   teaspoons olive oil
    3   ounces extra-sharp cheddar cheese, shredded
        (about ¾ cup)
    2   ounces Parmesan cheese, grated (about 1 cup)
    3   garlic cloves, minced
        Salt and pepper
 1¼   cups 2 percent milk
    ¾   cup low-sodium chicken broth
    2   teaspoons dry mustard
    1   teaspoon minced fresh thyme
    2   heads cauliflower (about 4 pounds), trimmed, cored,
        and cut into ¾-inch florets (about 12 cups) (see
        page 236)
    1   tablespoon cornstarch
    1   tablespoon water
    3   tablespoons light cream cheese

1. Adjust an oven rack to the middle position and heat the oven to 400 degrees. Pulse the bread in a food processor to coarse crumbs, about 10 pulses. Transfer the crumbs to a bowl and toss with the oil. Spread the crumbs on a rimmed baking sheet and bake, stirring occasionally, until golden brown and dry, 7 to 9 minutes.

2. Transfer the crumbs to a clean bowl and cool to room temperature. Stir 2 tablespoons of the cheddar, ¼ cup of the Parmesan, 1 teaspoon of the garlic, ¼ teaspoon salt, and ¼ teaspoon pepper into the cooled crumbs and set aside.

3. Meanwhile, turn the oven to 450 degrees. Whisk the remaining garlic, milk, broth, mustard, thyme, ¼ teaspoon salt, and ¼ teaspoon pepper together in a Dutch oven. Stir in the cauliflower and bring to a simmer over medium-high heat. Reduce the heat to low, partially cover, and simmer, stirring occasionally, until the cauliflower is nearly tender, 5 to 7 minutes.

4. Whisk the cornstarch and water together, then add to the pot, bring to a simmer, and cook, stirring

constantly, until the sauce has thickened slightly, about 2 minutes. Off the heat, stir in the remaining ⅔ cup cheddar, remaining ¾ cup Parmesan, and cream cheese until incorporated.

5. Pour the cauliflower mixture into a 13 by 9-inch baking dish and top evenly with the bread-crumb mixture. Bake until bubbling and the crumbs are well browned and crisp, 8 to 12 minutes. Let cool for 10 minutes before serving.

PER SERVING: **Cal** 160; **Fat** 7g; **Sat fat** 4g; **Chol** 20mg; **Carb** 16g; **Protein** 10g; **Fiber** 5g; **Sodium** 420mg

---

NOTES FROM THE TEST KITCHEN

CUTTING CAULIFLOWER INTO FLORETS

1. Pull off any leaves, then cut out the core of the cauliflower using a paring knife.

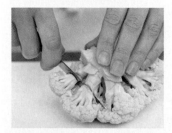

2. Separate the florets from the inner stem using the tip of a paring knife.

3. Cut the larger florets into smaller pieces by slicing them through the stem.

OUR FAVORITE SUPERMARKET PARMESAN

Can domestic Parmesan really stand up to imported Parmigiano-Reggiano? Simply put, no, it cannot. Our tasters effortlessly picked out the imports in our lineup of eight supermarket cheeses. The two genuine Parmigiano-Reggianos, sold by Boar's Head and Il Villaggio, were the clear favorites, and tasters deemed **Boar's Head Parmigiano-Reggiano** "best in show."

PUREED BUTTERNUT SQUASH

WITH ITS SILKY-SMOOTH TEXTURE AND EARTHY, lightly sweetened flavor, pureed butternut squash is a serious crowd-pleaser. Most recipes for pureed squash are similar in that the squash is cooked until tender, then pureed with some butter and/or cream in a food processor. Our questions about making a lightened recipe for pureed squash were fairly straightforward: Does the cooking method matter? What kind of dairy would deliver on taste without packing on the fat?

To start, we pitted four cooking methods against one another: roasting, steaming, braising, and microwaving. Looking for both ease and the best flavor, we found that roasting took too long (over an hour), and steaming and braising washed away some of the distinct squash flavor. Microwaving, however, in addition to being one of the easiest cooking methods, won tasters over for producing a clean, sweet squash flavor.

Next, we fussed with the best way to prepare the squash for the microwave. We tried microwaving it whole, halved, and cut into large chunks. Microwaving the squash whole was a disaster—it cooked unevenly and the puree tasted seedy. Microwaving squash halves worked better, but they were still somewhat unevenly cooked. Microwaving the peeled chunks of squash, luckily, worked very well, cooking evenly if they were given a simple toss halfway through cooking. We tried to save time by buying prepeeled chunks of squash, but we were sorely disappointed with the much less flavorful results.

After we microwaved and drained the squash (surprisingly, it released nearly ½ cup of liquid when cooked), it was time to puree it in the food processor with the dairy. We found that the squash puree needed only a small amount of dairy to help round out its flavor and add some complexity. Testing various types of dairy alone and in combination—including butter, heavy cream, half-and-half, and sour cream—we found the ideal flavor in a mix of butter and half-and-half; it added just enough richness to the puree without overpowering the squash flavor or tipping the calorie or fat scales. One squash (about 2 pounds) needs only 2 tablespoons of half-and-half and 1 tablespoon of butter.

Still, one nagging problem remained—some tasters complained that the puree was too thick, which made it seem heavy and gloppy. Not wanting to add more half-and-half, we wondered if we could skip draining the squash after microwaving it and use the released liquid to loosen the puree. We chopped up another butternut squash and gave it a try. While the resulting puree was certainly looser, the liquid had given our recipe an unappealing, slightly bitter flavor. Next we tested batches made by adding water and chicken broth to the food processor while it pureed. Chicken broth masked the flavor of the squash and tasted too chicken-y. Plain old water was the winner—our puree tasted clean and earthy, and the squash took center stage. We tested varying amounts of water and found that an additional 2 tablespoons was all it took to achieve a light consistency in our pureed squash. To complement the squash's sweetness, we found that 1 tablespoon of brown sugar lent just the right maple-y flavor and finished our dish perfectly.

Pureed Butternut Squash

SERVES 4

Don't buy precut squash for this recipe—the squash is usually dried out and fibrous. You can substitute delicata squash for the butternut squash.

- 1 **butternut squash (about 2 pounds), peeled, seeded, and cut into 1½-inch chunks (see photos)**
- 2 **tablespoons water**
- 2 **tablespoons half-and-half**
- 1 **tablespoon unsalted butter**
- 1 **tablespoon brown sugar**
  Salt and pepper

1. Place the squash in a large microwave-safe bowl. Cover the bowl and microwave on high until the squash

is tender and easily pierced with a fork, 15 to 20 minutes, stirring halfway through cooking.

2. Using potholders, drain the squash, then transfer to a food processor. Add the water, half-and-half, butter, sugar, and ½ teaspoon salt. Process the mixture until smooth, about 20 seconds, scraping down the bowl if necessary. Season with salt and pepper to taste and serve.

PER ½-CUP SERVING: **Cal** 150; **Fat** 4g; **Sat fat** 2.5g; **Chol** 10mg; **Carb** 30g; **Protein** 2g; **Fiber** 5g; **Sodium** 300mg

VARIATION

Pureed Butternut Squash with Sage and Toasted Almonds

Cook 1 tablespoon butter with 1½ teaspoons minced fresh sage in a small skillet over medium-low heat until fragrant, about 2 minutes. Follow the recipe for Pureed Butternut Squash, substituting the sage butter for the butter. Sprinkle 3 tablespoons toasted sliced almonds over the squash before serving.

PER ½-CUP SERVING: **Cal** 180; **Fat** 6g; **Sat fat** 2.5g; **Chol** 10mg; **Carb** 31g; **Protein** 3g; **Fiber** 5g; **Sodium** 300mg

NOTES FROM THE TEST KITCHEN

PREPARING BUTTERNUT SQUASH

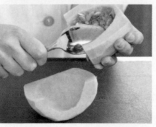
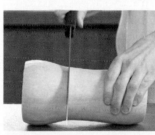

1. After removing the stem and root ends, cut the squash in half crosswise where the thinner neck meets the thicker base.

2. Use a vegetable peeler or paring knife to peel the skin from the squash, then cut the base in half to expose the seeds.

3. Use a large spoon to scrape the seeds and stringy pulp from the base of the squash. Chop each piece of squash as desired.

MASHED POTATOES

TEST KITCHEN
MAKEOVER

WHAT'S NOT TO LOVE ABOUT CREAMY, BUTTERY mashed potatoes? They are rich-tasting and easy to make, and they pair well with a wide variety of entrees. The problem, of course, is that this dish is notoriously fat-laden (a typical recipe can contain upward of 280 calories and 19 grams of fat), which is why it is often reserved for special occasions. We wanted to give mashed potatoes a makeover, but we still wanted the results to taste rich and silky. Sure, we could strip out the butter and cream and use skim milk, but we wanted our spuds to actually taste good. Enter buttermilk.

Some recipe writers tout buttermilk as a miracle ingredient for mashed potatoes, claiming that this naturally lean product (it has 110 calories and 2.5 grams of fat per cup, compared to the 830 calories and 89 grams of fat in an equal amount of cream) works such wonders it actually creates the illusion of butter and cream. What's the secret to getting buttermilk mashed potatoes just right? We headed to the test kitchen to find out.

A few tests proved that simply replacing the butter and cream with buttermilk doesn't work (unless you like curdled, parched spuds). The butterless, creamless recipes we tested may have been low-calorie, but they were so curdled, crumbly, chalky, and dry that we wouldn't consider eating them.

We sketched out a plan: First and foremost, we were going to add some butter. Because of the flavorful, creamy buttermilk, we wouldn't need to add a truckload, but we decided that almost-fat-free potatoes just aren't worth choking down. Second, we wanted an everyday recipe, streamlined enough for frequent dinner-table appearances. We also had to develop a curdle-proof technique. While most recipes instruct the cook to heat the buttermilk, what resulted was an unappealing mix of watery, coagulated liquid and grainy curds.

Tackling the curdling problem first, we tried to skip the heating step, but that wasn't the answer: Buttermilk curdles at 160 degrees, a temperature it reached almost instantly when it hit the steaming-hot potatoes. For our next batch, we pulled out an instant-read thermometer and added the buttermilk to the potatoes when they dropped below the 160-degree mark. This worked, but talk about fussy. We kept searching for a viable solution and came across sources suggesting pinches of baking soda (to neutralize acidity) or cornstarch (for stability). Neither trick worked. We knew that higher-fat dairy products like half-and-half aren't prone to curdling. What if we fattened up the buttermilk just a smidge (aware that we were still after keeping this recipe light) with some melted butter? Bingo. When mixed with room-temperature buttermilk, the melted butter acted as an insulating agent, with the fat coating the proteins in the buttermilk and protecting them from heat shock.

In previous tests, the test kitchen found that simmering whole russet potatoes in their jackets yields true potato flavor and a rich, silky texture; peeled and cut russets cook up with a thin taste and texture. But still, we liked the idea of the simpler, quicker-cooking peeled and cut potatoes. We wondered if switching the variety of potato we were using would make a difference. Peeled and cut red potatoes were dense and pasty when mashed, but peeled and cut Yukon Golds made creamy, smooth mashed potatoes. Why did the Yukon Golds behave so differently from the russets? Russet potatoes have more starch and therefore absorb a lot more water than lower-starch Yukon Golds. So while mashed russets become soggy if peeled and cut before cooking, the less absorbent Yukon Golds turn out just right.

Settling on amounts of butter and buttermilk was a delicate balancing act. Too much butter obscured the buttermilk flavor (not to mention it put us in danger of making our light recipe too fatty); too little tasted too lean. After many trials, we settled on 3 tablespoons of butter and ⅔ cup of buttermilk. These amounts allowed plenty of buttermilk tang to shine through without overwhelming or adding too much fat.

While the flavor of the potatoes was good, tasters were craving a bit more creaminess. Adding more butter was out of the question, so we tried adding some low-fat sour cream. Just ¼ cup folded in along with the butter and buttermilk gave our potatoes the creamy consistency we were after—and we didn't have to think twice when we wanted to go back for seconds.

MAKEOVER SPOTLIGHT: MASHED POTATOES

	CALORIES	FAT	SAT FAT	CHOLESTEROL
BEFORE	280	19g	14g	55mg
AFTER	200	6g	4g	20mg

BUTTERMILK MASHED POTATOES

To achieve the proper texture, it is important to cook the potatoes thoroughly; they are done if they break apart when a knife is inserted and gently wiggled. To reduce the chance of curdling, the buttermilk must be at room temperature when mixed with the cooled melted butter.

> 2 **pounds Yukon Gold potatoes (about 4 medium), peeled and sliced ½ inch thick**
> **Salt**
> ⅔ **cup buttermilk, at room temperature**
> 3 **tablespoons unsalted butter, melted and cooled**
> ¼ **cup low-fat sour cream, at room temperature**
> **Pepper**

1. Place the potatoes and 1 tablespoon salt in a large saucepan, add enough water to cover the potatoes by 1 inch, and bring to a simmer over high heat. Reduce the heat to medium-low and cook gently until the potatoes are tender but not falling apart, 15 to 18 minutes.

2. Drain the potatoes and return to the saucepan set on the still-hot burner. Using a potato masher, mash the potatoes until just a few small lumps remain. Gently stir the buttermilk and cooled butter together in a bowl until combined. Fold the buttermilk mixture and sour cream into the potatoes until just incorporated. Season with salt and pepper to taste and serve.

PER ⅔-CUP SERVING: Cal 200; Fat 6g; Sat fat 4g; Chol 20mg; Carb 28g; Protein 5g; Fiber 2g; Sodium 140mg

ROASTED SWEET POTATO WEDGES

ROASTING VEGETABLES IS ONE OF THE MOST FLAVOR-ful ways to cook them—it concentrates their flavor, coaxing out and intensifying their natural sugars—and as a bonus, it's also a naturally low-fat method because only a modest amount of oil is required. The recipe for roasting vegetables, if it can be called one, is basic and fairly universal: Toss vegetables in oil, season, throw onto baking sheet, roast at 450 degrees. But sweet potatoes don't work with this one-size-fits-all method. If you roast sweet potatoes this way, they usually taste washed out despite their abundant natural sugars. On top of that, thin wedges cook unevenly and become soggy inside and leathery outside. They never develop the caramelized exterior, creamy interior, and intense flavor of other roasted vegetables. With all their potential, we thought it was time to perfect a recipe for roasted sweet potato wedges.

We solved two of these problems right off the bat. First, we peeled the sweet potatoes; the leathery skins were history. Then we made the decision to cut them into thicker, more uniform wedges. Next, we turned our attention to the sogginess and lack of browning, which proved more formidable problems. As sweet potatoes cook, moisture leaks out, so the potatoes end up stewing in their own liquid instead of roasting—which means they never brown. (There's a complicated scientific explanation that concerns maltose, the boiling point of sugar solutions, evaporation, and more. The upshot is that sweet potatoes leak a sugary syrup that inhibits dry-roasting.)

To raise the potatoes out of that liquid, we roasted them on a wire rack set over a baking sheet, which took about 40 minutes. As we'd hoped, the potatoes were drier, but since they never came into contact with the hot baking sheet, they were pale and not particularly sweet. For our next attempt, we started the potatoes out on the rack, then after 30 minutes we wiped the baking sheet dry, dumped the potatoes directly on it, and returned them to the oven to caramelize the exterior right on the hot sheet. But by the time the potatoes developed any color—about 10 minutes per side—the insides were overcooked mush. Plus the potatoes stuck to the sheet pan. Tossing the potatoes with oil after their stint on the rack solved the sticking. To prevent over-cooking, we tried a shorter rack roasting period, but now we had the opposite problem: The outsides burned before the insides softened.

Maybe we could keep the temperature low while the potatoes were on the rack to prevent overcooking and then increase the heat to caramelize the outside once they were on the baking sheet. We turned the oven down to 325 degrees. After 30 minutes on the rack, the wedges looked weirdly dehydrated. Fearing the worst, we went ahead and cranked up the heat to

475 and let the oven come to temperature. For good measure, we put the baking sheet in the oven to heat up, too. Meanwhile, the partly cooked sweet potatoes sat on the counter on the wire rack. After 10 minutes, we tossed the wedges with the oil (any sooner and they soaked it up, tasted greasy, and stuck to the pan to boot), seasonings, and a little sugar to accelerate browning. Back in the oven they went. Twenty minutes and one flip later, they were creamy, tender, golden brown, and deeply sweet. Our method is unconventional, but you can't argue with success.

Roasted Sweet Potato Wedges

SERVES 6

Make sure to let the potatoes cool for 10 minutes before tossing with the oil. If the potatoes are too hot, they will absorb the oil and stick.

- 3 medium sweet potatoes (about 12 ounces each), peeled
- 1 tablespoon canola oil
- 2 teaspoons sugar
     Salt and pepper

1. Adjust an oven rack to the middle position and heat the oven to 325 degrees. Cut each potato in half crosswise, then cut each half into 6 to 8 wedges. Arrange the wedges on a wire rack set inside a rimmed baking sheet and bake until just tender, about 30 minutes. Transfer the rack (with the potatoes still on it) to the counter and let cool for 10 minutes.

2. Meanwhile, turn the oven to 475 degrees. Wipe off the baking sheet with paper towels and return it to the oven.

3. Transfer the cooled potatoes to a large bowl. Gently stir in the oil, sugar, ½ teaspoon salt, and ¼ teaspoon pepper until the potatoes are well coated. Remove the baking sheet from the oven. Carefully arrange the potatoes in a single layer on the hot baking sheet and roast until deep golden brown, 15 to 20 minutes, flipping the wedges halfway through. Season with salt and pepper to taste and serve.

PER SERVING: **Cal** 160; **Fat** 2.5g; **Sat fat** 0g; **Chol** 0mg; **Carb** 32g; **Protein** 3g; **Fiber** 5g; **Sodium** 290mg

VARIATIONS

Caribbean-Spiced Roasted Sweet Potato Wedges

Follow the recipe for Roasted Sweet Potato Wedges, adding ¾ teaspoon ground allspice, ¾ teaspoon dried thyme, ½ teaspoon garlic powder, ¼ teaspoon ground cinnamon, and ⅛ teaspoon cayenne pepper to the potatoes with the oil.

PER SERVING: **Cal** 160; **Fat** 2.5g; **Sat fat** 0g; **Chol** 0mg; **Carb** 32g; **Protein** 3g; **Fiber** 5g; **Sodium** 290mg

Curried Roasted Sweet Potato Wedges

Follow the recipe for Roasted Sweet Potato Wedges, adding 1 teaspoon curry powder, 1 teaspoon ground coriander, ½ teaspoon ground cumin, and ¼ teaspoon ground ginger to the potatoes with the oil.

PER SERVING: **Cal** 160; **Fat** 2.5g; **Sat fat** 0g; **Chol** 0mg; **Carb** 32g; **Protein** 3g; **Fiber** 6g; **Sodium** 290mg

Roasted Sweet Potato Wedges with Cumin and Lime

Follow the recipe for Roasted Sweet Potato Wedges, adding 2 teaspoons grated lime zest, 1½ teaspoons ground cumin, and ½ teaspoon garlic powder to the potatoes with the oil.

PER SERVING: **Cal** 160; **Fat** 2.5g; **Sat fat** 0g; **Chol** 0mg; **Carb** 32g; **Protein** 3g; **Fiber** 6g; **Sodium** 290mg

NOTES FROM THE TEST KITCHEN

SOLUTION TO SOGGINESS

Roasting sweet potatoes sounds like a great way to bring out their natural sweetness. In fact, they usually come out wet and soggy. We resolved the problem with a two-step, two-temperature cooking process.

START LOW
We start the sweet potatoes at a low temperature on a rack in the oven, so that they dry out and don't stew in their own juice.

FINISH HOT
We finish the potatoes on a preheated rimmed baking sheet in a hot 475-degree oven so the natural sugars in the potatoes caramelize on the exterior.

RASPBERRY-LIME AND STRAWBERRY SMOOTHIES

BREAKFAST & BAKED GOODS

M = TEST KITCHEN MAKEOVER

FRUIT SMOOTHIES

A FRESH FRUIT SMOOTHIE IS AN IDEAL HEALTHY, quick breakfast that you can feel good about enjoying any morning of the week, right? Well, not always. While fruit will give you a healthy dose of vitamins, antioxidants, and myriad other benefits, not all fruit smoothies are made the same. Often they are packed with sugar and are more fruit juice than fruit, not to mention that some smoothies contain large amounts of high-fat ingredients such as peanut butter or even ice cream. But nutritional flaws aside, we have found that most fruit smoothies have little honest-to-goodness fruit flavor, as they often contain more ice than fruit to get their bulk. Hoping to blend up the perfect fruit smoothie, we set out to develop our own version that was not overly sweet, had a smooth, refreshing consistency, and put the fruit front and center.

We quickly settled on using strawberries as the starring fruit in our master recipe since they appeal to most everyone. And while a fresh strawberry smoothie might at first sound like the obvious choice, we were well aware that frozen strawberries are harvested at the peak of ripeness and quickly frozen, which should mean that for much of the year they are a better bet than their fresh counterparts. But just to make sure, we made two batches of strawberry smoothies—one with fresh berries and another with frozen—mixing them with ice and just enough milk (dairy was a popular liquid choice in many of the recipes we found) to get everything spinning. A few things became apparent right off the bat. First, we found that smoothies made with frozen strawberries were more consistently flavorful than those made with fresh berries. Second, frozen berries could serve as the thickener, allowing us to ditch the ice. And because of this, we could pack in another full cup of fruit. The frozen fruit smoothies were an all-around winner.

At this point, our smoothies had all the fruit we could pack into them, but could we find a way to amplify the strawberry flavor even further? Up to this point, we had been using milk as our liquid component, but we wondered if a different choice might better complement the strawberries. Fruit juice struck us as a natural choice. We ditched the milk and blended up batches with apple juice, cranberry juice, and orange juice. Tasters agreed that the bolder, more acidic flavors of cranberry juice and orange juice detracted from the strawberry flavor, so they were

out. But apple juice was a winner, adding a mild sweetness without overpowering the strawberry flavor. But even though the flavor had taken a step forward, now tasters missed the creaminess the milk had provided.

To get the creamy dairy element back into our smoothies without making them too loose, we picked a few options from the supermarket dairy case to test. We tried adding milk, low-fat yogurt, and frozen yogurt to batches of our strawberry–apple juice smoothie. Not surprisingly, tasters panned the smoothies made with frozen yogurt as too sweet. Milk helped, but yogurt was the real winner. It provided an appealing tang, and its thicker consistency lent a rich texture.

At this point, a colleague suggested that since we were making strawberry smoothies, why not use strawberry yogurt instead of plain? It proved to be a great idea, taking the strawberry flavor up a level. But could we take the strawberry intensity even further? Some yogurts boast of "fruit on the bottom." This jammy substance added an off-taste to our recipe, but it gave us the novel idea to try incorporating strawberry preserves. Along with the frozen berries and strawberry yogurt, just 2 tablespoons of preserves packed our smoothies with a triple whammy of strawberry flavor.

With our strawberry smoothie perfected, we came up not only with a strawberry-banana variation, but also with a few recipes featuring peaches and raspberries instead of the strawberries since we could find relevant substitutes for each of the three flavor-boosting ingredients: frozen fruit, preserves, and yogurt. Packed with fruit flavor—and not with ice, sugar, or other distracting additions—these smoothies were a breakfast we could look forward to and really feel good about.

Strawberry Smoothies
SERVES 4

Add the strawberries last for easier blending. We prefer using frozen strawberries for these smoothies, but they will work with fresh as well. Substitute 3 cups fresh strawberries and add 10 ice cubes to the blender with the fruit.

1½ cups low-fat strawberry yogurt
1 cup apple juice
2 tablespoons strawberry preserves
3 cups (15 ounces) frozen strawberries

Combine the yogurt, apple juice, strawberry preserves, and strawberries in a blender, making sure to add the strawberries last. Process on low speed until the mixture is combined but still coarse in texture, about 10 seconds. Increase the blender speed to high and process until the mixture is completely smooth, 20 to 40 seconds longer. Serve immediately.

PER 1¼-CUP SERVING: Cal 160; Fat 1g; Sat fat 0.5g; Chol 10mg; Carb 34g; Protein 4g; Fiber 2g; Sodium 50mg

VARIATIONS

Strawberry-Banana Smoothies

Follow the recipe for Strawberry Smoothies, substituting 1 banana for 1 cup of the frozen strawberries.

PER 1¼-CUP SERVING: Cal 170; Fat 1g; Sat fat 0.5g; Chol 10mg; Carb 38g; Protein 4g; Fiber 3g; Sodium 50mg

Peach Smoothies

Follow the recipe for Strawberry Smoothies, substituting low-fat peach yogurt for the strawberry yogurt, frozen peaches for the strawberries, and peach preserves for the strawberry preserves.

PER 1¼-CUP SERVING: Cal 160; Fat 1g; Sat fat 0.5g; Chol 5mg; Carb 34g; Protein 5g; Fiber 1g; Sodium 60mg

Peach-Ginger Smoothies

Follow the recipe for Strawberry Smoothies, substituting low-fat peach yogurt for the strawberry yogurt, frozen peaches for the strawberries, and peach preserves for the strawberry preserves. Add ½ teaspoon grated or minced fresh ginger to the blender with the other ingredients.

PER 1¼-CUP SERVING: Cal 160; Fat 1g; Sat fat 1g; Chol 5mg; Carb 34g; Protein 5g; Fiber 1g; Sodium 60mg

Raspberry Smoothies

Follow the recipe for Strawberry Smoothies, substituting low-fat raspberry yogurt for the strawberry yogurt, frozen raspberries for the strawberries, and raspberry preserves for the strawberry preserves. Increase the amount of apple juice to 1½ cups.

PER 1¼-CUP SERVING: Cal 190; Fat 1.5g; Sat fat 0.5g; Chol 5mg; Carb 40g; Protein 5g; Fiber 5g; Sodium 60mg

Raspberry-Lime Smoothies

Follow the recipe for Strawberry Smoothies, substituting low-fat raspberry yogurt for the strawberry yogurt, frozen raspberries for the strawberries, and raspberry preserves for the strawberry preserves. Increase the amount

NOTES FROM THE TEST KITCHEN

FRUIT FLAVOR TRIPLE PLAY
Getting potent fruit flavor into our smoothies—whether strawberry, peach, or raspberry—is a product of combining three ingredients that feature the starring fruit.

FROZEN FRUIT
Not only does it have a more consistent flavor and texture year-round compared to fresh, but frozen fruit also works in lieu of the usual ice, ensuring undiluted berry flavor.

LOW-FAT YOGURT
It provides creaminess, and using the appropriate fruit-flavored variety lends even more fruit flavor.

FRUIT PRESERVES
Preserves made with real fruit pack loads of flavor in a small amount along with a hint of sweetness.

FROZEN STRAWBERRIES
Strawberry season is fleeting no matter where you live, and all too often the strawberries you find in the supermarket in the off-season are mealy and flavorless. On the hunt for the best frozen strawberries, we thawed and sampled three national brands, both plain and cooked in pie. Tasted plain, each brand had a surprisingly different flavor, and textures ranged from mushy to firm. And although the berries in all three brands were individually quick-frozen to preserve them at the peak of ripeness, two of the brands exhibited off-flavors. Our favorite? **Cascadian Farm Frozen Premium Organic Strawberries**, which tasters noted were the plumpest, juiciest berries, with good strawberry flavor and "balanced sweetness."

of apple juice to 1½ cups and add ½ teaspoon grated lime zest and 2 tablespoons fresh lime juice to the blender with the other ingredients.

PER 1¼-CUP SERVING: Cal 190; Fat 1.5g; Sat fat 1g; Chol 5mg; Carb 41g; Protein 5g; Fiber 5g; Sodium 60mg

HEALTHY SCRAMBLED EGGS

WHAT COULD POSSIBLY BE SO HARD ABOUT MAKING scrambled eggs? There are only a few ingredients involved, and the whole process—from walking into the kitchen to sitting down at the table—takes but a few minutes. But we all know the simplest things are not always the easiest, plain old scrambled eggs included. And you only make things harder when you try to make them healthier. The obvious way to lighten up scrambled eggs is to start removing yolks, since that is where the bulk of the cholesterol and fat is, but all too often the results are flavorless eggs that have the texture of crumbled rubber. We had a few challenges to tackle: We wanted to perfect our scrambling technique; we needed to find the perfect ratio of yolks to whites that would keep our recipe healthy without sacrificing flavor or texture; and we wanted to elevate this breakfast staple to supper status by introducing some healthy add-ins.

Before we could lighten scrambled eggs, we needed to make sure our basic technique was solid, so we started by perfecting a full-fat recipe. First, we tested beating eggs to varying degrees before cooking them. Muscling the raw eggs into a tight froth quickly proved to be a mistake. Why? Overbeating causes premature coagulation of the eggs' protein, which we realized meant these eggs were tough before they even hit the pan. We had the most success when we whipped our eggs until we had a smooth, consistent color and no streaks of white or yellow, and we made sure to stop while the bubbles were large.

Next we looked at the few basic ingredients often added before beating—salt, pepper, and either water or dairy. Seasoning was easy, and when we compared eggs made with water against those with dairy, we noted that scrambled eggs made with water were less flavorful, didn't fluff as nicely, and weren't as soft as those made with dairy (we used whole milk for the time being).

We tried scrambling our eggs over low heat, but by the time the eggs were cooked through, they had become tough, dried out, and overcoagulated, like a badly made meringue that "weeps." We found that a very hot pan was much better. The high heat began to cook the eggs instantaneously, which led to the quickest coagulation and created the steam essential for a light, fluffy texture. Of course, the problem with using high heat was that absolute vigilance was needed. To increase our margin of error, we scaled back to medium heat, which gave us relatively quick coagulation and sufficiently fluffy eggs without the constant fear of overcooking.

A folding method, rather than constant stirring, yields the creamiest, softest scrambled eggs with large, airy curds. A rubber or wooden spatula worked best; we used the flat edge to snowplow a 2- to 3-inch swath of eggs across the pan in one pass, lifting and folding as we went. Because the eggs continued to cook off the heat, we made sure they looked almost underdone when we made the final fold.

With our cooking technique set, we moved on to lightening our scrambled eggs. The dairy was an easy component to tackle first. In lieu of whole milk, we tested both low-fat and fat-free milk. We found that 1 percent low-fat milk gave us eggs that were sufficiently fluffy, though not quite so much as the whole milk; the skim milk had a negligible effect. Since there was only a small difference in fat and calories per serving between the eggs with skim and those with low-fat milk, tasters unanimously voted in favor of the low-fat milk.

Next up was the biggest challenge: removing yolks until we hit the right white-yolk ratio. We quickly learned careful balancing was required if we wanted eggs that still had an appealing consistency. Too many whites and the eggs ended up rubbery and unappealing. We whipped up a number of batches and eventually determined that two whites to one yolk was as low as we could go. Our resulting scramble was health-conscious, yet still rich enough to cook up light and fluffy.

Our eggs were finally ready for some add-ins to lend flavor, texture, color, and heft. We tested a range of additions to our scrambles, including vegetables, herbs, and lean meat, stirring each in at the end and allowing residual heat to cook them through. We learned that wet ingredients such as spinach, fresh tomatoes, and ham steak leached water into the eggs and caused the scramble to turn "weepy." However, drier ingredients like sun-dried tomatoes, shallot, asparagus, and basil did not water down our eggs and added flavor, texture, and visual appeal. Cheese is always a good match for eggs, and rather than consider low-fat cheeses, we picked a few full-fat cheeses that allowed us to minimize the calories and fat added while maximizing flavor. We created a few combinations, our favorite being a mix of shallot, feta, and basil. Tasters also liked the combination of goat cheese, sun-dried tomato, and oregano and another with asparagus, Parmesan, and lemon. These scrambles were loaded with texture, flavor, and color, and they were so satisfying we couldn't wait to have breakfast for dinner.

Healthy Scrambled Eggs with Shallot, Feta, and Basil

SERVES 4

To avoid wasting yolks, you can use 4 whole eggs and ½ cup store-bought egg whites. Don't substitute skim milk here. Be sure to remove the skillet from the heat as soon as the eggs are done to prevent them from overcooking. You will need a 10-inch nonstick skillet for this recipe.

- 4 **large eggs**
- 4 **large egg whites (see note)**
- ¼ **cup 1 percent low-fat milk**
- ⅛ **teaspoon salt**
- ⅛ **teaspoon pepper**
- 1 **teaspoon canola oil**
- 1 **shallot, minced (about 3 tablespoons)**
- 2 **tablespoons crumbled feta cheese**
- 2 **tablespoons chopped fresh basil**

1. Whisk the eggs, egg whites, milk, salt, and pepper together in a bowl.

2. Heat the oil in a 10-inch nonstick skillet over medium heat until shimmering. Add the shallot and cook, stirring occasionally, until softened, about 2 minutes. Add the eggs and cook, following the photo, gently pushing, lifting, and folding them from one side of the pan to the other, until large, shiny, wet curds form, about 2 minutes.

3. Quickly fold in the cheese and basil. Remove the eggs from the pan immediately and serve.

PER SERVING: Cal 120; Fat 7g; Sat fat 2.5g; Chol 215mg; Carb 3g; Protein 11g; Fiber 0g; Sodium 260mg

VARIATIONS

Healthy Scrambled Eggs with Goat Cheese and Sun-Dried Tomatoes

Follow the recipe for Healthy Scrambled Eggs with Shallot, Feta, and Basil, omitting the shallot. Substitute ¼ cup crumbled goat cheese for the feta and 1 tablespoon minced fresh oregano for the basil. Stir 2 tablespoons minced drained oil-packed sun-dried tomatoes into the eggs in step 3.

PER SERVING: Cal 130; Fat 8g; Sat fat 3g; Chol 215mg; Carb 2g; Protein 12g; Fiber 0g; Sodium 240mg

FOLDING SCRAMBLED EGGS

As the eggs cook, gently push, lift, and fold them from one side of the pan to the other, using a wooden spoon or heat-proof rubber spatula, until large, shiny, wet curds form.

PASTEURIZED EGG WHITES

Unless your weekly menu includes fresh egg pasta or homemade ice cream, you're likely tossing egg yolks down the drain when creating some of our healthier egg dishes. Could store-bought whites put an end to the waste? These products are pasteurized liquid egg whites—some brands are 100 percent egg whites and some include small amounts of xanthan gum and triethyl citrate, which according to the labels enhance whipping. We tested three widely available brands, alongside hand-separated whites, in scrambled eggs, omelets, and vegetable frittatas, and in these instances they made acceptable substitutes. We preferred the **Eggology 100% Egg Whites**. Two tablespoons of these egg whites are equal to one large egg white. Note, however, that we couldn't successfully whip the store-bought whites; for recipes like soufflés and meringue, it's best to use hand-separated whites.

Healthy Scrambled Eggs with Asparagus, Parmesan, and Lemon

Place 3 spears asparagus, sliced thin on the bias, and ½ cup water in a microwave-safe bowl. Cover the bowl and microwave on high until the asparagus is bright green and tender, 1 to 3 minutes. Drain, pat dry, and set aside. Follow the recipe for Healthy Scrambled Eggs with Shallot, Feta, and Basil, omitting the shallot. Substitute 3 tablespoons grated Parmesan cheese for the feta. Stir the asparagus, 1 teaspoon grated lemon zest, and 1 tablespoon fresh lemon juice into the eggs in step 3.

PER SERVING: Cal 120; Fat 7g; Sat fat 2g; Chol 215mg; Carb 3g; Protein 12g; Fiber 0g; Sodium 240mg

EGG ROULADE WITH SPINACH AND GRUYÈRE

EGG ROULADE

FOR MANY OF US, SUNDAY BRUNCH IS A CHANCE TO serve something a step beyond our normal weekday breakfast roster. But juggling sauté pans to make individual omelets or frittatas is certainly daunting for anyone who hasn't spent years as a short-order cook. Could we come up with an impressive egg dish that would simplify the brunch frenzy by feeding several people at once? During our research we spotted recipes for a super-size rolled omelet where the eggs are poured onto a rimmed baking sheet, a filling of gooey cheese and fresh vegetables is added, and then the whole thing is baked and rolled up like a jellyroll. This dish had all the appeal of a loaded omelet, with the additional benefit of feeding several people. It was a perfect candidate for a lighter, crowd-pleasing egg dish. All you need to do is roll, slice, and serve. We knew our challenge would be fine-tuning the cooking method and keeping things light.

First we turned our attention to the cooking method, keeping the filling out of the picture until we perfected the eggs themselves. We knew we wanted to feed six people with this dish, so we whipped up 15 eggs (an appropriate number to feed six, though we would need to lighten this base later) with ¼ cup of milk, poured it into our rimmed baking sheet, and baked it in the oven at 375 degrees. After about 10 minutes in the oven, the eggs were nicely cooked, but the whole thing stuck to the baking sheet, making it impossible to roll. In search of a solution, we cooked batch after batch of eggs and eventually found our answer. We lined the rimmed baking sheet with a large enough piece of greased parchment to come up the sides, a precaution that prevented the eggs from running under the parchment. It was crucial that the parchment be liberally sprayed with vegetable oil spray; if we skimped even a little bit, our eggs stuck, making rolling the omelet impossible. Additionally, the parchment aided the rolling process; we used the paper as a guide to roll the eggs into a tight pinwheel.

With a successful cooking method in place, it was time to lighten our roulade by removing yolks. Taking a cue from our Healthy Scrambled Eggs (page 247), we started with a ratio of two whites to one yolk, increasing the number of whites incrementally by one in each test. We wanted our eggs to have enough structure to be rollable, but not so much that they were rubbery and bland. It did not take long to reach the threshold of how many

we could add. A ratio of four whites to one yolk went too far and yielded an egg roulade that tasted overly lean and was rubbery and split when rolled. While a ratio of three whites to one yolk (5 whole eggs plus 10 whites) provided the best balance of flavor—these eggs tasted rich but remained lean—unfortunately it produced a roulade that also split when rolled.

Looking back at the rolled omelet recipes we had found, we noticed that in some flour was incorporated into the eggs. We hadn't analyzed why before, but now we understood its addition. The flour was there to strengthen the eggs and provide structure, allowing the roulade to be rolled without fear of cracking. We prepared several batches of eggs (using our determined ratio), incorporating flour in 1-tablespoon increments by whisking it with the milk before adding it to the eggs. Two tablespoons proved to be the magic number—eggs prepared with this amount cooked through and rolled seamlessly. Any more flour produced pasty, gummy eggs.

At this point, our method and egg mixture worked like a charm, so we moved on to the filling. Off the bat, cheese struck us as a natural fit, and it took only one test to prove that low-fat cheeses did not provide enough flavor to warrant their inclusion. As with our Healthy Scrambled Eggs, highly flavored cheeses were the way to go. Parmesan and Gruyère both worked well, and a little bit went a long way, boosting the flavor immensely and allowing us to keep the fat down. Gruyère was slightly preferred by tasters. For a healthy complement to the cheese, tasters agreed that spinach, with its earthy flavor and bright color, would do the job nicely. We tested roulades made with baby spinach and frozen chopped spinach; the subtler flavor of baby spinach won out, but it leached water into our eggs, ruining the texture. Microwaving the spinach until wilted, then squeezing it dry before sprinkling it over the eggs just before baking, fixed this issue. Just one clove of garlic added the depth our roulade needed. Once rolled, our spinach and Gruyère egg roulade was flecked with green, full of flavor, and an elegant presentation for Sunday brunch (not to mention it was easy to make).

For a few variations, a combination of ham, Parmesan, and scallion was a hit, as were sun-dried tomatoes, Parmesan, and scallion. These roulades looked fantastic and tasted great, but best of all, none of our brunch guests would know how light they were or how easy they were to put together.

MAKING AN EGG ROULADE

1. Coat a rimmed baking sheet with vegetable oil spray, then press a piece of parchment paper into the baking sheet, making sure to get the paper into the corners and up the sides. Coat the parchment with vegetable oil spray.

2. Pour the egg mixture into the prepared baking sheet, them sprinkle the spinach and cheese over the top. Bake until the cheese is melted and the eggs are set.

3. Once the eggs are cooked, starting at one of the short ends, roll the eggs into a tidy cylinder, using the parchment paper to lift and roll the eggs.

4. Gently roll the roulade backward into the middle of the parchment paper, then use the parchment paper as a sling to transfer the roulade to a cutting board.

MINCING GARLIC TO A PASTE

After mincing the garlic, sprinkle it with a pinch of salt, then drag the side of a chef's knife over the mixture to make a fine paste. Continue to mince and drag the knife as necessary until the paste is smooth.

Egg Roulade with Spinach and Gruyère

SERVES 6

To avoid wasting yolks, you can use 5 whole eggs and 1¼ cups store-bought egg whites (see page 247).

- 5 **ounces baby spinach (about 5 cups)**
- ¼ **cup water**
- ¼ **cup 1 percent low-fat milk**
- 2 **tablespoons unbleached all-purpose flour**
- 10 **large egg whites (see note)**
- 5 **large eggs**
- 1 **small garlic clove, minced to a paste (see at left)**
- ¼ **teaspoon salt**
- ⅛ **teaspoon pepper**
- 2 **ounces Gruyère cheese, shredded (about ½ cup)**

1. Adjust an oven rack to the middle position and heat the oven to 375 degrees. Following the photos, line an 18 by 13-inch rimmed baking sheet with parchment paper, liberally coat the parchment paper with vegetable oil spray, and set aside.

2. Place the spinach and water in a microwave-safe bowl. Cover the bowl and microwave on high until the spinach is wilted and has decreased in volume by half, 3 to 5 minutes. Using potholders, remove the bowl from the microwave, then transfer the spinach to a colander set over a bowl and press with a spatula to release any excess liquid.

3. Whisk the milk and flour together in a bowl. In a large bowl, whisk the egg whites, eggs, garlic, salt, and pepper together, then whisk in the milk-and-flour mixture until uniform. Carefully pour the egg mixture into the prepared baking sheet, sprinkle the drained spinach and cheese on top, and bake until the cheese is melted and the eggs are just set, about 11 minutes, rotating the baking sheet halfway through.

4. Remove the baking sheet from the oven and, beginning at a short end, use the parchment paper to roll the egg over itself into a tight cylinder. Use the parchment paper to transfer the roulade to a cutting board, slice, and serve.

PER SERVING: Cal 150; **Fat** 8g; **Sat fat** 3g; **Chol** 185mg; **Carb** 6g; **Protein** 15g; **Fiber** 1g; **Sodium** 320mg

VARIATIONS

Egg Roulade with Ham, Parmesan, and Scallion

Follow the recipe for Egg Roulade with Gruyère and Spinach, omitting the spinach and water and substituting ½ cup grated Parmesan cheese for the Gruyère. Sprinkle 2 ounces finely chopped ham steak and 1 minced scallion over the eggs before baking.

PER SERVING: Cal 130; Fat 6g; Sat fat 2g; Chol 185mg; Carb 3g; Protein 15g; Fiber 0g; Sodium 440mg

Egg Roulade with Sun-Dried Tomatoes, Parmesan, and Scallion

Follow the recipe for Egg Roulade with Gruyère and Spinach, omitting the spinach and water and substituting ½ cup grated Parmesan cheese for the Gruyère. Sprinkle ⅓ cup chopped drained oil-packed sun-dried tomatoes and 1 minced scallion over the eggs before baking.

PER SERVING: Cal 130; Fat 7g; Sat fat 2g; Chol 180mg; Carb 5g; Protein 14g; Fiber 1g; Sodium 330mg

MAPLE SAUSAGE AND WAFFLE CASSEROLE

TEST KITCHEN
MAKEOVER

IN ITS CLASSIC FORM, BREAKFAST CASSEROLE IS MADE by soaking day-old bread in a custard (a mixture of eggs and cream), layering it with sausage and cheese, and baking until golden and puffy. While they are a great way to feed the family or a small brunch gathering, most recipes turn out dense, fairly bland casseroles, hardly a good way to start the day. A few years ago the test kitchen developed a breakfast casserole using maple sausage and maple syrup (in lieu of some of the dairy) to boost the flavor, whole milk for a rich yet lighter custard, and toasted frozen waffles instead of the bread. Not only did the waffles offer greater convenience, but their airy, fluffy texture kept the casserole reasonably light, and the sweet flavor paired nicely with the sausage. Of course, while this revamped casserole had a light texture, it was still a heavyweight on the scales—a single portion tallied 550 calories and 35 grams of fat. Looking at all the cheddar cheese, the hefty amount of sausage, and the generous volume of eggs, we saw

plenty of room for change. We wanted to make over our popular casserole into a dish that was lighter and healthier but still maintained the full flavor and rich texture of the original.

We started with the custard, which calls for six eggs and 1¼ cups of whole milk. First, we wondered just how many yolks we could remove before tasters noticed a difference, so we made several batches of our casserole, each with one less egg yolk than the previous. We were able to remove four yolks; any fewer and tasters noted that the casserole tasted somewhat lean. For the milk, we tested swapping out the whole milk for skim and were surprised that tasters couldn't tell the difference. With just these two changes, we had already saved ourselves 50 calories and 5½ grams of fat per serving. We were off to a great start.

Up next was the maple-flavored pork breakfast sausage. We'd had great success substituting chicken sausage for pork sausage in other recipes we wanted to lighten, so we assumed it could be a viable alternative yet again. We compared casseroles prepared with breakfast sausage made from pork, chicken, and turkey. Tasters once again voiced approval of the chicken sausage; it made for a balanced, not overly greasy casserole that still had plenty of flavor (they also approved the turkey sausage). Next we tested the amount of sausage, making casseroles with 6, 8, 10, and 12 ounces of maple-flavored chicken breakfast sausage. Tasters thought the casserole made with 6 ounces lacked flavor and heartiness, while those with 10 and 12 ounces did not show enough improvement over the 8 ounces to warrant the extra fat (tasters also thought the larger amounts made for a heavy casserole). So we settled on 8 ounces of maple-flavored chicken breakfast sausage and moved on to the cheese.

Up until now, we had been using about 1½ cups of full-fat cheddar cheese, but we wondered if we could reduce our caloric intake here as well. To find out, we made a few more casseroles, this time building some with less cheese (we made batches with ¾, 1, and 1¼ cups of full-fat cheddar) and one with the full amount of reduced-fat cheddar. With the casseroles lined up against one another, tasters thought the reduced amount of cheese presented more problems than the reduced-fat cheese. Anything less than 1½ cups of cheese made casseroles that were noticeably lacking in cheesy appeal.

And while tasters noticed a slight drop-off in flavor with reduced-fat cheese, the casserole was rich and flavorful enough to take this small hit.

We were near the finish line, but then we realized there was one last adjustment we could make. On one of our last supermarket trips we spotted low-fat frozen waffles in the freezer section, so we tested these baked up in a casserole and compared it to one made with regular waffles. Happily, we found that for the most part there was little to no difference, whether we used plain or buttermilk low-fat waffles. We also tried multigrain and whole wheat varieties, hoping we might be able to give a nutritional boost to our recipe, but these waffles contributed a noticeable earthy flavor tasters did not like.

Our new lightened breakfast casserole tasted rich and satisfying, but with a lighter, healthier profile—we'd eliminated 330 calories and 14 grams of fat per serving—it wasn't about to slow us down.

MAKEOVER SPOTLIGHT: BREAKFAST CASSEROLE

	CALORIES	FAT	SAT FAT	CHOLESTEROL
BEFORE	550	35g	15g	290mg
AFTER	330	14g	5g	155mg

NOTES FROM THE TEST KITCHEN

THE WEIGHTING GAME
When developing our breakfast casserole, we found that a corner or two of waffle wouldn't fully absorb the custard, and some unlucky test cook would end up with a mouthful of dry waffle. To remedy the problem, we weighted the casserole, then refrigerated it for at least an hour. We found an easy way to weight the assembled casserole before baking.

Press plastic wrap directly onto the surface of the casserole, top with another 8-inch square baking dish, then weight with heavy canned goods.

Maple Sausage and Waffle Casserole

SERVES 6

Don't use Belgian-style frozen waffles for this recipe—they are too thick. Turkey sausage can be substituted for the chicken sausage. To avoid wasting yolks, you can use 2 whole eggs and ½ cup store-bought egg whites (see page 247). Heavy cans or a cast-iron pan can be used to weight the casserole in step 4.

- 6 **frozen low-fat waffles (½ inch thick; see note)**
- 8 **ounces maple chicken breakfast sausage, crumbled**
- 6 **ounces 50 percent reduced-fat cheddar cheese, shredded (about 1½ cups)**
- 4 **large egg whites (see note)**
- 2 **large eggs**
- 1¼ **cups skim milk**
- ¼ **cup maple syrup**
- ¼ **teaspoon salt**
- ⅛ **teaspoon pepper**

1. Adjust an oven rack to the middle position and heat the oven to 375 degrees. Arrange the waffles in a single layer on a rimmed baking sheet. Bake the waffles until crisp, about 20 minutes, flipping them halfway through.

2. Cook the sausage in a nonstick skillet over medium heat, breaking it apart with a wooden spoon, until well browned, 8 to 10 minutes. Transfer the sausage to a paper towel–lined plate.

3. Grease an 8-inch square baking dish. Add half of the waffles in a single layer, breaking them up as needed to fit. Sprinkle with half of the sausage and ½ cup of the cheese. Layer the remaining waffles, remaining sausage, and ½ cup more cheese into the dish.

4. Whisk the egg whites, eggs, milk, maple syrup, salt, and pepper together in a bowl until combined. Pour the egg mixture evenly over the casserole. Cover the baking dish with plastic wrap and, following the photo, place weights on top. Refrigerate the casserole for at least 1 hour or up to 24 hours.

5. Adjust an oven rack to the middle position and heat the oven to 325 degrees. Let the casserole sit at room temperature for 20 minutes.

6. Remove the plastic wrap and sprinkle the remaining ½ cup cheese over the top. Bake until the edges and center are puffed, 45 to 50 minutes. Let cool for 5 minutes before serving.

PER SERVING: **Cal** 330; **Fat** 14g; **Sat fat** 5g; **Chol** 155mg; **Carb** 29g; **Protein** 23g; **Fiber** 0g; **Sodium** 550mg

HAM AND CHEESE WAFFLES

AFTER DEVELOPING A BREAKFAST CASSEROLE MADE with frozen waffles (see page 252), we were inspired to create another waffle recipe, but this time we wanted to feature from-scratch waffles. And instead of the mildly sweet classic version (a sweetness amplified with maple syrup), we wanted to come up with a recipe for waffles that were salty and savory. During some initial research, we came across a waffle recipe that at first sounded implausible and just flat-out odd: ham and cheese waffles. But the more we thought about it, the more we saw potential for a great savory breakfast treat. We felt with a little work, we could develop a ham and cheese waffle that had a good balance of savory flavors, cooked up crisp, and appealed to both kids and grownups alike.

A classic buttermilk waffle recipe seemed like the right jumping-off point. We mixed together 2 cups of flour, 1 teaspoon of salt, and ½ teaspoon of baking soda in one bowl, 1¾ cups of buttermilk, 4 tablespoons of butter, and 2 egg yolks in a second bowl, and whipped the two egg whites in a third. We combined the wet and dry ingredients, then folded in the whites.

With a basic batter ready, we stirred in some diced, naturally-lean ham steak and cheddar cheese and put our waffle iron to work. After a few bites, tasters agreed that the tang of the buttermilk competed with the flavor of the cheese; the buttermilk needed to go. However, simply swapping the buttermilk for milk substantially changed things. Baking soda requires some acid to actually work, so without the acid provided by the buttermilk, these waffles were dense and gummy. We ditched the baking soda. One teaspoon of baking powder gave us the lift we sought, and it also brought along some unexpected side benefits—it provided enough lift to make whipping the egg whites unnecessary, and we were able to cut one of the eggs (and its extra fat and calories) from the recipe.

Finally we had a good waffle recipe, but we were still far off the mark when it came to the savory flavor we were after. We thought adding whole wheat flour might help by contributing a nutty flavor (and would also make our waffles healthier), so we made batches swapping in ¼ cup, ½ cup, ¾ cup, and 1 cup of wheat flour for all-purpose flour. Tasters thought the waffles made with ¾ cup and 1 cup of whole wheat flour were too dense and overly wheaty, but ½ cup provided a good nutty wheat flavor without making our waffles too heavy.

We then turned to the ham and cheese. Up until now, we had been adding diced ham steak and shredded cheddar, but we wondered if there were better options. First we tested two batches of waffles side by side, one with ham steak and one with sliced deli ham. The flavors of both were good, but the waffles made with ham steak were not as crisp. We realized the ham steak was leaching more liquid than the deli ham, resulting in a wetter batter that as a result could not cook up as crisp. We found that mincing the deli ham allowed it to blend seamlessly into the batter, ensuring a hint of ham flavor in every bite without any distracting texture.

For the cheese, we wanted to find out which type would have the most impact and best flavor match for our waffles without adding a lot of fat or calories. We made waffles with low-fat cheddar, full-fat cheddar, Parmesan, Gruyère, and Swiss. Tasters panned the low-fat cheddar (its flavor was unnoticeable) and the Gruyère (it was too potent). In the end tasters preferred the salty Parmesan cheese, but both full-fat cheddar and Swiss cheese were good alternatives. About ¾ cup of grated cheese was as much as we felt we could pack into our batter, but we wondered if we could somehow amplify the cheese's flavor even more. A colleague then suggested trying an old test kitchen trick: adding dry mustard powder. Indeed, a little bit of dry mustard complemented the cheese and boosted its flavor.

A final addition of a minced scallion completed our waffles, adding a nice bite that played well with the other

savory flavors. These waffles cooked up crisp on the outside and light and fluffy on the inside, and their one-of-a-kind flavor had people coming back for seconds faster than we could make them.

Ham and Cheese Waffles

SERVES 8

You can substitute ¾ cup shredded cheddar or Swiss cheese for the Parmesan. The number of waffles this recipe yields will depend on the size and style of your waffle maker; this recipe makes about 4 cups of waffle batter. You can serve these waffles plain or with maple syrup.

- 1½ cups (7½ ounces) unbleached all-purpose flour
- ½ cup (2¾ ounces) whole wheat flour
- 1 tablespoon sugar
- 1 teaspoon baking powder
- 1 teaspoon salt
- ⅛ teaspoon dry mustard
- 4 tablespoons (½ stick) unsalted butter, melted and cooled
- 1 large egg
- 1¾ cups 2 percent low-fat milk
- 4 ounces sliced deli ham, minced
- 1½ ounces grated Parmesan cheese (about ¾ cup)
- 1 scallion, minced

1. Whisk the all-purpose flour, whole wheat flour, sugar, baking powder, salt, and mustard together in a large bowl. In a separate bowl, whisk the melted butter and egg together, then whisk in the milk until uniform.

2. Make a well in the center of the dry ingredients, pour the milk mixture into the well, and whisk very gently until the milk mixture is just incorporated (a few lumps should remain). Fold in the ham, cheese, and scallion with a rubber spatula.

3. Heat the waffle iron according to the manufacturer's instructions. Lightly coat the hot waffle iron with vegetable oil spray, then, following the manufacturer's instructions, spread the appropriate amount of batter onto the waffle iron and cook until golden brown, about 3½ minutes.

4. Remove the waffle from the waffle iron and serve. Repeat with the remaining batter, spraying the waffle iron with vegetable oil spray as needed between batches.

PER SERVING (½ CUP BATTER; 1 TO 2 WAFFLES): Cal 230; Fat 9g; Sat fat 6g; Chol 55mg; Carb 27g; Protein 10g; Fiber 2g; Sodium 630mg

CHERRY-ALMOND COFFEE CAKE

CHERRY-ALMOND COFFEE CAKE IS A CAKE OF MANY moods, ranging from yeasted braids to cobbler cousins to triple-deckers of tender yellow cake, cherry filling, and crumbly almond streusel. We've always been partial to the last, with its promise of a moist yellow cake topped with a tart-sweet cherry filling and a crunchy, buttery almond streusel. But when we tried baking a few existing recipes, we were sorely disappointed. The cake was either bone-dry or so tender the cherries sank; the cherry topping tasted either bland or sickly sweet; and the almond flavor (usually provided by extract alone) was inevitably one-dimensional and barely noticeable. But on top of all these structural and flavor issues, we had another problem to contend with: Most recipes call for so much butter and sugar that they are a fatty, caloric nightmare. Nevertheless, we set out to make a recipe for a cherry-almond coffee cake with a sturdy cake base that actually tasted of almond, a cherry topping that was bright and fresh, and a nubby, nutty streusel blanket—all while keeping fat and calories within reasonable bounds.

Up first was the star of the dish: the cherries. One recipe we found relied on jarred cherry jam, an appealing option since we didn't want to deal with pitting fresh cherries and the cherry season is so fleeting anyway. But sadly, it lost its pizzazz once cooked. Maybe we could make a jam of our own that could take the heat. We tested jams made with frozen, canned, and dried cherries against one another, combining each type with water, sugar, and cornstarch and cooking them on the stovetop until jammy. Tasters gave the thumbs-up to canned sour (or "tart") cherries, which offered a bracing flavor that would provide a good counterpoint to the sweet cake. To reinforce the cherry flavor, we decided to add the syrup the cherries were packed in instead of water.

Moving on to the cake, we tested several traditional yellow cake recipes under our cherry topping (we would deal with lightening later), but all of these relatively thin batters buckled under the weight of the cherries. With nearly 2 pounds of fruit needing to be supported, we knew we would have to move on to a thicker crumb-cake-style batter, which contains less liquid (milk and eggs) in proportion to flour than the yellow cake batters.

This proved to be a good choice; the sturdier batter had no problems keeping the cherries afloat.

To lighten our cake, we looked at the list to see what we could adjust. The butter was really our only outlet for cutting fat and calories. We had been using a full stick of butter (granted, the cake served 16 people), so we tested cutting it back bit by bit. After a few rounds, we found we were able to cut out 2 tablespoons of butter before the cake became too dry.

Now we needed to infuse our cake with almond flavor. Many of the recipes we tried used nothing but almond extract, but we wanted to take it up a notch. First we tried incorporating ground almonds into the batter. Tasters liked the flavor, but the oil from the almonds affected the texture of the cake, making it overly tender. What about using marzipan or almond paste? It turns out the manufacturers of these products remove the oil before they produce the paste, so they were a better bet for our recipe.

On the labels, we read that almond paste contains 45 percent almonds; marzipan, 28 percent. As we expected, in a side-by-side test, the cake with marzipan was more sweet than nutty, but the almond-paste cake had outstanding almond flavor. Moreover, the dense paste improved the texture of the crumb. Looking for a little tang to balance the sweetness of the paste, we replaced the milk in the batter with low-fat sour cream. This made the batter so thick it had to be prodded into the corners of the baking pan, and it rose beautifully under the cherry topping, baking into a plush, moist, velveteen crumb.

At this point, with both our cake and cherry topping set, we focused on the streusel topping. Getting the almond streusel right was comparatively easy; for a full-fat starting point, we mixed flour, white and brown sugars, melted butter, and ground almonds. One test proved that the almonds made the streusel brittle, so they were cut from the mix. We had much more success when we reserved some almond paste from our batter and incorporated it into the streusel. However, when we began to lighten the streusel (by removing butter from the mix), it again turned brittle. A little bit of water stirred in solved the problem, allowing us to cut 3 tablespoons of butter from the topping. To seal the deal, we whipped up a quick almond glaze and drizzled it over the top. This coffee cake tasted so indulgent, it was a guilty pleasure but without any of the guilt.

Cherry-Almond Coffee Cake

SERVES 16

Tart cherries are sometimes labeled as "sour." Purchase cherries packed in syrup, not water, as the syrup is part of the recipe. Be sure to use almond paste in this recipe, not marzipan, which is much sweeter.

FILLING

- 2 (15-ounce) cans tart cherries in syrup
- ¼ cup (1¾ ounces) granulated sugar
- 2 tablespoons cornstarch

STREUSEL AND CAKE

- 2 cups (10 ounces) unbleached all-purpose flour
- 7 tablespoons (3 ounces) granulated sugar
- ¼ cup packed (1¾ ounces) light brown sugar
- ½ teaspoon salt
- 4 tablespoons (½ stick) unsalted butter, melted and cooled, plus 6 tablespoons (¾ stick) unsalted butter, softened
- 1 tablespoon water
- 1 (7-ounce) tube almond paste, crumbled into small pieces (about 1½ cups)
- 1½ teaspoons baking powder
- ⅓ cup low-fat sour cream
- 2 large eggs
- 1 teaspoon vanilla extract
- 1 teaspoon almond extract

GLAZE

- ½ cup (2 ounces) confectioners' sugar
- 1 tablespoon water
- ⅛ teaspoon almond extract

1. FOR THE FILLING: Combine the cherries with their syrup, granulated sugar, and cornstarch in a large saucepan. Mash the cherries with a potato masher and cook over medium heat, stirring occasionally, until the mixture is thick and measures 2 cups, about 30 minutes. Refrigerate until cool, about 30 minutes.

2. FOR THE STREUSEL AND CAKE: Whisk ¾ cup of the flour, 3 tablespoons of the granulated sugar, brown sugar, and ¼ teaspoon of the salt together in a medium bowl. Using a fork, stir in the melted butter and water until the mixture forms pea-size pieces. Stir in ½ cup of the almond paste and set aside.

3. Adjust an oven rack to the middle position and heat the oven to 350 degrees. Grease and flour a 13 by

9-inch baking pan and set aside. Whisk the remaining 1¼ cups flour, baking powder, and remaining ¼ teaspoon salt together in a bowl. In a separate bowl, whisk the sour cream, eggs, vanilla extract, and almond extract together. With an electric mixer on medium-high speed, beat the remaining ¼ cup granulated sugar, softened butter, and remaining 1 cup almond paste together until light and fluffy, about 2 minutes. Add the sour cream mixture and beat until incorporated. Reduce the mixer speed to low, add the flour mixture, and beat until just combined, about 1 minute. Return the speed to medium-high and beat until fluffy, about 1 minute.

4. Scrape the batter evenly into the prepared pan and smooth the top. Dollop the cooled cherry mixture over the batter and spread into an even layer. Sprinkle the streusel over the cherry mixture. Bake until a toothpick inserted into the center comes out clean, 30 to 40 minutes, rotating the pan halfway through. Let the cake cool in the pan, set on a wire rack, for 1 hour.

5. FOR THE GLAZE: Whisk the confectioners' sugar, water, and almond extract together in a bowl until smooth. Drizzle over the cake before serving.

PER SERVING: Cal 290; Fat 10g; Sat fat 5g; Chol 45mg; Carb 45g; Protein 4g; Fiber 1g; Sodium 140mg

ZUCCHINI BREAD

COME LATE SUMMER, THE ZUCCHINI CROP IS AT ITS peak, and while a simple steamed side or a summery vegetable gratin (see our recipe on page 233) is a great savory option for putting the abundant squash to use, zucchini can also shine when baked into a quick bread. Great zucchini bread is slightly sweet and moist and offers a hint of zucchini flavor. But more often than not, recipes fail to live up to the promise. Often calling for as much as a full cup of vegetable oil, four eggs, and 3 cups of sugar, these recipes (no surprise) produce dense, greasy, overly sweet loaves that hardly taste of zucchini. It wasn't hard for us to imagine a leaner, better-tasting version. We were after a brightly flavored, lightly sweetened quick bread with a moist crumb and subtle zucchini flavor in every bite. To give our loaf an added healthy boost, we also wanted to incorporate as much whole wheat flour into our recipe as possible.

Zucchini bread recipes generally follow a simple technique: Stir the dry ingredients (flour, leavener, spices, and salt) together in one bowl; stir the wet ingredients and sweetener (oil, eggs, sugar, and often yogurt or sour cream) together in another; fold the dry ingredients into the wet, while adding the grated zucchini. Since the vegetable oil was causing multiple problems—a greasy loaf and flat flavor—we started our overhaul there. We suspected that melted butter instead of the oil would better complement the zucchini and contribute a pleasant richness and better flavor, and a few preliminary tests proved our hunch was right. From there, we tested varying amounts and found that even ½ cup of butter was too much. Tasters agreed that just 5 tablespoons of butter contributed the proper richness without making our loaf too rich or greasy. And now, with butter as our fat of choice, we were able to use the creaming method, which produced loaves with a softer texture and good volume.

We had made some progress, but the flavor was still a bit flat. To brighten it up, we experimented with various acidic liquid ingredients that we have used in other quick-bread recipes: buttermilk, low-fat sour cream, and low-fat yogurt. While buttermilk worked well—and would be an acceptable substitute in a pinch—we preferred the texture and flavor of the bread made with plain low-fat yogurt. It added an appealing tanginess, and 1 tablespoon of lemon juice added a bit more acidity as well as a pleasant citrus note. In addition to improving the flavor of our zucchini bread, the yogurt and lemon juice reacted with the baking soda to produce a lighter bread with more rise.

For a heartier flavor and a healthier loaf, we tested substituting various amounts of whole wheat flour for some of the all-purpose flour. Loaves made with ⅔ cup of whole wheat flour and 1⅓ cups of all-purpose were perfect. Any more whole wheat flour turned out a dense loaf, and less than ⅔ cup was undetectable.

We had worked out a lot of issues, but we still had to face the biggest one of all, the zucchini itself. Zucchini brings two problems to the table: a lot of moisture, and a very mild flavor. Up until this point, we had been adding one small grated zucchini (which worked out to about 1½ cups, lightly packed). But the zucchini flavor and texture were too subtle; we wondered if the bread shouldn't have a more pronounced zucchini flavor. But when we tried increasing the amount of zucchini to 3 cups, we found ourselves with a loaf that was so moist it looked and tasted like mashed zucchini.

We wanted more zucchini flavor without the excess zucchini moisture. Clearly, if we were going to try to

ZUCCHINI BREAD

add more than that one small shredded zucchini, we were going to need to drain it first. Often we drain watery vegetables tossed with a little salt to help draw out moisture. Taking a cue from this technique, we shredded 1 pound of zucchini, tossed it with 2 tablespoons of sugar, and placed it in a fine-mesh strainer set over a bowl. After 30 minutes, we squeezed the shredded zucchini dry by wringing it in a dish towel. The sugar had helped to draw out nearly half a cup of liquid from the zucchini, and the resulting bread, dotted with green flecks of the squash, had a notably increased zucchini flavor as well as a moist, but not gummy, texture.

NOTES FROM THE TEST KITCHEN

REMOVING MOISTURE FROM SHREDDED ZUCCHINI

To prevent soggy zucchini bread, we sprinkle the shredded zucchini with sugar and let it drain for 30 minutes. Then we squeeze the zucchini between several layers of paper towels or a clean dish towel until it's dry.

THE BEST LOAF PAN

The array of loaf pans available is dizzying, with the options of different weights and finishes, not to mention price tags. We tested seven loaf pans made from a variety of materials, including metal, glass, and stoneware. Sticking was a problem in both glass and stoneware pans, so we took a closer look at the metal pans. Light-colored aluminum finishes yielded pale baked goods, and nonstick surfaces made the release of baked breads especially easy. Pans with handles at either end were hard to come by but were easier to work with.

The real star of the show, the **Williams-Sonoma 8½ x 4½-Inch Nonstick Goldtouch Loaf Pan** (left), $21, has a gold-coated nonstick surface that yielded baked goods with a perfectly even, honeyed-copper crust. For a more affordable option, the **Baker's Secret Loaf Pan** (right), $5, with its dark, nonstick surface, is a solid performer, and it comes in both 8½ by 4½-inch and 9 by 5-inch sizes. (Even though the surface of these pans is nonstick, we recommend spraying the inside of the pans with vegetable oil spray.)

Last, we tested incorporating other flavorings; ground cinnamon, grated nutmeg, ground allspice, ground ginger, vanilla, nuts, and raisins all went through the testing process. In the end, tasters liked a loaf made with the simple combination of cinnamon and allspice. Just a small amount of each added the right depth and brought out the zucchini's subtle flavor even more. This was one zucchini loaf that was light, tender, and actually tasted like zucchini.

Zucchini Bread
MAKES ONE 8-INCH LOAF

It is important to rid the zucchini of most of its moisture before adding it to the batter or the bread will have a gummy texture.

- 2 zucchini (about 1 pound)
- 1 cup (7 ounces) plus 2 tablespoons sugar
- 1⅓ cups (6⅔ ounces) unbleached all-purpose flour
- ⅔ cup (3⅔ ounces) whole wheat flour
- 1 teaspoon baking powder
- 1 teaspoon baking soda
- ¾ teaspoon salt
- ½ teaspoon ground cinnamon
- ¼ teaspoon ground allspice
- ¼ cup plain low-fat yogurt
- 1 tablespoon fresh lemon juice
- 5 tablespoons unsalted butter, softened
- 2 large eggs

1. Shred the zucchini on the large holes of a box grater. Toss the zucchini with 2 tablespoons of the sugar, transfer to a fine-mesh strainer set over a bowl, and let drain for 30 minutes. Following the photo, thoroughly squeeze the zucchini dry with paper towels.

2. Adjust an oven rack to the middle position and heat the oven to 375 degrees. Lightly coat an 8½ by 4½-inch loaf pan with vegetable oil spray and set aside.

3. Whisk ½ cup more sugar, all-purpose flour, whole wheat flour, baking powder, baking soda, salt, cinnamon, and allspice together in a large bowl. In a separate bowl, gently combine the dried zucchini, yogurt, and lemon juice.

4. Beat the remaining ½ cup sugar and butter together with an electric mixer on medium-high speed until creamy and uniform, 3 to 6 minutes, scraping down the bowl as needed. Beat in the eggs, one at a time, until combined, about 30 seconds.

5. Reduce the mixer speed to low. Beat in one-third of the flour mixture followed by half of the zucchini mixture. Repeat with half of the remaining flour mixture and the remaining zucchini mixture. Beat in the remaining flour mixture until just incorporated (do not overmix).

6. Scrape the batter into the prepared loaf pan and smooth the top. Bake until golden brown and a toothpick inserted into the center comes out with just a few crumbs attached, 55 to 65 minutes, rotating the pan halfway through.

7. Let the loaf cool in the pan for 10 minutes, then turn it out onto a wire rack and let cool for 1 hour before serving.

PER ⅔-INCH SLICE: **Cal** 200; **Fat** 6g; **Sat fat** 3.5g; **Chol** 50mg; **Carb** 35g; **Protein** 4g; **Fiber** 2g; **Sodium** 320mg

BRAN MUFFINS

THE IDEA OF THE BRAN MUFFIN CAME LONG BEFORE the recent whole grain craze. In fact, one of the first recipes appeared on the package of Kellogg's Krumbled Bran in 1916, when bran cereal was still fairly novel. Today, of course, bran cereals cover much of the supermarket cereal aisle, and bran muffins can be bought from grocers, coffee shops, and bakeries. But a bran muffin that is actually good—and good for you—might not be so easy to find. Many bran muffins are weighed down by sugar and fat, and of the recipes we've tried, both low-fat and full-fat, the results were almost always heavy, squat, and dry. Several years ago the test kitchen developed a great recipe for bran muffins, which were made with unprocessed wheat bran from our local natural foods store. But these muffins required a special shopping trip. We wondered, Could a commercial cereal sold at the supermarket deliver the same results? We wanted bran muffins that were moist, hearty yet not heavy, and redolent of bran's rich, earthy flavor.

Supermarket shelves are filled with a wide variety of bran-based cereals, fashioned in the shape of twigs, flakes, and granules, so first we set out to determine how each bran cereal functioned when baked into a muffin. We stitched together a recipe consisting of all-purpose flour, butter, sugar, molasses, milk, eggs, baking powder, and raisins and began testing cereals one at a time.

The recipes we tested with flakes came out flavorless and looked like springy cupcakes instead of the rustic muffins we had in mind. The muffins made with granules were also flavorless, and their texture was dense and pasty. The twigs offered the best potential. They provided a deep bran flavor, but getting them to bend to our will was another matter. They weren't fully dissolving into the batter and were even sticking out of the tops of the baked muffins.

Presoaking the twigs in the milk (as recommended in most recipes) didn't really work and made the muffins as dense as hockey pucks. The cereal was soaking up all the moisture, which dried out the batter. Heating the cereal in milk before adding it to the batter made it even worse, causing the muffins to bake up gummy. For our next test, we tried grinding the twigs to a powder in a food processor before adding them to the batter. Much better. These muffins had an even crumb, but they were a bit heavy. A compromise was in order. We pulverized half of the cereal and kept the other half whole. When we combined the pulverized and nonpulverized bran and added them to the batter, these muffins finally had the chewy, rustic texture we wanted.

Up to this point, we had been using Kellogg's All-Bran Original for our testing, but to make sure there wasn't a better option we circled back to try other brands of twig-style bran cereal. General Mills Fiber One produced bland muffins (which made sense when we read the label more carefully and saw that wheat, not bran, is the primary ingredient). Tasters had a hard time getting past Post 100% Bran's malted, fruity flavor (which was explained by an ingredient list containing malted barley flour as well as fig and prune juice concentrates). In the end, tasters deemed Kellogg's All-Bran Original the winner for its deep, complex bran flavor.

With the cereal mystery finally solved, we could fine-tune our recipe. We discovered that one egg didn't add enough structure, and two eggs made the muffins too springy. A whole egg plus a yolk worked best, giving the muffins a fluffy but not bouncy texture. Our muffins seemed too lean and dry, but more than 6 tablespoons of butter made them greasy, so we turned to the dairy element. Switching the milk for sour cream was overkill. Buttermilk was an improvement over plain milk, but low-fat yogurt was tasters' first choice. Replacing the baking powder with baking soda gave us a coarser crumb that tasters liked.

Mixing some whole wheat flour with the all-purpose

BRAN CEREALS

Bran is the outer layer of the wheat grain that is removed during milling. A good source of calcium, phosphorus, and fiber, bran cereal comes in various forms. Here's how they stack up in muffins:

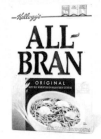

TWIG-STYLE

We found that All-Bran Original gave our muffins the most robust bran flavor.

FLAKE-STYLE

Bran flakes are made mostly of wheat and produced muffins with very little bran flavor.

GRANULE-STYLE

Small granules of bran cereal made very dense muffins with almost no bran flavor.

WITH RAISINS

These cereals seemed like a good idea, but the raisins cooked up dry and tough. If you want raisins, add your own and plump them first in the microwave.

GETTING BIG BRAN FLAVOR AND PERFECT TEXTURE

When we added the cereal directly to the batter, the muffins were marred by crunchy bits and twigs sticking out of the top. When we processed all of the cereal into a fine powder, the muffins were too dense. Our solution: By processing just half of the cereal and leaving the other half in twig form, we created muffins with an even, but not heavy texture.

WHOLE TWIGS

Leaving some twigs whole lends a rustic texture and ensures a light—not dense—muffin.

TWIG POWDER

Processing some twigs into a fine powder allows for a more even crumb.

flour reinforced the flavor of the bran, as did replacing the granulated sugar with brown sugar and increasing the amount of molasses. After complaints that the raisins didn't soften enough during baking, we plumped them in the microwave with a little water. With that, we had finally found a way to turn supermarket cereal into a moist, tender muffin with big bran flavor that was also genuinely light and healthy.

Bran Muffins

MAKES 12 MUFFINS

Dried cranberries or dried cherries can be substituted for the raisins.

- 1 **cup raisins**
- 1 **teaspoon water**
- 2¼ **cups (5 ounces) Kellogg's All-Bran Original cereal**
- ⅔ **cup packed (4⅔ ounces) light brown sugar**
- 3 **tablespoons mild molasses**
- 1 **large egg**
- 1 **large egg yolk**
- 1 **teaspoon vanilla extract**
- 1¾ **cups plain low-fat yogurt**
- 6 **tablespoons (¾ stick) unsalted butter, melted and cooled**
- 1¼ **cups (6¼ ounces) unbleached all-purpose flour**
- ½ **cup (2¾ ounces) whole wheat flour**
- 2 **teaspoons baking soda**
- ½ **teaspoon salt**

1. Adjust an oven rack to the middle position and heat the oven to 400 degrees. Lightly coat a 12-cup muffin tin with vegetable oil spray and set aside.

2. Place the raisins and water in a microwave-safe bowl. Cover the bowl and microwave on high until boiling, about 30 seconds. Using potholders, remove the bowl from the microwave and keep covered until the raisins are softened and plump, about 5 minutes. Spread the raisins on a paper towel–lined plate to drain and cool to room temperature.

3. Process half of the bran cereal in a food processor until finely ground, about 1 minute. In a medium bowl, whisk the sugar, molasses, egg, egg yolk, and vanilla together until uniform. Whisk in the processed and unprocessed bran cereal, yogurt, and melted butter and let sit until the cereal is evenly moistened (there will still be some small lumps), about 5 minutes.

4. In a large bowl, whisk the all-purpose flour, whole wheat flour, baking soda, and salt together. Gently fold in the cereal mixture with a rubber spatula until just combined (do not overmix). Fold in the cooled raisins.

5. Using a ⅓-cup measure lightly coated with vegetable oil spray, portion the batter into each muffin cup. Bake the muffins until dark golden and a toothpick inserted into the center comes out with just a few crumbs attached, about 16 to 20 minutes, rotating the muffin tin halfway through.

6. Let the muffins cool in the pan for 5 minutes, then flip them out onto a wire rack and let cool for 10 minutes before serving.

PER MUFFIN: **Cal** 280; **Fat** 7g; **Sat fat** 4.5g; **Chol** 55mg; **Carb** 50g; **Protein** 6g; **Fiber** 5g; **Sodium** 380mg

SWEET POTATO BISCUITS

IN THE SOUTH, WHERE BISCUITS ARE KING AND SWEET potatoes are a popular staple ingredient, it was only a matter of time before some inspired baker married the two. And it was a perfect match. The sweet potato adds earthy sweetness and moistness to a biscuit, setting it apart from the more familiar flaky buttermilk biscuit in a league of its own. But like buttermilk biscuits, sweet potato biscuits tend to be buttery and fatty. Could we come up with a lighter sweet potato biscuit, one that was still tender, moist, and with good sweet potato flavor?

First, we needed to come up with a basic sweet potato biscuit recipe before we tackled lightening it. Our research revealed many recipes that looked the part—tinged a pretty pale peach from the cooked, mashed sweet potato—but they were in fact wet and heavy and tasted nothing like sweet potato. We needed to head out on our own.

We wondered if we could introduce mashed sweet potato into a standard buttermilk biscuit recipe and make adjustments from there. We cobbled together a full-fat recipe that called for pulsing vegetable shortening (for tenderness) and butter (for flavor) together in a food processor with flour, salt, sugar, and leaveners until the fat was evenly dispersed. We transferred the mixture to a bowl and stirred in buttermilk, then briefly kneaded the dough, patted it into a circle, cut it into rounds, and baked.

Our main goal was to get as much sweet potato into these biscuits as possible without ruining them. To do so we boiled sweet potatoes and pureed them with the buttermilk to ensure a smooth texture (no one wanted little chunks of potato in their biscuits). We then made batches of biscuits incorporating ½ pound, ¾ pound, and 1 pound of pureed sweet potato into the dough. The batch made with ½ pound of sweet potatoes was barely reminiscent of the tuber, while the batch made with a full pound turned out so mushy and gummy we felt it was beyond help. Fortunately the batch made with ¾ pound had a nice subtle sweet potato flavor. However, it too turned out slightly gummy, but we knew we could rectify the situation. Clearly there was too much liquid in our recipe, so some would have to go.

Our first thought was that the method used to cook the sweet potatoes was contributing additional moisture. Up to this point, we had been peeling, chopping, and boiling the sweet potatoes before mashing them. Hoping that a drier environment would solve the problem, we prepared sweet potatoes by roasting them in the oven as well as cooking them in a microwave. Neither of these two methods produced significantly drier sweet potatoes, so we settled on microwaving purely for simplicity and convenience.

But with our moisture problem still unsolved, we saw only one other ingredient we could adjust; we would have to cut some of the buttermilk. After a few tests we found that cutting out ¼ cup of the buttermilk produced biscuits that were noticeably less gummy—but they still weren't quite there.

We needed to look beyond the ingredient list for solutions. What if we changed the size of our biscuits? Potentially, a smaller size could allow our biscuits to bake through more quickly and evenly, making them less gummy. So we tried downsizing from a 2½-inch biscuit cutter to a 2¼-inch cutter. Bingo! These biscuits were tender, moist, and packed with sweet potato flavor, and all without being gummy.

At this point, we had a great working recipe with nice sweet potato flavor, so it was time to cut fat from the recipe, tablespoon by tablespoon. We made batch after batch and soon found that removing vegetable shortening was much easier than removing butter. With the addition of a wet ingredient (mashed sweet potatoes), the tenderness contributed by the vegetable shortening was mostly negated (our biscuits were always less flaky and tender than the buttermilk version), making it unnecessary. However, tasters were quicker to notice when we began cutting back on the butter. Anything less than

LIQUID MEASURING CUPS

After testing a dizzying array of liquid measuring cups (11 models), we quickly discovered that clear glass or plastic cups with a pour spout and handle are preferable to metal liquid measuring cups—these cups are designed to make measuring liquids accurate and mess-free. We find the 2- and 4-cup sizes to be the most useful in the test kitchen. Our favorite is the plastic **Cuisipro Deluxe Liquid Measuring Cup**, $10.95 for the 2-cup and $14.95 for the 4-cup, and our best buy is the glass Pyrex Liquid Measuring Cup, $4.99 for the 2-cup and $5.99 for the 4-cup measuring cup.

BUTTERMILK SUBSTITUTES

Buttermilk is a decidedly misleading word. Many assume buttermilk is infused with butter and high in fat, when the truth is quite the opposite. The name refers to the watery end product of butter making—the "milk" left behind after the solid fat has been removed by churning cream into butter. Today buttermilk is a fermented product made by culturing milk. Buttermilk is naturally lean and is often used in quick breads because its acids activate chemical leaveners such as baking powder and baking soda—not to mention it lends many baked goods an appealing tang. We also use buttermilk in low-fat salad dressing for its rich flavor and creamy body. Although you'd never want to use anything but fresh buttermilk for a salad dressing, when baking there are a variety of options: liquid (or fresh) buttermilk, powdered buttermilk, and clabbered milk (milk mixed with an acid such as lemon juice or white vinegar). For baking, wee prefer fresh or powdered buttermilk; however, clabbered milk is a fine substitute in a pinch. To make clabbered milk, mix 1 tablespoon lemon juice or white vinegar into 1 cup milk and leave at room temperature until thickened, about 10 minutes.

| BEST ALL-AROUND | GOOD FOR BAKING | WORKS IN A PINCH |

4 tablespoons resulted in biscuits that were heavy and dense. And while 4 tablespoons was sufficient for a good texture, we felt it caused the flavor to suffer. Looking for a quick fix, we tried brushing 1 tablespoon of melted butter on the biscuits before they went into the oven. This easy step took the flavor of the biscuits up to the right level.

We wondered if we could work some whole wheat flour into our recipe to add not just nutritional benefits but also a nutty, rustic flavor. A few tests proved we could successfully swap in ½ cup of whole wheat flour for some of the all-purpose. Last, allspice was a natural pairing with sweet potatoes; just a little heightened the subtle sweet potato flavor and took our sweet potato biscuits from good to great.

Sweet Potato Biscuits

MAKES 16 BISCUITS

To chill the butter, place the pieces on a plate in an even layer and freeze until solid, 10 to 15 minutes. We much prefer the flavor of fresh sweet potatoes in this recipe, but in a pinch, you can substitute 1 (15-ounce) can sweet potatoes, drained thoroughly.

- 12 **ounces sweet potato (1 medium), peeled and cut into ½-inch pieces**
- 1½ **cups (7½ ounces) unbleached all-purpose flour**
- ½ **cup (2¾ ounces) whole wheat flour**
- 3 **tablespoons dark brown sugar**
- 1 **tablespoon baking powder**
- 1 **teaspoon salt**
- ½ **teaspoon baking soda**
  Pinch ground allspice
- 4 **tablespoons (½ stick) unsalted butter, cut into ½-inch pieces and chilled, plus 1 tablespoon unsalted butter, melted (for brushing)**
- ¾ **cup buttermilk, chilled**

1. Place the sweet potato in a microwave-safe bowl. Cover the bowl and microwave on high, stirring occasionally, until tender, 5 to 7 minutes. Using potholders, remove the bowl from the microwave and set aside to cool.

2. Adjust an oven rack to the middle position and heat the oven to 425 degrees. Line a baking sheet with parchment paper and set aside.

3. Pulse the all-purpose flour, whole wheat flour, sugar, baking powder, salt, baking soda, and allspice together in a food processor to combine, about 3 pulses. Scatter the chilled butter evenly over the top and continue to pulse until the mixture resembles coarse meal, about 15 pulses.

4. Transfer the flour mixture to a large bowl and wipe out the food processor. Pulse the cooled sweet potato and buttermilk together in the food processor until smooth, 10 to 15 pulses.

5. Stir the sweet potato mixture into the flour mixture with a rubber spatula until the dough comes together. Turn out the dough onto a lightly floured counter and knead until just smooth and no longer shaggy, 8 to 10 times. Pat the dough into a 9-inch circle, about ¾ inch thick.

6. Using a floured 2¼-inch biscuit cutter, stamp out 14 biscuits, gently patting the dough scraps back into a uniform ¾-inch piece as needed. Pat the small piece of remaining dough into 2 more biscuits with your hands. Arrange the biscuits, upside down, on the prepared baking sheet, spaced 1 inch apart.

7. Brush the tops of the biscuits with the melted butter and bake until golden brown, 12 to 15 minutes, rotating the baking sheet halfway through. Transfer the biscuits to a wire rack and let cool for 10 minutes before serving.

PER BISCUIT: Cal 110; **Fat** 3.5g; **Sat fat** 2.5g; **Chol** 10mg; **Carb** 18g; **Protein** 2g; **Fiber** 1g; **Sodium** 310mg

SOFT AND CHEWY DINNER ROLLS

FLUFFY, SOFT AMERICAN-STYLE ROLLS AND CHEWY, crusty European rolls both begin with flour, yeast, and salt, but the remaining ingredients and the technique make all the difference. American rolls include milk, butter, and eggs, ingredients that contribute tenderness, while on the other end of the spectrum, European rolls use water, the barest amount of fat (usually olive oil), and a lengthy rise and very hot oven for a sturdy crust. True, the leaner European rolls are the lower-fat option, but, while we love the crust on these rolls, we also crave the tender crumb of the American-style rolls. We were after something in the middle in terms of both fat/calories and texture: We wanted a dinner roll that was tender like the American-style but with the chew of the European-style.

We decided to begin with the test kitchen's recipe for Fluffy Dinner Rolls and work toward something leaner. Out went the full stick of butter and the egg. We replaced the 1¼ cups of whole milk with water and baked off a batch. Not surprisingly, the rolls were no longer rich or tender, but they weren't chewy either. The rolls were in fact tough, more akin to bad pizza dough.

Clearly, the recipe needed at least some fat. But even with just 2 tablespoons of butter, the rolls turned out too much like soft dinner rolls. Switching to an equal amount of olive oil moved us in the right direction, giving these rolls the chew we were after. But still, we wanted more tenderness.

During our research we came across dinner roll recipes in which, like potato bread, a boiled and mashed potato was incorporated into the dough. Potato bread has a soft, moist crumb, so we thought it was worth a try. When these rolls came out of the oven, they retained the pleasing chew attained from the oil, but they also had a nice supple texture thanks to the potato. Why? Because of the potatoes, the dough contained more starch than wheat, and this starch traps moisture during baking, thus creating a moister dough. Potatoes also contain less protein than flour, resulting in less gluten being formed in the kneaded dough. Less gluten yields a softer, more tender product.

These rolls were great, but could we find a way to skip the extra steps of boiling, cooling, and mashing the potato? A fellow test cook suggested we try using instant potato flakes. It sounded odd, but once reconstituted by the liquid in the recipe, the potato flakes worked just as well as the mashed potato had. These rolls were not only the perfect balance of tender and chewy, but they were also a snap to make.

Soft and Chewy Dinner Rolls

MAKES 12 ROLLS

You will need a standing mixer with a dough hook to make this recipe.

1¼   **cups warm water (110 degrees)**
2   **tablespoons extra-virgin olive oil**
1   **tablespoon sugar**
1   **envelope (2¼ teaspoons) instant or rapid-rise yeast**
3   **cups (15 ounces) unbleached all-purpose flour**
½   **cup instant potato flakes**
1¾   **teaspoons salt**
1   **large egg, lightly beaten**

SOFT AND CHEWY DINNER ROLLS

1. Adjust an oven rack to the middle position and heat the oven to 200 degrees. When the oven reaches 200 degrees, turn it off. Grease a large bowl and set aside. Line a baking sheet with parchment paper and set aside.

2. Whisk the water, oil, sugar, and yeast together in a liquid measuring cup until the yeast dissolves. Combine the flour, potato flakes, and 1½ teaspoons of the salt in a standing mixer fitted with a dough hook. With the mixer on low speed, add the water mixture in a steady stream and mix until the dough comes together, about 1 minute. Increase the mixer speed to medium and knead until the dough is smooth and comes away from the sides of the bowl, about 6 minutes.

3. Turn out the dough onto a lightly floured counter and knead briefly to form a smooth, cohesive ball. Place the dough in the greased bowl and cover with greased plastic wrap. Place the bowl in the turned-off oven until the dough has doubled in size, about 45 minutes.

4. Turn out the dough onto a lightly floured counter. Following the photos, divide the dough into quarters and cut each quarter into 3 equal pieces. On a clean counter, shape each piece of dough into a taut ball and transfer to the prepared baking sheet. Cover loosely with plastic wrap and return to the turned-off oven until doubled in size, about 20 minutes.

5. Remove the rolls from the oven and discard the plastic wrap. Heat the oven to 400 degrees. Brush the rolls with the egg and sprinkle evenly with the remaining ¼ teaspoon salt. Bake until the rolls are golden brown, about 15 minutes, rotating the baking sheet halfway through. Let the rolls cool on the baking sheet for 10 minutes before serving. (The rolls can be refrigerated for up to 24 hours instead of being returned to the turned-off oven in step 4. Remove the plastic wrap, heat the oven to 400 degrees, and proceed with Step 5 as directed.)

PER ROLL: Cal 140; Fat 3g; Sat fat 0g; Chol 20mg; Carb 24g; Protein 4g; Fiber 1g; Sodium 350mg

VARIATIONS

Soft and Chewy Cranberry-Pecan Rolls

Follow the recipe for Soft and Chewy Dinner Rolls, adding 1 cup dried cranberries and 1 cup pecans, toasted and chopped, along with the flour.

PER ROLL: Cal 230; Fat 9g; Sat fat 1g; Chol 20mg; Carb 34g; Protein 5g; Fiber 3g; Sodium 350mg

Soft and Chewy Sun-Dried Tomato and Basil Rolls

Follow the recipe for Soft and Chewy Dinner Rolls, adding ½ cup sun-dried tomatoes packed in oil, drained, patted dry, and minced, and 2 tablespoons chopped fresh basil along with the flour.

PER ROLL: Cal 150; Fat 3.5g; Sat fat 0.5g; Chol 20mg; Carb 25g; Protein 4g; Fiber 1g; Sodium 360mg

Soft and Chewy Rosemary-Olive Rolls

Follow the recipe for Soft and Chewy Dinner Rolls, reducing the amount of salt in step 2 to 1 teaspoon. Add 1 tablespoon olive brine along with the water. Add ¾ cup pitted kalamata olives, chopped and patted dry, and 2 tablespoons minced fresh rosemary along with the flour.

PER ROLL: Cal 160; Fat 4.5g; Sat fat 0.5g; Chol 20mg; Carb 25g; Protein 4g; Fiber 1g; Sodium 420mg

NOTES FROM THE TEST KITCHEN

THE SECRET TO SOFT AND CHEWY DINNER ROLLS

We use instant potato flakes to add tenderness and a little heft to our Soft and Chewy Dinner Rolls, without the bother of boiling and mashing a potato.

SPUDS IN SECONDS

FORMING DINNER ROLLS

1. Divide the dough into quarters, then cut each quarter into 3 equal pieces.

2. With a cupped palm, roll each piece of dough into a smooth, tight ball, then loosely cover with plastic wrap until the dough has doubled in size.

STRAWBERRY SHORTCAKE

BREAD PUDDING

CUBES OF BREAD, HEAVY CREAM, A TOUCH OF SUGAR, a few egg yolks—combine and bake and you've got

bread pudding: a borderline minimalist dessert. But it's not surprising that the calories and fat are hardly negligible. Each average serving boasts more than 700 calories and 35 grams of fat—and that's before it gets a drop of sauce or dollop of whipped cream.

At the opposite end of the calorie spectrum, "light" recipes for bread pudding would scare away all but the most desperate dieter. Some we tried were made from reduced-calorie bread, which did nothing but dissolve into the custard and create a bread pudding that was gummy and pasty. Other versions had no fat whatsoever, relying on whipped egg whites and nonfat milk to moisten bits of lean, flavorless bread. These were slimy and wet, and they curdled as they cooled—we could barely round up any tasters. Without fat to carry flavor, the puddings were depressingly bland. We imagined a silken yet sturdy makeover bread pudding, fluffy enough to fill out a baking dish—but not the eater. Heady vanilla and warm cinnamon would flavor it from the inside out, and it would be just sweet enough to call dessert.

As we often find when lightening desserts, we thought our best tactic would be to carve away calories from our favorite test kitchen bread pudding recipe, one that we loved for its floral vanilla scent and crunchy cinnamon-sugar topping. This recipe calls for eight large egg yolks, so first we tested reducing this number to four. But the yolks both thicken the custard and bind the casserole, so our pudding collapsed into a mushy heap. A better solution was to swap our four yolks for three whole eggs. The whites added the structure our pudding needed.

Finding a replacement for the silken, rich heavy cream was a bigger—but necessary—task, as the 3 cups in the original recipe contributed over 100 calories and 15 grams of fat per serving. We rounded up every potential replacement we could come up with: whole milk, evaporated milk, light coconut milk, fat-free half-and-half, buttermilk, low-fat sour cream, low-fat yogurt, and vanilla soy milk. We tested each alone and in various combinations, but none of the resulting custards were quite right. They had either the wrong texture or tangy off-flavors.

We settled on a dairy product that was "too thin" (i.e., skim milk) and looked for a way to thicken the custard without adding a ton of calories. Flour made the custard pasty and dull. Next, we whisked a couple of tablespoons of cornstarch into the milk, poured it over the bread cubes, and baked as usual. Although the custard lacked the sweet, buttery flavor of cream, its texture was improved. Still, it felt achingly lean. When a colleague commented that we had effectively turned the custard into vanilla pudding, we had an idea. Instead of cornstarch, we added 3 tablespoons of instant pudding mix to the custard. The mix's combination of cornstarch and milk powder transformed the bread pudding into a dessert that finally tasted rich and creamy. At the same time, the mix reinforced the bread pudding's fragrant vanilla flavor (we used 2 teaspoons of extract). To offset the sugar in the pudding mix, we reduced the amount of sugar in our working recipe by 3 tablespoons.

At this point, we had slashed so many calories that we decided to add a few back. Up to now, we had been using basic sandwich bread, which was our only way to ensure consistent fat and calories from loaf to loaf (unlike the varying loaves you get from a bakery). Scanning the aisle, we came up with a more flavorful alternative. At an increase of only 15 calories per slice, cinnamon swirl bread perfumed the pudding with its warm spice and

NOTES FROM THE TEST KITCHEN

NOT YOUR USUAL DIET DUO
Fat adds creaminess and also carries flavor. With drastically reduced fat, diet bread puddings are typically bland and disappointingly lean. We found two key ingredients gave our light bread pudding the satisfying creaminess and flavor we were after.

Just 3 tablespoons of vanilla pudding mix adds richness and flavor but few calories.

We cut so many calories that we could sneak a few back in, so we replaced sandwich bread with cinnamon swirl bread for more flavor.

added a hint of extra sweetness. Not a single taster could believe that we had cut a whopping 400 calories and 28 grams of fat per serving from the original dessert—but we just told them, "The proof is in the pudding."

MAKEOVER SPOTLIGHT: BREAD PUDDING

	CALORIES	FAT	SAT FAT	CHOLESTEROL
BEFORE	720	36g	21g	260mg
AFTER	320	8g	2g	105mg

Bread Pudding

SERVES 6

Both instant and "cook and serve" pudding mixes work here, but avoid sugar-free, which gives the bread pudding a chemical aftertaste. Look for any brand of cinnamon swirl sandwich bread that has about 80 calories per slice.

2 cups skim milk

3 large eggs

5 tablespoons sugar

3 tablespoons vanilla pudding mix (see note)

2 teaspoons vanilla extract

¼ teaspoon salt

12 ounces cinnamon swirl sandwich bread (about 12 slices), cut into ¾-inch pieces

¼ teaspoon ground cinnamon

1. Adjust an oven rack to the middle position and heat the oven to 375 degrees. Lightly coat an 8-inch square baking dish with vegetable oil spray and set aside.

2. Whisk the milk, eggs, ¼ cup of the sugar, pudding mix, vanilla extract, and salt together in a large bowl until combined. Gently stir in the bread. Let the mixture sit, tossing occasionally, until the liquid is mostly absorbed, about 10 minutes.

3. Combine the remaining 1 tablespoon sugar and cinnamon in a small bowl. Transfer the soaked bread mixture to the prepared baking dish and sprinkle with the cinnamon sugar. Bake the bread pudding until just set and the surface is golden brown, 35 to 40 minutes. Let the bread pudding cool for 15 minutes before serving.

PER SERVING: Cal 320; Fat 8g; Sat fat 2g; Chol 105mg; Carb 50g; Protein 12g; Fiber 4g; Sodium 450mg

CHOCOLATE CUPCAKES

FOR THE CHOCOHOLIC IN ALL OF US, NOTHING BEATS a decadently rich chocolate cupcake piled high with creamy chocolate frosting. But when we let the secret out—most cupcakes pack more than 25 grams of fat— tasters demanded we develop a lower-fat version. We quickly learned this would be no easy task. Most low-fat chocolate cupcakes we tested were either lacking in chocolate flavor or so dry and dense they were better suited as paperweights. We were after a lower-fat chocolate cupcake, one that didn't feel lean, remained moist, had great chocolate flavor, and was topped with a rich chocolate frosting.

Many low-fat cupcake recipes "solve" the fat issue by incorporating "alternative" ingredients like prunes, applesauce, or fat-free evaporated milk. But we found all of the cupcakes built around these replacement ingredients to be dry, crumbly, or overly dense. We unanimously decided our best bet was to start with the test kitchen's latest chocolate cupcake recipe and cut fat where we could—without ruining its appeal.

The easiest starting place in our minds was the chocolate. Our original recipe called for 3 ounces of bittersweet chocolate and ⅓ cup of cocoa, a large amount compared to most recipes, which we made possible by using bread flour rather than all-purpose. (Chocolate is a tenderizer and thus a large amount of it will make all-purpose-flour cupcakes overly tender; meanwhile, bread flour allows for gluten development, and thus a sturdier crumb that allows for more chocolate.) Since cocoa can provide a good amount of chocolate flavor without adding as much fat as bar chocolate, we wondered if we could boost the amount of cocoa and cut the bittersweet chocolate without causing problems. We made a batch in which we ditched all of the bar chocolate and increased the amount of cocoa to a full cup. (To account for the increased volume of cocoa, we also removed some flour from the recipe.) The results weren't promising. Unlike flour, cocoa powder contains no gluten-forming proteins, so the resulting cupcakes were dry and crumbly, not to mention the chocolate flavor wasn't up to par.

We felt we were heading in the wrong direction, so we went back to our original recipe and tested how much bar chocolate we could cut while leaving the cocoa as is. We compared cupcakes made with 1 ounce and 2 ounces of bittersweet chocolate. While those made with 1 ounce were tough, tasters agreed that those with 2 ounces had a nice, soft crumb and plenty of chocolate flavor. The addition of instant espresso brought out the chocolate flavor even more with minimal change to the nutrition. With the amount of chocolate as low as we wanted to go, we moved on to cutting back fat elsewhere.

Our original cupcake testing had discovered that canola oil (6 tablespoons of it) was a better choice than butter for a fat because the butter masked the chocolate flavor. Could we cut back on the oil? We knew a familiar textural issue would pop up as we cut oil because oil (like chocolate) acts as a tenderizer. If we cut too much, our cupcakes would be destined for the trash bin. After a few trials, we found we could cut only 1 tablespoon of canola oil from our cupcakes before they turned tough.

Now we had a great-tasting, moist chocolate cupcake, so we needed to tackle the icing. Our original recipe made a fluffy meringue-style buttercream, but with a stick and a half of butter and 6 ounces of chocolate it needed a major overhaul. We came up with a much lighter version using confectioners' sugar, cocoa, milk, and only 2 tablespoons of butter, but after a few rounds of testing we agreed that it was lacking in chocolate flavor. It took only 1 ounce of bittersweet chocolate to ramp things up to the right level. This single-serving chocoholic treat had shed fat and calories but maintained its moist crumb and rich chocolate flavor.

NOTES FROM THE TEST KITCHEN

THE POWER OF COCOA

Cocoa powder is chocolate liquor that is fed through a press to remove all but 10 to 24 percent of the cocoa butter. To counter the harsh, acidic flavor of natural cocoa, the powder is sometimes treated with an alkaline solution, or "Dutched." Cookbooks often claim that Dutching "mellows" chocolate flavor, but our tasters disagree. Without the distraction of natural cocoa's harsh acidity, the more subtle, complex chocolate flavors came to the fore. In every test we ran, making everything from hot chocolate and chocolate shortbread to low-fat chocolate pudding, devil's food cake, and chocolate pudding cake, the dutched cocoa won out. Our favorite is **Callebaut Cocoa Powder**; the more widely available Droste came in second. In the test kitchen, we often "bloom" cocoa powder in a hot liquid such as water or coffee. This dissolves the remaining cocoa butter and disperses water-soluble flavor compounds for a deeper, stronger chocolate flavor.

Chocolate Cupcakes

MAKES 12 CUPCAKES

For an accurate measurement of boiling water, bring a full kettle of water to a boil, then measure out the desired amount. You can substitute ¾ cup hot coffee for the boiling water and instant espresso.

CUPCAKES

- 2 ounces bittersweet chocolate, chopped fine
- ⅓ cup (1 ounce) Dutch-processed cocoa
- ¾ teaspoon instant espresso
- ¾ cup boiling water (see note)
- ¾ cup (4⅛ ounces) bread flour
- ¾ cup (5¼ ounces) granulated sugar
- ½ teaspoon salt
- ½ teaspoon baking soda
- 5 tablespoons canola oil
- 2 large eggs
- 2 teaspoons white vinegar
- 1 teaspoon vanilla extract

FROSTING

- 3 cups (12 ounces) confectioners' sugar
- ½ cup (1½ ounces) Dutch-processed cocoa
- 6 tablespoons 1 percent low-fat milk
- 2 tablespoons unsalted butter, softened
- 1 ounce bittersweet chocolate, melted
- 1 teaspoon vanilla extract

1. FOR THE CUPCAKES: Adjust an oven rack to the middle position and heat the oven to 350 degrees. Line a 12-cup muffin tin with cupcake liners.

2. Combine the chocolate, cocoa, and instant espresso in a large bowl. Pour the boiling water over the chocolate mixture, cover, and let sit for 5 minutes to melt the chocolate. Whisk the chocolate mixture until smooth, then set aside to cool slightly, about 2 minutes. In a separate bowl, whisk the flour, granulated sugar, salt, and baking soda together.

3. Whisk the oil, eggs, vinegar, and vanilla extract into the cooled chocolate mixture until smooth. Whisk in the flour mixture until smooth.

4. Using a large ice-cream scoop or measuring cup lightly coated with vegetable oil spray, portion the batter evenly among the muffin cups. Bake until a toothpick inserted into the center of a cupcake comes out with a few moist crumbs attached, 17 to 19 minutes, rotating the muffin tin halfway through. Let the cupcakes cool in the pan for 10 minutes, then transfer to a wire rack to cool completely before frosting, about 1 hour.

5. FOR THE FROSTING: Pulse the confectioners' sugar and cocoa together in a food processor until combined, about 5 pulses. Add the milk, butter, chocolate, and vanilla extract and process until smooth, about 15 seconds. Mound 2 tablespoons of the frosting on the center of each cupcake. Using a small icing spatula or butter knife, spread the frosting to the edge of the cupcake, leaving a slight mound in the center.

PER CUPCAKE: Cal 330; Fat 12g; Sat fat 4g; Chol 40mg; Carb 56g; Protein 4g; Fiber 3g; Sodium 170mg

PLUM-PEACH UPSIDE-DOWN ALMOND CAKE

BEFORE THE INTRODUCTION OF CANNED PINEAPPLE in the early 1900s, which sparked a craze for pineapple in baked goods, upside-down cakes were made with seasonal fruit such as apples, peaches, and plums. The technique was straightforward: Pour a mixture of melted butter and brown sugar into a pan, add sliced fruit, spread cake batter over fruit, and bake. The fruit caramelizes on the bottom of the pan, revealing a layer of burnished amber fruit when the cake is turned upright. To make a healthy version, we hoped to find a way to bring together a light yet moist and flavorful cake with a topping that showcased fresh in-season fruit that was perfectly caramelized and sweet without being cloying.

Tinkering with the fruit topping seemed like a good place to start. Right off the bat we chose a combination of peaches and plums for an elegant, summery cake. In most old-fashioned upside-down cake recipes, the specifics for turning the chosen fruit into a topping were roughly the same: Melt about 4 tablespoons of butter and up to ¾ cup of brown sugar in a saucepan, pour the mixture into a 9-inch round cake pan, and fan the thinly sliced fruit across the top. We gave this a try with our working cake recipe, but when we inverted the cake onto a plate, we found that the peaches and plums had cooked down to a shriveled layer, with patches of cake peeking through. Since we had sliced the fruit into ¼-inch-thick wedges, cutting it into thicker pieces was our first thought. This change improved matters greatly, and after more testing we found that cutting the fruit, unpeeled, into ¾-inch-thick wedges ensured that it

maintained its integrity and formed a solid layer for topping our upturned cake.

As for the butter, the copious 4 tablespoons was not going to pass muster for our healthy cake. We tested reducing the amount of butter in the topping 1 tablespoon at a time (as well as reducing the amount of brown sugar accordingly to keep the right gooey, caramelized results). We found that we needed only 1 tablespoon of butter and ¼ cup of brown sugar to provide the right richly flavored, perfectly caramelized topping.

With dishes piling up, we realized we could streamline by making the melted butter–brown sugar mixture right in the cake pan. We simply melted the butter in the cake pan in the preheating oven (which took only a minute or two), then sprinkled the brown sugar on top and patted it down. We arranged the fruit in concentric circles and proceeded with the cake. This worked well and saved us a little time along the way. So with our topping in place, we turned our attention to the cake.

First, we needed to fix the cake's structural issues. Up to this point, we had been using a standard butter cake recipe. While tasters enjoyed its tender texture, it was buckling under the fruit's weight. The creaming method for this cake—beating the butter with the sugar, beating in the eggs, and then alternately folding in the dry and liquid ingredients—was to blame. Creaming creates air bubbles, which produce lightness, volume, and delicate texture. For a coarser crumb, we needed to use the so-called quick-bread method, in which the butter is melted and the liquid and dry ingredients are mixed separately before being combined. The melted butter introduces less air into the batter than creamed butter, making for a sturdier crumb. Sure enough, the cake made with this approach was plenty moist but with a more substantial crumb that held up under the topping.

Now we needed to lighten our cake. From the full stick of butter, we were able to shave off 2 tablespoons with minimal effect on flavor. We tried using a combination of butter and oil instead of all butter to cut down on the saturated fat, but tasters missed the richness—all butter was worth keeping.

That said, compared to the flavorful fruit topping, the cake tasted a little lackluster. We tried trading the milk for other dairy products, and while both yogurt and buttermilk improved matters, low-fat sour cream was a standout. Its subtle tang balanced the sweetness of the cake and complemented the caramelized fruit. We also swapped out ¼ cup of white sugar for brown, which offered a hint of molasses. Given our cake's rustic nature, one test cook suggested incorporating ground nuts into the cake, as is done in classic Italian almond cakes. Adding a small amount of ground toasted almonds to the dry ingredients in lieu of some flour added a nutty, earthy flavor and pleasantly coarse texture that paired well with our topping. Although they added some fat, we agreed that since it was heart-healthy monounsaturated fat, the almonds were a good fit for our recipe.

After a number of tests, we realized that timing is key when unmolding an upside-down cake. When the cake was turned out of the pan hot from the oven, the fruit layer was too juicy and fluid, which resulted in the fruit layer sliding untidily over the cake layer. But if the cake cooled for too long, the fruit stuck in the pan. We found that a 10-minute cooling period was enough time to allow the fruit layer to firm up a bit so it adhered to the cake—and the cake was still warm enough to release easily from the pan. And once we turned over the cake pan, we allowed it to sit inverted over the cake for another minute, undisturbed. This step further ensured that the cake would release in one piece. Move over, pineapple, because this rustic summer-fruit rendition really takes the cake.

NOTES FROM THE TEST KITCHEN

MAKING UPSIDE-DOWN CAKE

1. After melting the butter in the cake pan and adding the brown sugar, arrange the plums and/or peaches in attractive concentric circles on top of the mixture.

2. Let the baked cake cool slightly. Lay a platter over the pan's top and invert the cake onto the platter. Let the cake release from the pan (do not shake or tap), which will take about 1 minute. Then let the cake cool completely.

THE BEST ROUND CAKE PAN
Does the type of cake pan you use make a difference? Yes, and we've baked our fair share of pale cakes or, even worse, ones that have refused to turn out of the pans regardless of how diligently we greased them. We baked three of our basic cakes in 17 different pans, which ranged widely in price and construction, testing each one for quick release, even browning, and overall appearance. For the neatest and most attractive appearance, we prefer cakes baked in pans with straight sides. Of the 17 brands we tested, we liked the **Chicago Metallic Professional Lifetime 9-Inch Nonstick Round Cake Pan**, $15.95, the best. In addition to promoting the best browning, the nonstick surface ensured the quickest and best release every time.

Plum-Peach Upside-Down Almond Cake
SERVES 10

You will need a 9-inch nonstick round cake pan with sides that are at least 2 inches high to make this cake. If your cake pan is not tall enough, the batter will overflow in the oven.

TOPPING
- 1 tablespoon unsalted butter
- ¼ cup packed (1¾ ounces) light brown sugar
- 1 pound plums and/or peaches (2 to 4), pitted and sliced into ¾-inch-thick wedges

CAKE
- ¼ cup slivered almonds, toasted
- ½ teaspoon salt
- 1 cup (5 ounces) unbleached all-purpose flour
- 1 teaspoon baking powder
- ¾ cup (5¼ ounces) granulated sugar
- ¼ cup packed (1¾ ounces) light brown sugar
- 2 large eggs, at room temperature
- 6 tablespoons (¾ stick) unsalted butter, melted and cooled
- ½ cup low-fat sour cream
- 1 teaspoon vanilla extract
- ¼ teaspoon almond extract

1. FOR THE TOPPING: Adjust an oven rack to the lowest position and heat the oven to 350 degrees. Place the butter in a 9-inch nonstick round cake pan and heat in the oven until melted, 1 to 3 minutes.

2. Sprinkle the brown sugar into the cake pan, then pat into an even layer with a spatula. Following the photo, arrange the slices of fruit in concentric circles on top of the sugar.

PLUM-PEACH UPSIDE-DOWN ALMOND CAKE

3. FOR THE CAKE: Process the almonds and salt together in a food processor until very finely ground, about 15 seconds. Whisk the almond mixture, flour, and baking powder together in a bowl.

4. In a large bowl, whisk the granulated sugar, brown sugar, and eggs together until thick and homogeneous, about 45 seconds. Slowly whisk in the melted butter until thoroughly combined. Whisk in the sour cream, vanilla extract, and almond extract until uniform. Whisk in the flour mixture until just combined.

5. Spoon mounds of batter evenly over the fruit and gently smooth the top. Gently tap the pan on the counter to settle the batter. Bake the cake until golden brown and a toothpick inserted into the center comes out with a few moist crumbs attached, 35 to 40 minutes.

6. Let the cake cool slightly in the pan, about 10 minutes. Place a platter over the top of the cake pan, invert the platter and pan, and let sit until the cake releases itself from the pan (do not shake or tap the pan), about 1 minute. Gently remove the cake pan and let the cake cool completely, about 2 hours, before serving.

PER SERVING: Cal 280; Fat 11g; Sat fat 6g; Chol 65mg; Carb 41g; Protein 4g; Fiber 1g; Sodium 180mg

STRAWBERRY SHORTCAKES

GIVEN ALL THE FRUIT, IT'S EASY TO FOOL YOURSELF into believing that strawberry shortcake is a healthy dessert. But when you realize the biscuits have a full stick of butter in them, the strawberries are drowned in sugar, and the whipped cream that is light as air is heavy with fat, you are brought back to reality. A single serving adds up to almost 700 calories and 40 grams of fat. Could we cut fat and calories from this summer classic and still maintain its true essence: fresh, bright berries, tender, flaky biscuits, and a lighter-than-air whipped topping?

To start, we put a few low-fat recipes to the test. The chief complaint among tasters was that not one produced an acceptable shortcake. Made with little fat, these cakes were tough, squat, pale, and dry. As for the whipped toppings, they were anything but creamy. A meager drizzle of artificially sweetened yogurt (the route most took) was a long way from a billowy cloud of whipped cream. We opted to forgo these low-fat failures and find a better

TEST KITCHEN
MAKEOVER

solution. The test kitchen has no shortage of strawberry shortcake recipes, so we felt it best to start with a full-fat version and pare it down.

Our original shortcake recipe used a stick of butter, one egg, and ½ cup of full-fat sour cream for six biscuits. Each tablespoon of butter adds about 100 calories, so we set out to reduce the amount of butter in the recipe by half. At 4 tablespoons, we could still taste the butter, but the shortcakes were dry. To combat the moisture problem, we added ¼ cup of skim milk, but upping it to ½ cup allowed us to omit the egg. We often use Greek yogurt in light recipes when we need a thicker dairy product, and 6 tablespoons of fat-free Greek yogurt successfully replaced the sour cream. Our biscuits were much better, and definitely light in terms of fat and calories, but they still weren't as tender as we would have liked.

Up until now, we had been cutting the butter into the flour in the food processor to distribute it. Normally, when the bits of butter melt, steam escapes, which puffs the shortcake up and out. But with so little butter in our lightened recipe, the method barely worked. A test kitchen drop biscuit recipe gave us the idea to whisk slightly cooled, melted butter with the milk and yogurt. The melted butter clumped into droplets and distributed more evenly throughout the dough, which in the oven acted like the butter pieces in the original recipe, yielding lean yet tender shortcakes.

Our next change was a simple one. We cut the amount of sugar in the berry portion by half. Three tablespoons, tasters agreed, was plenty sweet and enough to create a syrupy glaze on our berries.

Finally, we needed to confront the whipped-cream topping, which accounted for about 200 calories per serving in our original recipe. Finding a suitable substitute for whipped heavy cream turned out to be nearly impossible. We tried beating chilled evaporated milk with powdered sugar and vanilla extract. In no time, it whipped into light, airy foam. In even less time, it disintegrated into a puddle of deflated bubbles. We tried to firm sweetened low-fat milk with gelatin, but the result was wiggly, clotted, and nothing like whipped cream. We then tried cutting a small amount of whipping cream with different light ingredients, including reduced-fat cream cheese, reduced-fat ricotta, pureed cottage cheese, and fat-free Greek yogurt. The cream cheese, ricotta, and cottage cheese all yielded heavy, deflated, and grainy whipped toppings that were nothing like the real deal. Only the Greek yogurt produced a light, airy whipped topping that was nearly as good as the original.

We had cut 260 calories and 22 grams of fat from our original recipe, but one thing was certain: These shortcakes were certainly not short on flavor.

MAKEOVER SPOTLIGHT: STRAWBERRY SHORTCAKES

	CALORIES	FAT	SAT FAT	CHOLESTEROL
BEFORE	680	37g	23g	150mg
AFTER	420	15g	10g	50mg

Strawberry Shortcakes

SERVES 6

Greek yogurt makes the topping taste creamy and rich; don't substitute regular fat-free yogurt. Allow the berries and accumulated juice to soak into the shortcakes for a few minutes before serving.

STRAWBERRIES

- 6 cups (30 ounces) fresh strawberries (2 cups hulled plus 4 cups hulled, halved, and sliced thin)
- 3 tablespoons sugar

SHORTCAKES

- 2 cups (10 ounces) unbleached all-purpose flour
- 2 tablespoons sugar
- 1 tablespoon baking powder
- ½ teaspoon salt
- ½ cup skim milk
- 6 tablespoons fat free Greek yogurt
- 4 tablespoons (½ stick) unsalted butter, melted and cooled slightly

TOPPING

- ½ cup heavy cream
- ¼ cup (1¾ ounces) sugar
- 1 teaspoon vanilla extract
- ½ cup fat-free Greek yogurt (see note)

1. FOR THE STRAWBERRIES: Mash the hulled whole berries in a large bowl with a potato masher. Stir in the sliced berries and sugar and let sit at room temperature until the sugar has dissolved and the berries are juicy, about 30 minutes.

2. FOR THE SHORTCAKES: While the strawberries sit, adjust an oven rack to the middle position and heat the oven to 400 degrees. Line a baking sheet with parchment paper and set aside.

3. Whisk the flour, sugar, baking powder, and salt together in a bowl. Whisk the milk, yogurt, and melted butter together in a large bowl until small clumps form. Stir the flour mixture into the yogurt mixture until the dough comes together and no dry flour remains. Turn the mixture onto a lightly floured counter and knead lightly until smooth, 8 to 10 times.

4. Pat the dough into an 8-inch circle, about ½ inch thick. Using a floured 3-inch biscuit cutter, stamp out 4 shortcakes. Press the remaining dough together and stamp out 2 more shortcakes.

5. Arrange the shortcakes on the prepared baking sheet, spaced about 1½ inches apart. Bake the shortcakes until golden brown, 12 to 15 minutes, rotating the baking sheet halfway through. Let the shortcakes cool on the baking sheet until warm, about 10 minutes.

6. FOR THE TOPPING: Meanwhile, whip the cream, sugar, and vanilla extract together in a large bowl with an electric mixer on medium-low speed until frothy, about 1 minute. Increase the mixer speed to high and continue to whip until the cream forms soft peaks, 1 to 3 minutes longer. Gently fold in the yogurt.

7. TO ASSEMBLE: Split each shortcake in half and lay the bottoms on 6 individual serving plates. Spoon a portion of the berry mixture over each bottom, dollop with the whipped cream, and cap with the shortcake tops. Serve.

PER SERVING: Cal 420; Fat 15g; Sat fat 10g; Chol 50mg; Carb 62g; Protein 9g; Fiber 4g; Sodium 500mg

---

NOTES FROM THE TEST KITCHEN

THE KEY TO TENDER, FLUFFY, LOW-FAT SHORTCAKES
Our light shortcakes don't have enough butter to make them puff in the oven as would normally happen with full-fat shortcakes. Here's how we got fluffy shortcakes without the fat.

We melt 4 tablespoons of butter, then combine it with the yogurt and milk. The clumps that form evenly distribute in the dough and create the steam needed for tender, fluffy shortcakes just as good as the full-fat variety.

PEACH BROWN BETTY

COBBLERS, PIES, AND CRISPS MAY BE THE GO-TO BAKED fruit desserts, but don't be too quick to count out brown betty. It's a homey sweet traditionally made by layering sliced apples and buttery bread crumbs in a deep dish and baking them until the apples are tender and the crumb topping is crisp. The crumb layers are there to sop up the fruit's juice, and we figured they'd serve the same function if we used juicy, in-season peaches instead of apples. But a few tests proved that the crumbs weren't up to the task. Our peach version was wet and washed out; the crumbs were soggy and the peaches tasted canned. We set out determined to solve these problems and give this old-fashioned dessert a lighter, fresh peach profile.

First, we tried the usual tactics for dealing with excess fruit juice. We tried adding both cornstarch and flour to the peaches, but both dulled the fruit's flavor. Tossing the peaches with sugar and draining them—a method we sometimes use to draw out liquid—worked but took about an hour, more time than we were willing to devote to what should be an uncomplicated dessert (not to mention we'd be throwing flavorful peach juice down the drain). Precooking the peaches in a skillet with just 1 tablespoon of butter proved best. As the peaches cooked, they released their juice, and after a few minutes of cooking the juice began to thicken and the natural sugars in both the fruit and juice began to deepen and caramelize, intensifying the peach flavor. We wondered if sprinkling in more sugar would magnify the results. It did, but we opted to wait until after we had precooked the peaches to add the sugar, off the heat to avoid scorching. A combination of white and brown sugar—just ⅓ cup of each—lent the right amount of pure sweetness and maple flavor.

At this point, we decided to abandon the concept of transferring everything to a baking dish and instead would turn our Peach Brown Betty into a skillet recipe. While traditional brown betties call for layers of buttery crumbs to help bind the dessert together, we hoped our thickened, reduced peach juice would be binding enough, allowing us to use the bread crumbs only for a topping (saving us not only labor but also calories and fat). Crossing our fingers, we sprinkled fresh bread crumbs over the fruit and put the skillet into the oven. To our dismay, the topping drowned in the bubbling juice; we would have to stir at least some bread crumbs into the filling for structure and support. We took some of the crumbs from the topping (instead of adding more) and stirred them into the peaches. That did the trick; our bread-crumb topping stayed on top where it belonged.

Our topping was now staying put and keeping dry enough to brown, but it still wasn't crisp enough to lend the right contrast to the tender peaches. Up until now, we'd been tossing fresh bread crumbs with melted butter. Toasting the fresh crumbs first made the topping too dark. Going back to raw bread crumbs, we wondered if the melted butter was weighing them down. We processed the crumbs with 3 tablespoons of cold butter (anything less and the crumbs did not brown well), stirred some of this coarse, shaggy mixture into the peaches, then sprinkled the rest on top and placed the betty in the oven. About a half-hour and one bowl of Peach Brown

NOTES FROM THE TEST KITCHEN

PEELING PEACHES

1. With a paring knife, score a small X at the base of each peach. Then lower the peaches into boiling water and simmer until the skins loosen, 30 to 60 seconds.

2. Transfer the peaches immediately to ice water and let them cool for about 1 minute.

3. Use a paring knife to remove strips of loosened peel, starting at the X on the base of each peach.

Betty later, we could definitely say our crisp topping was a suitable match for the juicy, fragrant peach filling. A little lemon juice added the right brightness, a splash of vanilla extract brought out the flavor of the peaches, and a sprinkle of cinnamon sugar at the end added flavor and even more crunch. We were ready to introduce our guilt-free Peach Brown Betty to our friends.

Peach Brown Betty

SERVES 6

You can substitute 3 pounds frozen sliced peaches, thawed and drained, for the fresh peaches. If you don't own an ovensafe skillet, transfer the peach filling to a 2-quart baking dish at the end of step 2 and continue with the recipe as directed.

TOPPING

- 4 slices high-quality white sandwich bread, torn into pieces
- 3 tablespoons unsalted butter, cut into ½-inch pieces and chilled
- 1 tablespoon granulated sugar
- ¼ teaspoon ground cinnamon

FILLING

- 1 tablespoon unsalted butter
- 3½ pounds ripe but firm peaches (7 to 10), peeled (see page 276), pitted, and cut into ½-inch-thick wedges
- ⅓ cup (2⅓ ounces) granulated sugar
- ⅓ cup packed (2⅓ ounces) light brown sugar
- 1 tablespoon fresh lemon juice
- 1 teaspoon vanilla extract
- ⅛ teaspoon salt

1. FOR THE TOPPING: Adjust an oven rack to the middle position and heat the oven to 400 degrees. Pulse the bread and butter in a food processor to coarse crumbs, about 10 pulses; set aside. Combine the granulated sugar and cinnamon in a bowl and set aside.

2. FOR THE FILLING: Melt the butter in a 12-inch ovensafe skillet over medium-high heat. Add the peaches and cook, stirring occasionally, until beginning to brown, 8 to 12 minutes. Off the heat, stir in 1 cup of the bread-crumb mixture, granulated sugar, brown sugar, lemon juice, vanilla extract, and salt.

3. Sprinkle the remaining bread-crumb mixture evenly over the peach mixture, then sprinkle the cinnamon-sugar mixture over the top and bake until the topping is golden brown and the juice is bubbling, 20 to 25 minutes. Let the brown betty cool for 10 minutes before serving.

PER SERVING: Cal 310; Fat 9g; Sat fat 6g; Chol 20mg; Carb 59g; Protein 4g; Fiber 4g; Sodium 140mg

SKILLET LEMON SOUFFLÉ

TO HOME COOKS, FEW THINGS SEEM AS DAUNTING TO make as a soufflé. Towering like chefs' toques over the fluted rims of porcelain ramekins, they seem too difficult to prepare for a casual weeknight menu. Recipes we tested that propose to simplify the process by having you bake the soufflé in a 10-inch skillet just didn't come close to the lightness we were looking for—they inevitably ended up wet and underrisen. And like most lemon soufflés (skillet or traditional), they didn't have a truly bright taste. Hoping to rectify these obvious pitfalls, we wanted to streamline this naturally light French classic, turning it into an easy, low-fat dessert that could make regular appearances in the home cook's repertoire without fear of falling flat.

The most time-consuming part of any soufflé is making the base, a cooked mixture of flour, milk, butter, sugar, and egg yolks. Whipped egg whites are then folded into this base and the soufflé is baked. The base provides stability, and the whipped whites offer lift.

Not willing to take anything for granted (particularly stodgy French tradition), we attempted a lighter soufflé without a true base—saving us, we hoped, both labor and several grams of fat in the process. We whisked together five egg yolks and ⅔ cup of sugar, but we omitted the traditional butter and replaced a full cup of milk with ⅓ cup of lemon juice (not only did these steps cut fat, but we also thought the dairy elements might be dulling the lemon flavor). A typical soufflé contains about 1 tablespoon of flour per egg. But with far less liquid in the mix, we settled on just 2 tablespoons of flour altogether. With such a small amount, adding raw flour to the base (versus cooked in a true béchamel) wasn't likely to be a problem. We folded the meringue into the base and poured the mixture into a skillet to bake at 375 degrees.

It worked, sort of. Tasters couldn't detect the presence of raw flour and found the lemon flavor far brighter without the muting effect of dairy. Plus, the soufflé rose dramatically above the rim of the skillet. But, as with all the skillet soufflé recipes we had tested in our research, the bottom of ours was undercooked. Clearly the thick metal of the skillet (unlike a traditional soufflé pan, which is thinner) was protecting its underside, preventing it from cooking properly.

Dropping the oven temperature to 300 degrees in an effort to promote more even cooking between the top and the bottom was a bust. A soufflé needs high heat to cause the air inside it to expand quickly and create its signature rise; otherwise, it turns out more like a lemon pancake. Then our thoughts shifted to another one of France's great desserts (also cooked in a skillet): tarte Tatin. In this rustic dish, apples are first caramelized in the skillet on the stovetop, then topped with a layer of pastry and transferred to the oven. The double whammy of heat from below and then from above ensures that the dessert is fully cooked through, top to bottom. It sounded crazy, but could we use this method on our soufflé?

NOTES FROM THE TEST KITCHEN

THE IMPORTANCE OF CREAM OF TARTAR
Recipes that call for whipping egg whites often add cream of tartar to the whites, but what is it, and why is it added? Cream of tartar, also known as potassium bitartrate, is a powdered byproduct of the wine-making process and, along with baking soda, is one of the two main ingredients in baking powder. Cream of tartar's acidic nature lowers the pH of egg whites, which encourages the eggs' proteins to unfold, thus creating more volume, greater stability, and a glossier appearance. We compared whipped egg whites and cooked meringue (an egg white and sugar mixture) prepared with and without cream of tartar. For the whipped egg whites, the volume of the batch with cream of tartar was nearly double that of the batch without it. Both versions of the cooked meringue were similar right out of the oven, but after two days the meringue without cream of tartar had begun to separate and exude liquid (or "weep"), and the meringue made with cream of tartar was fully stable. The moral of the story? That small amount of cream of tartar makes a big difference.

We gently heated a mere tablespoon of butter (just enough to prevent sticking) in a 10-inch skillet and poured the batter directly into the pan. It immediately started to set and after about two minutes was lightly puffed and gently bubbling on the edges. We quickly transferred the skillet to the oven and kept a careful watch through the oven window. Not 10 minutes later, we pulled a golden brown, perfectly puffed soufflé from the oven. After dusting it with powdered sugar, we scooped into it with a spoon, revealing a light, moist, and creamy interior that went all the way from top to bottom. Even though every soufflé will eventually fall, our streamlined skillet lemon soufflé was so good, tasters made sure it never had the chance.

Skillet Lemon Soufflé
SERVES 6

Don't open the oven door during the first 7 minutes of baking, but do check the soufflé regularly for doneness during the final few minutes in the oven. Be ready to serve the soufflé immediately after removing it from the oven. Using a 10-inch traditional (not nonstick) skillet is essential to getting the right texture and height in the soufflé.

- 5 **large eggs, separated**
- ¼ **teaspoon cream of tartar**
- ⅔ **cup (4⅔ ounces) granulated sugar**
- ⅛ **teaspoon salt**
- ⅓ **cup fresh lemon juice plus 1 teaspoon grated lemon zest (about 2 lemons)**
- 2 **tablespoons unbleached all-purpose flour**
- 1 **tablespoon unsalted butter**
  Confectioners' sugar, for dusting

1. Adjust an oven rack to the middle position and heat the oven to 375 degrees. In a large bowl, whip the egg whites and cream of tartar together with an electric mixer on medium-low speed until foamy, about 1 minute. Increase the mixer speed to medium-high and whip the whites to soft, billowy mounds, about 1 minute. Gradually whip in ⅓ cup of the granulated sugar and salt, and continue to whip the whites until they are glossy and form stiff peaks, 2 to 6 minutes. Gently transfer the whites to a clean bowl and set aside.

2. In a large bowl, whip the egg yolks and the remaining ⅓ cup granulated sugar together with an electric

SKILLET LEMON SOUFFLÉ

mixer on medium-high speed until pale and thick, about 1 minute. Whip in the lemon juice, lemon zest, and flour until incorporated, about 30 seconds.

3. Fold one-quarter of the whipped egg whites into the egg yolk mixture until almost no white streaks remain. Gently fold in the remaining egg whites until just incorporated.

4. Melt the butter in a 10-inch ovensafe skillet over medium-low heat. Swirl the pan to coat evenly with the melted butter, then gently scrape the soufflé batter into the skillet and cook until the edges begin to set and bubble slightly, about 2 minutes.

5. Transfer the skillet to the oven and bake the soufflé until puffed, the center jiggles slightly when shaken, and the surface is golden, 7 to 11 minutes. Using a potholder (the skillet handle will be hot), remove the skillet from the oven. Dust the soufflé with confectioners' sugar and serve immediately.

PER SERVING: **Cal** 180; **Fat** 6g; **Sat fat** 2.5g; **Chol** 180mg; **Carb** 28g; **Protein** 6g; **Fiber** 0g; **Sodium** 105mg

VARIATION

Skillet Chocolate-Orange Soufflé

Grating the chocolate fine is key here; we find it easiest to use either a rasp grater or the fine holes of a box grater.

Follow the recipe for Skillet Lemon Soufflé, substituting orange juice for the lemon juice and 1 tablespoon grated orange zest for the lemon zest. Gently fold 1 ounce (about ½ cup) finely grated bittersweet chocolate into the soufflé batter after incorporating all of the whites in step 3.

PER SERVING: **Cal** 210; **Fat** 7g; **Sat fat** 3.5g; **Chol** 180mg; **Carb** 32g; **Protein** 6g; **Fiber** 1g; **Sodium** 105mg

LEMON YOGURT MOUSSE

THOUGH MOST EVERYONE LOVES A COOL SCOOP OF ice cream, every now and then we want something a little lighter. Lemon mousse, with its sunny flavor and creamy yet fluffy texture, offers a refreshing alternative. However, while its texture is light, like any traditional mousse its egg yolk–enriched base combined with whipped heavy cream, egg whites, and sugar is actually heavy on the fat (a ½-cup serving can contain up to 12 grams). Could we cut some of the fat from the traditional mousse yet maintain the same appealing creamy, smooth texture and bright flavor?

We started by rounding up a few existing recipes, in all of which yogurt was substituted for the heavy cream. Some also cut out the yolks entirely, and others involved whipping the egg whites with sugar over the heat, a technique that creates a creamy yet airy texture, similar to the technique for making what is commonly known as seven-minute icing. While the icing technique showed good promise (it offered more structure than standard whipped egg whites), in general the results revealed a host of problems. Some versions were stiff and springy like a creamy Jell-O; others were foamy, and almost all were watery and separated. And then there were the issues with the lemon flavor. Some mousses were lip-puckeringly sour, and others barely registered any lemon flavor at all. Clearly, we needed to set out on our own. We wanted a smooth, creamy mousse and bright lemon flavor.

We made two decisions up front. First, we would proceed without egg yolks. While the yolks contribute richness and a silky texture to the standard mousse, we didn't want the added fat and would find a way to create similar satisfying results without them. Besides, they made for a heavier mousse and we were after lightness. Second, we would rely on Greek yogurt for the yogurt component. It has a dense, creamy texture that the test kitchen has found works well in a number of lighter creamy desserts.

With those two decisions made, we were ready to experiment. We began with the texture and structure. There are two main components of a standard mousse: whipped cream and whipped egg whites. When folded together, they provide a suspension of fat and protein that gives mousse its distinctly creamy yet airy texture. Obviously we would need to find a way to achieve similar results with yogurt in lieu of the heavy cream. We already knew from early tests that a simple swap of one for the other wouldn't work. Unlike whipping heavy cream, whipping yogurt will not do much in terms of lightening and aerating. As a result, the whipped egg whites can't incorporate with the heavier yogurt to create the proper suspension. You end up with a dense, separated lemon pudding with the lemon juice pooling at the bottom of the dish.

Whipping the egg whites with the sugar, icing-style, offered more structure, but not enough. We would need to create more suspension and lift. First we tried adding more egg whites to the standard three found in most mousse recipes. We tested incorporating four and five whipped egg whites (sweetened with sugar) into a basic mousse base made with Greek yogurt and a few tablespoons of lemon juice. But each added egg white only made things worse, resulting in mousse that tasters pronounced "too eggy," with an unappealing texture. We went back to three egg whites—and to the drawing board.

We often use gelatin in the test kitchen to give structure to custard-based desserts like panna cotta and chilled soufflés. It seemed worth a try here. We started by soaking a packet of gelatin (2½ teaspoons) in water until dissolved, then we added it to the cooked egg whites. The results told us we were heading in the right direction; this mousse held together and the wateriness was gone. But this mousse was too stiff. Working backward from 2½ teaspoons, we tested lesser amounts in ½-teaspoon intervals. We found that the perfect structure came from ¾ teaspoon of gelatin, giving us a creamy, smooth mousse.

Up to this point, we had been using full-fat Greek yogurt. We wondered if the texture would suffer if we used 2 percent or fat-free Greek yogurt instead, so that we could cut a few more calories and grams of fat. We couldn't. Tasters unanimously agreed that the full-fat yogurt was essential to the creaminess. The lower-fat versions lacked flavor and created a spongy texture.

But even with full-fat yogurt, tasters felt the recipe was missing some of the richness that they expected in a mousse. Crunching the numbers, we found we had a little wiggle room to add back some fat, so we whisked ¼ cup of heavy cream (full-fat recipes call for 1 cup or more) into the yogurt. This gave the mousse just the richness tasters craved.

Finally, we could focus on flavor. We wanted a bright lemon zing that would complement the tanginess of the yogurt; however, we knew we had to be careful. Lemon juice whisked in with the yogurt added great lemon flavor, but too much liquid created a watery mousse. A few tests proved 3 tablespoons was the limit. Still, we wanted more lemon flavor. Lemon zest packs a powerful lemony punch, and 1½ teaspoons added the right amount without making the mousse bitter.

Tasters liked the mousse as it was, but we thought it might be nice to dress it up a bit so we developed three easy berry sauces. We simply cooked blueberries, raspberries, and strawberries with a little sugar, pureed

them, and strained them through a fine-mesh strainer. But spooning these sauces over the mousse didn't look as attractive as we had hoped; they looked more like an afterthought. Then a fellow test cook mentioned fruit-on-the-bottom yogurt. What if we put the sauce in the ramekins before adding the mousse and letting them set? It was easy enough to do, and tasters loved swirling the sauce into their mousse at the table. Of course, they also loved that each serving had half the fat—just 6 grams—of full-fat lemon mousse. This dessert was the perfect treat for a hot summer day.

Lemon Yogurt Mousse with Blueberry Sauce
SERVES 6

You can substitute 1 cup frozen blueberries for the fresh berries.

SAUCE

¾ cup (3¾ ounces) fresh blueberries
2 tablespoons sugar
2 tablespoons water
   Pinch salt

MOUSSE

3 tablespoons water
¾ teaspoon unflavored gelatin
½ cup whole-milk Greek yogurt
¼ cup heavy cream
3 tablespoons fresh lemon juice plus 1½ teaspoons grated lemon zest
1 teaspoon vanilla extract
⅛ teaspoon salt
3 large egg whites
6 tablespoons sugar
¼ teaspoon cream of tartar

1. FOR THE SAUCE: Bring the blueberries, sugar, water, and salt to a simmer in a medium saucepan over medium heat, stirring occasionally. Cook until the sugar is dissolved and the fruit is heated through, 2 to 4 minutes.

2. Transfer the mixture to a blender and process until smooth, about 20 seconds. Pour the puree through a fine-mesh strainer, pressing on the solids to extract as much sauce as possible (you should have about ½ cup).

Discard the solids. Spoon the sauce evenly into six 4-ounce ramekins and refrigerate until chilled, about 20 minutes.

3. FOR THE MOUSSE: Meanwhile, pour the water into a bowl, sprinkle the gelatin evenly over the top, and set aside to let the gelatin hydrate for 10 minutes. In a separate bowl, whisk the yogurt, cream, lemon juice, lemon zest, vanilla extract, and salt together until smooth.

4. Whisk the egg whites, sugar, and cream of tartar together in a large heatproof bowl. Set the bowl over a large saucepan of barely simmering water, making sure the water does not touch the bottom of the bowl. Heat the mixture, whisking constantly, until it has tripled in size and registers about 160 degrees on an instant-read thermometer, 5 to 10 minutes.

5. Off the heat, quickly whisk in the hydrated gelatin until melted. Whip the warm mixture with an electric mixer on medium-high speed until it forms stiff, shiny peaks, 4 to 6 minutes. Add the yogurt mixture and continue to whip until just combined, 30 to 60 seconds.

6. Divide the mousse evenly among the chilled ramekins with the blueberry sauce, cover with plastic wrap, and refrigerate until chilled and set, 6 to 8 hours or up to 24 hours. Serve chilled.

PER SERVING: Cal 150; **Fat** 6g; **Sat fat** 4g; **Chol** 20mg; **Carb** 21g; **Protein** 4g; **Fiber** 1g; **Sodium** 110mg

---

NOTES FROM THE TEST KITCHEN

MAKING LEMON YOGURT MOUSSE WITH BERRY SAUCE

1. Pour the berry sauce into the bottom of six 4-ounce ramekins and let them chill in the refrigerator for at least 20 minutes.

2. Spoon the mousse into the chilled ramekins on top of the sauce. Cover with plastic wrap and refrigerate the mousse until chilled and set, 6 to 8 hours.

VARIATIONS

Lemon Yogurt Mousse with Raspberry Sauce

Follow the recipe for Lemon Yogurt Mousse with Blueberry Sauce, substituting fresh raspberries for the blueberries.

PER SERVING: Cal 150; **Fat** 6g; **Sat fat** 4g; **Chol** 20mg; **Carb** 21g; **Protein** 4g; **Fiber** 1g; **Sodium** 110mg

Lemon Yogurt Mousse with Strawberry Sauce

Follow the recipe for Lemon Yogurt Mousse with Blueberry Sauce, substituting 1 cup (5 ounces) fresh strawberries, hulled and halved, for the blueberries and reducing the amount of water to 2 teaspoons.

PER SERVING: Cal 150; **Fat** 6g; **Sat fat** 4g; **Chol** 20mg; **Carb** 21g; **Protein** 4g; **Fiber** 1g; **Sodium** 110mg

POACHED PEARS

SERVED CHILLED WITH A SWEET, FLAVORFUL SYRUP made from the cooking liquid, poached pears are a classic dessert perfect for finishing a meal without making you feel bogged down, and with their elegant presence on the plate, they are a great choice for entertaining. Poaching is an ideal cooking method for fruit because, unlike other cooking methods, it allows the shape and texture of the fruit to remain intact while improving its tenderness and enhancing, rather than washing out, its flavor. Though simple in appearance, poached pears are not easy to get just right. Most recipes we tried yielded fruit that was either too mushy or still rock hard, and all were accompanied by a sickly sweet syrup that was hardly palatable. Brushing these failures aside, we set out to develop a recipe for poached pears that were soft and tender, infused with aromatics, and perfect when served chilled with the poaching liquid as the sauce.

We began our testing by poaching different common types of pears (Bosc, d'Anjou, Comice, and Bartlett) in varying states of ripeness. Unripe pears (of any variety) never attained a tender texture no matter how long they simmered, and if the pears were too ripe, they were difficult to handle and easily cooked to mush. Moderately ripe pears became our favorite to work with, as they cooked quickly and their slightly underripe texture turned perfectly tender once cooked. Of the types of pears tested, our favorites were the Bartlett, for its floral, honeyed notes, and the Bosc, because it tasted like a sweet, ripe pear should taste. The other two varieties were unremarkable in flavor and the least attractive in appearance, as they experienced some discoloration during poaching.

With our pear varieties selected, we went about trying to bolster their flavor by testing different poaching mediums. Most of the recipes we came across used either a simple syrup of sugar and water or a sugar-sweetened wine for poaching the pears, but we were curious about other poaching liquids. We tried both of these common options as well as juice and combinations of the three. The pears poached with water tasted flat and dull, and the fruit juice added a generic-tasting "fruit" flavor to the pears. The wine-poached pears, however, were bright and far more interesting, the unanimous winner. These early tests proved that cutting the wine with another liquid was not only unnecessary, but a mistake—it simply watered down the bright wine flavor.

Attempting to decide between red and white wine was difficult. We liked the flavor of each in its own right, so we developed a recipe for each. Tasters noted milder, floral flavors in the pears poached in white wine, making poaching aromatics such as herbs (we settled on a combination of mint and thyme) and lemon a logical match. Meanwhile, we found the deep, robust flavor of red wine paired better with more savory spices like black peppercorns and whole cloves. But in both recipes, tasters agreed the addition of cinnamon and vanilla to the poaching liquid (and thus the resulting sauce) was a must.

So with our pears and poaching medium settled, we moved on to fine-tuning our recipe. After poaching numerous batches of pears, we determined two things. First, depending on the ripeness, poaching the pears, covered, at a gentle simmer could take anywhere from 10 to 20 minutes. Second, the pears had to be cooled in the poaching liquid. This gave the pears the chance to absorb some of the syrup; they took on a candied translucency, and they became plump, sweet, and spicy. However, if the pears were plucked from the poaching liquid while hot, they did not have a chance to absorb the syrup into their flesh, resulting in a less appealing, drier texture.

Finally, we tested sugar amounts. Most of the recipes for poached pears that we found made achingly sweet poaching liquids. After extensive testing, we chose a light syrup made with just ¾ cup of sugar to 3 cups of wine. However, because our syrup was so light, it was too thin to cling properly to the fruit as it should. To fix this, we removed the pears from the syrup after poaching and turned up the heat to boil the liquid and reduce and thicken it to a saucy consistency. We then poured the hot, thickened syrup over the pears. Once cooled, this sauce napped the pear in a thin coat of syrup that was so flavorful and refreshing, we didn't miss the whipped cream or ice cream.

White Wine–Poached Pears

SERVES 6

Look for pears that are ripe but firm, which means the flesh at the base of the stem should give slightly when gently pressed with a finger.

1	(750-milliliter) bottle dry white wine (about 3 cups)
¾	cup (5¼ ounces) sugar
6	(3-inch) strips lemon zest plus 2 tablespoons fresh lemon juice
5	sprigs fresh mint
3	sprigs fresh thyme
1	vanilla bean, halved lengthwise, seeds scraped out and reserved (see page 284)
½	cinnamon stick
⅛	teaspoon salt
6	Bartlett or Bosc pears (about 8 ounces each)

1. Bring the wine, sugar, lemon zest strips, mint sprigs, thyme sprigs, vanilla bean seeds and pod, cinnamon stick, and salt to a simmer in a large saucepan over medium heat and cook, stirring occasionally, until the sugar dissolves completely, about 5 minutes; cover and set aside off the heat until needed.

2. Meanwhile, fill a large bowl with water and add the lemon juice. Peel, halve, and core the pears following the photo on page 284, adding them to the lemon water to prevent browning.

3. Drain the pears, discarding the lemon water, and add to the wine mixture. Bring to a simmer over high heat, then reduce the heat to low, cover, and cook until the pears are tender and a toothpick or skewer can be inserted into a pear with very little resistance, 10 to 20 minutes, gently turning the pears over several times.

4. Using a slotted spoon, transfer the pears to a shallow casserole dish. Return the syrup to medium heat and simmer until thickened slightly and reduced to 1⅓ cups, about 15 minutes. Pour the syrup through a fine-mesh strainer, discarding the strained solids, then pour over the pears.

5. Refrigerate the pears until well chilled, at least 2 hours or up to 3 days. To serve, spoon the pears and syrup into individual bowls.

PER SERVING: **Cal** 300; **Fat** 0g; **Sat fat** 0g; **Chol** 0mg; **Carb** 56g; **Protein** 1g; **Fiber** 6g; **Sodium** 55mg

NOTES FROM THE TEST KITCHEN

CORING PEARS

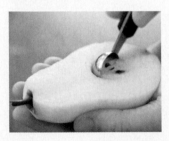

Use a melon baller to cut around the central core of a halved pear with a circular motion and remove the core. Then draw the melon baller from the central core to the top of the pear, removing the interior stem, leaving the blossom end intact.

REMOVING SEEDS FROM A VANILLA BEAN

1. Use a small, sharp knife to cut the vanilla bean in half lengthwise.

2. Scrape out the seeds by placing the knife at one end of one bean half. Press down to flatten the bean as you move the knife away from you and catch the seeds on the edge of the blade.

VARIATION

Red Wine-Poached Pears

Follow the recipe for White Wine–Poached Pears, substituting dry red wine for the white wine. Omit the lemon zest and add 25 black peppercorns and 3 whole cloves to the saucepan with the wine. Omit the lemon juice in the water bath in step 2.

PER SERVING: **Cal** 310; **Fat** 0g; **Sat fat** 0g; **Chol** 0mg; **Carb** 56g; **Protein** 1g; **Fiber** 6g; **Sodium** 55mg

BISCOTTI

THE TWICE-BAKED ITALIAN COOKIES KNOWN AS biscotti make a perfect light finish to a meal, great on their own but ideal for dunking in coffee or an after-dinner drink—and it doesn't hurt that they are low in fat. Their longer-than-average baking time not only yields a uniquely crunchy texture (which is what makes them ideal for dunking) but also gives them an unusually long shelf life. This makes biscotti an excellent choice for home bakers who want to have a simple, light dessert at the ready. To come up with our own recipe, we started by testing a few dozen of the countless existing recipes we found to find out what separates the good from the bad.

When we compared the recipes side by side, we noticed they called for a fairly constant ratio of sugar to flour to flavorings. The major difference among them boiled down to the use of butter and eggs. We found three different styles. The most traditional recipes contained whole eggs, sometimes supplemented by additional yolks; the richest variety contained both butter and eggs; the third style (and the leanest) were made with just egg whites—no yolks or butter. After sampling batches of all three types, we learned that this "fat factor" had a dramatic effect on both the taste and the texture of the resulting biscotti.

While the recipes calling for both eggs and butter produced satisfyingly crunchy cookies, they were somewhat softer and richer—more cookie-like—than the dunkable biscotti we had imagined. Biscotti with whole eggs and additional yolks were also fairly cookie-like, and those

CHOCOLATE-HAZELNUT BISCOTTI

MAKING BISCOTTI

1. Using floured hands, quickly shape the dough into two 13 by 2-inch loaves, spaced about 3 inches apart, on a parchment-lined baking sheet. Pat the loaves smooth and bake.

2. Cool the baked loaves on the baking sheet for 10 minutes, then transfer to a cutting board and cut on the diagonal into ½-inch-thick slices. Be sure to slice the loaves while they are still warm.

3. Lay the slices about ½ inch apart on the baking sheet and bake until crisp, 15 to 20 minutes, flipping them over halfway through. Transfer the biscotti to a wire rack and let cool completely before serving, about 1 hour.

SKINNING HAZELNUTS

1. Toast the hazelnuts in a 350-degree oven until fragrant, about 15 minutes, then transfer them to a clean kitchen towel. Rub the warm nuts together in the towel to scrape off as much of the brown skin as possible.

2. Once you open the towel, you'll see that the skins have come away from the nuts. It's fine if a few patches of skin remain.

made with whole eggs only—without additional yolks—were noticeably less cake-like, with a more straightforward crunch. And finally, there were those made with just egg whites. While appealing from a light-eating point of view, these cookies were so hard and dry they were more like hard candy. We weren't sure if dunking them in coffee could even save them. We cut the last option from the list and considered the remainder.

Tasters agreed that while the texture of the egg-and-butter biscotti needed some tweaking, the butter provided a superior and irresistibly rich flavor. We needed to cut out some of the butter and yolks to make the cookies less cake-like but still keep enough for some tenderness and good flavor. After testing various combinations, we arrived at two whole eggs (no extra yolks) and just 4 tablespoons of butter. Given that this dough yielded 30 biscotti, these cookies were still plenty light. And any less butter or egg and our biscotti crossed the line from appealingly crunchy to too hard and dry.

With our fat factor settled, we wondered if there was another way to make this cookie healthier. We decided to revisit the flour—would it be possible to substitute whole wheat flour for some or even all of the all-purpose flour? Several batches of biscotti later, we found that we could indeed incorporate whole wheat flour into our recipe. However, if we used too much, the wheaty flavor took over our delicate biscotti. In the end we arrived at 1⅓ cups of all-purpose flour combined with ½ cup of whole wheat flour for a healthier cookie that did not sacrifice flavor or texture.

Most biscotti recipes share a common preparation and baking method. They typically require simply mixing the wet ingredients with a whisk in one bowl, whisking the dry ingredients in another, then folding the dry into the wet along with flavorings. First they are baked in loaves for 30 to 40 minutes to allow the dough to firm up and set, then they are sliced and baked again for an additional 10 to 15 minutes until they reach the proper crisp texture.

Biscotti's simple neutral-flavored dough adapts beautifully to literally dozens of flavor combinations. We started with a basic almond biscotti (nuts are a classic addition in Italian recipes), and from there we developed a few variations, one with orange zest and anise, and one with chocolate and hazelnuts. With three great options ready to go, we knew we'd always keep some biscotti on hand.

Almond Biscotti

MAKES ABOUT 30 COOKIES

The batter may at first appear rather sticky, but resist the urge to dust it with flour—too much and the biscotti will become dense. Use a rubber spatula, waxed paper, or plastic wrap if you have trouble handling the dough. Make sure to cool the biscotti completely before storing them to ensure that all the moisture has escaped so the cookies maintain their crunch.

1⅓ cups (6⅔ ounces) unbleached all-purpose flour

½ cup (2¾ ounces) whole wheat flour

1 teaspoon baking powder

¼ teaspoon salt

1 cup (7 ounces) sugar

4 tablespoons (½ stick) unsalted butter, softened

2 large eggs

½ teaspoon vanilla extract

½ teaspoon almond extract

¾ cup almonds, toasted and chopped coarse

1. Adjust an oven rack to the middle position and heat the oven to 350 degrees. Line a large baking sheet with parchment paper. Whisk the all-purpose flour, whole wheat flour, baking powder, and salt together in a bowl.

2. In a large bowl, beat the sugar and butter together with an electric mixer on medium speed until creamy and uniform, 3 to 6 minutes. Beat in the eggs, one at a time, until combined, about 30 seconds, scraping down the bowl and beaters as needed. Beat in the vanilla and almond extracts.

3. Reduce the mixer speed to low and slowly mix in the flour mixture until combined, about 30 seconds. Gradually mix in the almonds until just incorporated.

4. Following the photos on page 286, use floured hands to shape the dough into two 13 by 2-inch loaves on the prepared baking sheet, spaced about 3 inches apart. Bake the loaves until golden and just beginning to crack on top, about 35 minutes, rotating the baking sheet halfway through.

5. Let the loaves cool on the baking sheet for 10 minutes. Turn the oven to 325 degrees.

6. Transfer the loaves to a cutting board and cut each on the diagonal into ½-inch-thick slices with a serrated knife. Lay the slices about ½ inch apart on the baking sheet. Bake until crisp and golden brown on both sides, 15 to 20 minutes, flipping the slices over halfway through. Transfer the biscotti to a wire rack and let cool completely before serving, about 1 hour. (The biscotti can be stored in an airtight container for up to 2 weeks.)

PER COOKIE: Cal 90; Fat 3.5g; Sat fat 1.5g; Chol 20mg; Carb 13g; Protein 2g; Fiber 1g; Sodium 45mg

VARIATIONS

Chocolate-Hazelnut Biscotti

Instant coffee can be substituted for the instant espresso.

Follow the recipe for Almond Biscotti, reducing the amount of all-purpose flour to 1 cup. Omit the almond extract and substitute hazelnuts, toasted, skinned (see page 286), and chopped coarse, for the almonds. Add ⅓ cup Dutch-processed cocoa and 1 teaspoon instant espresso to the batter with the vanilla extract in step 2.

PER COOKIE: Cal 90; Fat 4g; Sat fat 1.5g; Chol 20mg; Carb 12g; Protein 2g; Fiber 1g; Sodium 40mg

Orange-Anise Biscotti

Follow the recipe for Almond Biscotti, omitting the almond extract and almonds. Add 1 tablespoon toasted anise seeds and 1 tablespoon grated orange zest to the batter with the vanilla extract in Step 2.

PER COOKIE: Cal 70; Fat 2g; Sat fat 1g; Chol 20mg; Carb 12g; Protein 1g; Fiber 0g; Sodium 45m

CONVERSIONS & EQUIVALENCIES

SOME SAY COOKING IS A SCIENCE AND AN ART. We would say that geography has a hand in it, too. Flour milled in the United Kingdom and elsewhere will feel and taste different from flour milled in the United States. So, while we cannot promise that the loaf of bread you bake in Canada or England will taste the same as a loaf baked in the States, we can offer guidelines for converting weights and measures. We also recommend that you rely on your instincts when making our recipes. Refer to the visual cues provided. If the bread dough hasn't "come together in a ball," as

described, you may need to add more flour—even if the recipe doesn't tell you so. You be the judge.

The recipes in this book were developed using standard U.S. measures following U.S. government guidelines. The charts below offer equivalents for U.S., metric, and Imperial (U.K.) measures. All conversions are approximate and have been rounded up or down to the nearest whole number. For example:

1 teaspoon = 4.929 milliliters, rounded up to 5 milliliters
1 ounce = 28.349 grams, rounded down to 28 grams

VOLUME CONVERSIONS

U.S.	METRIC
1 teaspoon	5 milliliters
2 teaspoons	10 milliliters
1 tablespoon	15 milliliters
2 tablespoons	30 milliliters
¼ cup	59 milliliters
⅓ cup	79 milliliters
½ cup	118 milliliters
¾ cup	177 milliliters
1 cup	237 milliliters
1¼ cups	296 milliliters
1½ cups	355 milliliters
2 cups	473 milliliters
2½ cups	592 milliliters
3 cups	710 milliliters
4 cups (1 quart)	0.946 liter
1.06 quarts	1 liter
4 quarts (1 gallon)	3.8 liters

WEIGHT CONVERSIONS

OUNCES	GRAMS
½	14
¾	21
1	28
1½	43
2	57
2½	71
3	85
3½	99
4	113
4½	128
5	142
6	170
7	198
8	227
9	255
10	283
12	340
16 (1 pound)	454

CONVERSIONS FOR INGREDIENTS COMMONLY USED IN BAKING

Baking is an exacting science. Because measuring by weight is far more accurate than measuring by volume, and thus more likely to achieve reliable results, in our recipes we provide ounce measures in addition to cup measures for many ingredients. Refer to the chart below to convert these measures into grams.

INGREDIENT	OUNCES	GRAMS
Flour		
1 cup all-purpose flour*	5	142
1 cup cake flour	4	113
1 cup whole wheat flour	5½	156
Sugar		
1 cup granulated (white) sugar	7	198
1 cup packed brown sugar (light or dark)	7	198
1 cup confectioners' sugar	4	113
Cocoa Powder		
1 cup cocoa powder	3	85
Butter†		
4 tablespoons (½ stick, or ¼ cup)	2	57
8 tablespoons (1 stick, or ½ cup)	4	113
16 tablespoons (2 sticks, or 1 cup)	8	227

* U.S. all-purpose flour, the most frequently used flour in this book, does not contain leaveners, as some European flours do. These leavened flours are called self-rising or self-raising. If you are using self-rising flour, take this into consideration before adding leavening to a recipe.
† In the United States, butter is sold both salted and unsalted. We generally recommend unsalted butter. If you are using salted butter, take this into consideration before adding salt to a recipe.

OVEN TEMPERATURES

FAHRENHEIT	CELSIUS	GAS MARK (imperial)
225	105	¼
250	120	½
275	130	1
300	150	2
325	165	3
350	180	4
375	190	5
400	200	6
425	220	7
450	230	8
475	245	9

CONVERTING TEMPERATURES FROM AN INSTANT-READ THERMOMETER

We include doneness temperatures in many of our recipes, such as those for poultry, meat, and bread. We recommend an instant-read thermometer for the job. Refer to the table above to convert Fahrenheit degrees to Celsius. Or, for temperatures not represented in the chart, use this simple formula:

Subtract 32 degrees from the Fahrenheit reading, then divide the result by 1.8 to find the Celsius reading.

EXAMPLE:

"Roast until the thickest part of a chicken thigh registers 175 degrees on an instant-read thermometer." To convert:

$175°\ F - 32 = 143°$
$143° \div 1.8 = 79.44°C$, rounded down to $79°C$

INDEX